Sobremesa

A MEMOIR OF
food and love
IN THIRTEEN COURSES

Dear Wanda,
From my table to yours!
¡Buen Provecho!

Josephine Caminos Oría

Scribe Publishing Company

Pontiac, Michigan

Scribe Publishing Company
29488 Woodward, #426
Royal Oak, MI 48073
www.scribe-publishing.com

Sobremesa: A memoir of food and love in thirteen courses

This is a work of nonfiction. All of the persons and locations described in this book are real, but in some cases, in order to preserve privacy, the names of persons and places have been changed. Timelines, dialogue and the descriptions of incidents and events are based on the author's recollections and reflect the author's impressions of what occurred. The author's perspective by no means represents those of the population of Argentina and the United States, including her own bicultural family. In some cases, dialogue and timelines and sequences of events have been consolidated or condensed.

Editing by: Allison Janicki, Jennifer Baum and Mel Corrigan
Cover photo: Maya Tuttle
Back cover and author photos: Jonathan Boncek
Cover and interior design: Aerocraft Charter Art Service

PRINTED IN THE UNITED STATES OF AMERICA

ISBN: 978-1-7353051-8-9

Publisher's Cataloging-in-Publication data

Names: Caminos Oría, Josephine, author.
Title: Sobremesa : a memoir of food and love in thirteen courses / Josephine Caminos Oría.
Description: Royal Oak, MI: Scribe Publishing Company, 2021.
Identifiers: LCCN: 2020945224 | ISBN: 978-1-7353051-8-9 (print) | 978-1-7353051-9-6 (ebook)
Subjects: LCSH Caminos Oría, Josephine. | Argentina—Description and travel. | Cooking, Argentine. | Food habits—Argentina—Anecdotes. | Cooking, Latin American. | Cooking—United States. | Argentine Americans. | BISAC BIOGRAPHY & AUTOBIOGRAPHY / Cultural, Ethnic & Regional / Hispanic & Latino | BIOGRAPHY & AUTOBIOGRAPHY / Personal Memoirs | COOKING / Regional & Ethnic / Central American & South American
Classification: LCC TX716.A7 .C36 2021 | DDC 641.5982/092—dc23

Contents

Dedication

For my abuelos,
Alfredo and Dorita Germain, mi Argentina . . .
and the one they call Doll,
my Mom, Poupée.

And finally, Gastón.
My love for you knows no borders.

"Andábamos sin buscarnos,
pero sabiendo que andábamos para encontrarnos."

"We went about without looking for each other,
but knowing we went about to find one another."

Julio Cortázar

Foreword

*F*ood is a celebration, a way of bringing people together. It evokes two of our most urgent desires: to be nourished and to belong. We eat with all our senses—not just taste, but sight, smell, touch, memory and imagination. Sometimes, what we crave most—that moment of joy—carries with it the story of a village, a culture or a community.

Like the United States, Argentina is comprised of immigrants: Italians, Spaniards, French, Germans, Arabs and Jews (among many others) who've blended with the natives. Gathering around a table and sharing meals has always been—and continues to be— the glue that connects all these families together. Food is their shared point of commonality, that moment of synthesis in which cooking and love pass through fingers: from mother to daughter, from grandmother to granddaughter or to the menfolk with their fire and bread. They eat for more than sustenance. Food is an offering of heart and heritage for family, friends and guests alike. The table is where love is expressed, friendship is honored and, in an expansive way, a new cultural identity is born.

Argentina is a disorganized country in many ways, but we have a fantastic knack for putting together a sumptuous meal for our friends. It's one of our greatest characteristics—simple yet exuberant. This tradition is a matter of national pride, something at which we are world leaders. It's what we miss the most when we go abroad to work, live or travel. And it's something to which any visitor to our homeland can attest. Eating *asado* with your loved ones is close to a religious experience; having a place at that meat-laden table is to occupy sacred space. The people we love most sit with us there. Meals are shared. Stories are told. And retold. We laugh together and cry together. We reminisce about where we've been and what's to come. And we live to tell about it at the next *sobremesa*.

In Argentina, *sobremesa's* tableside chats can last for hours, often longer than the meal itself, thanks to the never-ending offerings of sweets, savory snacks, teas, coffees and sparkling wine. *Sobremesa* contains an air of ceremony. It provides a state of calm, along with a chance to shine. In this ritual of flowing conversation, one's true self is revealed once the food has been enjoyed and wine continues to flow. *Sobremesa* shatters the walls that separate us, blending—transcending—language altogether, opening pathways to intimacy and lifetime bonds with one another.

I agree with Josephine that *sobremesa* is where family is built. It's a place where we express ourselves with the affectionate tones of Italians and analyze one another as if in a Woody Allen film or group therapy session, where cultures, cuisines and flavors merge. It leaves us with a melting pot of ideas, customs and traditions to hang our hats on.

I met the Caminos family as a young girl when my family moved to Pittsburgh. They were among the few other Argentines who lived there, although they had a huge advantage over us as a family already comfortable moving between both cultures. While an unspoken complicity always existed, both of our families knew that we belonged to two worlds—the new world that was Pittsburgh, and the world of *asados*, *gaucho* cowboys and vineyards surrounded by mountains; the world of *medialuna* pastries made from fat and *vitel toné* Christmas recipes; the world of our dear grandmothers—Josephine's *abuela* Dorita and my Tete and French grandma Meme; the world where both our grandmas, with their love and patience, helped our mothers overcome their respective uprooting to raise their multicultural families.

I love the fact that Josephine didn't just find a love for Argentina in reconnecting with her family's past and heirloom recipes. She's uncovered a sisterhood in *sobremesa* and wants to extend it to those who don't yet know about it, or who don't know what they're missing. It's in the intimacy of our own kitchens that we join forces, connecting in the place that, for so many people and families, is a meeting point, a place where culture lives on and transforms itself.

Sobremesa taps our commonalities: the need to eat, the desire to share, the longing to belong, the craving to embrace a slower way of life. Today, during the unprecedented quarantine that has gripped our nations and world, I can't help but think taking the time to practice *sobremesa* could be a small step towards helping us navigate these uncertain times. While most of us are confined behind closed doors, we are also more connected than ever on a global level. We can't put words to the fear, isolation and loss—of loved ones, of jobs, of our homes, of our support systems—that we collectively awaken to each morning. We must bravely hold onto hope, love and, most importantly, one another.

Argentina's time-honored *sobremesa* tradition encourages us to do this. The down time and connectivity it fosters is essential to both our humanity and sanity.

Sofia Pescarmona

ENTREPRENEUR AND VITICULTURIST

CEO and Owner, Lagarde Winery and Fogón Restaurant in Mendoza, Argentina

Introduction

so·bre·me·sa /so.ßre'mé.sa /

(noun): time spent being present at the table,
lingering over a meal in conversation
well after the food is gone.

With parents who spoke between tongues, indiscriminately switching on and off between their native, River Plate *Castellano*, their learned English with heavy accents and their assault on both—*Spanglish*, which often surfaced in the same conversation—our family decidedly did not blend in. My parents made sure we never did. That we never would. Instead, day after day, year after year, we pledged allegiance to *sobremesa*, the lesser known ingredient of our Deep South, Argentine cuisine. *Sobremesa* set the table for a future I never saw coming, like the legions of ghosts and ancestors past who frequented my family's dining room. They'd come in, pull up a chair and make themselves at home among rumpled napkins splotched with wine, Tang or coffee, glasses harboring the last dregs of a plump Malbec and torn sugar and Sweet'N Low packets. Some, from a distant past, were unknown to us. Others we loved and missed with every breath.

Our ghosts had always been there, whether or not we chose to recognize them. They still are. Their spirits hung on the edge of multiple conversations until the last drops percolated over the table, offering up crumbs of information here and there. Morsel by morsel, I savored each moment, until they became imprinted on my taste buds.

I've since come to understand that our mystical visitors, always at the ready to be conjured back to mind through taste and smell, were guiding me down *los caminos de la vida*—the path that ultimately upended my world and led me back to the home I never knew on the bank of el Río de la Plata, where the open fires of the Argentine *asado, dulce de leche*, Andean Malbec and *fútbol* are national obsessions.

* * *

I was raised straddling two cultures, between America's city of bridges—Pittsburgh, Pennsylvania—and Argentina's endless, yawning plains. The same mother country that at once defined me and made me feel as if I were living in a foreign language. But no matter where I awoke, we ate like Argentines. Hardwood charcoal, *gaucho*-style open-fire cooking on my dad's Weber grill was a requisite at least once a week, and most Sundays when the weather cooperated. Also required: sitting down at a table, napkin in lap, and staying a while to share the meal with family, friends, coworkers and neighbors. We faithfully adhered to our *sobremesa* tradition, yet to others it remained lost in translation. It didn't—still doesn't—have an English equivalent. The attempts at translations—the literal: *over the table*; the subjective: *the post-meal equivalent of pillow talk*; the succinct: *table talk*, among others—described it, but barely. My parents, like most Argentines, were suspicious of guests who ate-n-ran. "*Pájaro que comió, voló*," they'd comment under their breath, comparing the culinary offense to a bird that flies the coop after eating. Their loss—the first to leave the table often missed out. Conversation always took a turn for the real once the napkins made their way back onto the table. That's when true connections were forged and *la verdad de la milanesa*, hidden truths, were uncovered.

Sobremesa was how I learned to make sense of the world— the good, *lo malo*, the beautiful, *lo feo*, the unexpected, *lo esperado*. With the exception of the *choripán* (*chorizo* in a bun, the perfect answer to street food) and the occasional frozen Lean Cuisine or Stouffer's Spinach Soufflé, our childhood home was not a grab-

and-go sort of place. Whether it followed a late breakfast, lunch, dinner or even a *picada*—the Argentine version of *tapas*—*sobremesa* happened spontaneously. It was also an unspoken obligation. *Sobremesa* wasn't reserved for holidays or weekends; it happened any day of the week, though it was often longest on Sundays. In Argentina, it was even thought to be necessary for proper digestion. People genuinely didn't want to leave the table. Me included, until, like most children, I got older and it started eating into my weekend plans. Plans or no plans, my parents still expected us to partake. At least for a while. They were Argentine down to the bone. With the exception of the movie *Grease* being on TV or a spontaneous dance party breaking out to Blondie's "The Tide is High," the Village People's "YMCA," anything by Billy Joel or Julio Iglesias or the soundtrack to *Camelot*, *sobremesa* was non-negotiable. To them, food and wine weren't the end goal of any evening, but a conduit to something else. There was no use in rushing. Mom would pass around *cafecitos* or digestive *Cachamai* herbal teas. I always accepted the latter. Depending on the day, a Limoncello or Cointreau might be uncorked. Just another excuse to stay awhile and retell our stories over and over until they became our truth, or at least our own version of it. And, believe me, we Caminos love to tell the same anecdotes on repeat, as if they're landing on virgin ears for the first time. Mom, especially. She could tell a story to the grave, making it better and better each time. Especially when it served her purpose. I've since carried on the tradition. We can't help ourselves.

Still, no matter the occasion or evening, there was always room for two or three more people at my parents' endless table. *Donde comen dos, comen tres*—where two eat, there's always room for another. As for my siblings and I, we were held to *sobremesa's* three unspoken tableside rules: First, stay seated until formally excused. The dishes could always wait. Second, speak in Spanish or Argentine *Castellano* if you wanted to get a word in. Otherwise my parents would snipe back, "*No hablo inglés,*" pretending not to understand, even if someone were simply asking them to pass the bread. And, finally, if Mom or Dad covertly stepped on your foot underneath the table, that was code for "cut it out" or "change the subject. Now." And you never dared say "ouch." But truth be told, few topics were off-limits. We talked about anything from Reagan versus Mondale, to Clinton's word or Lewinsky's, to the British invasion of Argentina's Malvinas Islands (*what were the Brits thinking?*), to whether or not O. J. did it (Mom and Dad had polar opposite opinions on this one that often led to screaming matches). *Sobremesa* brought out the funny in the least funny of us. Jokes never landed better than when your audience was well-fed and, preferably, a bit boozy. Lighter issues, such as the latest crazy antics our free-spirited housekeeper who we loved like our own, Star (Crystal Gayle hair and all), came up with, to the latest *chisme* or gossip buzzing among Mom's faithful group of Latina friends, "*las chicas*," or some family drama or another would round out the conversation. And your own personal life or issues were almost always fair game, whether you liked it or not. If you had a beef with someone, *sobremesa* was the time to *irse a los bifes* or go to the steaks and pick a fight. Then, at the very end of it, you'd kiss and make up. On and on the conversation went until someone finally got up and left the table, breaking its spell.

But above all, *sobremesa* was a means for my parents to pass on their Argentine traditions and culture beyond DNA. It satiated a hunger in me that food alone never could, tethering me to an Argentina that had always seemed worlds away.

* * *

Mom and Dad were in their respective late twenties and early thirties when they moved their young family of five children from Argentina to Pittsburgh, Pennsylvania in 1974. I was six months old. My real name is Josefina. It's still the one listed on my Argentine and US passports. Once I started school, Mom thought it would be easier for my fellow classmates to say Josephine with a hard "J." And it stuck. When I was older, she confided in me that she didn't like the way they pronounced HOE-zefina. She was raising me to be a lady.

We grew up in the States but were raised in the bicultural homes my parents created for us in Pittsburgh and Miami Beach, Florida. During the holidays, we often spent weeks upon weeks between

Buenos Aires and my parents' *estancia* La Santa Elena, a working cattle ranch tucked away in the Province of Santa Fé's *pampas*. My maternal grandparents, Alfredo and María Dora, "Dorita," Germain, were an integral part of our family. Growing up, they became my Argentina. Dorita and Alfredo visited often, sometimes up to six months at a time. During their extended visits to Pittsburgh, they always stayed in the apartment over the detached garage of our family home. Mom had to referee the fights among me and my sisters as to who got to sleep with them each night. Dorita would put curlers in our hair and heat up milk with honey or *dulce de leche*, while she showed us a complicated needle stitch point or told us tales of their latest travels. She loved speaking of Cuba's Hemingway and how his spirit was more present than ever as she walked arm in arm with Alfredo along the Malecón, Havana's majestic coastal road that circles half the city. As Dorita got lost in her thoughts, *Abuelo* would scour the *New York Times* and *Wall Street Journal* for any snippet or mention of Argentine news. Alfredo was always commenting on how little news from Argentina made it to the States. Argentine headlines were rare, to say the least, and when one did appear it was typically the same news, an assassination or political trial of some military figure or other, who, unlike their more popular predecessor, Evita Perón, the Argentine people didn't cry for. During his visits, in the pre-internet and mobile phone era, my *abuelo* found himself anxiously disconnected from life as he knew it for months at a time.

On the other hand, Dorita did everything possible to bring Argentina to our home in Pittsburgh. She made sure that her grandchildren spoke Spanish fluently. *"R con r guitarra"* was one of the tongue twisters she'd make us recite over and over to get us in the habit of rolling our double *r*'s properly. But trilling never came naturally to me—a dead giveaway that, like *sobremesa*, part of my bicultural heritage simply didn't translate. I was fully neither, nor fully both. At home in Pittsburgh, I was considered Spanish or Argentine, but in Argentina, I was branded *"la Yanqui,"* whose Levi jeans hung a little too loose for their own liking.

Into their second or third month of visiting, Alfredo would begin to plant the seed for their return home, but Dorita always fought him on it. This was, after all, pre 9/11, which meant the duration of their stay in the US wasn't bookended by a visa. Dorita usually got her way. She felt at ease in Pittsburgh. Like her faithful apron, she carried Argentina with her, no matter the destination. She and Mom helmed our homes from the kitchen. Mom as the cruise director, juggling a demanding workday that included helping Dad build his cardiology practice in the earlier years, then managing their Argentine cattle ranches in the later ones. All the while coordinating the demanding schedules of six children, seeing to Dad's needs, renovating her latest real estate find, co-chairing the Ibero-American Pittsburgh Opera Guild under the artistic direction of fellow Argentine Tito Capobianco, talking to her travel agent to iron out the details for her next overseas trip with Dad, making weekend plans with friends to see a show or dinner and dancing and, last but not least, jotting down a grocery list, packing school lunches and greeting the milk man with a smile as she planned out the day's menu. Not to mention getting herself dressed and all of us out the door before the clock struck eight. Some days Mom prepared dinner in the morning so it would be one less thing to worry about when she got home later that evening. Polynesian chicken and a slow-cooked *peceto* (eye-of-round) stew were among her faithful go-to dishes. Other days she'd leave directions for our housekeeper to get dinner started. Unless Dorita was in town. That's when we ate best.

Everyone took a back seat to Dorita in the kitchen. Back at home in La Plata, Dorita volunteered countless hours cooking for and serving at-risk children at the non-profit organization, Casa Del Niño Esperanza (Child Hope House). In the States, she focused all of her attention on my family, preparing the Argentine dishes I now cook for my children. Dorita's food was from scratch—every meal, every day. She spent hours in the kitchen. Elbow-deep in flour, Dorita would tell us her deepest secrets and family stories, while we attempted to teach her English. She never did quite get it right, but it didn't matter. She didn't need words. Dorita had a way that transcended language altogether.

I can still see Dorita now, with her perfectly manicured nails and freshly coiffed platinum white hair, effortlessly whipping up dozens upon dozens of beef *milanesas* with the skill and ease of a trained seasoned chef during the dinner rush hour. Ever an *abuela* of contrasts, Dorita was both cosmopolitan and *casera*. Equal parts *abuela glamorosa* and Betty Crocker homebody, Dorita taught us that as women we could be both. She was unusual for her time because she stressed the importance of being independent to her granddaughters. She also engrained in us the pride she took each day in taking care of her family. Dorita showed us we could go out and take on the world, then strap on an apron and be a culinary goddess at home. One didn't take away from the other.

After Mom, Dorita was the closest and dearest person in my life. My three older sisters, Valentina, Camila and Laura, came in a close third. Together, and to the dismay of my dad and brothers Oscar and Federico, we formed a tribe of outspoken women. When we got together, I'd often find myself explaining to others, "We aren't arguing. That's just how we talk." No one rivaled my love for my band of *chicas*.

Through the years I savored our family *sobremesas*, meal after meal. They've left me with an edible memory that connects me to my past and now, twenty years later, continues to guide me on a culinary journey that, like ancestors past, seemingly showed up out of nowhere. This detour came at me out of left field when, at thirty-five, with four children under the age of five in tow, I awoke one morning with an innate and somewhat irrational desire to make *dulce de leche*—Argentina's ubiquitous golden milk jam. The same *dulce de leche* my *abuela* Dorita fed me as a child. It began to haunt me. I'd walk into a room and smell burnt sugar or wake up and taste warm milk with honey on the tip of my tongue. The scent always seemed to be coming from the kitchen. Then it suddenly dawned on me: I'd been smelling home. Argentina was calling, and my team of angels made sure I was paying attention. In the kitchen. At *sobremesa*. Willing me to plant the roots that would prepare me for what lay just ahead—no matter how frightening starting over from scratch would be. In my quest to find myself, I learned that to move forward, I had to return to the place where it all began.

Seven years after that first impulse, I left a fifteen-year, C-level career in healthcare to make *dulce de leche*. At forty-three. Most of my friends and family thought I was crazy, myself included. I, too, grew up drinking the Kool-Aid that told women it's too late, or even selfish, to change the course of our lives after our mid-thirties, even if we intuitively felt something was missing from them. Looking back now, from the vantage point of years gone by, it's hard to believe a single ingredient could have the power to divert the course of an entire life, to rewrite the hundreds upon thousands of decisions made—some on a whim, most carefully thought out—on which it was built. But that's how it happened. It was greater than me, and there was nothing I could do to stop it.

And while I have nothing but respect for Argentina's slow-food tradition of preserving milk into *dulce de leche*, perfecting it came with its own challenges. Raw milk is unpredictable. Just a few seconds of neglect can cause a pot of milk to boil over, scalding everything and everyone it touches. When done right, *dulce de leche* offers up a golden *Castellano* flavor, resulting in guilty pleasure. But it can also create disharmony. One can never know with certainty how the milk will behave, at what point it will burn or if it will spill over. It all boils down to a question of time and alchemy.

For this reason, today more than ever, *sobremesa's* post-meal tradition is just the elixir I need to center myself and feel one step closer to the spirits of loved ones who may no longer be with us but live on in my family traditions. I've found the connection *sobremesa* fosters reaches far beyond this world, as does the tragedy that can ensue when it is neglected.

This is my story. According to me. That's the thing about *sobremesa*—we all leave the table on our own terms. Some of us take our leftovers, while others leave everything on the table. Some prefer to sweep things under the rug, or table linens—whichever is more convenient. Out of sight, out of mind. We take with us the ingredients and conversations that mattered most to us when we get up from the table, the ones that filled us up or left us longing for more in that specific moment of our lives. But the truth is, there is no *one* truth. We each have our own version of a story, or interpretation of the same. Just as some of us choose to recognize and acknowledge the ghosts we carry with us, while others prefer to ignore mystical encounters with the spirit world or altogether relegate them as non-existent.

I should also add that my family members—myself included—have all inherited a generation-spanning genotype that makes us—unintentionally, of course—prone to fully exaggerate stories to our own liking. Like a childhood game of telephone, or in Argentina, *teléfono descompuesto*, details become distorted, names get changed or forgotten, conversations get recreated from memory and different stories meld so that no one is quite sure who said what, or what actually happened, and we are left with a wonderfully complex stew of truths and flavors that only gets better with age, like a fine wine or cheese.

This is all part of the allure of *sobremesa*. Yet, its story—and the power *sobremesa* wields—remains largely untold. My hope is that mine will inspire you to slow down and do as the Argentines do. Stay awhile at the table. Indulge in two-bite *facturas* and uncork another bottle of wine as you surrender into the mysterious and meaningful that happens tableside between people—past, present and even future. But not to worry. Besides contemplating your next drink, *sobremesa* is all about being present in the moment, even if you're not quite sure where the conversation is going.

So for now, ¡*buen provecho!*

Prologue

Al pan, pan, y al vino, vino
Bread Is Bread and Wine Is Wine

Abuela Dorita used to always say that God has a way of showing up at tables—why else would he have gifted each of us with thousands upon thousands of taste buds? If it's true that food is God's love language, then one of his greatest masterpieces had to be Dorita's *sopa pastina*. Trapped in the domestic confines women of her generation had become accustomed to, Dorita had learned to masterfully wield the power that food offered her. A pot of *sopa pastina* steaming on the stove for hours on end was a common fixture of her faithful kitchen arsenal. The bone broth could cure most illness, heartbreak or even mental anguish. It brought me back to life after the car crash that, for all intents and purposes, should have ended my life when I was sixteen, along with the lives of my *abuelo* Alfredo and brother Oscar.

* * *

My second chance at life came in December 1990, just before Christmas. Not even two days had gone by since I'd passed my driver's license test on my birthday. My family, minus Dad, was caravanning in three vehicles from Pittsburgh down to our house in Miami Beach to spend the holidays. A cardiologist, Dad had a packed patient schedule, and as usual, would be flying in a day

1

or two before Christmas. My brother Oscar, nineteen at the time, *Abuelo* Alfredo and I headed the group in Ol' Bessie, our brown-and-beige striped Chevrolet Suburban SUV, one of the few cars from the early '90s large enough to seat my family of eight. We'd begged Mom to mount Texas Longhorns to the car's front grille, but she wouldn't hear of it. "*Que* tacky, *chicos.*"

The car was packed to the brim with suitcases, Christmas decorations and presents. In the middle of the caravan were my three sisters, Valentina, Camila and Laura, in their own vehicle. Mom, *Abuela* Dorita and my younger brother Federico brought up the rear.

It was just after midnight. We were about eighteen hours into the twenty-hour trip, cruising on Interstate 95, just past Port St. Lucie.

"Two hours to go," Mom had said at the last refuel. "We can all sleep in tomorrow."

When you're part of a larger family, it's often too expensive or simply too complicated to fly. Mom and Dad could swing the airfares, especially as I got older. But it all boiled down to one question: why fly when you can drive? I don't know, maybe it was an Argentine thing. So through the years, we'd become used to pulling off long, nonstop driving distances. Between all of us, we had six drivers, but as a newly minted driver myself, Mom had forbidden me to get behind the wheel.

"It's out of the question. Oscar can handle the rest of the drive," she'd said earlier that evening as I polished off my spicy chicken sandwich with a side of fries at a Wendy's just off the interstate.

Once we were back on the road, however, Oscar didn't agree. He was exhausted, and instead of pulling over, began begging me to drive.

"Oscar, Mom will kill me. You heard her."

"Come on. She doesn't have to know. Just jump over the seat and I'll move over."

The Suburban had a wide bench-style front seat, which sat three adults across. I was sitting in the second row, directly behind Oscar in the driver's seat. The space immediately next to him was empty. After several minutes of his incessant pleading, I did the unthinkable and heeded my brother's risky request. I took a look at my *abuelo* in the front passenger side seat. He was sound asleep, snoring away. *He'd never have to know,* I thought.

"Okay. One hour max. That's it. Then we switch again before getting to Miami, that way neither Alfredo nor Mom finds out."

The rest is a blur; it happened so fast. As I hopped over the front seat, Oscar scooted right towards the middle, making room for me. He was holding onto the steering wheel while I got settled. But as I sat down behind the wheel, I realized my legs were too short to reach the pedals. My chest tightened. Oscar had the car on cruise control; it was set at seventy-five mph, so at this point it was driving itself. As I reached down to pull the seat closer to the dash, it became suddenly clear it was too heavy. Oscar and Alfredo's weight together made it impossible for me to adjust it. Because it was a bench seat, the entire row had to move together. Panic set in, and I told Oscar to grab the wheel. He'd just started his descent to the back seat.

"Let me jump in the back so I can push the seat from behind," he assured me. "Just keep your eyes on the road."

That's when it happened. The car swerved as I slid down the seat in an attempt to reach the brakes. I never again regained control. Ol' Bessie struck a sharp left and we plowed into the middle guard rail. We'd later learn the car's axle broke, causing us to spin and roll over, and over, and over until we finally came to a stop, landing on the shoulder of the highway, facing north.

As this surreal scene unfolded in slow motion, the life I never knew flashed before my eyes: *I'd never go to college . . . live on my own . . . walk down the aisle with Dad.* I did the only thing I could. I clutched the steering wheel and set my intention to live. As I hung on with all my might, I remember seeing *Abuelo's* face. Our eyes met for only a moment, his filled with sheer terror. He'd been jolted from a deep sleep with no time to react. *This can't be happening!* I desperately tried to pin my grandpa back to his seat with my legs. It was then that I saw Alfredo's forehead ricochet off the dashboard, his black eyeglasses breaking in two. I had lost sight of Oscar at this point, but managed to yell, "Hold on. Grab onto anything you can."

Then everything went silent. Time stopped. The car filled up with luminescent particles of light, as if a million lightning bugs had come to join us in the fight of our lives. Suddenly the three of us, Alfredo, Oscar and I, were suspended in air. It seemed like we were floating in a nebulous cloud. The whole car appeared to be made out of light. Looking back, I'm sure that angels descended upon us and hugged each one of us tightly. Each time the car flipped, they twirled us in the other direction, keeping us from harm's way. And when the car began to spin, they held us in a tight chest-to-chest *abrazo*; they embraced each of us, intertwining their bodies with ours to keep us from getting jolted from the car as its doors unhinged, one by one. It felt like a dream, yet I was fully aware of the imminent danger we faced. *Is this what it feels like to die?* As my head met the cold glass of the windshield, everything went dark.

My sisters later told me that they were just minutes behind us and the first to witness the aftermath. It was late, so there were few cars on the highway. I always thank God for that. They first saw the suitcases, Christmas decorations and gifts strewn across I-95. The interstate looked like a holiday bazaar, or as it's coined in the famous Argentine tango, *un cambalache*. Then they spotted Ol' Bessie flipped over on the side of the road, facing traffic. Once they recognized her, they started screaming, thinking there's no way we could have survived. But God gave each one of us a second chance that day. Oscar walked away with a broken arm and battered conscience. Alfredo survived with a neck brace, an ugly gash on his forehead and a prescription for replacement eyeglasses. They found me in the grass near the car, but miraculously, hours later when I awoke in the hospital, I'd sustained only minor scrapes and bruises, a sore neck that got crankier with time and a scratched retina that branded me with a lifelong astigmatism from glass that perforated my eye as I hit the windshield.

The following day we were all home in Miami Beach, recovering. Dad had flown in early that morning after receiving news of the accident. I spent several days in my parents' bed, with bandages covering both of my eyes, allowing the scratched one to properly heal. As I lay there, days passed before I could bring myself to utter a word.

"She's in shock," Dad whispered to Mom behind closed doors. "Give her time."

It was then agreed, through whispers loud enough for me to hear, that they would never ask any of us for the blow-by-blow details of the accident. "*Lo pasado, pisado.* What's done is done," Mom said.

Dad was right; I needed time, as I couldn't seem to process my thoughts. As Mom sat by my bedside, I'd pretend to be asleep to avoid her trying to get me to talk. It was just easier that way. I couldn't find the words—at least not until the third or fourth day, when I heard *Abuela* Dorita's footsteps carefully climbing the Spanish-tiled cement stairs that led to the bedroom.

With each step she took, I could smell the *sopa pastina*. Its steam enveloped the hallway, curling its way under the door jamb as it playfully stumbled into the room like a royal court jester announcing his majesty's imminent arrival. The soup's aroma tickled my throat, awakening my appetite. Dorita sat on the side of the bed, carefully placing the large room-service tray over my legs. She stroked my hair as she fed me by the spoonful. I didn't resist. The broth, singing with the aroma of laurel leaves, chicken, semolina, carrots, onions, celery and garlic, penetrated all of my senses. I didn't need to see what I was eating; layer upon layer of velvet silkiness allowed me to decipher each ingredient separately. Each spoonful melted away the fear that had taken hold of my tongue and imprisoned my thoughts.

As Dorita scraped up the last bits of noodles at the bottom of the bowl, she asked me, "Josefinita, what is it you're not telling us? Your *abuelo* and Oscar are fine. They're downstairs. Everyone made it out okay. Tomorrow is Christmas."

I took off my bandages. "I thought I killed them, *Abuela*. What if I'd killed them? It scares me to death to think that I had the power to do so, with that one, stupid decision. What if someone else had been on the road that night?"

Dorita handed me a piece of the baguette she'd brought to sop up the remains of the soup. "*Al pan, pan, y al vino, vino.* When it comes to life and death matters, I don't mince words." *She never did.* "You didn't kill anyone. Most importantly, you didn't kill yourself. The car is replaceable. But other than our caravan, there weren't any cars in sight. *Gracias a Dios.* I don't want to ever hear you blame yourself again. An accident's an accident. Whatever happened that night, next time you'll know better. That's that."

"But that's just it. I can't even begin to understand what happened. How we survived. As we were flipping, the car all of a sudden filled with the brightest light I've ever seen. We weren't alone. I couldn't process it at the time, but we danced with angels that night. They kept us safe. Something or someone was in the car, protecting us."

"I'm certain, we all have angels watching out for us. It makes perfect sense," *Abuela* said, readjusting the bandages back onto my eyes.

"Did Mom thank the man who pulled me out? I'd like to write him a letter."

"*¿Quién?* What man? We were the first there. Except for the medics that arrived in the ambulance, no one else was there. At least not that I'm aware of."

"But an older man helped me out of the car. He picked me up in his arms and laid me down on the grass. That much I remember. He crouched by my side and held my hand until everything went blank again. Then I woke up later in the hospital."

"You know it's perfectly normal to have some hallucinations after the trauma you experienced."

"He was there. I saw him," I said with certainty and a tinge of annoyance. He was seventy-ish years old with a silver-white beard, and he was wearing a khaki windbreaker and some sort of cap.

Dorita and I sat in silence for a long while at that bedside *sobremesa*. Just as I was about to fall asleep, she placed her hand over mine. "Do you think he was your guardian angel?"

I shook my head no. "He was there. In the flesh. Watching over me with the ghost of a smile, no doubt trying to console me. I tried talking to him, to ask him what happened and how the others were. But I couldn't get the words out."

Dorita squeezed my hand. "Oscar says he kicked what was left of the windshield out so you could all crawl out of the car. But he hasn't said a word more. Your grandfather is mum, too. It seems to be a blur for everyone. Or simply too much right now. I'm not saying how you remember it didn't happen. I don't know who that man you saw was. Or how he got there. But, if he was there, there's a reason. The only thing that matters now is that you're home safe. Now, get some rest. *Feliz navidad.*" Dorita kissed me goodnight, taking the bed tray as she closed the door behind her.

I tried to sleep, but like most Christmas Eves, couldn't. Except this had nothing to do with the anticipation of whether or not *Papá Noel* was coming and everything to do with the accident. I had a haunting feeling I couldn't shake. The man who helped me—where did he go? Did I imagine him? I couldn't have. I would have never been able to get out of that car by myself. And had I been thrown from the vehicle as it tumbled, I'd have broken bones to show for it. But who was he? He seemed to know me, but I'd never seen him. How could he have vanished into thin air? Could I have mistaken him for my brother Oscar? Was he a figment of my imagination, even if I wanted to fool myself into thinking otherwise? According to my family, he was. But I remembered the tight grip of his hand as he held mine in his. Yet my family swore up and down that other than a couple of policemen and two EMTs, no one else was at the scene that night. I left it at that. So did Oscar and Alfredo. From that day on, we rarely spoke of the accident, but the three of us forged an unspoken bond that would last a lifetime.

From then on, I slept with a sliver of light on. And every once in a while, day and night, I'd catch a glimpse of movement from the corner of my eye that would make the hairs on my arms and back of my neck rise. But whenever I turned, there was never anyone or anything there that could explain it. Until there was.

Sopa pastina (Pastina Soup)

SERVES 7. *Or 1. If you think you've plumb lost your mind.*

I like my broth velvety rich, so I cheat when making this soup by adding store-bought chicken stock. You can certainly use water or chicken bouillon cubes, but you will likely need to simmer the broth for several more hours to obtain the same result. For Thanksgiving, I substitute the chicken legs with the turkey neck and giblets that come stuffed into the cavity, and it creates an equally luxurious soup. I like to start this soup in the morning hours and then finish preparing it in the evening, about a half hour before serving dinner. While you may be tempted to add more pastina, tread cautiously as the pasta continues to expand in the soup and may disrupt your broth-to-noodle ratio. My family prefers a brothy soup, but feel free to add chunks of the cooked chicken back into the pot.

2 teaspoons extra-virgin **olive oil** (or enough to coat bottom of stock pot)

2 teaspoons **salt**

5 **chicken legs**, skin removed (1½ pounds)

1 large **onion**, chopped roughly

5 large **celery stalks**, chopped roughly

3 large **carrots**, chopped roughly

1 teaspoon freshly ground **black pepper**

5 **garlic cloves**, smashed

16 cups low-sodium **chicken broth**

4 cups **water**

2 **bay leaves**

Juice of 1 **lemon**

1 large **egg**

1 cup **semolina pastina #70 noodle**

Freshly grated **Parmesan cheese** (optional)

Place a large stock pot over medium heat and heat oil. Add one teaspoon salt. Remove skin from chicken legs and sauté in oil, turning them until golden brown. Remove legs from heat and reserve on a plate.

In the same pot, add the onion, celery, carrots, black pepper and remaining salt, stirring with a wooden spoon while scraping up any brown bits and sauté until translucent. Add garlic, cooking two to three more minutes. Add chicken broth, water, bay leaves and lemon juice. Bring stock to a boil, cover with a tight-fitting lid and reduce to a simmer. Allow stock to simmer for a minimum cook time of 5 hours. Remove pot from the heat and strain the broth, reserving the vegetables and chicken legs. Transfer the broth back into the stock pot, reserving one cup, and simmer on medium-low heat. Discard the bay leaves and chicken bones. Transfer the remaining vegetables and a cup of the stock to a high-speed mixer or food processor and blend until velvety smooth. Allow to cool for a couple of minutes prior to adding the egg, once again blending until smooth (you want the mixture to be cool enough to avoid scrambling the egg). Transfer the blended mixture back into the stock pot, whisking until fully incorporated into the broth. Cover and allow to simmer 5 more minutes. Add the pastina, mixing so it does not stick. Cover and allow to simmer another 15 minutes prior to serving.

OPTIONAL: Garnish each bowl with freshly grated parmesan cheese.

Part One

HERE

Chapter 1

Puñados, dedos, pizcas y tacitas
Handfuls, Fingers, Pinches and Teacups

If there's ever an American holiday that encapsulates the spirit of *sobremesa*, it's Thanksgiving. *Día de acción de gracias* is one of the few days that most Americans allow themselves the luxury of disregarding the clock to devote an entire day to gathering around the table and stuffing their mouths like the turkey on it. Mom packed her Thanksgiving stuffing year after year with walnuts and loads of mushrooms, my absolute favorite. She didn't cook it inside "Big Bird," as Mom called it, but she used the turkey's juices to create the perfect consistency—a golden brown, crunchy top that was soft and moist in the center. Mom made her stuffing once a year—it didn't quite fit into our Argentine meal repertoire. So for me, Thanksgiving was as much about the stuffing as it was the turkey. As a child, I'd get so excited the night before, knowing that I'd wake up to the smell of turkey in the oven. Mom would still be in her blue terry cloth monogrammed robe, making a huge pan of scrambled eggs as she prepared to iron the special tablecloths she'd hand selected for the evening.

No matter the occasion, Mom always insisted on crisply starched and pressed table linens that she'd iron herself. Mom collected tablecloths. She had hundreds, some with intricate, hand embroidered patterns, for every occasion. She faithfully handwashed and pressed them before and after each use. The keepers of secrets, they were her must-have ingredient to throwing a successful soiree. The heavier the faultless Niagara Spray Starch, the better to safeguard the stories and stains our family table had collected throughout the years.

* * *

When it came to my family, our unspoken assigned seats around the dinner table conveyed volumes about our upbringing. The men would congregate on the end of the table farthest from the kitchen. Dad always took his seat at the head, pretending to be famished, but the mustard stains on his starched white button-down always gave him away—a telltale sign that he'd picked up two, maybe three, hotdogs at the local Exxon gas station on his way home from evening rounds at the hospital. Dad often enjoyed his first scotch on the rocks with a splash of water at *sobremesa*. The second one he'd nurse while ripping ballads on his baby grand piano well into the night. His oldest son, Oscar, sat to his right. He got Dad's musical talent and quick wit, and, according to most everyone we met, my looks (even though I'm three years younger). Our uncanny resemblance foiled Oscar's yearslong plot to convince me I was adopted, as if he were unveiling a dark family secret for the first time, each and every time.

While Mom and Dad threw their four daughters lavish *quinceañeras* at the ripe age of sixteen (mine was actually at seventeen—they were quite tired by the time mine rolled along), Oscar's only birthday request was to celebrate in a corner booth at Denny's with item J from the kids menu, a tomato soup and grilled cheese combo, as his guest of honor. My baby brother Federico faithfully sat to Dad's left. The youngest of the family, Federico, or Fede as Mom called him, was the spitting image of Dad in every way.

Then came the women in the workers' seats closest to the kitchen. Mom, the only almost-natural blonde among a table of brunettes, sat across from Dad at the other end of the table. One of the smartest people I've ever known, Mom loved to go at it hammer and tongs with Dad. And he dished it right back. Their banter was playful and passionate and, depending on the topic, could quickly take a turn for the fierce. Mom always told my sisters and me to find a man that challenged us. She'd certainly found that in Dad. There was always a general underlying mood of competition between them. They'd talk over one another in *Castellano*. In English. In Spanglish. Neither was ever at a loss for words.

Mom was also the gatekeeper. She was the one who'd declare *sobremesa* over and done with. Tableside, Mom was a stickler for proper manners, often threatening my sisters and me with Miss Manners' finishing school (if that was even a thing). Among her greatest pet peeves was when we said we were full. "Satisfied, girls. We say we're satisfied in this family when turning down second helpings." We obliged. Sometimes. Mom's best feature was her smile. But it didn't mean she was always happy. It wasn't until I had five kids of my own that I really came to understand her. Her crazy. Her generosity. Her love. Her frustration.

Then came Mom's girls. The four of us. I'm the youngest and the only leftie of my immediate Caminos family. I always sat to Mom's left, across from her "right-hand person," Laura. Just a year and a half older than me, Laura and I were like oil and water until we lived together in college and became the best of friends. Laura was the independent one. Mom constantly bragged she was potty trained at eleven months—I'm pretty sure her age kept getting younger and younger as Mom got older. She loved to tell stories of Laura as a child, and constantly reminded us all that she was always the silent mastermind behind Oscar's constant mischiefs as a kid. I, on the other hand, was the possessive one—particularly of Mom. Until I hit puberty, I wouldn't let anyone sit next to her. In the car. At the movies. Certainly not at the dinner table. It exhausted Mom. She also loved it, or at least loved the attention.

In the middle of the table sat the peacekeepers, my two oldest sisters, Valentina and Camila. Their birth order and double X chromosomes meant they bore the most responsibility. Valentina, the firstborn, was like a second mother to Federico and me. That landed her between the two of us at dinner. My Billy Idol-loving, president and founder of her school's David Letterman Fan Club, portrait-painting sister was a conundrum of brilliant. The shortest and most petite of all of us, Valentina was the only one who could fill my parents' shoes. All four of them. When the girls-only private school she attended called my parents to suggest Valentina skip her senior year and head straight to college, Mom and Dad declined the offer. Like the dishes, graduation could wait.

Last, but in no way least, Camila sat across from Valentina. Second in line, Camila was the sister who turned the most heads. That didn't mean the rest of us didn't warrant a turn or two. But Camila was different. She was a Scorpio like Mom. The two of them shared a magnetic charisma that commanded attention wherever they went.

It was always understood that there was a reason the five women of the family naturally sat together, closest to the kitchen. When we'd ask Mom why our brothers could keep on playing while we cleaned the house, or why they got to get up from the dinner table and do as they pleased while we were relegated to the kitchen, we always got the same answer: "*Chicas*, they're boys." Latin to the core.

Thanksgiving was no different. The women spent the day in the kitchen while the men patiently waited to be called to the table. But we wouldn't have had it any other way. *La cocina* was where all the action was. It was where *we* called the shots. We reveled in the juicy anecdotes. The taste testing. The secrets we uncovered only to carefully iron them away into the evening's heavily starched table linens trimmed with hand-woven fruit and gourd cornucopia borders.

Aside from the food, or maybe because of it, Thanksgiving was always a big to-do at our home. We faithfully celebrated with four other *Latino* families who, through the years, had become our extended family in the States. Some years we'd escape Pittsburgh's gray winters and meet up for the long holiday weekend in Miami Beach. Fed up with the bone-chilling cold, Mom and Dad had bought a waterfront home at auction when I was in eighth grade.

As Mom served her famous scrambled eggs every Thanksgiving morning, she did her usual recitation of the dinner menu (as if she'd changed it up from the year before) and assign my sisters and me our sous-chef roles for the day. "Valentina, *mi artista*, is on table setting. Camila, my star anise, is on salads. My *Laurita Stewart* (a play on Martha Stewart's name she had given Laura due to her meticulous craftiness) is on the carrot and spinach soufflés. And Josie, my baby girl, is on *puré de papa* (mashed potatoes), stuffing and gravy."

The turkey was always Mom's task—and hers alone. She'd cook it to perfection, covering it in loads of gratitude, along with oranges, butter, fresh herbs and white wine. Mom was always proud of her cooked bird and happy to pass the carving knife to my father; but the truth is, she did much of the pre-carving in the kitchen to make sure it was done the right way—*her way.*

The Friday after turkey day was always a notoriously lazy day in my family, as we all recovered from the previous day's cooking, eating and cleaning. One particular Friday in my early twenties, the day after Thanksgiving of 1997, I was sitting with Tripp—my on-and-off boyfriend of eight years—in the family room alongside Dorita, channel surfing. I was holding my nephew, Anthony, barely two months old, in my arms. He was sound asleep, purring against my chest. I didn't want to move for fear of waking him and breaking the spell of the moment.

More than a year had passed since my maternal grandpa Alfredo's long, drawn out death. My sisters Laura and Camila had also both recently given birth to their first children, Daniel and Anthony, born just two days apart. We were all over the moon with their arrival, making frequent trips between their homes in Key Biscayne and Savannah, Georgia. *Abuela* Dorita had been staying at our home in Miami Beach since her husband's passing, but that Thanksgiving weekend she desperately longed to go back to Argentina to her little backyard cottage in La Plata. Mom, however, knew better.

"*Mami,* the girls need you to help with the babies," I heard Mom say to Dorita. "How many women your age do you know who get to hold their great-grandbabies?"

Mom knew Dorita would go home to an empty house in Argentina, and the moment she got there she would be calling, asking when she could come back to visit. This had been the story of her life since my parents immigrated to the States. Her heart was always in two places at once—and never quite felt whole. Dorita's father had abandoned her and her family when she was barely a teenager. Gone without a trace. She never spoke of him but we all knew it to be true. Dorita made sure history wouldn't repeat itself. She couldn't—wouldn't—do the same to her oldest child and only daughter. She would follow Mom to the ends of the earth.

As I cradled Anthony, Tripp was sitting on the blue leather couch just next to the patio doors that led out to the yard and pool overlooking the Miami skyline across Biscayne Bay. It had been almost a year since he'd moved from Pittsburgh to Florida in an attempt to make it on the PGA tour. Tripp was a legend in his own right in our hometown—homecoming king, captain of the State Cup champion Fox Chapel Area High School soccer team and golf club champion at the local country club located next door to my parents' home in Pittsburgh. But in Florida, he was just another one of the many tour hopefuls trying to make it. While I hated the distance between us, I'd always admired his relentless determination to follow his dream. He had a tournament the following Sunday, so we had decided to spend the holiday together at my parents' Florida home, just two hours south of his place.

The Richard Marx song, "Right Here Waiting," pretty much summed up my relationship with Tripp. God knows that's what I had been doing for those past several years. We met our sophomore year in high school, just after spring break. Barely sixteen, he was a newly minted driver. I was fifteen. It wasn't often that Shady Side Academy and Fox Chapel High School kids mingled, at least not my year. But in our case, my best friend Taylor—the flirtatious girl that all the boys wanted to make out with, whether or not they admitted it—had transferred to the public high school in tenth grade and was the reason Tripp and I got together.

We met at her house. I was walking down Taylor's stairs, dressed in a red-and-white striped mini skirt and sheer white tank top that showed off my just-back-from-the-beach tan. As I rounded the staircase, my eyes met his and my breath caught, causing me to almost fall. Suddenly it felt as if we were the only ones standing in Taylor's kitchen. I took a deep breath, steadying myself on the doorknob.

"What happened to your leg?" I asked, pulling down my skirt.

"Broke it in Sun Valley over the break." He adjusted his crutches so he could move his leg, clad in a full-length cast, out of my way. "I'm Tripp. It's Josephine, right?"

The morning after, I was back in Taylor's kitchen, feeling giddy. After a couple of bites of her Fruity Pebbles, Taylor started in.

"Tripp likes you, you know. He wants to see you again."

The next weekend, Taylor invited me to a party at the house of a girl I didn't even know. My memories of that night are foggy, to say the least. I was so nervous to see Tripp that I'd decided, for the first time ever, to have a couple of drinks to gain my courage. I knew I was playing with fire. I had a boyfriend at the time, Owen. We'd been dating since my freshman year. The only problem was that he was no longer in Pittsburgh. It had been six months since his parents moved his family to Orchard Park, New York. It only took three Seagram's wine coolers for me to lose all inhibition and sneak upstairs with Tripp. That night, too tipsy to go home, Taylor and I went back to her parents' house. I awoke the following morning in her room with a dry mouth and pounding headache.

Taylor came out of the bathroom, toothbrush in hand, wearing an old white T-shirt that barely covered her underwear. Her sun-kissed glow showed off her thin legs and long blonde hair even more than usual. I was still nursing my headache in bed.

"Hi, sleepyhead. How are you feeling this morning?"

"Hey, okay, I guess."

"So, about last night? Tripp's cast? I mean, Jesus, it goes all the way up to his hip. The kid can barely walk. How'd you two manage?" Taylor barely got in a breath, spurting out question after question, pausing only to quickly spit and rinse.

"Creative positioning, I guess. It must run in the family. Did I ever tell you I was conceived while my dad was in a full-body cast?" I asked, attempting to get the spotlight off me.

"What? No."

"It's a running joke between us. Dad was in an accident back in '72. He got hit head-on in a Fiat 600. They're tiny. When the ambulance came, he realized his leg was facing the wrong way. Two operations later, it landed him in bed with a full-length body cast for a year. I was born seven months after he got it off."

"No way. Is that why your Dad has a limp?"

"Yeah. His left leg is two inches shorter than his right."

"What about Owen? Are you breaking up with him?" Taylor added with a look that said she hoped the answer was yes. She'd made that clear more than once. We were all over my long-distance relationship.

I didn't answer. God knows I hadn't planned on being with Tripp, at least not consciously. I hadn't intended for this to happen. I pulled the covers over my head and abruptly turned to face the wall, pretending to fall back asleep to avoid dealing with Taylor's inquisition. Barely fifteen, I'd managed to get buzzed and lose my first boyfriend, among other things, in just a matter of hours. I wondered how many other firsts in my life I would manage to screw up so quickly.

As life would have it, I ended up falling hard. Tripp and I soon became inseparable—until our family routines and lifestyles continuously conspired to separate us. We lived just two blocks away from one another in Pittsburgh, yet our relationship also soon became long-distance. I spent my summers at our family's summer home on the Calibogue Sound in Hilton Head Island's South Beach. He spent most of his weekends during the school year at his parents' ski-in/ski-out hillside chalet in Upstate New York. After high school graduation, I headed south to Duke University in Durham, North Carolina. Tripp went north after being recruited to play Division 1 soccer in Maine. One day during our sophomore year, he called to let me know he would be transferring to a college closer to me.

"There's no future in soccer," he said. "I'm transferring this fall to Greensboro, just an hour away from Duke. I made their golf team. The coach saw me play and is letting me walk on. We'll finally get to be together. We can see each other every weekend."

It broke my heart to tell Tripp that I'd just enrolled for a semester abroad in Madrid, Spain. "I leave August first," I said. It seemed as if the universe was colluding to keep us apart. But once we were both back in North Carolina, it soon became clear that the distance was the least of our problems.

* * *

It became especially obvious that particular Thanksgiving, back in the TV room as I cradled my nephew Anthony. Dorita broke my train of thought by asking me for the roll of white yarn that had fallen off of her lap as she was attempting to undo a stitch that had gone awry. Nearing eighty, her arthritic hands were giving her trouble as she tried to grasp the knitting needles, yet she was intent on making matching vests for her newborn great-grandbabies.

"Can you reach that ball of yarn for me, Josie?"

"Of course, *Abuela*. Tripp, can you grab it? I don't want to wake the baby."

"Sure," he said, bending down. The sun shone like a spotlight through the patio doors, revealing Tripp's scalp through his closely shaved hair. His naturally striking blonde mullet he had when we first started dating—the standard soccer player haircut—had taken on more of a reddish undertone through the years. Always chasing summer, Tripp sported a golfer's tan over his tight arm muscles.

"What do you want to watch?" Tripp asked, looking at me with his crystal blue eyes from behind wire-rimmed glasses. He had particular difficulty pronouncing *s* and *z* sounds, often replacing them with an erroneous *th* or out of place *sh*. Our friends often commented on his lisp, harmlessly teasing him in good fun, but I never seemed to notice it, or at least care enough to pay attention. His looks and sheer athleticism rendered it a moot point. That's the thing about love: aside from being blind, it also often falls on deaf ears.

"Josie, how's the baby?" Camila asked, popping her head into the living room to check on the two-month-old. Her dark, shampoo-shiny curls followed closely behind.

"Still asleep," I whispered.

"Great. I'm going to have a coffee with Mom in the kitchen. Let me know if you need me to get him. He should be getting hungry soon."

"No problem, I'll bring him to you."

Just then a commercial for the box office hit *Titanic*, featuring Kate Winslet and Leonardo DiCaprio's ill-fated love affair on the maiden voyage of the unsinkable ship, came on. "I want to see that movie," I whispered to Tripp, careful not to wake the baby. "It comes out just after my birthday, right before Christmas."

"I don't know if I'm going home for the holidays. It all depends on my tour schedule."

It was the same old song that played over and over in my head, "Right Here Waiting." Lately, it seemed to be all I'd been doing. Waiting. What concerned me most was that it didn't seem to bother him in the least. I'd always known I came in second to golf. Why then did it seem to catch me off guard in that moment? Wasn't it his steadfast determination that had drawn me to him in the first place?

"Why don't you come down and see me?" he asked, as if I had nothing else going on in my life. By then, I was working as a medical assistant at Dad's outpatient diagnostic medical company in Pittsburgh.

"You do realize I have a job? A real one that allows two weeks' vacation a year." After graduation, Tripp went South to pursue a career in golf while I stayed behind in Pittsburgh, applying to med school while earning some money. But my aspiration at the time to pursue medicine as a career wasn't turning out as I'd imagined. Once I did the math, I realized that I wouldn't become the pediatrician I'd dreamed of becoming until I was twenty-nine. Where did that leave marriage? And kids? Just as I'd always imagined Tripp one day going down on one knee, I figured we'd have at least one by thirty.

"I know. We'll figure it out. We always do. By the way, I keep meaning to ask you. Have you seen our ghost again? I keep replaying that night over in my head."

"No. It still spooks me."

An out-of-this-world experience had left us dumfounded during his last visit to Pittsburgh a couple of months back. It happened so fast, we couldn't process it. I was still living at my parents' home in Fox Chapel, just outside of Pittsburgh. They were out for dinner when Tripp came over. Catching up on months of longing for one another over late night calls, we figured we had time to spare until my parents got back. We were lying arm in arm on the green Chesterfield leather couch in the family room when all of a sudden the back door alarm beeped and the door swung open. Tripp jumped faster than I imagined possible, grabbing his pants and shirt from the floor. I rolled off the couch and hid under the mahogany coffee table while trying to clasp my bra. Tripp's face went pale. We'd assumed it was my parents coming home, but it was someone else entirely. He was there, standing in the hallway. Staring at us. A silver-haired, bearded man. Hat in hand.

Tripp shot me a wide-eyed look, totally perplexed. "Who's that?"

I didn't know, but there was something vaguely familiar about him. He looked to be in his seventies, with bowed legs, a khaki windbreaker and matching herringbone flat cap. I watched in awe as he closed the back door softly behind him and began to walk slowly towards us down my parents' long, white Carrera marble-lined hallway. His gaze never veered from ours. I could hear my heartbeat pounding in my ears.

"Hurry, fasten my bra!" I whispered frantically, trying to make out the man's face.

"Say something," Tripp suggested. "Maybe he's looking for the bridge game at the country club. You know it's happened before. Remember last year when that band of old guys crashed your breakfast asking for the card room?"

I abruptly rose to my feet. "Hello," I yelled, but he just kept slowly walking toward us, his steps deliberate as my heart raced faster and faster. As the stranger walked effortlessly toward us, hands in pockets, that nagging sense that I knew him from somewhere didn't abate. But I couldn't place him. Not yet.

I stumbled, but even as Tripp caught me, I felt myself trembling, the hairs of my neck alert and on standby. "Can I help you? If you're looking for the country club, it's next door, up the hill from the golf course. You need to leave."

That, he seemingly understood. The white-bearded man stopped and fixated his eyes on mine. At just under six feet tall, he had my full attention. He didn't look away. Instead, he lifted his arm and pointed straight at me. Adrenaline poured through my veins.

I looked at Tripp as I finished tucking in my shirt and combing my long brown hair back with my hands. "What does he want?"

"I don't know, but look, he's leaving," Tripp pulled me towards him, wrapping a protective arm around my shoulders.

So it seemed. Without uttering a word, our uninvited guest turned to leave. Except, he didn't. He stopped when he reached the hallway door to the basement, and after shooting a piercing glance our way, put his cap back on and nodded, as if to say goodbye. Then he opened the door and closed it behind him, disappearing down the stairs. Tripp and I looked at one another. *Now what?*

"We need to go down there and see what he wants," I said.

Tripp ran to the back door and got two large umbrellas. "Okay, take one just in case."

"Should we call the police?"

"He's an old man. What could he possibly do to us? He's probably just lost or confused."

My heart raced as we prepared to go look for him, when the back door opened. My parents. *Thank God!*

I ran to the door. "Mom, Dad, there's a strange man in the house. He's downstairs. I told him the country club was next door, but he just kept walking around, as if he didn't understand. Or care to," I said, panicking.

Perplexed, Dad opened the door to the basement and went to take a look, Tripp in tow. Dad turned and looked at him, his thoughts clear as day. *I can handle this on my own.*

Moments later, they reappeared from the basement. "Josie, are you sure you heard the door open?" Dad asked in his deep Argentine accent that he'd been unable to shake, even after twenty years of living in the States. It worked to his benefit, and he knew it. The ladies found it charmingly sexy. The boys who crossed the threshold into his home, looking to date one of his daughters, found it terrifying. In that moment, I wondered what rattled Tripp most: Dad or the ghost? "No one's down there. The back door was locked when your mother and I came in, and we just checked the entire basement."

"Should we call the police?"

"And say what? You want me to file an official police report that claims an old man entered our house uninvited, pointed you out and then disappeared into our exit-less basement? Never to be seen again?"

Well, when you put it that way . . .

Dad was annoyed. He looked at Mom as if to say, *Did you know these two were going to be alone in the house? Because I sure as hell didn't.*

It didn't matter how old I was. Until I was married, it was never proper for me to be alone with a man, no matter how many years we'd been together. The four years I'd lived on my own at college didn't matter, nor did the one following graduation when I lived in Aspen, Colorado in order to "find myself." Now that I was back home, I was still under Dad's rules.

One of Mom and Dad's favorite *sobremesa* teachings during my teenage and young adult years was the bovine, rhetorical question, "Why buy the cow, when you can get the milk for free?" My parents must have asked me this question dozens of times. They never expected an answer in return, but instead meant only to repeatedly remind me that even the slightest promiscuity on my part was not only considered unladylike but could derail any chances I had of marrying at all. Mom didn't need me to marry. Of course, she hoped I'd meet Prince Charming, but on my own terms and on my own two feet. She didn't want me to screw up my chances of living happily ever after. Not after the personal sacrifices they'd made to give their six children a better life in the States.

* * *

The late Miami sun was setting, flooding the family room with a golden hue. Lost in my thoughts, Tripp tapped my shoulder. "Josephine. Earth to Josephine."

Baby Anthony began to stir in my arms. "Do you think we imagined him? Our ghost?" I asked.

"No. He was definitely there. I can still hear his footsteps hitting the marble floor. Where he went is a mystery to me."

"Well, if he is a ghost, I suppose they don't talk back. My parents think we imagined the whole thing. They don't seem to find it at all unusual that a total stranger walked into their house and disappeared into the basement. There's no way to get outside from down there. Not even a window. They kept saying our home is one of Fox Chapel's original farmhouses and we probably just heard the old floorboards creaking."

But we both knew what we saw and heard. And Mom never did say why she started keeping a hand axe at the ready in her everything-but-the-kitchen-sink drawer. Still, months later, there was no logical explanation. The only thing I knew in that very moment on the couch was that I all of a sudden really had to pee.

Abuela Dorita was knee-deep in yarn, so I handed Anthony to Tripp, whispering in my softest baby voice, "Go with your uncle while *Tía* Josie runs to the bathroom."

"I'm not his uncle," Tripp corrected me, "but here, give me him." He held out his arms to cradle my nephew.

Dorita had never quite mastered the English language, yet somehow she never missed a beat. She was looking down, contemplating a complex stitch in the pattern, and after shifting her glance over her bifocals looked up at me and said candidly, "*Tu novio, querida mía, no te quiere.*" Your boyfriend, my dear, is not in love with you.

"What? What'd she say?" Tripp asked, smiling at *Abuela* as he cradled the baby. It looked especially good on him. Tripp knew she was talking about him. The "*novio*" part he got, but the rest was foreign to him.

"Whatever. Nothing important. I'll be right back."

I took my time in the bathroom, splashing water on my face as my thoughts hung on every one of Dorita's words. *Your boyfriend, my dear, is not in love with you.* She was looking out for me, that much I got—trying to make me see what I couldn't see for myself, but at that moment I hated her for it. *But how does she know?* The voice in my head quipped back, *she just does. She always did.*

Dorita knew things beyond the familiar realm of the senses. Take her cooking. Like most grandmas, she never used a recipe.

Instead, she eyeballed amounts using *puñados* (handfuls), *dedos* (fingers), *pizcas* (pinches) and teacups of all different sizes—"*Un dedo de aceite, dos dedos de agua,*" she'd always say. "One finger of oil, two fingers of water." Dorita tasted, tested and felt her way through the kitchen. She never required a timer; the smell alone wafting from the oven was enough for her to know whether or not a cake was ready. And if she suspected the crumb was a little dry, she'd reach for a bottle of Cointreau and brush on a smidgeon here and there to moisten it. Anyone who has chased their own grandmother around the kitchen, trying to capture the secret behind her beloved *torta de nuez* walnut cake or *ñoqui*, understands this magic. Her instincts were always spot on. She only had to look at a pastry dough to know what it needed. "*Un dedo más de leche, querida, si no se te quiebra la masa.*" One more finger of milk, my dear, otherwise your dough will crack on you.

For the most part, Dorita was sweet as could be. We always said she was made of sugar and spice. But that didn't mean she was always nice. Regardless of her intentions, her words could cut like a knife. Especially that day.

Like a good pastry dough, I needed the advice *Abuela* Dorita had so readily dished up—*your boyfriend, my dear, is not in love with you*—with another finger or two of milk, or even better, heavy cream. I closed the bathroom door and headed towards the kitchen. I needed comforting, and I sure as hell wasn't going to find it back in the family room.

"Josie, come sit down. Your sister and I are just about to have a tea and *café con leche,*" Mom said as I entered the kitchen.

"You mean *café con* coffee creamer? I don't know how you drink that stuff."

"Now, what can I get you?" Mom and Camila were sitting quietly at the kitchen table tucked away in a glass-encased alcove, overlooking the bay. Even the dining table was glass. You couldn't hide anything here. It had always been one of my favorite spots in the house for intimate conversation.

"*Manzanilla,* chamomile, for me. And, Camila, don't worry about the baby. Tripp and Dorita have him. He's still sleeping. I'll check on them in a few."

It was just before five p.m., and like clockwork, Mom was sitting down for her daily *merienda*. It was like Dorita always said, "You can take the girl out of Argentina, but you can't take Argentina out of the girl." For a half hour or so, between 4:30 and 6:30 every afternoon, Argentines enjoy *la merienda*—a time to recharge with tea or coffee and sweet and savory snacks while partaking in an abbreviated version of the mealtime *sobremesa*. This can be as formal as an afternoon tea, but more often than not, it's shared with family or friends around the kitchen table or in a local café. Children call it *la leche* and will often have warm or cold milk with chocolate powder or a teardrop of coffee—also known as a *lagrima*. With the dinner hour typically pushed back to nine, ten or eleven o'clock, most Argentines need this mid-afternoon refreshment. Grandma Dorita was also a faithful *meriendera* teatime aficionada, but I didn't bother to invite her to join us that day, as I was still working on digesting the words of wisdom she so freely offered up. "*No te quiere*. He doesn't love you."

"Camila, have a *palmerita*," Mom said, pushing the plate on my sister.

The best part of any *merienda* is the *facturas*, a variety of popular mini pastries that you can find in any café or neighborhood *panadería*. That day, Mom had Spanish *palmeritas*—mini elephant ears. They were her favorite.

"You're too thin, Camila. You need to eat when you're breastfeeding to make more milk."

Mom always tended to exaggerate and wanted more than anything to feed anyone that crossed her path, another generation-spanning gene among most of the women in my family. But, in this instance, she was right. Camila looked thin and tired. She was still navigating being a first-time mom and was working on little to no sleep.

"*Palmerita?*" Mom asked, handing me my piping hot chamomile tea.

"*No gracias*. I'm in the mood for something salty. Do we have leftover stuffing?"

"Teatime stuffing?" Mom reached into the fridge. "*Claro*. Of course. It makes perfect sense," she said, shooting me one of her coy side-eye glances. "Give me a second." Mom began spooning the stuffing and rolling it into little balls that she pan-fried in butter. "*Voilà . . . torrejas*," she announced, placing them alongside the *palmeritas*. I loved how Argentines, Mom and Dorita especially, had the uncanny ability to turn most any leftover into a crazy good fried fritter. "Camila, eat one. The walnuts will make your milk nice and rich." But Camila opted for the safer option, an elephant ear.

As I took a bite of stuffing followed by a sip of chamomile, the combination of earthy flavors came together so beautifully on my tongue that they went straight to my head and before I knew it, they unleashed a well of tears. I tried to push them back, but they continued to pool, forcing me to noticeably wipe them away.

"I know you love my stuffing, but crying?" Mom asked inquisitively. "*¿Que pasa?*" She reached over to grab my hand. As I replayed Tripp's and Dorita's words, Camila and Mom listened intently.

"Josie, don't worry about it. *Abuela* gets cranky. She's really intent on knitting the babies' matching vests and is probably just frustrated. You know how she is. One minute she loves you, the next you're her punching bag. Since Alfredo's been gone, she has no one to take her moods out on. Don't mind her. She doesn't mean anything by it."

"But she did mean it. She can be such a bitch."

"*Mami's* always said whatever's on her mind." Mom grabbed my chin and gave it a tug. "Like someone else I know."

"The thing is, I think she might be right. Even last night at *sobremesa*, as we went around the Thanksgiving table and each person was sharing what they were most thankful for, Tripp leaned over and mentioned something about getting engaged soon. But as much as I want to believe him, I just don't. Too much has happened. Even though he denies the rumors I keep hearing about other women, I can't shake my doubts. I turn twenty-four in three weeks. What am I going to do?"

"Keep your voice down. He's just down the hallway." Mom hushed me. "Do you really want to have this conversation here? Now?"

But it was too late. There was no going back. True to herself, Mom was going to speak her mind whether I liked it or not. "You know we love him, Dorita included. We've watched him grow up. And he does love you. He's been most everywhere with us—Hilton Head, Buenos Aires, San Martín de los Andes in the Patagonia. Now he's in Florida. And while you wait, he always comes back, sooner or later. Now what about you? I know you love him. But do you love him for him, or do you love the person you think you can make him?"

I said the three magic words all moms hope to hear, "You were right. I actually don't want to have this conversation. Let's forget about it."

"No, *hija*. Now that you brought it up, it's time we talked about it. Like you said, you're almost twenty-four, and yet you still don't know what you want to do with your life. You decided not to continue on to med school after college graduation because you want to get married and have children when you're still young. Now you're considering a career as a physician's assistant while you work for your father in Pittsburgh as a medical assistant. Imagine, with your Duke degree, you're doing jobs that don't even require four years of college. Look at your sisters. Valentina has her MBA. Camila, her CPA. Laura, a law degree. What are you going to do? You're the only one I still worry about."

"Camila and Laura may have degrees, but neither of them have jobs."

Camila put down her coffee. "Josie, I just had a baby."

Mom lightly stepped on my foot under the glass table—code for *cut it out*. "It doesn't matter. Your sisters have something to fall back on. The degrees they got are insurance policies for their future. I made sure of it. I promised myself I would raise you girls to be able to stand on your own. I don't want any of you to ever have to depend on a man. The moment things take a turn, that's a position you never want to be in."

"Like you?"

Mom paused. "Josie! And you complain about *Mamí* saying whatever she pleases. That mouth of yours is going to get you in trouble. Always so *impertinente*. Just what is it you're trying to say?"

"Nothing. Just that you've told me on more than one occasion that you often wish you would have followed your own career in law or returned to teaching."

"True, but I don't have any regrets. Your father and I wouldn't be where we are today if I hadn't been by his side helping him build his medical practice, and then the ranches. I know that. But I also wouldn't have been able to help him, raise you all, and forge my own career on the side. And imagine, I had *Mami* helping me. But a career on top of that simply wasn't a choice I could make. And I'm okay with that. I chose my path. But your generation of women has so many more professional opportunities at your disposal. Not to mention a pool of men—if you pick the right one—who are sharing the responsibility of bringing up the next generation."

I got it. Mom was arming me with the strength to become my own person. Many women of her generation weren't afforded that same opportunity. Sold on JFK and Jackie O's version of Camelot, they were raised to marry well. It was like the late Supreme Court Justice Ruth Bader Ginsburg once said, "For most girls growing up in the '40s, the most important degree was not your BA, but your MRS." But that nuptial degree didn't come with a lifelong to-have-and-to-hold guarantee, leaving some women stuck or unable to leave for lack of their own plan B. Mom had seen one too many of her friends succumb to this same fate. For that reason, she made sure that my sisters and I could leave, if and when needed.

I drank the last of my tea, staring into my cup as I tried to reconcile my feelings. "I'm going to go check on the baby."

"No. Wait," Mom motioned for me to stay seated. "Tripp will bring him if he wakes up. I need you to answer me one thing. Why do you keep settling? Tripp's not asking you to. He's chasing his dreams to become a pro golfer. And he hasn't asked anything of you that would keep you from doing the same. Are you going to wait until he makes it? Or are you waiting for him to not make it so your life with him can finally start?"

"I've invested more than eight years into this relationship. It's all I know. He's all I know. We're planning on getting married. At least I am."

"Okay, but have you ever stopped to think that maybe your relationship's gone stale? Like the bread in that stuffing?"

"I love this stuffing." I grabbed another *torreja*. *Even if it's fried in gobs of butter and regret.*

"*Claro*. For a weekend. Once a year. You wouldn't eat it day after day. How about Tripp? Would you be able to live with him day in and day out?"

"He hasn't asked me to. Honestly, we've never been in the same city long enough to know."

"You don't need him to ask. This is your home. I'm here more than I'm in Pittsburgh. You're bilingual. And with your marketing and pre-med degrees, you could get a job here in a heartbeat. Something's holding you back. If he makes it on the golf tour, are you prepared to give up your dreams and ambitions and follow him? Because the daughter I know is not a follower. And what if he doesn't make it? What then? Will he be enough? Let's not forget when we took him skiing to Chapelco in Argentina. He paid seven dollars for a *New York Times*, took out the sports section and threw the rest of the paper away. And what did you do? You went and fished it out of the waste bin without saying a word."

"Really, Mom? That damn *New York Times* story again? You read way too much into that." But deep down, I knew Dorita and Mom were right. I only saw what I wanted to see.

"No, it's you who's not paying attention. This is what your *abuela* is trying to tell you. Even if it hurts." Mom took a sip of her tea.

I took a long look at her. Mom had always had a voracious appetite for reading and film, learning new things, seeing new places. At fifty-two, she still did. On her nightstand you could always find the two or three latest books she was reading along with that day's newspaper, a dog-eared *Architectural Digest* or two, and a marked-up *Michelin Travel Guide* plotting her and Dad's next adventure. I never knew when Mom found the time to devour all of that information, but she did. At my age, she'd already had two kids—with another on the way—and a husband who spent most of his living and breathing time clocking hours at the hospital so he could get ahead. I didn't disagree that Mom would have been a damn good lawyer. But back then as a newlywed in Argentina in the late '60s and early '70s, the Catholic priests preached to Mom and her friends that it was a sin to use birth control. That their lives now belonged to their husbands. That the only insurance they needed was God's plan and a mastery of the calendar-counting rhythm method for birth control.

I took a deep breath and jumped back into the conversation. There was no use in fighting it. Mom was going to drill me until she was done. "I don't know if I can give him up. It's been too long. And I'm in love with him. I don't want to end up living with the ghost of what might have been if I'd just waited a little bit longer for him to take the next step."

"Just be careful, little sis," Camila said, barely able to get a word in. "When you can't seem to make a decision, life tends to step in and make it for you. And usually, it only makes it worse. You know if you can't trust him now, once you're married things only get more complicated. There's no plan B when you say 'I do.' *If you mean it.* Now where's that *bebo* of mine. My milk just let down."

"Camila's right," Mom said, shifting in her seat. "If you can't trust him now, a ring won't fix that."

"But an insurance policy will?" *Ojalá.* Hopefully.

I didn't know then, but Mom's and *Abuela's* words would become an ironic foreshadowing of turmoil to come. Mine lay just ahead, waiting for me in the new year. Camila's would be delivered two years later, on the heels of the birth of her second son, Phillip, that left her reeling to chart out her own plan B. But that's her story to tell, because unless it's your own to do with as you please, what happens at *sobremesa* stays at *sobremesa.*

Mom's Thanksgiving Stuffing

SERVES 7. *Or one, if you find yourself unexpectedly plotting out an Emergency Plan B over a long, drawn-out holiday weekend.*

Whether you call it stuffing or dressing, you probably feel inclined to make it once and only once per year: on Thanksgiving. But this really is a versatile side dish for almost any protein and is a great excuse to use stale bread. True to Mom's recipe, I've listed packages of seasoned bread stuffing cubes. But as an adult I prefer to hand-tear a day-old French bread loaf into ¾-inch pieces and slowly finish drying it out in a low oven. Mom probably would have preferred to make her own croutons as well, but as kids, we wouldn't let her—similar to the way we would get mad at her when, God forbid, she'd peel and boil potatoes and hand-mash them instead of making the boxed Hungry Jack instant potatoes we all loved.

2 tablespoons extra-virgin **olive oil**

4 bunches **green onions**, finely chopped

4 tablespoons **unsalted butter**

3 large **garlic cloves**, finely chopped

1 pound fresh **wild mushroom blend**, sliced

½ pound **walnuts**, finely chopped

1 cup **white wine**

Salt and freshly ground **black pepper** to taste

1 cup **boiling water**

1 envelope **onion soup mix**

1 cup **milk**, warm

1 cup fresh-squeezed **orange juice**

1 cup low-sodium **chicken stock**, warm

½ bunch fresh **sage**, finely chopped

Two 12-ounce bags Pepperidge Farm herb seasoned cubed **stuffing** (or white bread, crust removed)

Preheat the oven to 375°F and butter a two-quart baking dish.

In a large skillet over medium heat, sauté the green onions in olive oil with a pinch of salt. When they begin to glisten, add butter, garlic, mushrooms and walnuts, stirring occasionally for approximately 2–3 minutes. Increase the heat to high and carefully add wine. Cook for another 3–5 minutes until most of the moisture has evaporated. Season with salt and pepper to taste.

Meanwhile, in a large bowl, dissolve onion soup mix in 1 cup boiling water. Mix in milk, orange juice, chicken stock, sage and mushroom mixture. Slowly add breadcrumbs (or bread) and carefully fold into the mixture.

Pour into a roasting dish and bake for 30–35 minutes until golden brown on the top (if it gets too brown before the 30 minutes is up, tent with foil).

Chapter 2

Estar al horno con papas
Caught Red-Handed

Since as far back as I can remember, Mom had a torrid love affair with *palmitos*. Otherwise known as hearts of palm, swamp cabbage or burglar's thighs, the innocuous milky white batons were the lobster to her vegetables. I could walk into the kitchen any time of day and find her eating them straight from the jar. I could tell her mood just by the way she ate them. If she sat slowly peeling back the outside flavorful flesh in anticipation of arriving to the tender, slightly nutty core as she watched CNN or perused the morning paper, all was good in that moment. But if I walked in to see her standing at the kitchen counter, chomping on them like a beaver eating stems, then I knew something was gnawing at her. The churning movement and constant munching subconsciously calmed the ever-present anxieties of raising six children while managing a household, working with Dad and countless social obligations.

* * *

My *abuela's* ill-fated words from the previous Thanksgiving holiday had revealed themselves to be true, just four months later in March when Tripp took a family vacation—a cruise of all things—and returned only to confess he'd fallen in love with a woman he met aboard. She was everything I wasn't—blonde with bright blue eyes, as American as apple pie. She was a perfect match for Tripp, whose aspirations to be a professional golfer led him to spend hours on end at distinguished old guard WASPy country clubs. His home turf was the Harts Run Club. If he wasn't on the course, you could find him in the mahogany-lined Men's Grill that was off-limits to women and children. Ironically, I grew up next to Harts Run's golf course. My parents' home sat on three acres adjacent to the course. Tripp would swing by on his golf cart, and I'd jump the white picket fence separating our lawn from the course and join him.

"Josephine, I told you. You need to wear a collared shirt."

"Really? No one will notice," I'd smile back, adjusting the spaghetti straps on my tank top. *But he noticed.*

"Come on. You know I don't care. I love the way you look. But rules are rules. I don't want anyone to say anything or call us out." And off we'd go to the club, the only way a girl like me could be admitted—as a guest, or with a little luck, a wife. I'd found this out the hard way at just seventeen.

One night, my parents and I were invited to dinner at Harts Run Club's Grill Room by friends of the family who also happened to have a daughter my age, Bridget. We were in class together at Shadyside Academy. We'd been good childhood friends but grew apart in high school. Probably because I spent most of my time with Tripp. But that night we fell right back into our friendship, bonding tableside. I can still taste the buttery poached salmon with homemade hollandaise sauce and fresh avocado chunks that I relished bite after bite. *Sobremesa* was even better since it gave us time to catch up. The whole night was a treat, until I abruptly came to understand the real story behind that fabled dinner.

A couple of weeks later, Tripp and I were celebrating his first inner-club tournament win at the local hangout, Harris Grill, with a group of friends when Bridget walked in. Foregoing a greeting, she immediately announced to the table how sorry she was that her parent's attempts to sponsor my family for membership at the club had been thwarted. "Turned down. Just like that. And we all know why. I mean, you can't help where you were born. My parents are just furious."

"Enough, Bridget," Tripp cut her off. "We don't know what you're talking about."

But Bridget kept at it. "You said you were going to tell her? You know, break it to her gently?"

"I mean it. Enough." Tripp grabbed my hand. It was clear Bridget meant well, but with each word she muttered, she dug herself deeper and deeper into a hole.

"Thanks, Bridget. I don't really know what you're talking about, but I'm sure it's some sort of misunderstanding. You know we've always belonged to our club in Churchill." It was true. I grew up down the street from the country club back in Churchill, swimming and playing tennis days on end in the summer. We loved it there. We were accepted there. But I was coming to learn that things worked differently in Fox Chapel. We were moving on up, but did we want to be there?

Bridget shrugged her shoulders. "Okay, but don't say I didn't try to warn you," she said before walking away.

I choked down a swig of my Arnold Palmer as I looked at Tripp, asking under my breath, "What's she talking about? You knew about this? Is it true?"

Tripp grabbed my hand and took me aside. "I heard a rumor. That's all I know. I'm sorry, Josephine. I was looking for the right time to tell you."

"And still you want me to get all dressed up tomorrow night to celebrate your win at the club, even after I know what I know?"

"You know I don't care about any of that stuff. I just want to play golf and have you by my side. Those are the only two things I care about. I don't want any part of their politics or this bullshit. Especially if it hurts you."

I didn't want it to hurt. But I can't say it didn't sting. Through the years I'd been to countless events at the club next door with Tripp, not to mention other friends. Taylor's family included. We'd spent countless days poolside, lounging around with friends. It just never dawned on me I was only welcome as a guest. But mostly, I didn't really know how I felt about trying to fit into a world—Tripp's world—when it didn't want me as I was.

Tripp squeezed my hand. "I really think you should come so we can show them we don't care."

"So you want me to get dolled up in a collared shirt and plaid skirt, put on a smile and pretend I don't know?"

"Come on, *you* wouldn't be caught dead in plaid. That's why I love you. No. I want you to wear a slinky dress and hold your head up high. The only thing that matters is you and me."

* * *

Tripp's betrayal made me begin to doubt everything—my own judgement, my other relationships, why I stayed, why I ignored my *abuela's* admonitions.

That last Thanksgiving weekend we spent together in Miami Beach before the breakup, I vividly remember praying to God on the flight home to Pittsburgh. I said my usual roundup since my Catholic CCD days growing up: three Hail Marys, followed by an Our Father, topped off with my Miraculous Medal prayer. "Oh Mary conceived without sin, pray for us sinners who have recourse to thee." My intentions were for God to make the turbulence go away, and while He was at it, help me to meet someone else so I could move on from Tripp.

Ironically, just after New Year's, I tried to break up with Tripp—just three months before he managed to finish the job himself. I couldn't get Dorita out of my head. But he convinced me otherwise. It was just after Tripp's twenty-fifth birthday in January. He was in Florida and I was back home. We'd gotten into a fight over the phone for some reason or another. I don't even remember about what. We'd been together for the better part of a decade. Sometimes off. But mostly on. It didn't matter. Somewhere along the way we picked up too much baggage to carry with us. Tripp had admitted his past infidelities in so many words. He promised me there wouldn't be a third time. *A third time? Was that all?* I couldn't say I hadn't had a minor indiscretion here or there. Too many years had gone by to have a perfect track record, but I didn't want to spend the rest of my life fighting. It was painful, not to mention exhausting. But when push came to shove, Tripp insisted he couldn't live without me, without us. He said everything I wanted and needed to hear one night over the phone.

"I'm flying in for Valentine's Day in two weeks. We can spend the whole weekend together."

"Don't come on my account. I mean it. I can't do this anymore. The fighting. It's not good for either of us."

"I know. But I'm coming. We can work this out. We have to."

"That doesn't mean we're staying together."

"I get in on Friday the thirteenth at six o'clock. Can you pick me up at the airport or not? Either way, don't make plans."

I didn't. "Friday the thirteenth? Are you sure you want to get on a plane?"

"I know, I thought about that when I was getting my ticket. It doesn't matter. I'm coming."

"You know in Argentina, Tuesday the thirteenth is the unlucky day. Not Friday. It'll be fine," I said, thinking how interesting it was that the fear of the number thirteen seemed to be a cultural phenomenon without borders. For me, it was among my luckiest.

As promised, I met Tripp at the airport. The sight of him made me forget my breakup plan altogether. I melted into his arms. We drove straight to Harts Run Club where we were meeting his parents for dinner. Between rounds of Chardonnay for the women and Seagram's VO and beers for the men, we caught up on Tripp's latest tournaments and spoke of their family's upcoming vacation. Tripp's parents had invited him, his younger brother and their two grandmothers on a ten-day Caribbean cruise and were looking forward to spending a week with just family.

Later that night when we were alone, Tripp mentioned he'd wanted to invite me on the cruise, but his parents felt it might be their last opportunity to have a family vacation alone. "You know, before we get engaged."

"I get it," I said, wondering if and when this pending "engagement" would ever happen.

That night, in bed, we listened to Bryan Adam's latest hit, "Please Forgive Me."

"This is us. Listen to the words," Tripp pressed up against me as he whispered in my ear, "Still feels like our first time together."

What neither of us realized is that would be one of our last together. Through the years, we'd come to know each other's every mole, scar, birthmark and imperfection. We knew each other's scents. We reveled in them. He knew my neck, the slope of my shoulders, the rise of my breasts as I'd lower myself to his chest.

We decided to stay in for Valentine's. I was living in my parents' cottage house, the detached garage and adjacent two-floor apartment across the driveway from the main house. It had two small bedrooms, a full bathroom, dining room, a small living space and tiny kitchen. Way more space than I needed at twenty-four. I made Tripp's favorite, *fondue bourguignonne*: cubes of beef and raw vegetables cooked in hot oil with an arrangement of different sauces, and for the side, my favorites—cheese fondue with apples, broccoli florets and French bread.

"By the way, when I was looking up fondue recipes, I read that if you drop your bread from your fork while dipping, you have to kiss someone at the table. Otherwise you face years of bad luck." I grabbed the piece of bread I'd just speared onto my fondue fork and tossed it back into the melted cheese.

"Good thing you're the only one here. Otherwise, who knows who I'd end up kissing," Tripp joked, pulling me towards him.

My thoughts, exactly.

After dinner, we decided to watch a movie. "Look for a good one. Something funny," I said as I headed to the kitchen, plates in hand. "But first, dessert." Anticipating some foreplay at *sobremesa* that evening, I'd prepared a chocolate fondue with strawberries, pound cake and sliced apples.

But when I emerged from the kitchen, Tripp was fast asleep on the couch. *There goes our romantic evening. I should have left the dishes for the following morning.* Once again, *Abuela* Dorita's voice was there in my head. This time forewarning me, "Josefinita, be wary of the bird that eats, then flies the coop." As much as I loved him, Tripp never had been one for table talk.

The following morning, Tripp was headed back home to Florida. We stopped by his parents' house before driving to the airport. As he showered, I sat upstairs on the corner of his bed waiting for him. My stomach was in knots as I folded his golf shirts, placing

ESTAR AL HORNO CON PAPAS

them neatly in his carry-on. Even though he said otherwise, something told me this goodbye was for good. I could feel it in my gut and in the weather outside. The barometric pressure was dropping, which meant a storm was brewing. The last time I'd felt this way, things ended disastrously. I was eighteen and just finishing up my freshman year at Duke. The morning of my last final, I called home to talk to Mom to see if she could put some money in my bank account. A bunch of us were going to Myrtle Beach the following day to celebrate the end of the year before heading home for the summer. Dorita answered the phone that morning in her broken English and thick Spanish accent.

"*Hola. Hallo.* Who is?"

"Dorita, *soy yo.* Josie."

Relieved she could switch to Spanish, Dorita and I talked for several minutes. I told her about my Spanish literature final that I'd be taking later that evening and asked how things there were.

"*Y*, as best as can be expected with everything going on with your *abuelo* Caminos. We're all praying everything turns out well tomorrow."

"What? What's wrong with him, and what's happening tomorrow?"

I heard Mom's voice in the background ask Dorita who she was talking to. Dorita immediately realized that Mom hadn't told me about my grandpa on Dad's side, who I'd soon find out was headed into open-heart surgery the following morning.

"*Hay, Mami.* You weren't supposed to say anything. Josie has an exam today. We need her to get through it without drama," Mom scolded as she grabbed the receiver.

"Josie, everything's going to be okay. Your *abuelo* Caminos is just having a minor heart procedure tomorrow to open up one of his stents." Caminos was Dad's father. More than a father, he was my dad's idol. He never wanted us to call him grandpa or *abuelo*, so from the time we were very young we called him by his—and our—last name. Somehow it stuck. He was eighty years old, but was a solid man with a prominent Roman nose that preceded him. He wore it proudly. It meant he never sought the approval of others and didn't take shit from anyone. Dad loved that about him. Caminos and my dad's mom, Buby, divorced after their kids were grown. He later married a concert pianist, Pía Sebastiani, twenty years his junior, and often traveled the world with her. Caminos visited us once a year, working his yearly cardiology appointments into his travel plans. Dad took care of his heart, always wanting the best for him.

"Mom, you weren't planning on telling me. Really? This doesn't seem like a minor thing."

"I was planning on telling you after finals. We all know how you worry. Your father says he'll be okay. He's found the best surgeon. The operation's tomorrow. Now, what time is your exam?"

We hung up shortly after and instinctively I began to pack. Not for Myrtle Beach, but for home. I called Mom an hour later to tell her I'd talked to my professor, who was letting me take the exam earlier that morning. I wanted to go home and see Caminos before he went into surgery.

"I know you too well." Mom said. "I've already booked a six p.m. direct flight on US Airways. You'll need to go to the airport right after your exam."

"Thanks, Mom. What's that you're chomping on? Let me guess. ¿Palmitos?" She said she wasn't worried. But she was.

* * *

I arrived at West Penn Hospital just before visiting hours were over. Caminos' wife Pía, Mom, Dad, my sister Valentina, brother Federico, Dorita and Alfredo were all gathered around him, joking about the things he'd be doing after his surgery.

"China awaits!" Caminos stated confidently. Pía was holding his hand.

I felt better immediately. As we all said our goodbyes that evening, my grandfather called to me.

"Josefina, come here. I want to tell you something." I was eighteen at the time, though we'd never been particularly close. But that didn't mean I didn't love him.

Caminos grabbed my hand and held it tight. "*Te veo en el cielo*, I'll see you up there. You know what I mean, ¿*Sí?*" He smiled, pointing his right index finger upwards.

"But what about China? Why are you saying these things?" I softly argued with him.

"It's going to be okay. I want to thank you for coming to wish me goodbye. Your *mamá* told me how worried you were when you heard the news. But don't you worry. We'll see one another again. But only after you're old and gray and have lived a full life, like me." Caminos pointed upwards again with a serene smile.

Haunted by his words, I didn't sleep that night before his surgery. The following day, we arrived at the hospital at four a.m. Six hours later, the surgeon came out to speak with Dad. Caminos had made it through surgery beautifully, and they were just stitching him up. Dad delivered the good news to us.

"He's like an ox," the surgeon said. We all took a deep breath, relieved that the worst was over. *Why did I always assume doom when challenging situations arose?*

We remained in the waiting room for another hour when suddenly the surgeon burst through the doors with a grim look on his face, removing his surgical cap with resignation. Dad rose from his chair to meet him. After a moment, all we could see was Dad collapsing into his legs, using his arms to steady himself against his thighs, his head hanging low, so he could breathe. Caminos had made it through the surgery with flying colors, but without any explanation or warning, flatlined just as they finished closing him up. For more than thirty minutes, the surgical team worked on resuscitating him. Unsuccessfully. Caminos had known all along that his time was up.

Since my car accident my junior year of high school, this sense of premonition seemed to become more and more prevalent. I'd get a sense of something in my gut and hard as I might try, I couldn't shake the feeling or make it go away with logic. If I didn't acknowledge my intuition about something, it seemed to only make the situation worse. For instance, what would have happened had I not flown up to visit Caminos? I would have never forgiven myself. Mom always said I worried too much; that it was in my head. *Was it?* It's as if I experienced a different realm of this world that night I flipped our Suburban over and over on the highway. Whatever it was, it stayed with me. I came out a different person. Even more perplexing was that my grandfather Caminos knew that I knew.

* * *

Now, back in Tripp's bedroom, that unshakable feeling was back again. Pressed on time to get him to the airport, I sat folding his clothes, placing them in his carry-on while he showered. I couldn't help but wonder what my gut was trying to tell me this time, when, standing before Tripp's bedroom dresser, I sensed a movement out of the corner of my eye. There they went again: the hairs on the back of my neck telling me I wasn't alone. I looked straight ahead into the dresser mirror and saw the reflection of the silver-bearded man. Our ghost, the one Tripp and I saw months before at my parents' home, was looking back at me. *That half smile. I knew that half smile.* It seemed friendly enough. Still, it chilled me to the bone. Our ghost was between Tripp's closet and bed in his cap, brown tweed pants and perfectly trimmed beard and mustache. He stood there, hands in pockets with his head slightly tilted, looking at me, this time with concern. I hadn't been able to forget his penetrating stare since our first encounter. But this time I was much closer to this ghostly gentleman. Just a couple of steps and I could reach him. I turned around abruptly.

"Who are you? What do you want?" No one was there. Back in the mirror, I saw only my reflection. But he'd been there. Just seconds ago. I was sure of it. His stare went right through me, sending a shudder through my body. I stood there motionless, mentally drawing a chalk outline of where exactly I'd seen him—just as police did in movies, piecing together evidence to recreate the crime scene.

I was a whiter shade of pale when Tripp walked in with a towel around his waist, still wet from the shower.

"What's the matter?"

"Did you see him? The man we saw that night at my parents'?"

"What? No. Where?"

"I was standing here, folding your shirts, when I noticed him staring at me in the mirror. He was standing right there. Where you are. The man we saw at my parents' house."

"Where'd he go? I didn't see anyone in the hallway."

"I don't know. He was there one second. I saw him in the mirror. And then when I turned around, he was gone."

Tripp hugged me. "Could it be last night's wine speaking? In all of the years I've lived here I've never experienced anything strange in this house."

"Maybe, but I swear he was standing right there." I was visibly shaken.

Tripp hugged me tighter. "You okay?"

"I don't know. Does this mean I'm seeing ghosts now?" I buried my face in Tripp's chest. "I really don't want you to go. I hate this long-distance thing. I can't take it much longer."

"We'll figure it out. Soon. We always do. You'll see." Tripp said, gently kissing my lips.

I didn't know it then, *did I*? That was the last I'd see of Tripp. As my boyfriend, at least. But I can't say the same for my mysterious vanishing Gentleman Caller. Over the coming decades, he'd follow me everywhere, always showing up unannounced. The only thing I could make of him was that he seemed to be of a different generation—one where men raced ahead to hold a door for a lady, gave up their seat for women and children and, without fail, removed their cap when entering a room. It's almost as if his hauntings were politely calculated. He never overstepped his boundaries.

* * *

Later that March, the very week that Tripp went on the cruise with his family, I was invited to Washington, DC for an admissions interview for the Physician Assistant Program at the George Washington School of Medicine and Health Sciences. My longtime friend Hope, who was always like a fourth sister growing up, lived in Georgetown, so the plan was to interview that Friday and then spend the weekend together. Tripp and I had made plans to call one another the following Saturday at seven p.m. But just before boarding the cruise ship, he called me one last time from a payphone.

"I can't go three days, let alone ten, without talking to you. It's killing me. I love you. Never forget that. And if you do decide to spend the weekend with Hope, leave a message on my machine with her number so I can call you as soon as I get home."

"I promise. Have a great trip with your family. I love you too," I said one last time before hanging up the phone.

The following Friday night in DC, I was fast asleep on Hope's couch, when suddenly an eerie, prickly feeling came over me. Someone was staring at me. Every hair on my body sensed it, jerking me awake. There he was again. The ghost. The Gentleman Caller. Closer than ever. I blinked. He didn't. Clad in his same tweed pants and silver-white beard, he took off his cap, revealing a receding silver hairline. His hand was on my leg, as if he'd been trying to gently stir me awake.

Wake up, Josephine, I thought. *Wake up. Scream for help.* But I was paralyzed, by fear or by sleep. Like the other times, he didn't make a sound. As our eyes locked, I tried to scream, but nothing came out. Instead I heard a still small voice: *Go home. It's important. You need to get home.* I can't tell you if he spoke in English or Spanish, or at all. He didn't use words. His lips didn't even move. But something told me I should listen to him. And in an instant, as I came to, he was gone. He was really good at disappearing before I had time to react.

My watch said it was just after five a.m. I got up and made myself some coffee as I sat watching the sunrise. I waited until eight a.m. before I woke up Hope, kissed her goodbye and let her know something came up. I had to go.

"I'll explain later. It has nothing to do with you. I love you. I'm so sorry we can't spend the weekend together." I didn't bother to tell Hope I'd been seeing ghosts, most recently in her apartment of all places. I was starting to convince myself he was, like Mom always said, just a figment of my imagination. Mom had almost convinced me he was, until I'd remember that Tripp also saw him in the flesh that night at my parents' home. I wondered why he didn't show himself to the both of us that second time I saw him, in Tripp's bedroom. *Was it me alone he was haunting?*

There was a reason I was being summoned. For the first time, I began to wonder if the visits by the silver-bearded man might have some greater purpose. As I got into my car, I couldn't help but notice the beautiful blue sky overhead, paved with cobblestone-like white fluffy clouds that seemed to nearly kiss one another. It looked like it was going to be a sunny day, but I could hear *Abuela's* voice telling me otherwise. "Josefinita, grab an umbrella. *Cielo empedrado, suelo mojado.*" A cloud-flecked, mackerel sky always means rain is on its way. Dorita had always been intrigued with clouds. She'd look to them each morning, sticking her head out of her bedroom window that hung above the headboard of her bed, to tell her how to dress for the day. She understood that clouds were fragile, fleeting and powerful, and that in a few short moments they could change from a fair-weather cumulus to an angry, ominous, hail-producing nimbus. Rain was definitely on the horizon. The beautiful morning was the calm before the storm I was heading straight into. And something told me it had Tripp's name written all over it.

I made it home to Pittsburgh in just under four hours, right around lunchtime. I had an uneasy feeling all day. As I waited by the phone that evening, Tripp never called. Seven o'clock turned into 7:30, then 8:30. By nine I started incessantly calling him. *What had happened to our phone date and his romantic plea that he couldn't go ten days without talking to me?* He finally picked up my call at 11:30 p.m. The tone of his voice said everything.

"Josephine, we have to talk." Tripp didn't need to say anything else. I already knew.

"Oh, God, you did it again! Let me guess. I've been missing you like hell for the past ten days. How about you? You met someone, didn't you? That's why you haven't called?"

"I swear I didn't mean to hurt you, Josephine. It just happened. I'm so sorry . . ."

Enraged, I cut him off, yelling from the depths of my soul, "No! How could you do this? You promised me there wouldn't be a third time. You begged me to believe you. Despite all my doubts. You promised! I trusted you. Even when I knew better! How could you do this to me? To us? We grew up together. It's always been you and me." I was shaking, barely able to take in a breath, when Mom suddenly appeared at my door and, grabbing the receiver from my hands, hung up the phone. The life I'd imagined with Tripp flashed before my eyes.

"Let him go. *Está al horno con papas*. You caught him red-handed. It's time to close that door. For good this time. He made his choice. It'll likely burn him. But that's not your problem anymore." Mom wrapped her arms around my convulsing body, trying to calm the rage pulsing through my veins.

It was just as my sister Camila had warned. When you put off making a decision for yourself, you can sure as hell be certain that life will step in and make it for you, and you'll probably be that much worse for it. God answered my prayers that night, just not in the way I'd hoped. I couldn't help feeling my Gentleman Caller had woken me up that morning to warn me this was coming. He must have known that if I stayed in DC that I'd have been too upset to drive home the following day. Since my accident, I'd become prone to panic attacks while driving. Like my friendly ghost, they'd show up unannounced. Was that what my mystical visitor was doing? Warning me? About Tripp? Ironically, almost nine years to the date, I'd done the same to my first love, Owen. I left him without warning when I met Tripp. Life is like a garden; you reap what you sow.

* * *

Three months had passed since our breakup that April. *El Niño* started that summer of '98 off with a bang. The global wind pattern was wreaking havoc all over the East Coast, causing floods, mudslides, tornadoes and unusual weather-related phenomena. Just two days into June, an outbreak of nine tornados had touched down in Pittsburgh, tipping over cars, damaging homes, toppling trees and uprooting lives. When ghosts weren't calling on me, I was haunted by memories of Tripp. I felt blindsided. Lost. As if I was in a crowded room screaming for help with no one to hear. But my *abuelo* Alfredo, Mom's dad and Dorita's husband, heard me, and he'd make sure I would get through one of my darkest times. It didn't matter that he'd been dead and gone for two years now. *Abuelo* Caminos' passing had been a terrible day in my life, but even more painful was the passing of Alfredo, whom I had always been closer with. His loss touched me profoundly. And now, he was back—at least in my dreams.

I was sound asleep that first night when Alfredo visited. I must have dozed off watching *Titanic*, the ill-fated movie that was all too painful of a reminder of my own star-crossed love. I'd dreamt that I was immersed in the obscure abyss of the ocean, clinging for dear life to a large block of ice. I could see people and lights in the background slowly fading away as a large ship's stern sunk farther and farther into the sea. Then, just as my hands began to slip, Alfredo grabbed me, pulling me from the water in one fell swoop.

"Take my hand," *Abuelo* appeared out of nowhere, standing on the thick piece of ice I'd been clinging to. "Hold on." He pulled me up from the water and, wrapping a large blanket around me, held me tight. *Oh, how I missed his touch.*

"*Te tengo.* I've got you. I'm not going to let anything happen to you, Josie."

That's when I suddenly jerked awake, muscles tense and gasping for air, unsure of where I was. I sat upright, running my fingers through my matted hair, wet with panic, and placed my hands on my chest. My heart was beating a mile a minute. Looking around, I soon realized I was safe and warm in my bed. It had all been a bad dream.

A week or so later, *Abuelo* Alfredo visited me again. I was drifting in and out of sleep after binge-watching TLC's home decorating show *Trading Spaces* when, out of nowhere, he appeared on my bedside. He was wearing his old faithful tan V-neck cashmere sweater and white turtleneck. Never mind it was summer. His black-framed wayfarer glasses sat upright on his nose, as he smiled at me. I tried to utter "*¿Abuelo?*" but my lips wouldn't move. I was mesmerized by the energy he radiated, which I can only compare to the feeling of sipping a steaming cup of Dorita's *sopa pastina* on a cold winter day that heats you from within.

Alfredo was just as I'd always remembered. There he sat with his perfect posture and tall, broad shoulders; his silver hair neatly combed back and donning his impeccably trimmed signature mustache. He'd always been an elegant man of few words—he said only what needed to be said or didn't say anything at all. Unless, of course, someone uttered a negative comment about his Argentina, to which he would be immediately offended and quick to passionately and verbosely defend. As I took in his breath and reveled in his scent that hinted of tobacco, I was eleven years old again, wearing my green-and-white striped Ellis School for Girls uniform, sitting on Alfredo's lap. We would often watch Little House on the Prairie together. Alfredo would smoke his perfectly polished pipe—his favorite pastime, until Dorita forbade him to smoke. Then he'd try to sneak a cigarette or two in the car as he was driving one of us to a playdate or after school activity. He'd light his cigarette, and no sooner after he placed it in the console ashtray, one of us would immediately put it out, giving him a stern, accusatory look.

That night was no different as he sat beside me on the bed. Grabbing my hand, he cupped it within his. I couldn't help but notice his fingernails were still perfectly manicured.

"*Querida* Josefina, I have you. Don't worry. I've got you. *Tengo tu corazón en la palma de mi manos.* I have your heart right here. In the palm of my hands. It's time to go home."

But I was home.

"Argentina. He's there. Waiting for you."

Who? Who's waiting for me?

As I went to speak, Alfredo quietly got up, smoothed out his pants and, clasping his hands together behind his back, winked before turning and walking out of my room. He was gone. If only I had opened my eyes a moment sooner, I would have seen him for sure. I had been dreaming, yet every sense of my being had never been more awake.

I looked at my clock—8:30 a.m.—and jumped out of bed, not bothering to throw on a robe as I ran outside and crossed the driveway to my parents' house. I peeked through the window and was so relieved to find Mom in the kitchen, clad in her faithful light blue terry cloth robe monogrammed with her initials, BGC—Beatriz Germain Caminos. Few knew her as Beatriz. To all who loved her she was Poupée.

Mom was standing at the stove, sipping her *café con* coffee creamer (she'd given up *leche* a while back). As customary, she was scrambling a large pan of eggs and feeding slices of salami to our caramel-colored golden retriever, Sonny (short for *Sonrisa*, meaning *smile*). While breakfast tended to be a lighter, continental affair in Argentina—strong black coffee or *café con leche* with *tostadas* (thin slices of French bread toasted with butter, jam or *dulce de leche*)—Mom scrambled a carton of eggs several days a week. Eggs were a blank canvas for her. She loved experimenting with them to keep them interesting—often mixing in part of last night's leftovers—ratatouille and *chorizo* among her favorite add-ins.

"Josie, *buen dia*. Eggs?"

"Morning," I said, kissing Mom's cheek. "I'd love some. I'm suddenly starving." I sat down at the breakfast table, patting Sonny on the head. Her tail fanned in the air as she greeted me back.

Mom looked up from the pan and served me a generous portion of scrambled eggs along with her other usual, an English muffin with whipped cream cheese and pan-fried Canadian bacon. She was about to douse my plate with her usual lemon-pepper when I stopped her.

"Mom, just once can you hold the lemon-pepper?" I scooted my stool closer to the table.

"I'll just sprinkle on a little. Mother always knows best." At least she thought she did. Even if you told her otherwise. There was no point in telling her what to do. Mom always did as Mom pleased. No matter how crazy the outcome, her intentions were always good. They always came from the heart. I'd been able to count on that since I was a kid.

"Here you go. Watch, *está caliente*. Careful not to burn yourself." Mom handed me a mug of piping hot water, plopping a bag of *Cachamai* tea, a traditional Argentine infusion made from a mixture of common herbs and *yerba mate*, into it. "Now, to what do I owe the pleasure of your visit so early on a Saturday?"

"I saw Alfredo. He was with me last night in the cottage house. I must have been dreaming, but it was so real. He sat on the side of my bed holding my hand. I could see him. I felt him. He's still with us, Mom." I blew on my tea, trying to cool it down.

Mom sat a while, nursing her own mug. I'd definitely caught her off guard. For once, she was speechless.

"You don't believe me. *Do you?*"

Mom clasped her mug, staring down into her coffee. "*Todo lo opuesto*. I do. I believe you. All too well."

"Has he visited you too?"

"No. But I know the feeling. Your great-*abuela* Josefina, your namesake, has visited me a couple of times." Putting down her coffee, Mom combed her hair back into a ponytail, settling in to tell me a story. "I loved my grandma very much. We were very close. Like you girls with Dorita. I was pregnant with your sister Camila when she died. Her passing haunted me for years. I was the one who found her. *Muerta*. Dead. Knitting needles in hand, in the wooden rocking chair your Dad and I bought her after losing her left leg to diabetes. I can picture her now. The ball of white chenille yarn she'd bought to make a receiving blanket for the arrival of her much anticipated second great-grandchild lay unwound on the floor, next to the chair. What struck me most was that she was clearly gone, but the chair continued to rock back and forth. As if she was still alive."

"That's terrible, Mom. I can't imagine losing Dorita. Or you."

"Certain goodbyes stay with us forever. But I've always felt Josefina guiding me. She was the one who woke me up that night our house caught fire all those years ago, when you were in the first grade. She'd been gone for almost ten years at that point. But there she stood by my bed, shaking me awake. I can still hear her now. '*Los chicos*, Poupecita. The kids are asleep in their beds. The house is burning down. You need to go get them. Now. Before it's too late.' She's the reason we made it out alive."

Chills ran up my spine as I sat listening to Mom. She and Dad did manage to get us all out that fateful snowy night when an electrical fire sparked in the pump room of our indoor pool in the middle of the night. According to my parents, the entire house became engulfed in flames within minutes. Mom and Dad rushed to get the six of us out. I've never forgotten the panic in Dad's voice when he ran into the bedroom I shared with my sister Laura. My bed was closest to the door. He scooped me in his arms, covering me with a blanket as he ran through the smoke-filled hallway. He stopped when he reached the top of the stairway.

ESTAR AL HORNO CON PAPAS

"*Hija*, make yourself into a tight ball. Poupée, catch her. It's Josie. I'm going back for Laura," Dad yelled.

Mom was waiting for me at the bottom. I could see flames encroaching on her. My oldest sister and Oscar had already gotten downstairs. Mom handed me off to Valentina, who shoved me off to Oscar, who ran me out the back door. There was no time for niceties. Our neighbor Polly, always like a great aunt to us, stood there knee-deep in the snow waiting for me. She ran me over to her house where I joined my pajama-clad baby brother, Federico, in her front yard. Barefoot, we both stood there watching our large Tudor-style home succumb to flames while Polly motioned to her son to run and get us blankets. Waiting in silence and shivering as my family members emerged one by one. Camila was the last of my sisters to get out. Mom was right behind her.

"Where's *Papi*, Mom?" We cried. Minutes passed, and as Mom tried to console us, she stood staring at the scene unfolding in front of us. There were more flames than house. *Where was he?* Mom tried to go back in to look for Dad, but Polly grabbed her arm, holding her back by force. "Think of the kids, Poupée. You can't leave them." That's when we saw the outline of Dad's figure emerging from the smoke. In his boxers, wading through the snow. Carrying a box full of things he'd gone back for. His and Mom's US naturalization certificates. Our passports. A wedding portrait. The book he'd almost finished writing on congenital heart disease.

Dad collapsed just before reaching us. The firemen arrived seconds later. He'd inhaled a lot of smoke and the soles of his feet were singed to a crisp. Still, Dad found the will to help the firemen locate the fire hydrant buried under the snow. We all got out unscathed that night. Now I understood it was thanks to my great-*abuela* Josefina's ghost who beckoned to Mom. And she followed. That night was a stark wake-up call that our world can tilt on its axis in just a moment. You never can know with certainty when a fire will spark, how hot it will burn, where it will spread or how long it'll be before all that remains are cold ashes. It took more than a year to rebuild our home.

"I never knew she was the one who woke you up. That's incredible. Did Josefina ever visit you again?"

"No. Not since that night." Mom grabbed my hands. "Now. *Dale. Contáme todo.* Tell me everything. But first take a bite of your breakfast. You know what they say, you shouldn't share your dreams on an empty stomach or else nightmares may come to pass and good dreams might not."

Always a superstitious one, Mom loved talking about *Abuelo* Alfredo. Dorita had always told me that Mom had him wrapped around her finger from when she was just a girl. She was his *Poupée*, which means *doll* in French. Alfredo had coined Mom's lifelong nickname.

"He was there. On my bed. Next to me. I could feel him. He took my hand in his and told me it was time to go home to Argentina."

"Argentina was always on his mind. But this is your home. Here with us."

"I thought the same thing. And then he said something else. That *he*—someone—was there waiting for me."

"Did he say who? I don't think this is the time to be rushing into another relationship."

"Believe me, I know. And, no, he didn't. I must've been dreaming. But it's strange. He was so real. I miss him."

"I miss him too. Every single day. You know, I love *Mamí* with all of my heart. Sometimes I even think she's been a better mom to all of you than me. But your *abuelo*, somehow, we understood one another on a whole other level. I could do no wrong in his eyes, and I miss that."

Like us, I thought, *except for the "I can do no wrong" part.* My mind wandered to a recent Tony Robbins show I had seen on TV. As the self-help guru spoke to the crowd, he asked, "Whose love did you crave most as a child, and who did you have to be to get it?" Mom craved Alfredo's. And she only had to be herself to get it. Me, I craved Mom's. But that meant I couldn't always be fully honest with her. Because, as she so often reminded me, she was raising me to be a lady. Dad was always closer with my younger brother and sister Laura. He even said so in so many words when he gave his father-of-the-bride speech at Laura's wedding.

"*Check . . . check*," he said, tapping his finger against the mic to make sure it was on. "My wife Poupi says that to me all the time. It's not every day a father has the extreme privilege of giving his favorite daughter away . . ."

Camila called him out on it. Dad chalked it up to a Scotch-induced slip, but his words never came as a surprise to me. We all knew them to be true. And that was okay. I had always been a mama's girl.

Mom and I sat at the breakfast table that day talking well into the morning. She reached over the table to grab a jar of *palmitos* and opened it. She knew I was still mourning my relationship with Tripp. She knew I was scared that I'd never be able to trust a man again. "Josie, did I ever tell you that your father wasn't my first boyfriend?"

"No. I don't think so."

Mom reached for another *palmito*, stripping the peel from its dense white flesh. "I met him when I was just fourteen. Around the same age you met Tripp. His name was José Luis. We dated for several years. His family was one of the wealthiest in La Plata. Everyone, including me, thought we would marry."

"Really? So, what happened?"

"Your dad. That's what happened. I was at a party one night when I had just turned seventeen. José Luis and I were dancing, until out of nowhere your dad, who was a couple of years older, began sauntering across the dance floor straight for us. He was everything my boyfriend wasn't. Confident, tall, thin, with jet black hair slicked back so perfectly that a penny could bounce off it. He looked straight at me with his dark eyes, completely ignoring the fact that I was dancing with someone else. Then, before I knew it, he cut in. I don't remember if José Luis had any words with him. I just remember dancing with your dad for the rest of the evening. That one moment changed my entire destiny."

"How scandalous, Mom. I didn't know you had it in you," I said jokingly, thoroughly enjoying one of the juiciest and unforeseeable *sobremesas* we'd had to date, as I followed along sipping on my now nearly cold tea.

"So that's when you and Dad started dating?"

"Oh, no. I gave him my number, but your dad never called. Neither did José Luis. He never spoke to me again. My parents, well, *Mamí* at least, were furious with me. José Luis was from a well-to-do family. He was marriage material. *Mamí* reminded me over and over. But whatever it was worth, your dad made me realize I didn't love him."

"So, how did you and Dad finally get together?"

"A year or so later we ran into one another at the Jockey Club horse races. I was with your godmother, Graciela. We were dressed to the nines. Your dad was with Jorge Luis. You know? Graciela's husband."

"Of course. How incestuous you all were."

"Ay, Josie," Mom laughed. "Anyway, your dad had just graduated from medical school. I pretended not to remember him. He kept at it, trying to remind me of the dance we'd shared. But I brushed him off."

"You know, Dad always says you were the most beautiful girl of all of La Plata. That you could have had any man you wanted."

Mom blushed. She knew it was true, but played it off. "He just says that to show you *he* could have anyone he wanted. But that day at the tracks, he offered to place my bets on the horses I'd chosen."

"What happened next?"

"Your dad called me. But I pretended not to be home to see if he'd call back."

"Did he?"

"Oh, he did. You know your Dad—over and over. Until one day your *abuelo* Alfredo suggested we invite him for tea. 'That, or I'll have to change our number,' he said."

"So, Alfredo had a hand in getting you two together?"

"You could say so. In those days, things were different. A man courted you, but never without first meeting and having the approval of your parents."

It wasn't often I got to see this schoolgirl side of Mom. Her story made me feel all warm and cozy. She loved Dad. *For better, for worse, till death do they part.*

"Speaking of being happy, Mom, I don't want to be a physician's assistant. I flopped my interview in DC."

"Your dad and I have been waiting for you to figure that out. You have to decide what it is you want to do."

I grabbed my kitchen stool and pushed it closer to the breakfast table, leaning into Mom so no one else could hear and softly said, "You know, I always suspected Tripp was unfaithful. I just didn't want to believe it. I never saw it for myself, so I didn't pay attention when I heard rumors here and there. I'm not as strong as you think."

Mom took a sip of coffee. "Did you ask him about it?"

"Of course. Many times. But like Ross to Rachel on *Friends*, he always swore we were on a break."

"Were you?"

"I don't know. Maybe. But I don't think so. Who knows. We were together so long I never really did know." *But I did. At least my gut told me I did.* And while I'd always hated ironing, throughout the years Mom's all day table-linen pressing sessions sometimes came at the most opportune moments.

A far-off look came over Mom, followed by a moment of silence. She'd seen her own share of infidelity. She was the only first wife left standing in the Caminos family. Thankfully, she'd been spared. That didn't mean it was easy. Marriage never was—never is. Dad was the only one among his brothers and father who hadn't divorced. The other first, and in some cases, second, wives weren't so lucky.

"Well Josie, *ojos que no ven, corazón que no siente.* You two were really young when you met. Sometimes we fool ourselves into thinking what we don't know, what we can't see, can't hurt us. But it usually does, sooner or later. It catches up to us. What does it matter now? You're moving on."

"It just feels good to finally admit it to someone else. Since the beginning, the one thing I couldn't compete with was golf. It was never just one round. Then there was the nineteenth hole in the Men's Grille afterwards. I was never going to be his first priority."

"You've always needed to be number one. In your own quiet way. Do you remember when you were a little girl? You didn't let anyone sit next to me. You always had to be by my side. You don't love easily. But when you do, you're all in. It's not that easy to turn off, just like that."

"I spent years waiting for him. Most days and evenings I'd wait hours for him to finish up his second round. I was always working around his schedule. But I'm done waiting—for any man."

"Josie, there's a reason some women describe themselves as golf widows. I'm just thankful you won't be one of its latest victims. You would have been bored. You might not be able to see it, but you aren't cut of country club cloth. I'm not sure any of us are. We may live next to one, and—don't get me wrong—it's nice to go for dinner or a wedding every once in a while, but the white picket fence separating our land is the only thing we share in common." Mom got up from her stool and walked over to the pantry to retrieve several more jars of hearts of palm from her arsenal of canned goods.

"What are you doing with those?"

"I'm meeting *las chicas* for lunch at Olga's house." Mom always tried to get together with her true-blue girlfriends when she was in Pittsburgh. "We're each bringing a dish. I'm making a *palmito* salad with *salsa golf.* Can you slice them up for me while I whip up the salsa?" She handed me a cutting board and knife. "And put some heart into it. It's for *mis chicas.*"

Ensalada de palmitos con salsa golf
(Hearts of Palm Salad)

SERVES 7. *Or 1 restless heart.*

Salsa golf is an Argentine obsession of sorts. It's a cold sauce, somewhat resembling Thousand Island dressing or the Japanese Steakhouse-inspired Yum Yum sauce. But Argentines claim it as theirs. It was invented by the Nobel laureate Luis Federico Leloir in the mid-1920s at the golf club in the Argentine resort town of Mar del Plata. A chemist, he was supposedly bored of eating shrimp and prawns with mayonnaise and asked the waiter to bring him various ingredients to the table that he could experiment with. The waiter brought him vinegar, lemon, mustard and ketchup, among other things. And it was at that very table overlooking the golf course that *salsa golf* was born. There are several recipes, but it's usually homemade mayonnaise with a tomato base like ketchup. You can cheat by using store-bought mayo, but the taste will not be nearly as good. *Salsa golf* is used to dress salads or meats, or as a dip for French fries and other food, and it is the main ingredient in the following typical Argentine dish.

Not a fan of mayonnaise? I haven't been, either, since the day I got a terrible perm at age thirteen. My best friend Taylor's mom swore the mayo would relax the curl, but the only thing it did after I doused my scalp in it was make me throw up. So, I've offered an alternative orange vinaigrette that pairs beautifully with the hearts of palm. It's also lighter on our burglar's thighs.

SALSA GOLF

2 large **eggs**

¾ cup **canola oil** or a Mediterranean blend of Italian sunflower with extra-virgin olive oil

Juice of half a **lemon**

½ teaspoon **salt**

2 tablespoons **heavy whipping cream**

¼ teaspoon **Dijon mustard**

3 tablespoons **ketchup**, preferably Heinz

ORANGE VINAIGRETTE

2 tablespoons freshly squeezed **orange juice**

2 tablespoons fresh **lime juice**

3 tablespoons extra-virgin **olive oil**

¼ teaspoon fine **sea salt**

¼ teaspoon freshly ground **pepper**

SALAD

2 14-ounce **hearts of palm**, jarred or canned, drained

2 **tomatoes**, roughly chopped

2 **Hass avocadoes**, sliced

4 tablespoons **scallions**, sliced

3 tablespoons **cilantro**, roughly chopped

Make the salsa golf. Put eggs in a medium bowl. Using a hand-mixer or blender, beat the yolks on medium speed. Add the oil in a very thin, steady stream, beating continuously until the mixture has emulsified. Add the lemon juice and salt to taste.

In a separate bowl, whip the heavy whipping cream until thick and creamy. With a spatula, fold in the mustard and ketch-up until combined. Carefully fold in the emulsified egg mixture until combined. Chill until ready to serve.

Make the vinaigrette. Combine orange juice, lime juice, oil, salt and pepper, and stir or shake.

Assemble the salad. Slice the hearts of palm in ½-inch rounds. Add tomatoes, avocado, scallions and cilantro to bowl; gently toss with choice of *salsa golf* or vinaigrette to coat.

Chapter 3

Las penas con pan son menos
Sorrows With Bread Are Less

Mom's mushroom sandwiches stuffed with loads of *champiñones a la Provenzal* needed no introduction or titles. Any dish with a French or Spanish name sounds more delicious and sexier, in my opinion, but these sandwiches speak for themselves in any language. Mom started with everyone's childhood favorite: plain white sandwich bread. Not the gourmet kind; not the farmhouse loaf, but the Town Talk kind that forms a soft ball and sticks to the roof of your mouth as you chew. Then she sautéed plain old white button mushrooms with garlic and a dash of thyme, usually dry, in salted butter on high heat, so the mushrooms would be crispy on the outside and soft and juicy on the inside. Mom liked to quote Julia Child, failing terribly at Julia's signature transatlantic accent, as she stirred. "Remember, don't crowd the mushrooms. Otherwise they won't brown." Mom piled the mushrooms high between the two sandwich slices and served it up, unadorned. Eating the sandwich was an art in itself; a race against time before the bread became too soggy to pick up as it continued to soak up the butter and richness with each bite. I'd come to rely on Mom's white button sandwiches when things weren't going as planned. They were like an old friend who rolls out of bed and greets you at the door as they are, whose support you can always count on.

* * *

"Happy Fourth of July, my little Yankee Doodles!" Mom faithfully greeted us each Independence Day morning before breaking out in song, belting out an entire rendition of "*I'm a Yankee Doodle Dandy . . .*" while whipping up a large pan of scrambled eggs. She never did learn the words.

The Fourth of July came and went that summer of 1998. Four months had passed since Tripp and I broke up. My whole family was in Pittsburgh, a feat that was becoming rarer due to conflicting busy schedules. We were winding down from my parents' annual party. Once a year, hundreds of people would descend upon our yard, making their way onto the golf course to watch the club's fireworks. We were all still recovering from a day of eating and drinking, followed by a night of more of the same, as my brother Oscar, who'd taught himself how to play the guitar when he was twelve, played music into the wee hours of the fifth. Midsummer's lightning bugs had settled into the landscape, hovering among the grass and maples, oaks and pines, creating a twilight glow as if by magic. The lazy summer days and nights seemed to stretch on infinitely. So did the family's *sobremesas*. For the good and the bad.

Lately, our family's after-dinner conversations seemed to revolve around the same topic: *El Niño* and the irreparable damages it was doing to the herds on my parents' cattle ranches in Santa Fé, Argentina, one of the country's central provinces rich in agriculture and livestock. As I often tuned out, they'd argue about La Santa Elena, the main ranch, and I'd randomly catch words like *alfalfa*, *sorgo* (sorghum), *molinos* (windmills), *alambrado* (fencing), Braford and Hereford cattle . . . on and on it would go. I grew up hearing about the ranches, yet it was still all foreign to me. My parents had begun to talk about Marco and Gastón Oría, the two brothers they had hired the year before—Marco as the ranch's large animal veterinarian and his older brother, Gastón, as its administrator. Gastón had just recently graduated and received his CPA when he decided to visit Marco at Santa Elena before settling into a full-time job. My parents had dinner with the two one evening and hired Gastón on the spot. He didn't have any agricultural experience and had never worked with cattle, but he seemed to have a good financial head for managing the books and inventory. And, simply put, he could charm the pants off of anyone. Or so Mom said. Plus, he had his brother there. They'd be able to keep one another company. Ranch life, after all, was pretty lonely, especially for two young single men.

My parents trusted the two brothers. As the sons of two of their closest childhood friends, Jorge Luis and Graciela Oría, they were almost like family. Graciela was the friend Mom had been with that fateful night she reconnected with my dad. She was always a super attentive godmother. Graciela would send me letters on my birthday and invite me to tea or take me shopping when I'd visit Argentina as a girl. Still, I'd never met her older boys. We'd typically get together with her three younger daughters, who were closer to my age. Graciela always promised me she'd travel to the States the day Tripp and I married. "*Es un hecho.*" It's a done deal. Now that we were no longer together, I wondered what other reason I could come up with to get her to visit.

Mom, visibly tired from the night before, was making her *salmon en papillote*. She tucked the fish into the parchment paper, along with freshly chopped dill, thinly cut lemon slices and julienned red and yellow peppers. "*Chicas,* why don't you do something useful and set the table?" she asked, walking away, muttering to herself. "As usual, *todo el mundo esta haciendo picnic alrededor.* No one's helping."

"What's that, Mom? You want to have a picnic?" Laura walked into the kitchen, her son Daniel in her arms, chewing on a Gerber teething biscuit.

Always running late and overwhelmed with having to cook for the whole family, Mom shot Laura a seething glance. She wasn't in the mood.

"What? What'd I miss?"

"Nothing. I'll set the table, Mom. Are we eating inside or out?" I asked, thinking of the hand axe that Mom kept at hand in the catch-all drawer underneath the kitchen phone. I once asked her what it was doing there, and she told me it was her own personal defense system. "I also have one under my bed," she'd once confessed.

I was glad to know they were there in case my ghost decided to sneak up on me. I tried to imagine my five-foot-three mom, clad in her terry cloth robe and large black Chanel sunglasses that she never took off—"They're prescription, Josie"—slinging an axe at the site of an intruder entering the back door. *Who would she hurt more, herself or the trespasser?* I wondered.

That night, well after the salmon was gone, *sobremesa* dragged on. As I rocked Daniel to sleep in his baby pram, I felt as if I'd fall asleep myself. Hoping to sneak away unnoticed, I stood to take him to his crib.

"Where are you going?" Dad cleared his throat.

"I'm going to put my godson down to see if he'll stay asleep for the night."

"He's sleeping. You can take him up in a little when we finish talking." When Dad spoke, his word was final. I sat back down at my usual seat at the table and reached for the bottle of Malbec. I ended up drinking a little too much. Malbec always did that to me. The last thing I remember was stumbling across the driveway to the cottage house and falling asleep with my clothes on. Then I had the strangest dream.

Laura and I were sitting on the white picket fence separating our yard from the golf course. The fence was covered with purple azaleas. We sat there talking, just hanging out with our backs to the golf course. Then, out of nowhere, I noticed two men leaving the cottage house where I lived, just across the other side of the yard and driveway. One, tall and thin, was in his twenties or early thirties, with dark, wavy hair. He was wearing a worn-in button-down with faded jeans that hung low on his hips. He was walking with an older man who seemed vaguely familiar, but I couldn't quite make him out. *I know that cap from somewhere,* I thought, squinting to get a better look. The two stopped in front of the garage, turning towards us. They both seemed to be staring right at me, as if I was their main topic of conversation. The older man appeared to be pointing me out to the younger one. And while I'd never met either of the two, I felt as if I knew them from somewhere. My eyes then met the younger one's piercing gaze. He didn't look away. I looked at Laura, "Who are those men? They just came out of my place."

"That's Gastón. From the ranch. I don't know who the older one is."

His penetrating stare was so intense that it woke me up, nearly knocking me off the bed.

The next morning, I was in bed still sleeping soundly when my friend Megan came bursting through the garage door. *I shouldn't have given her the door code*, I thought, pulling the sheets over my head.

"Let's go, Josie. Get your butt out of bed. We have a 9:30 spin class to make." She was that friend who always looked like a million bucks without doing anything. She could even pull off wearing an eighties-style sweat band, Olivia Newton John-style, across her forehead and still look fantastic. Everything about Megan was petite, except for her smile and hair that seemed to be perpetually in motion, as if she were being followed around by a lovesick breeze. She was all teeth, hair and spirit. "Come on," she said, pulling back my sheets. "I'm not taking no for an answer. Let's go and *get jiggy wit' it* so we can burn off some calories and drink all the *sangria* we want tonight at Mallorca." Sangria, *ugh*, I thought, remembering that we had plans to go to our favorite Spanish restaurant that night. I was still feeling the effects of the Malbec from the night before.

"I just had the strangest dream, Meg. I dreamt that my godmother's son, Gastón, the one who works on my parents' ranches in Argentina, was here in Pittsburgh. In the cottage house, just outside the garage. He was looking for me."

"What'd he want?" she asked, pulling her blonde hair back into a ponytail. "Is he cute?"

"I don't know. I've never met him. I don't even know what he looks like. But in my dream he was."

"I think you'd better lay off the *vino* for a while, Josie. Good thing we're drinking *sangria* tonight," she said, winking as she flashed me her megawatt smile.

Megan always had a golden tan. She seemed to possess the same magic as the lightning bugs, like something warm and bright was glowing inside of her.

"Now get dressed. I've already started calling the girls, so we can all meet for some *rrrrrrroasted* suckling piglet tonight."

While on the outside Megan looked like an all-American pin-up girl, what you couldn't see was that she had Greek passion coursing through her veins. She loved to roll her double *r*'s as much as I wanted to be able to, and would always make the waiter at Mallorca recite their lengthy daily specials, sometimes twice, which often came with a healthy dose of double-*r* trilling.

"Sorry, what was that last dish? Do you mind repeating them one more time?" she'd ask, knowing full well that we'd be splitting the *mariscada*, ocean fare served up in a simmering pot of fish sauce, brandy and wine broth, with a side of crispy, Spanish-style fried potatoes and saffron rice.

Megan was also extremely compassionate. She was used to taking care of people, which is why, since my split with Tripp, she'd made it a point to get me to the gym with her at least three days a week. I was her project of the moment. She'd often have to drag me there, but after an hour spin class, I always felt better. The spin room was small and dark, and the music so loud that you could feel it thumping in your chest. The lights-off combination of our hearts beating in rhythm with the music mixed in with the scent of sweat and determination always moved me, and I'd leave the class feeling lighter, as if I'd purged some of my toxicity. That day was like all the others at class, except Megan had a secret.

As we left the gym, Megan took off the sweat band that held her hair off her face. It was perfectly dry and styled, as if she hadn't broken a sweat. I, on the other hand, was drenched from head to toe. She grabbed my hand and looked at me with her light hazel eyes.

"I need to tell you something. I wanted to make sure you heard it from me, so you don't feel blindsided," she said, grabbing a Pepsi out of her bag. "There's no easy way to say this. Tripp's moving in with his new girl. He's in town and she's here with him. I saw them the other night eating at Hamfeldt's and he told me that he's asked her to move down to Florida."

"Moving in? She's with him, what, four months and they're going to live together? I waited more than two years for him to ask me."

"I know. But there's nothing left for you to do. You're going to meet someone else. I just know it."

As we drove home, Blondie's "Heart of Glass" played on the radio. Megan cranked it up, singing along. "What's *mucho* mistrust mean, anyway?"

I looked at her, half smirking. "You know what it means."

"Yup. Just making sure you do too."

That was Megan for you. Always setting me straight. "Thanks for the reminder. And ride. I'll see you tonight," I said, wiping away a tear as I kissed Megan on the cheek and then hopped out of her Jeep.

"Oh, yeah you will." She yelled back to me from her car window. "See you at the rrrrrrrrestaurant."

I ran into the house looking for Mom.

"Josie? Is that you? We're out back on the patio."

Mom and Dad were sitting under the awning having a heated conversation on speakerphone. On the other line, a man with a deep voice was speaking swiftly, his double r's dancing effortlessly off his tongue. Something in his voice stopped me in my tracks. It was mesmerizing, similar to a first bite of velvety smooth chicken liver *paté* that would always keep me coming back for more. I never did like liver, but somehow *paté* was one of those things I couldn't get enough of.

"Gastón, I'm going to have to call you back," Mom interrupted him.

She took one look at me and knew tears weren't far behind. "*Mi hija* just walked in and I have to talk to her. Josie, do you remember Gastón?"

"No, I can't say I do. *Hola.*" Even though I'd never met him, lately I couldn't seem to escape this guy. His name was everywhere . . . at the dinner table, on speakerphone, in my dreams.

"Josefina, *Hola. ¿Que tal?* How are you? I'm sure we probably met years ago. I've heard so much about you from our moms. *Mamá* has a picture of you on her nightstand. Poupée sent her a new one every year."

Mom nodded in agreement. "That's right. Since she was young."

"I've grown up looking at them." Gastón's sinewy voice showered me in a cascade of smooth *Castellano*.

I didn't even want to imagine the hideous photos Mom must have sent Graciela. She lived her life in pictures. She'd become obsessed with collecting family photos since the fire that burned down our house robbed her of a lifetime's worth of memories captured on film. The scorches left behind rendered Mom incapable of weeding out bad pictures from the good. Instead, she'd framed each one she got back from the rolls of film she'd sent out to be developed. Growing up, I'd hide framed photographs of me under cushions, in drawers or behind the rows and rows of photos that covered any inch of free tabletop real estate.

The tears started rolling as soon as Mom hung up the phone. "He asked her to move in with him, Mom. She's moving down to Florida. Can you imagine? We were together for almost a decade and he never asked me to live with him. She's with him for not even a couple of months and they're planning on living together." I slumped miserably into the chair next to Mom, still in my sweaty workout clothes.

"Who?" Mom asked.

"Tripp! *Really*?"

"Are we still talking about him, Josie?"

"It's been four months, Mom. I dated him almost nine years. Give me a break."

And as if on cue, Mom looked at Dad, who chimed in, "You know we would have never allowed you to live with him. Why buy the cow if you can get the milk for free, *hija*? You're better off without him." This coming from the man who, if I brought a boy over, would make us sit in the living room with several feet between us. God forbid we had a blanket draped over our legs. That in itself was considered a carnal sin. But if one of my brothers, no matter older or younger, brought his girlfriend over, they could have her in his bedroom and close the door, and no one would think twice about it. There was a general understanding between my parents: "He's a man. It's different. Your brothers can't get pregnant."

"Whether or not you would have let me live with him is beside the point. He didn't ask me. But he asked her." It struck me that this sort of inherent Latin *machismo* I'd come to expect at home was a blind spot in my parents' rearview mirror. I couldn't help but think it wasn't of their own doing—this same type of gender bias had been ingrained in them since birth. It was paradoxical at best since Mom and Dad made sure to give their daughters the best education possible. They were bringing us up to break barriers and fend for ourselves. But if there was anything I'd learned on the basis of sex, political correctness and *machismo* growing up in a bicultural home, it's that things are not always as they seem. In a land where catcalls and *piropos* are the norm, Argentina has not one, but two female presidents—no matter the way they rose to power—in its history books. Not to mention a staunch female activist and screen actress turned immortal First Lady, Evita Perón, who, in her own words, demanded more rights for women because she knew what women had to put up with. Somehow, Argentines' general disdain for saying "the correct thing" or self-censoring has led them to embrace a more open and tolerant society. The US, on the other hand, a country that prides itself on equal rights and a culture of staunch political correctness, has had zero female leaders at the helm. It goes to show so often we take situations at face value and don't recognize that they are not what they appear.

"Josie, are you listening to us?" Mom placed her hand on my leg. "We've talked about this over and over. It doesn't matter. You're better off."

"That's right, *hija*" Dad said. "I understand how disappointed you are. That all of a sudden your life took a turn you never saw coming. But the only thing you can do is move forward now. You can't go back to someone who would treat you like that."

"See Mom, at least Dad understands me. You could stand to be a little more compassionate."

Mom rolled her eyes, but like Argentina, she and Dad weren't always what they seemed. Often times, when I least expected it, Dad would be the more tolerant of the two. Especially when it came to matters of the heart. But then, just like that, the tables would once again turn.

"Josie, what are you doing out here like that? The golfers are looking."

"I just came from the gym, Dad. Give me a minute and I'll throw something on." *Of course the golfers were going to look. They always did; safely, from their side of the picket fence.* I could only imagine the things they'd say while they waited to tee off. Talk comes cheap when the story is good.

Dad was becoming noticeably uncomfortable. "Poupi, tell your daughter to put some clothes on."

"Josie, your father's right. We're raising you to be a lady."

I looked down at the sight of me, and thought that for once, I didn't look half bad. In fact, I liked what I saw. Breakups seemed to be good for at least one thing: getting back into shape. And thanks to Megan, I was in the best shape of my life. My normally size six frame had shrunk to a size four after her incessant pushing, prodding and spinning. I was wearing a strappy exercise bra that barely held in my size B breasts. On the bottom, I had thrown super worn Levi's jean shorts over my bike pants. They hung around my hips, showing off my summer tan. My long brown hair, streaked golden from the summer sun, hung tousled past the middle of my back. I hadn't brushed it since yanking my ponytail out after spin class.

"Come on inside, Josie," Mom said. "Let me make you a mushroom sandwich." She grabbed a blanket from the basket next to the couch and wrapped it around me. "You're getting too thin. Are you eating?"

"Mom, stop. It's at least eighty degrees out here." I pulled the blanket off as we headed inside.

Growing up, I hated mushrooms. I'd pick them out of anything I ate, one by one, until I was eleven or so, when Valentina and Camila, fed up with my complaining that Mom was adding them to some dish or another, pinned me down to the kitchen floor and force-fed me some that Mom had just finished sautéing. Lucky for me, Mom didn't stop them. And I haven't stopped eating them since.

Mom's mushroom sandwich soon became my ultimate comfort food. Whatever occasion arose—my first boyfriend moving away, failing a test, getting denied from most grad schools I'd applied to—Mom was there, mushroom sandwich in hand. After the car accident, she fed them to me almost daily until I was back to myself. They were also a cause for celebration—the day I got accepted to Duke, my first car, the day I brought our golden retriever Sonny home from Aspen, Colorado. She'd preheat a pan on high heat, add loads of butter and pile on umami mushrooms until they crackled and sizzled, turning a golden brown. Then, just before they were done, she'd add chopped garlic, thyme and a generous dusting of cracked black pepper, tossing it all together for a minute or two until the smell of garlic filled the room. Even today, just a whiff of sautéing mushrooms with garlic, butter and salt takes me right back to my childhood.

I closed my eyes for the three minutes it took me to eat my sandwich, savoring the woodsy, buttery mushrooms that exploded on my tongue with each bite. The sandwich never could fill my void of longing and emptiness, but it certainly took a bit of the edge off, even if for just a fleeting moment.

"Eat. You know what they say. *'Las penas con pan son menos.'*" Sorrows with bread are less. Mom could tell things about people just by the way they ate. She got that from *Abuela* Dorita. She could feel their pain, sense their unhappiness and longing. From the first bite, she could tell whether they would embrace their pain, run, lash out or crumble. But today she was certain of one thing: she wouldn't let me crawl into a ball and hide. Instead, she'd serve me up a delicious plate of umami, straight from the earthy forest, in the hopes it would restore a sense of balance and harmony within me. Mom handed me another piece of bread, soft as a white handkerchief, to wipe clean my plate. She had no more words. She understood all too well that love, and the deception of it, always leaves ripples, and that I would have to find my own way. But it hurt her to watch.

Mom got up from the kitchen table to heat the kettle for chamomile tea. "Josie, have you noticed that since you and Tripp broke up, you haven't had one panic attack? It's been more than four months, and not one. Don't you find that interesting? Your dad and I were talking about it earlier today. I know you're depressed, but I don't think it's a coincidence that the panic is gone."

Mom was right. I hadn't thought about it, but along with my Gentleman Caller, the panic *was* gone. *For the moment.* At least, I hadn't had an episode since the split. I'd been so consumed with my newfound heartbreak that I had forgotten to worry. Up until the attacks manifested, I'd always been able to keep my anxiety to myself. Only my thumbs, always victim to my compulsive *tick, tick, tick,* picking until the skin on the sides past the knuckles was painfully raw, gave me away.

My first panic attack came on as they always did, without warning or any apparent reason, around the same time I started dating Tripp again for the last time, when I was twenty-two. I was doing what I did most days, driving my usual commute home on Interstate 76, or the Pennsylvania Turnpike, from Monroeville to Fox Chapel. The nine-mile stretch between the two exits was such an easy twenty-minute commute that I often felt I could do it with my eyes closed. I often had no memory of the drive. So what was different about that day in particular? Nothing out of the ordinary had happened; I was sitting at the wheel, driving my new red Jeep Cherokee Sport that I'd finally saved up enough money to buy, when about halfway home my heart started pounding. It was so insistent, I could hear it in my ears—thump, thump, thump; I could feel it palpitating in my throat. Then I noticed my hands trembling over the steering wheel. They were tingling, slowly going numb. My vision followed, becoming blurry as I tried to focus on the road. Suddenly, I was hot and sweaty, so much so that I steadied the wheel with my left knee as I struggled to strip off my medical assistant's lab coat. I had to really focus to get my hands to do as I told them. My heart seemed to pound even faster, even harder. I tried taking a deep breath to calm myself, but my breaths were sharp and shallow and didn't seem to fill my lungs. I was hyperventilating. My vision got darker and narrower and I felt as if I were looking through a kaleidoscope—I was seeing stars. It was as if the world tilted off its axis for a moment. I managed to pull my Jeep over to the side of the road. *This is what death feels like, and you're going to die here, alone, on the turnpike.* Then I noticed an emergency call box sitting on top of a mile marker post (this was years before smartphones). As I got out of the car, I felt unsteady on my feet but managed to get to the phone. I picked up the receiver and an operator immediately answered. "How can I help you?"

"I think I'm having a heart attack. I'm in a red Jeep. Please send help."

And then I slowly sank to the shoulder of the road and all went blurry from there. I don't know how much time passed before the ambulance arrived—it could have been thirty seconds or ten minutes. After an EKG test and a once over in the ambulance, I was told I'd had a panic attack. The EMT crew called Mom, who came to get me. She brought Federico along so he could drive my car home, while I settled into the front passenger seat of Mom's car.

As I buckled my seatbelt, Mom pulled a bottle of Johnnie Walker Black Label out of her worn and faded brown leather Gucci purse that as a child always reminded me of Mary Poppins' magical carry-all carpetbag. She poured some into the cap. "Drink this. You won't like the way it tastes, so drink it all at once. It will calm your nerves."

Mom was of the generation that swore a splash of whiskey could solve anything. Colicky baby? Put a drop of whiskey in their bottle of milk or formula. Feeling a little too full after a meal? Sip on a finger or two of whiskey as a *digestivo*. Can't sleep? Add a splash of whiskey to your chamomile tea. And now, having a panic attack? Throw back a capful of Johnnie to ward off impending doom.

That was the first of many attacks. While they were infrequent, they always seemed to appear when something was awry with my life. Perhaps one of the worst things about them was the uncertainty of their arrival. They'd come knocking at any time, always unannounced, often at the most inopportune moment, leaving me to stash brown paper lunch bags in purses, desk drawers and the center consul of my car in case of emergency. Mine always seemed to come when I was driving alone. I'd have to talk myself out of having them most times I was behind the wheel, which had become more and more infrequent.

My parents assumed I was having a post-traumatic reaction to the stress of the car accident. But why so many years later? It made sense and sounded logical, but it didn't feel right to me. There was something I just couldn't put my finger on. I'd nod anyway, agreeing with them.

After a year or so, once she realized the attacks weren't going away, Mom reluctantly decided to take me to see a psychiatrist. While the late and much-missed Anthony Bourdain, host of CNN's food-focused television show *Parts Unknown*, noted that Argentina has the distinction of being home to more headshrinkers per capita than anywhere else in the world, my Argentine parents didn't seem to agree. They didn't believe in therapy outside the home or airing dirty laundry in public. In our home, everything could be solved in private, behind closed doors or tableside at *sobremesa*. Then, when we were done, we'd sweep it under one of Mom's beautiful embroidered tablecloths and call it a day.

After a quick fifteen-minute consultation, the doctor I met with was quick to diagnose me as suicidal, which is why, she said while handing me a prescription, the attacks seemed to be triggered while driving, since I could be easily tempted to take my life while behind the wheel. I didn't agree. It had almost been taken from me behind the wheel all those years ago—and I miraculously survived. I wasn't one to tempt fate.

"The funny thing, Mom, is that I'm scared to die," I said as we left her office. "When the attacks come on, all I can think is, 'Please God, don't let me die. My life hasn't even really begun.'"

The psychiatrist prescribed Prozac but we never bothered to fill it. Not because we didn't take my attacks seriously, but because my parents didn't want me taking any meds unless it was absolutely necessary. And it wasn't. From that moment on, we decided we would stick to Bach Flower Rescue Remedy, setting aside time for a daily *sobremesa* and a couple of other tricks Mom had up her sleeve—including her tried-and-true remedy of a capful of Johnnie Walker. It did seem to de-escalate the attacks when they came on. Even now, when every once in a while a panic attack shows up, uninvited.

Champiñones a la provenzal
(Mom's Mushroom Sandwich)

SERVES 1. *For the sandwich to wield its magic, it must not be shared.*

This might be the easiest dish you'll ever prepare, but that doesn't mean it's not important. It's a love letter from my Mom. So *oye*, listen up. There are occasions when only a bag of sliced white bread will do. This is one of them. This sandwich tastes of home, hangovers or both. The bread takes a back seat to the snowcapped mushrooms, allowing their umami goodness to shine through. Further, a reliable white sandwich bread won't crumble, even when it's the only thing that stands between you and a tidal wave of tears. There's one last requisite: this sandwich is best eaten in pajamas or old sweats, in bed or in a comfy chair in front of the TV while watching a Hallmark or Lifetime movie or two, back to back. You'll need only half of the roasted mushrooms for one sandwich, but you'll find a good use for the rest of them, I'm sure. Like, perhaps, a second sandwich.

3 tablespoons **salted butter** (If you must, you may substitute with extra-virgin olive oil)

1 12-ounce package **mushrooms** (white or cremini), sliced

½ teaspoon fresh **thyme leaves**

1 **garlic clove**, finely chopped

Pinch of fine **sea salt**

¼ teaspoon freshly ground **pepper**

2 slices **white sandwich bread** (Suggested: an additional two for reserves)

Melt butter in a heavy-bottomed sauté pan over medium-high heat. Add mushrooms and thyme. Sauté for 5–7 minutes or until they're fully coated with butter and start to crackle and pop. Add garlic and cook for another 2–3 minutes, stirring frequently, making sure not to burn the garlic. Once mushrooms take on a golden-brown color but are still nicely soft and juicy, remove pan from heat. Season to taste with salt and pepper. Serve immediately between two slices of white sandwich bread.

Chapter 4

Con las manos en la masa
Hands in the Cookie Jar

Whether or not you were brought up eating frittatas or *tortillas* depended most entirely on your grandmother. If she was Italian, it was frittatas. Spanish, *tortillas*. Many had grandmothers who were both Argentine and Italian. Like the US, Argentina was once a New World magnet for Old World immigrants. Today, both countries are a mixing pot of the millions of emigrant Europeans who, at the end of the nineteenth century, were torn between the two: *Buenos Aires or New York? The prairie or las pampas?* Many Italians chose the latter, bringing with them their sing-song rhythmic way of talking, along with architecture, music, dance and most of all: their food.

Tortillas were a staple in my home. "The secret to *tortilla*," Dorita would always say, "is in the flip. If you time it correctly you'll get that soft, custardy center that keeps you coming back for more." Second to Mom's mushroom sandwiches, *tortilla* was comfort food par excellence. As a child, I'd often find myself watching Dorita as she prepared it, first frying the potatoes and then the onions. I was always amazed how a couple of humble ingredients could transform into a nuanced and soul-satisfying dish fit for a queen.

* * *

They say time heals all wounds. As the end of summer approached, I found my grief over the loss of my relationship with Tripp was like the wind. It was always there, always changing. It would pick up dust, suddenly leaving me unable to see my hand in front of my face as it enveloped me in a whirlwind of memories I'd rather just forget. Or it could be still for days, suddenly knocking me to my knees, making me turn, heart racing, certain I'd heard the one I'd been missing call my name.

Lying in bed, having just awoken, I could hear Megan's voice in my head telling me to get my ass moving. *It'll make you feel better.*

So that's what I did. I threw on a sports bra and running shorts and grabbed a handful of Cracklin' Oat Bran that I immediately spit out. It had lost its crackle due to all of the moisture in my non-air-conditioned cottage house. That summer I'd relied on cracked windows and three fans going at once to cool the place down. But instead of offering relief, the fans mostly recycled the heat, leaving my anguish to stew in the air and hover over the dark-paneled shiplap lining the cottage walls.

I grabbed a leash and made my way to the street with Sonny by my side. I'd decided to run the wooded three-and-a-half-mile loop that connected Field Club, Fox Chapel and Squaw Run roads. Sonny was my faithful pacer. She always made sure I'd get to the finish line. Each time she'd pull taut on her retractable leash, exhausting its length, I had one of three choices: let go and risk her getting hit by an oncoming car, fall flat on my face or get my ass in gear and keep up. About three-quarters into the run, Sonny just about knocked me over as she took off chasing after white flashes of fluffy tails. Up ahead, three whitetail deer leapt across the windy road, jumping the fence bordering Riding Meadow Park. By the time I had time to react, I had no other option than to release my grip on the leash as Sonny darted ahead in pursuit of them. Sonny was no stranger to the place. Known as Fox Chapel's off-leash dog park, Riding Meadow had an extensive trail system carved into heavily wooded hillsides that residents often spent hours exploring alongside their furry friends.

As I sprinted after Sonny, attempting to grab hold of her trailing leash before she disappeared into the woods, I became hyper-vigilant of everything around me—as if time somehow slowed, even stopped. I smelled the wet, earthy mud below, the dewy moss and skunk cabbage lining the bumbling stream ahead. I could spot the chipmunks scurrying through the lush green fern-covered forest floor; above I could hear the crows cawing, birds chirping in the trees, wild turkey squabbling in the distance and the steady cadence of gunshots coming from the club's shooting lodge. I was so entranced by the lush forest around me that I lost sight of Sonny and the deer. Bending down, I placed my hands on my knees to catch my breath. There hadn't been any wind for days, but a breeze quickly picked up, rustling the canopy of oak, myrtle and locust trees. As the trees danced in the wind, twisting and churning around me, I spotted flashes of whitetails skirting among them. The deer seemed to be playing hide and seek, turning to look at me from behind tree trunks. But I wasn't moving. The loud swoosh of the leaves along with the percussive hammering of a woodpecker who seemed to be speaking in Morse code filled my head with the strangest feeling of déjà vu. I was awake but fully immersed in a dream, as if I were a child again on vacation in Argentina's Patagonia, standing in the heart of the magical deep forest of *Arrayanes*—ancient cinnamon-colored Myrtle trees with irregular, flaky white spots, smooth cool barks and trunks that seemed to twist in all directions. The trees, numbered in the thousands, are said to be so bewitching that they served as inspiration for Walt Disney himself, who used them as a muse for his rendition of *Bambi*. That day the Argentine myrtles had come knocking, beckoning me back to the home I never really knew.

The jingling of Sonny's collar tags as she emerged from the stream ahead broke my trance. "Sonny, come on. Let's go!" I yelled sternly. She looked my way, but Sonny brushed me off, insisting on stopping and saying hello to an older man sitting alone atop a wood bench made of two railroad ties sitting on large stones flanking the stream. He patted Sonny's head as she wagged her white, crimped tail in gratitude.

"Sonny, come on!" I approached the man, who, overdressed, was clad in a khaki windbreaker and cap. "She's super friendly," I said. "I hope she didn't get you wet. She just loves the water. Can't keep her out of it."

The man looked up, smiling and shaking his head as if to let me know all was good. Our eyes met. His were kind but seemed distant. He didn't say a word. Instead, he began contentedly playing tug of war with Sonny with his white handkerchief as he pensively stroked his closely trimmed platinum white beard with the other hand. Now that Sonny was preoccupied, I was able to hook the leash back on her collar. *He must be boiling,* I thought as I tugged on Sonny's leash. "Let's go, girl. Time to head home."

When I thought about it, the man's outfit made perfect sense. He seemed of a different era, the kind that would never wear shorts or show their bare legs in public. He was one of the men who always wore dress shoes, no matter the occasion, and no longer had hair on the bottom third of his legs due to daily use of polyester black knee-high socks. The kind that offered a lady a just-pressed kerchief at the sound of a sniffle, took their cap off when entering Sunday Mass or dedicated black-and-white photos of themselves to their one and only true love.

"Well, goodbye," I said, turning around one last time as Sonny urged me ahead. With a brief nod of his chin and wave of his handkerchief, he motioned back towards the trees on the other side. I looked again towards the wooded forest, wondering if he too saw the mystical orange glow of my Argentine *Arrayanes. Did he know what they were trying to tell me?* Our eyes met once again. His lips didn't move, yet his message came through loud and clear. *"La está esperando."* He's waiting for you.

What? Who? Who is this guy? He seemed to have the same message for me that *Abuelo* Alfredo gave me at the beginning of the summer, when he told me I needed to go home. I was home— at least I thought I was.

And just like that, with a fixed stare he tipped his herringbone cap and bid me farewell. The hairs on my arm and the back of my neck perked straight up, figuring out who he was before my mind had a chance to catch up. I turned and ran as fast as I could back onto the road, holding Sonny on a taut leash as I unhooked the entry gate door. I couldn't get out of there fast enough. As I turned to close the gate behind me, I stopped. Why run? It was time I finally faced this mystical Gentleman Caller. He'd been MIA since Tripp and I broke up. Now what? What did he want, other than to show up and catch me off guard in the most unassuming moments?

I turned back to the stream, but the bench was empty. I looked around, but no one was in sight. That was the thing about ghosts—mine at least. He appeared and disappeared just like that, without making a sound.

Certain I was going crazy, I ran as fast as I could around the remaining loop and up the long final hill back home. The wind was blowing in our favor. About halfway, fatigue began setting in and Sonny, never one to complain, was heavily panting. I couldn't stop thinking that she, too, had seen him. She was playing tug-of-war with him, for God's sake. I couldn't have been imagining him. I now had two witnesses—Tripp and Sonny. Too bad only one of them could actually corroborate our ghost sightings, and we didn't speak anymore. *God, I missed him.* What I would've done to call him and tell him all about our ghost. I couldn't help but wonder if he'd had any more sightings. Something told me he would've called me if he had.

My legs got heavier as our steps got slower. When we reached the house, I unleashed Sonny and made a detour into my parents' kitchen for a drink of ice water and to enjoy the air conditioning for a moment before heading home to change. As I walked into the kitchen, a blast of cool air hit my face. It felt and smelled like heaven. I was met with the scent of fried onions, potatoes and fresh cut parsley. On the counter was an enormous *tortilla Española* (potato frittata) that *abuela* Dorita had just taken out of the oven. I snuck around the counter, peeking under the towel covering it to get a better whiff, when suddenly I heard a familiar voice coming from the back patio. That damn wind was playing mind games again. *Could it be? It couldn't. What would he be doing here? He wouldn't dare.*

And yet, he did. As I walked towards the chatter, I heard Mom and *Abuela* laughing along with Tripp and a woman whose voice I couldn't place. I felt my heart pounding in my face. Then I heard my sister Laura's voice. *What? Her too?*

I presumed Tripp had been golfing, and when he arrived at the tee next to our home, he casually hopped over the white picket fence to say hello, *uninvited*. Still inside, I reached the dining room table, placing my hand on it to steady myself, and as I looked up, our eyes met. There he was, plain as day, standing just outside the open French doors leading to the patio. Tripp was leaning on a golf club, his left foot planted on the patio floor and right foot propped up behind the club's head. He looked better than ever. Our eyes locked, almost knocking Tripp off his balance. *Now he wasn't feeling so confident, was he?*

My family was out of sight, sitting on the couches just left of the patio doors, and another person was standing just out of my sight to the right of him. I heard a woman ask if he was okay. Tripp didn't bother to answer.

It was her. I could vaguely make out his girlfriend's reflection against the open door. Tripp was there, introducing my family to the acquisition from his family cruise, who was tidily dressed in a knee-length golf skort and short-sleeved Polo, her straight blonde hair meticulously pinned back with a headband. I could see her but she couldn't see me. At least I didn't think she could.

But Tripp could. With his mouth wide open, he looked at me as if for the first time, taking in my flushed cheeks and tousled hair that brushed over my caramel-colored skin, glistening with sweat. I knew that look. He drank me in with his eyes, traveling up and down my body. *Thank you, Megan. Thank you for this moment.*

His eyes said it all. *I remember the smell of your skin. I remember everything.* Giving the reflection of his new conquest the once-over, I suddenly understood. Tripp stood torn between two very different worlds—one of tawny, sweet *dulce de leche*, and another of comforting and familiar milky-white vanilla pudding. He loved diving into the *dulce de leche*, with its complex flavor teasing him in large creamy spoonfuls straight from the jar. But while he loved it, he didn't fully understand it; he didn't even really know how to pronounce it. It wasn't a part of his world. Vanilla pudding, on the other hand, was nice. Served neatly in a clear, small parfait glass, it's as American as apple pie.

The intensity of our stare and cascade of emotions came to a point of overload. It made me look away. My mind went back to that evening all those years ago when Tripp and I, just seventeen, were confronted head-on with the unspoken rules separating our two worlds as we sat celebrating the first of what would become many golf tournament wins. I'd always wished I could erase that moment. Sometimes there are some things we're better off not knowing. But no matter how much I wanted to pretend it didn't happen, it did. And it never sat well with me. *Did I really want to be a part of his world if it meant playing down who I was?*

I remembered how hurt Tripp was. The way he'd held me tight that night. And so many nights afterwards. We were young at the time and didn't yet know Tripp was on his way to becoming a pro golfer, but the cultural divide between us had already begun to slowly fissure our relationship. We came from different sides of the white picket fence that separated my family home from the golf course where he spent most of his time. Maybe we weren't equipped to overcome it. Perhaps we didn't want to, or had to chalk it up to bad timing. Tripp wanted to play golf. He needed to play golf. He couldn't have cared less about the rest of the country club antics. That much I'd always known. But that was his playing field and he was a determined professional athlete. I was coming to understand he had to choose between his world and mine. At that time, Argentine Malbec hadn't yet come into fashion in the States, especially not in my hometown. Looking back, I can only imagine Harts Run Club and its members weren't quite ready back then for a party of eight at Sunday brunch on the porch eating at full volume—in *Castellano*. Thankfully, times have changed. Now, some twenty years later, Spanish-breathing wines are generous-ly poured on most porches, no matter their view. But in my heart I knew that to really move forward, I'd have to forgive Tripp—in time, but not yet. That first run in with him made my blood boil.

I reminded myself to breathe as I turned around and walked back into the kitchen before Tripp mustered up the courage to say hello. Suddenly, all I could think about was the huge piece of *tortilla* I was about to devour, and how I hoped he'd gotten a glimpse of my newly toned backside before his new girl grabbed his hand, letting him know it was their turn to tee off.

"*Chau*, Tripp. Thanks for popping in to say hello, enjoy the rest of your golf game. It was so nice to see you. And nice to meet you as well." Mom, always gracious, saw them both off back to their side of the fence, offering cheek kisses here and there.

"Always good to see you, Mrs. Caminos," he said, as he swiftly hopped over the fence and turned to help his girl over.

That's when it hit me: *she* was his girl. I no longer was. Love might not go away, but it has its seasons—and we'd had ours. *It was time to move on. For good.*

Back in the kitchen, I took a bite of *tortilla*. Still hot, its nutty flavor melted in my mouth. It would be better in an hour or so once it cooled to room temperature, but I couldn't wait. I felt so jumpy I could crawl out of my skin. I needed a good amount of carbs to ground me.

I was on my third sliver when Laura came into the kitchen. She was in town visiting Dorita before she headed back to Argentina in a couple of days.

"Oh my God, Josie. That *tortilla* is for a going away lunch Mom's having for Dorita this afternoon. Did you see Tripp? How awkward." Laura told me how he hopped over the fence to say hello, after he and his girlfriend pulled up to the seventh tee in a golf cart. "As if the past couple of months never happened. But what was I supposed to do? Not say hello? I feel like that would have made you look worse."

She was right. It would have. Slightly annoyed, I was thankful my family had played it cool.

"Josie, put down the knife!" Mom shrieked as she came into the kitchen. "That *tortilla* is for *las chicas*. The girls are coming over for a going away luncheon for *Mami*. *Ay, ay, ay*, now I'm going to have to make another one," she complained, wrapping her hands around my neck jokingly as if to choke me.

"Sorry, Mom. I couldn't resist. But let's be honest. Dorita's going to have to make it. *Not you*." I quipped back.

"I know, but you know *Mami* needs a 'Juanita.' I'm going to have to peel the potatoes and chop the onion and parsley for her," Mom said, referring to the kitchenhand of the ubiquitous Argentinian TV cook and cookbook author, *Doña* Petrona—our very own Julia Child, if you will. Her first cookbook, *How to Create a Common Table*, published in 1933, was an instant bestseller and on most Argentine bookshelves. True to her generation, many of Petrona's early kitchen recipes lacked precision—she'd instruct to add a teacup of water, for instance, but didn't say how big the cup should be; or on her television show, would indicate that a recipe needed "three eggs, this size, no smaller."

A mere three years younger than my namesake and great-grandma Josefina, the celebrity chef was born Petrona Carrizo de Gandulfo in La Banda in the province of Santiago del Estero in 1896. One of her first jobs was making personal shop-front appearances, demonstrating gas ovens to prospective buyers with the then-named Primitiva de Gas company. She not only showed them how the ovens worked, but she also took questions about what to cook and how to cook on it—and more importantly, how to cook it economically. The company produced a brochure advertising her advice and their stoves. With that simple printing, her career began.

I can't help but think in our day and age she would have been coined the culinary world's *Doña* Oprah. She started giving all sorts of advice and tidbits over the radio. Her first cookbook included kitchen prescriptions *al estilo Argentino*, without any measurable details, along with page after page of home ec advice and tips on how to put together a common table and entertain guests, husbands included. At the time, the kitchen was a woman's domain.

Petrona's fame catapulted in 1960 when she launched her cooking show, *Buenas tardes, mucho gusto,* a name that became a popular cliché among Argentines. Women watched in awe at the sheer size of her onscreen delicacies. *Vol-au-vent al chantillí* pastry cream, savory and sweet molds of all sorts, cakes of all kinds—for weddings, birthdays or whatever the occasion. Among them, a four-tiered 1978 *Copa Mundial* World Soccer Cup *torta.*

Men and women alike were hooked on her show. As *Doña's* fame grew, Juanita Bordoy, her culinary assistant, became an icon herself. They watched as *Doña* bossed her about in menial tasks. Juanita was the Gayle to *Doña* Petrona's Oprah. Except she wasn't as nice to her. But that didn't mean they didn't love one another. *Doña* Petrona would ask Juanita for opinions. Then she'd often dismiss them, but mostly in good fun. Some didn't agree, but their quick banter became a national joke of sorts, landing Juanita an eternal trade name in her own right. To this day, Argentines refer to sous chefs as "Juanitas." When it came to Dorita, my sisters and I jumped at the chance to be hers. It always came with benefits, taste-testing and licking the bowl among them.

* * *

"Mom, Josie saw you hugging Tripp," Laura chimed in, egging her on. She sat down, grabbing a sliver of *tortilla* herself. To partake in the *sobremesa*, you must share in the food, *sí o sí*, no matter what.

"How could you and Dorita kiss him like that after what he did? Laura, I get. She was in the wrong place at the wrong time. But you could have made it clear to Tripp that he's no longer welcome in our home! Not yet. We've never even spoken since that night."

"What would you have had us do?" Mom asked. "You know what they say. When you don't know what to do, kill them with kindness. So that's what we did. Anyway, the first run-in is always the worst after a breakup. But I'm glad Tripp didn't see you like that. Or did he?" Mom cut herself a slice of *tortilla*. "He seemed to get awfully quiet towards the end," she said. "I mean, you're half naked in that sports bra. Did you run around Fox Chapel like that? Your father would not be happy."

"Really, Mom? Don't try to divert the real matter at hand here by commenting on my exercise attire, which is nothing out of the ordinary. It's not going to work," I snapped back.

"What you don't understand is that your *abuela* and I respect Tripp's decisiveness more than ever now. I'll always hold that boy up on a silver platter. And you know why? He did what you wouldn't. He did what you couldn't. The way I see it, he saved you from years of unhappiness. I don't like the way he did it, but that's his new girlfriend's issue. And believe me, it will be an issue," Mom answered, peeling a new batch of potatoes. "Now, get over here and help me chop some onions so you can cry all you want."

It was useless to argue. Mom was never big on remorse or apologies. Half an hour later, I was still in the kitchen watching

Dad polish off the remainder of the potato *tortilla* while *Abuela* effortlessly flipped the new one she was making. It seemed she was born to do this.

That afternoon, I decided to call my high school friend Robert, who had come back home to Pittsburgh to attend Duquesne Law. Megan, Taylor and I had gone out with him and a couple of other friends most nights that summer, and at least once a night he'd ask me out. Every time I'd turn him down, but ever persistent, he'd ask me again the next time we saw each other, thinking he'd wear me down. His senior year of college, Robert was named captain of Penn State's men's ice hockey team. Now, when he wasn't studying, he trained as a triathlete in his spare time. He wasn't used to getting turned down. Ever. I was a challenge, and Robert loved challenges.

I dialed his number. "Rob, Hey. I've been thinking about it, and yes."

"Hey, Josie. Yes what?" He asked on the other line.

"Yes, I'll have dinner with you. When?"

"Okay. All right then. Give me a second to gather my thoughts. How about tonight?"

"Perfect. I don't have any plans. What time do you want to pick me up?"

"Let me make you dinner. I'll be there around seven, groceries and all. I've got it covered."

"Are you sure? Do you really want to go to all that trouble? I have to warn you, I don't have air conditioning. It may be an oven in here. Literally."

"Even better. I'll see you at seven."

"Rob, it's just dinner."

"I know. You've made that loud and clear all summer. See you tonight."

"Do me a favor and park up the street at the Presbyterian Church. I'm going to tell my family I'm going out for the night so they don't bother us."

That evening, I couldn't seem to calm the rage burning inside me since seeing Tripp earlier that day. As I turned off the water in the shower, one side of the bathroom was barely visible from the other, leaving me to feel my way through the palpable mist in search of a towel. I dried off and sat naked on my bed staring at my closet, wondering what to wear. It was so hot that my choices were limited. I also didn't want to make it seem like I was trying too hard. *This isn't a date*, I reminded myself. But I wanted to look good. I needed to look good. I kept thinking about Meg, who always joked, "The best way to get over a bad breakup, Josie, is to get under someone." After trying on three or four sundresses, I decided on a sleeveless Nicole Miller black cotton sheath dress with a deep scoop neck that hugged my curves in all the right places. I tied up my wet hair in a loose bun—it was way too hot to pull out the hair dryer—and threw on mascara and lip gloss. Since we were staying in, I skipped wearing shoes altogether and painted my toenails blood red to match my mood.

While I waited, I uncorked a cold bottle of Sauvignon Blanc and poured a glass. Its crisp, citrusy zing felt refreshingly vivacious on my tongue and kept me going back for more. It took only a glass for the wine to kick in and calm my second thoughts. It had been forever since I'd been with anyone other than Tripp. Did I really want to do this? I didn't know if I knew how, but I'd soon find out.

Robert knocked at the door. I took a deep breath and counted to three before opening, trying to calm my pounding heart. There he stood, holding two grocery bags, in a white T-shirt, jean shorts he had cut himself and worn Birkenstocks. His sandy-blonde wavy hair was cut short around his ears, showing off his straight, prominent eyebrows that said *what you see is what you get*. His incredible looks gave him a hall pass on the jean shorts. It's like *Abuela* Dorita always said, "*Lo que importa es la percha, no la ropa.*" The hanger is what counts, not the clothes. I closed the door behind him, locking it, and offered him a glass of wine.

"I see you've already gotten started," he said, planting a kiss on my cheek. He smelled of soap and fresh towels pulled warm from the dryer.

"Just a glass. Let me help you," I said, reaching into one of the grocery bags.

"No way. Sit over there. Tonight, I'm doing all the work." Robert motioned to the stool on the other side of the kitchen pass-through counter that connected the dining room to the small galley kitchen that comfortably fit one. I walked past him, just brushing his arm, letting him feel the undercurrent of electricity.

Robert set down the groceries and began lining the ingredients up on the counter: bone-in chicken thighs, a few Granny Smith apples, one Honeycrisp apple, a Vidalia onion, garlic, fresh ginger root, apple cider, apple cider vinegar, Dijon mustard, a wedge of St. André triple cream brie and two chilled bottles of Pinot Grigio. *This was a man after my own heart.* Just the sight of him made me hungry.

"What's for dinner? Everything there looks delicious."

"Chicken Normandy, or *Poulet à la Normande,* as the French would say. Sounds sexier that way, doesn't it?" Robert reached for the cutting board, then began slicing the Honeycrisp apple alongside thick slices of the softened brie.

"Yum. Never tried, but I love French food so I'm sure I'll love it. Let me do something. Hand me the other cutting board and knife by the sink and I'll slice up the other apples."

Robert shooed my hand away. "Then you'll love this dish. It's shamelessly French: chicken thighs braised in cider. The dish is usually deglazed with brandy and finished with a splash of cream, but I figured with this heat I'd lighten it up with apple cider and vinegar."

Robert reached through the pass-through window as he fed me a slice of Honeycrisp generously smeared with brie. The sweet-tart apple burst instantly against the meltingly smooth and buttery triple-crème, drenching my mouth in its juice.

"Oh my God, so good. You don't even need to cook. I could literally just eat this all night," I said, grabbing another slice of apple with brie. "My grandfather Alfredo was part French, and he used to eat an entire wedge with some crusty French bread for lunch. That and a glass of red wine was all he ever needed."

"So, the apple doesn't fall far from the cheese in your family?" Robert glanced at me with his grayish-blue eyes as he chopped the onions, confidently wielding a chef's knife.

I watched intently as he snapped off the arm of the ginger root, gently peeling back its thin tan skin. The bob of his knife cast a mildly hallucinatory effect over me as it yielded against the firm inner flesh of ginger. The root emitted a spicy, woodsy aroma each time it succumbed to the blade, moistening the cutting board with its creamy juice. I felt almost as if I shouldn't be watching, but I couldn't look away. My eyes traveled up Robert's strong hands to his forearms, broad shoulders and chiseled face, tracing his pronounced jawline, then staying a while on his dimpled chin until meeting his eyes, which looked back at me looking at him. Embarrassed, I quickly looked away, dabbing my mouth with my napkin. His crisp white T-shirt began to soften and become translucent against his skin as he sautéed the onion, garlic and minced ginger. His eyes became weepy from the chopped onion, so he grabbed a dish cloth that was tucked into his back jeans pocket and wiped away the tears, flashing me a vulnerable smile.

There was something profoundly sexy about watching him make dinner. Food, after all, has been the language of lovers since Eve offered Adam her forbidden fruit. Until that evening, I'd never had a man cook for me. Other than the after-school Ritz cracker *canapés Abuelo* Alfredo made me as a child, the men in my family didn't cook . . . ever. They were accustomed to being served. Apart from wielding a barbeque paddle, I'd never seen my dad or two brothers prepare anything in the kitchen. It was always fun watching Dad cook. When grilling, he often ate standing *gaucho*-style by his Weber, knife in hand, eating bites of meat here and there from the grill. "Otherwise it gets cold," Dad would say. But he often had his fill by the time he sat down to join us at the table.

It felt almost voyeuristic to watch Robert handle the tongs as he flipped the chicken thighs, searing each side to a perfect golden brown in a mixture of butter and extra-virgin olive oil. The mix of aromas and wine that enveloped me made my mind go somewhere it shouldn't have.

While he cooked, I began mentally taking off Robert's clothes. The way he moved about so effortlessly among the cutting boards, skillets and saucepans stripped away every inkling of a thought I might have had in the back of my mind about running into Tripp earlier that day.

Robert came from good genes. His Dad had been a Pittsburgh Steelers number one defensive back draft pick in the early '60s. But athleticism was among the few things Robert and his father had in common. Robert was a family man. He was his mom's son, and she had taught him how to treat women. From the looks of it, she'd also taught him how to cook, effortlessly—and quite seductively.

"Whatever you're doing is going straight to my head," I swooned. "Let me at least prepare the salad." I reached over the counter and grabbed the butter lettuce and candied pecans, hoping the freshly washed leaves would cool me down.

Robert slowly shook his head, took a sip of his wine, set down the goblet and grabbed my hand. He looked into my eyes and the thread of electricity between us burned with desire.

"No. Tonight is my treat. The whole evening. Even the dishes. I'm taking care of everything."

"Okay, but we have a rule in my house. The dishes can wait. I can get them tomorrow."

"That's a good rule. I like that." He handed me my wine glass, topping it off. Our ensuing conversation, like the wine, flowed easily.

I could really get used to this, I thought. Too bad I'd sworn off relationships for good since Tripp. After close to a decade of being with one person, the last thing I needed was to jump into another serious relationship. Months back, when Tripp and I were still together, I'd prayed to meet someone else so I could muster the courage to leave him without the inevitable heartache. But now that I'd waded through it and felt myself coming out on the other side, I wasn't interested in having a man in my life for the moment. Somewhere along the way, I'd lost myself to Tripp's own needs and desires. It wasn't anyone's fault but my own. I'd spent too many years living my life based on someone else's terms. Now I wanted to discover and live according to my own.

Robert set the seared chicken thighs aside on a plate as he prepared the evening's crescendo. A cloud of steam enveloped the kitchen as the apple cider and vinegar splashed into the searing pan. He mixed in a teaspoon of Dijon mustard and deglazed the golden-brown bits from the pan's bottom, creating a tantalizing scent throughout the cottage house. I was intoxicated—and not just from the wine. Suddenly, my appetite turned ravenous, so I reached for another slab of brie and slice of apple. Robert combined all of the recipe ingredients back into the golden sauce—the sautéed vegetables and ginger, seared chicken and plump Granny Smith apples—before sliding the pan into the 325-degree oven to braise.

As I stood up to set the table, the back of my legs stuck to the stool from the heat. I lowered the overhead lights, hoping to cool down the room, and lit some candles. It felt as if the sky had fallen into the cottage house and a micro-mist of apple cider seeping with desire had overtaken our table for two. Robert uncorked a second bottle of wine. As he made his way from the kitchen to the dining room, I met him halfway. Both of my palms landed on his broad, firm chest. We pressed up against one another and then began stripping off our clothes. Robert wound his arms around me with the same ease he showed when moving among the skillets and saucepans. I felt his hot breath on my neck as he began to kiss it. I bit his bottom lip as I ate his kiss.

"Rob, whatever you do, don't fall for me."

"I won't," he said, breathing heavily.

Robert looked at me with lustful eyes as if to devour me. As he pushed up against me, I wound my legs around him, my breasts flattening against his chest. He picked me up and pinned me against the shiplap walls, taking hold of me. As he clung to me, his fingers moved slowly up my thighs, just as I'd imagined. The curtain of fog clung to our entwined bodies, encouraging our hands to explore further and further.

"Are you sure you're ready for this?" Robert asked, catching his breath. "I really like you, and I don't want to mess anything up."

I wasn't ready. Maybe it was my inbred Catholic guilt. "Not tonight. It's not that I don't want to. I just can't. Not yet."

Robert kissed me tenderly on the lips. "I can wait as long as you need. Hungry? I'm starved."

We never did make it to the table. It was too hot. Instead, we sat half naked on the wood floor atop a white bed sheet we'd stripped from my bed, sharing the fall-off-the-bone Chicken Normandy straight from the pan. Robert ripped bite-sized pieces of a baguette and threw them in the pan to absorb the sultry, slightly tart juices. Sopping wet, the bread melted upon impact as it hit our mouths. As we finished eating, the fog that had overcome the cottage house and the late August heat slowly began to dissipate, lulling us back to the bedroom where we slept, arm in arm.

The following morning, I awoke to an empty bed and hurried to get to work. When I got home later, my bed was covered in roses. Robert had spent the day installing two window air-conditioning units in my place—one in my bedroom and another in the living room. He had set the thermostat at sixty-eight degrees and blanketed my bed in red rose petals that pranced atop the bedspread as they were gently tossed by the blowing cool air. On my nightstand was an arrangement of three dozen red roses with a card. "I forgot the dessert last night. Can't wait to share it with you. Call me."

I was tempted, but I didn't. No one had ever done such a bold, romantic gesture for me. It felt so grown up. But I had some growing up of my own to do before I got involved with someone else. *How'd Robert manage to get in?* Megan must have given him my garage door code. *What else did she know about our evening together?* I was mostly touched but also slightly annoyed about cleaning up the rose petals as I crossed the driveway to my parents' home to get a broom and vacuum. Sonny stopped me halfway. Never to be outdone, she'd brought me a gift of her own.

"What do you have there, girl?" I crouched down and Sonny gently laid a brilliantly red-crested cardinal at my feet, its reddish bill, black face and vibrant plumage perfectly untouched. "Oh no! What'd you do?" She nudged the bird closer to me as if to say, *Here. I brought him just for you.*

"Thank you. You're such a good girl." I beckoned Sonny to follow me into the garage so she wouldn't continue to play with the poor asphyxiated bird. I grabbed a garden shovel and scooped up the bird. As I walked to the garbage bin, I looked up and saw *Abuela* watching me from the kitchen window.

When I went into my parents' home, Dorita was waiting for me in the kitchen. "*Hola, Abuela,*" I said, kissing her on the cheek. She was in her apron making *milanesas* for that evening. It would be one of the last meals she'd make before her trip home in two days.

"Josie, what was it that Sonny brought you?"

"A cardinal. Poor thing. I was hoping it was alive, but Sonny scared it to death. Its eyes were still open. Sonny didn't leave a mark on it. Such a beautiful bird."

"*¿Un cardenal? Pobrecito.* You know what they say about cardinals: they're messengers. If you're single and one comes to you, it's a sign that you're about to meet someone."

"Oh, really, *Abuela*? The last thing I need is to fall for someone. I may rethink it, however, if I can find a man that cooks for me."

"Now, that would be a first in our family!" Dorita pounded the sirloin steaks into thin sheets that she would soon dip in egg and cover in breadcrumbs before frying. "So, do you like him?"

"Who?"

"That boy that kept going in and out of the cottage house today?"

"You saw him?"

"Your *mamá* and I watched him all day. All those flowers. *Dios mío*, good God, what did he do with all of them?"

"Well, uh . . ."

"Your *mamá* wanted to ask him to leave. She said it was too much, but I stopped her. I know how hot it is in there. Anyway, the only thing we agreed on is that he is a *churro.*"

I couldn't help but laugh, "*Abuela,* how modern of you. He is cute, isn't he?"

"I might be old, but that doesn't mean I don't have good taste. So . . . tell me. Who is he?"

"No one. Just a friend. He told me he had a couple of old air conditioners he could lend me."

I wasn't about to tell her that my friend decided to install air conditioners in my place after our steamy evening together. He was obviously expecting to come back again and hoping to make his stay more comfortable.

"*Cada loco con su tema*, Josie. To each his own," she said, looking at me as if she knew something I didn't. "Just be careful collecting all those rose petals. They'll clog the vacuum."

"Okay," I said, realizing Dorita had caught me *con mis manos en la masa*—with my hands in the dough. Even worse, the cookie jar.

"Josie, is that you?" Mom called from the family room as I rummaged through the hallway closet.

"It is. I'm just borrowing a broom."

"Can you come to the family room? We need to talk to you."

I grabbed a broom and some garbage bags and found Mom sitting next to Dad. He'd just arrived from the office. They were talking softly to one another, as if conspiring about something.

"Josie, stop there. Bring me a scotch on the rocks. Two fingers scotch, one finger water." *As if I didn't know that.* Dad sat back, kicking up his feet in his usual spot on the couch. I'd been serving him his nightly scotch since I was eight years old, yet he still felt the need to explain the ratio of scotch to water each time he requested it.

After I handed him the glass, he asked me to sit.

"Sure. What's up?"

"Your future is what's up," Mom said. "Your father and I have decided that you're going to Argentina on Wednesday with your grandmother and me."

"What?" I interrupted Mom. "I'm not going . . ."

But Mom continued talking right over me. "*El Niño* has done a number on the ranches, taking out crops and herds with heavy flooding. The Argentine government is offering subsidies, so we need you at the ranch to help. There's a lot of money at stake here. Gastón, the administrator, is doing most of the paperwork, but we need you to audit his work and help inventory the cattle for the seven ranches."

"Is this about the roses? You do realize I'm twenty-four? Anyway, what makes you think I'd even know how to audit? My degrees are in marketing and pre-med, with a minor in Spanish lit. I wouldn't even know where to begin."

"Yes, you would." Mom crossed her arms over her chest. "You've been helping me with the books and taxes in Dad's office for years now. You're trained in Microsoft Money. We use it at the ranches, too."

"Your brother Oscar is going too," Dad butted in. "I've asked him to help me liquidate the herds of remaining cattle before we lose them. He'll help you. Between the two of you, you'll get the job done."

"Are you serious? You both decided? Don't I have a say in the matter? I have a job and friends here. No! I'm not going. It's not just that I know nothing about cattle herding and crops. I have no one to take care of Sonny," I said, standing up in a show of might.

"You're going, and that's that," Dad concluded, setting his scotch glass down hard on a coaster.

"No, I'm not," I responded defiantly. "You can't tell me what to do. I'm no longer a child." It was of no use, though. The thing was, he *could* tell me what to do. He was quite literally my boss. I'd been working at his office as a medical assistant for the past year.

"Sit down," Dad continued. "It's part of the family business, and I'm not asking. If you don't go, you can turn in your lab coat. You'll be gone until the end of September. I'll be meeting you all in Argentina the last two weeks of the month. That should give us enough time to deal with this mess."

Whose mess? Yours or mine? I couldn't imagine leaving my friends for an entire month to be held prisoner in the remote solitude of the ranches. I'd have no choice but to be alone with my thoughts at Santa Elena, where the closest town, just over a half-hour away, had less than seven thousand residents. At the moment, my friends and our nightly drinking escapades were the only thing sustaining me. I picked up the broom and bags and went to leave without saying another word.

"Josie, one last thing," Dad said, clearing his throat. I turned and looked at him.

"While your mom and I agree that it's a good idea for you to put some distance between yourself and your life here in Pittsburgh, the only thing is, *hija*, I'm afraid it could backfire on us, and you'll meet an Argentine guy and never come back," he said, with a twinkle in his eye.

Looking back now, maybe he knew things, like his father Caminos, who, the night before open-heart surgery, told me he'd see me up there in *el cielo*. But in that moment it seemed Dad was looking at me as if seeking reassurance that I wouldn't fall in love and run away from home forever. I didn't offer it. There'd always been an invisible wall separating the two of us, built layer upon layer of words that went unsaid.

* * *

The following morning, I met Megan at the gym for a spin class before heading into work. "I'm leaving tomorrow for a month in Argentina," I said, wiping the sweat from my face with my towel. "Guess I should place my membership on hold until the first of October."

"What? A month? Why are you just now telling me?" Megan asked.

"I honestly didn't know. I found out last night. My parents aren't giving me much of a choice. First thing I'm going to do when I get back to Pittsburgh is look for another job and an apartment of my own. I love my parents, but they feel they can't control me, so their solution is to simply send me away."

"Something tells me you aren't coming back," Megan hugged me. "I don't know what happened between you and Robert the other night, but something in you is different. I can see it in your eyes. I'll check in on Sonny for you. We're both going to miss you."

"Why does everyone keep saying that? I'm definitely coming back. My life is here," I reassured Megan, hugging her back tightly.

As for Robert, he was my perfectly beautiful rock bottom. I never did get to tell him that. Our night together made me realize that there are few virtues a man can possess that are more erotic than culinary skill. Though our timing wasn't right, Robert's affection lifted me from the fog I'd been aimlessly walking through those past months. It was time to move forward, so I decided that's what I would do and began packing for Argentina.

Tortilla española (Potato and Egg Frittata)

SERVES 7. *Or one, nearing rock bottom.*

A Spanish *tortilla* is so much more than the sum of its humble parts. Potatoes are the star, but the onions come in a close second. Although my *abuela* Dorita preferred them simple, *tortillas* welcome variation. Many mix in Spanish *chorizo* or red bell peppers. Some prefer them *rellenos*, stuffing them to the gills with loads of mozzarella and boiled ham. Do as you please. There's no right or wrong way. *Tortilla* makes an excellent breakfast, lunch, dinner, snack or crowd-pleasing *tapa*. How you choose to eat it—hot, cold, in small cubes as an hors d'oeuvre, in a hefty wedge for dinner, inside a *bocadillo* or baguette sandwich or standing at the kitchen counter stuffing slice after slice into your mouth—is entirely up to you and your mood.

6 cups of **canola oil**, pre-heated to 350°

4 pounds of **Idaho potatoes**, peeled and cut in ½-inch cubes

3 large **Spanish onions** (2 to 2½ pounds), cut in ½ inch cubes

12 large **eggs**

3 teaspoons **salt**

1 teaspoon **pepper**

1 tablespoon extra-virgin **olive oil**

Handful of fresh flat-leaf **parsley**, chopped coarsely

Smoked **paprika** for garnish (optional)

Carefully place potatoes into pre-heated canola oil and fry until golden brown, about 15 minutes. Remove potatoes with a slotted spoon and place on a paper towel to soak up any excessive oil.

Carefully place the onions in the same oil until translucent, about 15 minutes. Remove onion with a slotted spoon and place on a paper towel to soak up any excessive oil.

In a bowl, whisk together the egg, salt and pepper.

Pour olive oil into a large, 12-inch, ovenproof nonstick skillet with a tight-fitting lid and heat over medium-low heat, swirling to coat the pan.

Meanwhile, mix in the slightly cooled potatoes and onions to the egg mixture and pour evenly into the skillet. Shake and swirl the pan the first minutes to keep the *tortilla* in motion so that it cooks evenly. Cook, covered, for approximately 20 minutes, until the bottom half and outer edge of the *tortilla* are set, and the egg on the top is no longer runny, but still fluid.

At this point you can decide to either flip the *tortilla* to properly brown it, or to place it in the oven under the broiler. A *tortilla* of this size is difficult to flip, so we often prefer the broiler method.

Flip method: Run a spatula around the edge to loosen it. Set a large plate over the skillet (use one that's slightly larger than the pan). In one swift, confident motion, lift the skillet up, placing your hand flat on top of the plate, and invert the *tortilla* onto the plate. The faster you do this, the better, since hesitation is exactly the thing that will make your *tortilla* slip and hit the kitchen counter or floor.

Put the pan back on the burner and carefully slide the *tortilla* in, cooked side up. Use a spatula to tuck in the edge, creating a neat, rounded appearance. Cook just until set, about 5–10 minutes longer. Leave it a little longer if you want a more fully cooked center, or less if you want it runny.

Broiler method: While the *tortilla* cooks on the cooktop, preheat the oven to 350°, placing the oven rack on the top shelf. After 20 minutes, remove the lid from the skillet and transfer the skillet to the oven, placing it on the top shelf to brown the top of the *tortilla* for five to ten minutes. Leave it a little longer if you want a more fully cooked center, or less if you want it runny.

Run a spatula around the edge to loosen the *tortilla*. Carefully flip the *tortilla* out onto a serving plate. Garnish with freshly chopped flat-leaf parsley and smoked paprika (optional).

Part Two

ALLÁ
(THERE)

La verdad de la milanesa
The Truth and Nothing But the Truth

Growing up, *milanesas*—breaded, thin slices of prime beef from the *colita de cuadril* sirloin roast—were always served at our family table when there was no one around to impress. If red meat wasn't your thing, chicken, soy or sliced eggplant *milanesas* took its place. This was the default dinner when Mom and Dorita were too tired for ideas, but that didn't mean they worked any less. It took love, time and bloody knuckles to make one really good *milanesa*, nonetheless three dozen at a time—especially when your husband and sons could each down five in one sitting. Mom likened them to Argentina's culinary foot soldiers. You could find *milanesas* most anywhere—in train stations, subway *kioskos*, rolling food carts, roadside cafés and, as I would soon discover, gas stations, too.

* * *

"*Damas y caballeros*, ladies and gentlemen, *bienvenidos* to Córdoba. Please stay seated with your seatbelts fastened until the plane comes to a full stop." The moment the announcement began, I reached for the carry-on I'd shoved under the seat in front of me. I couldn't get off that plane fast enough. Between the four Advil I'd taken with the two airplane-sized complimentary bottles of

Malbec I'd had for dinner, I was sure I'd get some shut-eye on the twelve-hour flight. Instead, I got my period at forty thousand feet while I sat wide-eyed, stewing in my middle seat watching that evening's in-flight movie selection, *Titanic*. The movie that I'd wanted to see once was now one I couldn't get away from. As if it weren't enough that I was facing a month of solitude alone with my thoughts at our ranch, La Santa Elena, where the closest town of Suardi had a population of 6,933, the movie selection was a stark reminder of the shipwreck of my ill-fated love life.

I must have prayed more than a hundred Hail Marys and Our Fathers by the time the plane came to a stop. I'd always had a borderline neurotic fear of turbulence—the coffee-spilling, luggage-jostling, belly-dropping kind that makes you contemplate whether you've been good or bad. The kind that makes you question if St. Peter will step aside and allow you passage through Heaven's pearly gates. Because the next step was certainly that. Or hell. *Ojalá* it's the first and not the latter.

Flying was one of the few instances that Dad and I saw eye to eye. In fact, he and Mom were mile-high juxtapositions. Dad, the oldest son of my *abuela* Buby, a devout Catholic who attended Mass each morning, was a self-proclaimed atheist. But at the first midair tremor or bump, he'd grab the hand closest to him and desperately begin praying. Mom, on the other hand, normally high strung with a side of stress, was calm and collected once airborne. She'd tell me to sit back, relax and *tomármelo con soda*, or in her case, tonic with a splash of vodka and twist of lime.

As soon as the pilot turned off the overhead seatbelt sign, I was among the first in line to deplane. I'd sat by myself for the last leg of the trip. Mom and Dorita had flown business class from Miami to Buenos Aires while Oscar and I traveled in coach. But after saying our goodbyes to Dorita in Buenos Aires, Mom asked if we could switch seats as we headed back north to Argentina's heartland, Córdoba. The way I saw it, it was a win-win. I'd gotten bumped up to business class for the first time ever, and Mom got some alone time in with Oscar. Smack dab in the middle of Mom's four girls, he was the one she felt had gotten away—she worried she hadn't spent the same amount of energy and time mothering

Oscar as she did her daughters. Or was it simply that our double X chromosomes required more attention?

As I disembarked the plane, the crisp, cool, Argentine winter air hit my face. It felt refreshing but was also a blatant reminder that I'd been robbed of my highly coveted last month of summer back home in Pittsburgh. I reached the tarmac, finally on solid ground, and stepped aside to fish my jacket out of my carry-on. Suddenly the creepy, prickly feeling I got when someone was staring at me grabbed ahold of my senses.

I looked up. He was there, standing just inside the gate's floor-to-ceiling window. The silver-haired man.

My ghost.

In Argentina.

His hauntings, while brief, had always been sporadic. But I'd never imagined they would be transcontinental. He was the same as always, in his windbreaker and gentleman's cap. Except this time he wasn't alone; he was with a younger man. The image of the two of them standing side by side—one taller and more casual, one shorter and more formal—made my head fill with a deafening white noise. Adrenaline poured through my veins as my Gentleman Caller stood inside the airport terminal, looking down at me through the glass. It appeared as if he was pointing me out to the younger one. His companion stood in a faded button down, arms crossed along his broad chest, looking at me. When our eyes met, he didn't look away. I looked around, but the other passengers descending from the aircraft seemed oblivious to them. So I, too, pretended not to notice and headed inside. My entire body seemed suspended as I walked towards the gate. I didn't dare look back. *But who was the other man? He was at once new and also familiar.* While I couldn't put my finger on it, I also couldn't shake the feeling that I knew him.

I'd soon find out. He was waiting for me as I entered the gate: a tall, thin man in his late twenties with silky, dark, wavy hair, hazel eyes and a prominently curved nose that gave him an air of confidence. He was standing behind the glass doors, brazenly looking straight at me, his hands tucked away in his worn Levi's jeans. He was handsome—not in a pretty way but in that rugged way some men are, when together, the sum of their parts makes you look twice. His full lips formed a smile, the punch of which made him seem even more familiar.

"*Hola, flaca. Soy Gastón,*" he said, placing his hand on my shoulder as he bent down and kissed my right cheek hello. "Josefina, right? How was the flight? *Y tu mamá* and brother?" he asked. His calloused hands brushed over mine as he grabbed my bag.

I froze. The stubble from Gastón's five o'clock shadow left my cheek tingling. He was at least a head taller than me, yet I was somehow looking straight into his eyes that were yellow and green with swirls of grayish brown. Thinking back to when I'd first heard his deep voice over the phone, it was even more sensual in person. I didn't know what caught me off guard most—that he knew my name or that he called me *flaca*. All my life I'd been *la gordita.* Until then, I had never been the skinny sister. I had Megan to thank for that.

Notorious for emphatically assigning nicknames tied to physical traits, Argentines somehow always got away with calling friends and loved ones *gordo* or *gorda*—fatty, chubby one, *tubalub*—regardless of their shape or girth. And instead of getting a good old slap in the face, they're received as terms of endearment. Most times it didn't even matter what you looked like. You could be blonde and fair skinned and be called *negra* (black one), be a thirty-five-year-old mom and be known as *vieja* (oldie but goodie) to your children, or have packed on the pounds in recent years, yet be lucky enough to have your tenured nickname *el flaco* or *la flaca,* the skinny one, stick. It was when a loved one called you by your actual name that you began to worry.

"*Hola* Gastón. Sorry, I didn't recognize you. Have we met before? I asked, scanning his face and my memory.

"Only in pictures. They're all over the ranch. I'd recognize you and your brothers and sisters from anywhere."

I didn't remember ever seeing a photograph of Gastón. Yet he seemed so familiar.

"Plus, *mi vieja* always filled us in on her faraway goddaughter's life."

"*Claro*, Gastón. She's so sweet. I've also heard so much about you. It's nice to finally put a face to the name." *Especially a face like yours.* "Thanks for picking us up. Mom and Oscar should be coming any minute."

* * *

Mom and Gastón's mom, Graciela, were childhood friends who'd stayed in touch even after Mom moved to the States. Our families went way back. Our grandfathers, Merardo on Gastón's side and Alfredo on mine, worked together for years at the large petroleum company, YPF. Our *abuelas* became quick friends and often got their families together. I'd always get together with Graciela and her three daughters for lunch during our yearly family trips to Argentina. But the five-year age gap between Gastón and me kept us from meeting. Until that day.

"Are you alone? I thought I saw you through the window standing with an older man."

"Nope. Just me. Between the luggage and the four of us, there isn't much room in the truck for anyone or anything else. We've got a good three-and-a-half-hour trip to Santa Elena," he said, turning to greet Mom and Oscar, "Ah, here they are now. Poupée, Oscar, *¿como les va?* How was the trip?"

He didn't see him. He couldn't see him. My Gentleman Caller. From first glance, it looked as if they were discussing something. As if they were discussing me. But Gastón couldn't hear him. He was oblivious to the conversation. That's the thing about ghosts, at least mine. They don't make a sound. You don't always know they are there, or in my case, who they are or what they want. I'd been living with the silent ghost of my Gentleman Caller long enough to know.

As I watched Gastón greet Mom and Oscar with cheek kisses, it hit me. *That wasn't the first time I'd seen him with my Gentleman Caller.* I'd dreamt about them together weeks before. I was sitting with Laura on the white picket fence separating our parents' home in Pittsburgh from the golf course. They were the men we saw from across the driveway looking for me. When our eyes locked, the force of Gastón's pull almost knocked me off the fence. So much that it jerked me awake. They were the same men that I'd seen just moments before as I walked from the tarmac to the gate. I was sure of it. Even if Gastón assured me he was alone, he hadn't been.

I was exhausted and crampy, not to mention hungry. "Is it lunch time yet?" I asked as Mom and I climbed into the front bench seat of the Ford F-150 pickup. I was sandwiched between her and Gastón, who was driving, while Oscar squeezed into the small half-back seat.

"I know just the place," Gastón said. "It's just off the route about a half-hour into the trip back. They've got the best *milanesas* in town."

"*Dalé* Gastón, that sounds perfect," Mom said, cleaning her large black prescription sunglasses that she wore regardless of the sun's mood or reach.

Before we knew it, Gastón was turning into an Esso gas station. "*Llegamos*. Here we are. Hope you're hungry."

"I don't understand, are we getting gas?" I whispered to Mom.

Gastón beat her to the punch. "They've got a small restaurant inside. Let's go."

"It's been at least twenty hours since I've had a decent meal. Can't we go somewhere with real food?" I whispered back to Mom.

"I'm starving," Oscar chimed in from the back, rubbing his hands together as he often would when he was excited about something—just as my *abuelo* Alfredo used to do. "A *milanesa* would hit the spot just about now."

"Exactly, Oscar," Gastón quipped back as he turned off the ignition, shooting me a coy side-eye as if we were friends who went way back. There was a lightness to him that was magnetic, even if I wasn't in the mood. But he didn't give a shit. *Was he always this confident and comfortable with people he didn't even know?*

"Your *hermana* has a lot to learn about Argentina. It's easy to find good *milangas* on the road. Just follow the trucks." I found myself having to pay extra attention to Gastón's fast-paced slang, quickly realizing *milangas* was lingo for *milanesas*. He got down from the pickup, all *compinche* with Oscar, joking around as if they were old buds. "I bet *la Yanqui* here wouldn't know a good *milanesa* if it smacked her in the face." Gastón laughed, putting his arm around my shoulders as he pulled me into him.

I moved away, looking down at my spanking new Nike running shoes, a sure giveaway that I wasn't from here. Argentine girls wouldn't be caught dead in them, unless, of course, they were actually running. By now, Gastón must have realized I couldn't roll my double *r*'s. Even though we shared the same heritage, the differences between us were glaring. Suddenly I found myself feeling overly self-conscious. "We grew up eating *milanesas*. My *abuela* Dorita would make stacks and stacks of them. No one knows their way around a top sirloin like Dorita. She'd slice it perfectly thin and then pound it even thinner, making the most tender *milanesas* ever." *So there.*

I'd made sure to leave out the part about how in her day, Dorita wielded her meat mallet relentlessly and often pounded away the frustration she had felt each time *Abuelo* Alfredo tightened his purse strings. They were the only control he had over Dorita. Money made her dependent on him. But women of her day and age didn't dare work, unless, of course, they were an aging spinster and had to. (With the exception of *Doña* Petrona, who was both married and paving the way for Argentina's next generation of female chefs.) A woman's place was in the kitchen, and any other place she could see to her husband's every whim. That drove Dorita crazy. Beating out pound after pound of *colita de cuadril* was her therapy, and, after two minutes on each side in the frypan, our nourishment. I always loved helping Dorita make *milanesas*. Mostly I loved eating the fried *milanesa* balls she'd make from the leftover egg and breadcrumb mixture. They were the benefits you reaped if you helped, like getting to lick the cookie bowl. I made sure to leave that part of the story out, too.

"Dorita's *milanesas* were the best," Oscar said. "Poor Dori. We'd grab them right out of the pan. She couldn't keep up with how fast we ate them."

"You mean how fast you and Dad ate them?" I quipped. Dorita and Mom would hide piles of *milanesas* in the microwave, in kitchen cabinets, on top of the fridge—anywhere they could think of to save us girls some before the men ate them all. But by that time, Dorita barely made *milanesas* anymore. Her arthritic hands had forced her to concede the meat mallet to Mom. But that was okay. While hers weren't Dorita's *milanesas*, Mom also needed the therapeutic benefits of pounding the meat. At some point, we all do.

"*Vamos* Josie. Try to improve your attitude please," Mom whispered, putting her arm around me as we entered the mom-and-pop restaurant attached to the Esso gas station. It was surprisingly packed. "I know you don't want to be here, or in Argentina at all for that matter, but that's not Gastón's fault."

Wasn't it, though? If I remembered correctly, they had sent me to Argentina to audit Gastón of all people. Being there in that foreign place felt, in so many ways, like being a child again, traversing a playground of the unfamiliar. Even though my parents began livestock and cattle ranching when I was in the eighth grade, our trips to Argentina primarily consisted of visiting family in the Buenos Aires area. We rarely spent more than a week at Santa Elena, their working *estancia* in *las pampas*. In that moment I felt like I was ten years old, dragging my feet because things didn't go my way. *Didn't anyone care that I was starving? And on my period?* I needed food more than anyone, but this place wasn't appealing at all. It wouldn't be another decade until author and journalist Michael Pollan articulated my thoughts exactly: "Don't get your fuel from the same place your car does." That was the fifty-seventh of sixty-four culinary mandates he'd later include in his *Food Rules: An Eater's Manual.* My Dad didn't agree. For as far back as I could remember, he'd frequented our local Rodi Road gas station, sneaking those hotdogs on his way home from the office.

Apparently, Gastón wouldn't have agreed with Michael Pollan either. He snagged us a table that had just become free. When the waitress arrived, we immediately ordered. There was no need for menus. I'm not even sure they had any. Mom ordered a *milanesa completa* with lettuce, tomato, cheese and ham. Gastón chose a *Napolitana*—a *milanesa a la pizza* topped with tomato sauce, oregano and melted mozzarella. Oscar followed suit. When it came my turn to order, I asked the waitress for a *suprema de pollo*, Argentina's emblematic chicken *milanesa*, plain, with lemon wedges, and a side of *papas fritas*. French fries always hit the spot that time of the month.

"No, no, no," Gastón shook his head. "Bring her a *milanesa de carne de vaca* instead," he said to the server, winking at her. Then he turned to me and squeezed my hand. "Trust me. Go with the beef."

My skin felt so jumpy in that moment that I wanted to crawl out of my body. *Who the hell is this guy, ordering for me as he flirts with the waitress?* Like most Argentine women, she had a stunning figure and light brown hair that had just enough natural curl to make it look like ribbons of *dulce de leche* spilling off the sides of a perfectly shaped cake. But in an effort to avoid another under-the-table foot altercation with Mom, I went along with Gastón's bovine suggestion. "*Dalé*, sure. Bring me the beef *milanesa* with extra lemon."

The waitress brought out *milanesas* so big they spilled over the sides of the plates. I had to contain myself. These were the kind of country-fried steaks that made you want to kick back your chair, stand up and belt out, "*Don't cry for me Argentina . . . the truth is I never left you.*" But I wouldn't give Gastón the satisfaction. After polishing mine off, I had to admit I had been too quick to judge. This pump-side hole-in-the-wall restaurant had some of the best *milanesas* I'd ever eaten—after Dorita's, of course. That particular Esso served up Argentine soul food at its best.

Sobremesa that afternoon was an abridged version, consisting of *cafés dobles* for Gastón and Oscar and *cortaditos*, coffees "cut" with milk, for Mom and me, served up with a sideshow of Gastón charming the pants off of Mom. And Oscar, one to never miss an opportunity to throw in his nonsensical, game-show-worthy, two-cent banter into a good conversation, was right there with them while I stayed on the sidelines. I couldn't remember the last time Mom genuinely laughed like that. She seemed younger and freer. The moment was interrupted by the handheld telephone ringing in her travel bag.

"*Hola*. Are you there? Hello?" Mom said, but the line was dead. It was Dad, calling from the States. Mom was the first to get up from the table in search of cell service in the parking lot, weaving in and out between the rows of parked trucks.

As Gastón signaled to the waitress for the check, he turned to Oscar and me. "So, are you taking some time off? Or learning the family business? You're the first Caminos children to come since I've been here. I don't blame you. It's in the middle of nowhere. You know what they say, foreigners escape to the Argentine *pampas* for one of three reasons: for work, for love or to run away from the law."

I sat sipping my coffee as Oscar answered.

"I'm helping my parents get some paperwork in order. I also make it a point to never pass up a free trip. But Pheenie, here," Oscar patted me on the back. "They forced her to come. She was partying a little too much back home." When he wanted to annoy me, Oscar always made sure to pull out the old childhood nickname, Pheenie Fries, that he and a friend gave me years ago as I sat eating French fries during swim team practice one day.

"Speak for yourself, Oscar. I'm here for one reason and one reason only—work. I figured you knew, Gastón? We're here to audit you. We'll be spending a *lot* of time together."

Oscar shot me a look. "She got her period on the plane. Just ignore her. We're here because of *El Niño*. Dad says it's caused havoc and tremendous losses of crops and livestock. We're here to help with whatever's needed."

Gastón wasn't the least phased. "So, *la verdad de la milanesa* comes out. No worries, Oscar. I like straight shooters. Your sister can dish it out. Maybe there is a tinge of Argentina in her after all. I respect that. It's why we eat and drink, to have conversations like these. The kind that rip a tablecloth out from under you, uncovering the filth below."

"Speaking of ripping things off, did you check out our waitress?" Oscar changed the subject.

"Very nice. She's like a good fruit salad. *Tiene todo menos limón.* She's got it all, minus the lemons," Gastón said, shamelessly looking her up and down.

Wow. I'd found myself in the throes of Argentine *machismo* at its best. How convenient, I thought, that while us women wore our lemons front and center, men had the advantage of conveniently tucking theirs away from public scrutiny—leaving us to size them up half naked, when it was often too late to politely decline their advances. *No thanks. I think I'll pass.* Back home in Pittsburgh, with her figure, the waitress would have had her pick of the litter with most of the men I knew. She also didn't seem to mind Gastón's subtle advances in the least. Yet, I felt suddenly obligated to defend her. Because as *Abuela* Dorita used to say, *when life gives you lemons, you* sobremesa—*with limoncello, of course.*

"And your *limones*, Gastón? I'm curious, would you say you're more fruit salad material or straight up limoncello?" *Match point: me.*

"Straight up, of course, just like your *milangas*. Except you like yours with extra lemon. Right?" *His point—deuce.* Gastón laughed, holding out his arms as if he was carrying two heavy shopping bags. "*¡Que hincha pelotas!*" What a ballbuster!

Unable to hold back laughter, Oscar joined in, "You know, Gastón, I've been trying to tell Pheenie for years now that she's adopted. That's why she's the only southpaw in the family. But she doesn't want to hear it."

"Other than the fact that I'm the better-looking version of you?" I shot back. If we were comparing lemons to lemons, Oscar might have had a case. I was, after all, the fruit salad among the Caminos women in my family—my sisters, Mom, even *abuelas*. But as for my acidic attitude, Dad had started calling me "Li'l mean Josephine" years ago. Jokingly, of course, *but was he really?*

"I don't know, Oscar. I'm with *Princesa* Josefina on this one. You can't ignore the fact that she looks exactly like Poupée. And you. You both definitely got your *mamá's* genes."

"*¿Princesa?* Surely you can do better than that, Gastón? Come on." The first and only time I'd ever been called a princess was in the summer going into tenth grade. A friend and I went on a three-week Student Hosteling Program trip biking from Montreal, Quebec to Burlington, Vermont. The only girls of a group of twelve, the guys had coined us Princess One and Princess Two. I was the latter. It didn't matter, though. Into the second week, once we started passing them up in the peloton, leaving them eating our dust, the boys had no option but to retire our royal monikers. We, however, continued to wear our royalty proudly as we proceeded to lead the pack into the finish line.

Now, as for the part about looking just like Mom, I'd take that. Other than the extra pounds that had begun weighing Mom down over the years—pounds that multiplied as a result of the stress of having six kids (some with kids of their own), an aging mom of her own that also required her all, and of course the pressures of running an agro-beef company from across the world while taking on countless volunteer and social obligations—I couldn't think of a better compliment.

Gastón slapped the table with the palms of his hand and pushed his chair back. "Okay then. Let's hit the road or it will be dark before we get back," he said, reaching his hand out to shake mine, American style. "*Encantado*, Josefina. What's your middle name?"

"Ursula. Why?" I don't remember a guy ever asking me that. *Ever.*

"Okay. Josefina Ursula Caminos," he repeated. "It's been enchanting. You're exactly as I imagined you from *Mamá's* bedside picture—every bit the princess."

I shook his hand back, shaking my head. "There it is again—*Princesa*. What's that all about? You don't even know me."

"It's what my brothers and sisters and I call you at home. You know. Because of the picture of you in the white dress with puffy sleeves, posing. That must have been one *fiesta de quince*."

"*Quinceañera*? I never had one. Unless I count the surprise party my parents threw me when I was seventeen. But that was in the dead of winter and I definitely wasn't wearing a white dress."

"Well in *Mamá's* picture, you look like you're wearing a wedding gown and posing as if you're in some sort of Miss America pageant."

"Oh, the Cinderella Ball. God, she sent your mom that picture?" No wonder Gastón was intent on calling me princess. Of all the pictures Mom could have sent Graciela, she'd sent the one of me all made up as a debutante in the Cinderella Ball. A far cry from Argentina's coming of age *fiesta de quince* fifteenth birthday party celebrating a girl's transition from childhood to womanhood, Cinderella Ball was Pittsburgh's who's-who society event. While I was always up for a party, I never understood why our fathers had to formally introduce us to society when we already knew the majority of people there. But I had to admit, it was super exciting playing dress up for a night and being presented to some of my favorite people with Dad and Tripp on each arm. And Mom, well, it was important to her that her girls be invited to attend. I imagine she and Dad wanted to level the playing field for their daughters in a society where they'd never had the home-field advantage.

That afternoon at *sobremesa*, one thing was for sure: Gastón and I had each laid our cards out on the table. Me? I wasn't going to hold my tongue anymore. For any man. But while I might have been able to dish it out, Gastón was no stranger to food fights. He could serve it right back. I didn't quite know what to make of it. I'd never met anyone like him.

* * *

Knowing where each one of us stood, we got back on the road. As we drove kilometer by kilometer into *las pampas'* sleepy open skies, the road leading to our *estancia* seemed to go on forever, as if it got swept up into the horizon. Other than trucks carrying livestock or the occasional car or pick-up that passed by, the route was a lonely place. I spotted a couple of *gauchos* silhouetted against the bleak expanse of the endless *pampas*. The lone riders were at one with the horses they sat upon. Mom always said that *gauchos* clad in their *bombachas,* or loose-fitting pants, carried their prized possessions with them at all times: a yerba *mate* gourd, saddle, poncho, *boleadores* or *bolas,* three balls of hide-covered wood, stone or other hard material and lasso. The *facón*—the *gaucho's* always-sharp knife kept in the back of his *faja,* the woolen sash worn around the waist— was his most prized possession after his horse. The knife was used throughout the day for anything that might come their way—be it to help a *novillo* or calf who had gotten tripped up in barbwire fencing, or for skinning, self-defense or an impromptu *asado.* I squinted at them in the distance: infinite freedom, infinite loneliness. *What,* I wondered, *would I carry around if I did as the gauchos did, toting my prized possessions with me at all times?*

Winds of change were blowing wide and free through the vast swathes of long, succulent grasses and endless flatlands surrounding us. In the truck, the 1980s song "Life in a Northern Town" by Dream Academy played on the radio. I'd always thought it hauntingly beautiful and, lost in my own thoughts, found myself humming along. I was a Northern girl, but in that moment, I felt Pittsburgh and the possibilities of what my life there could have been fading away into the dark rim of the horizon. The problem, I realized, wasn't necessarily my breakup with Tripp. It was the suddenness of it all: the trajectory of my life disappeared suddenly before a new one rushed in to replace it. There, in the middle of *las pampas*, was nothing but space. The vast, empty grasslands were the perfect place to wipe the slate clean as I began my next chapter.

Gastón looked over at me. "You like this song?"

"It's one of my favorites. I haven't heard it in years. It reminds me of high school. I'd fall asleep listening to it on my Walkman on the 6:30 evening bus home. It was dark by then, sometimes even snowing. It always made me kind of sad. But in a good way."

"Me too." Gastón snuck a glance at me. "Maybe our worlds aren't that far apart after all."

* * *

La Santa Elena was a distance off the bumpy, *gaucho*-beaten track. Other than the stench from the hog farm bordering the kilometers-long, winding dirt road that led to the ranch, you'd never know you had finally arrived at the turn-off. Tucked away at the end of a canopied, century-old, eucalyptus-lined avenue, only those who knew to look for the *estancia* could find it. Once you did, it felt as if you were taking a step back in time as you approached the white Spanish colonial home covered in terracotta ceramic roof tiles. It was built around a main courtyard with a panoramic gallery running the length of the home that opened onto the ranch's vast pastures studded with Hereford and Braford cattle and the *gauchos* who worked the herds and land. No matter the time of our arrival, the *gauchos* always awaited, forming a receiving line on horseback to welcome us. Up close, as Mom greeted each one by name, I could make out the landscape etched into each line of their hands and faces.

By the time we arrived, I'd been chasing sleep for more than twenty-four hours. I laid down for a *siesta* but ended up sleeping through dinner. My room butted up against the dining room. The voices and clatter woke me up around ten o'clock. I tried getting up, but my eyes fought to stay closed.

"¿Y Josefina? She's not eating?" I heard Gastón ask Mom.

"I tried waking her, but she's out."

"Oh well, more for us, I guess," Oscar joked.

I couldn't bear another meal with Gastón. Not yet, at least. I'd only known him one day, yet the *sobremesa* we'd shared earlier that afternoon had left me mentally exhausted. I didn't know if it was his quick wit and record-speed *lunfardo* that left me hanging on each and every word, trying to keep up with his Argentine modern-day slang, or that the way he spoke to me so forthrightly, as if we were longtime friends, was leagues beyond how even Tripp and I communicated. I couldn't quite get a pulse on why I was having such an adverse reaction to Gastón's presence. Somehow he'd gotten under my skin and triggered my body's fight-or-flight response. *But why?*

Still, as I lay there in bed, half-asleep, I couldn't seem to escape him. Gastón's deep *Castellano* hummed around the dining room, curling its way under my door sill. It tucked me in, lulling me back to sleep, like Dad's late-night scotch-infused piano ballads used to as a child.

Milanesas (Beef Milanese)

SERVES 7. *Maybe. If you hide them well enough.*

Like so much in Argentina, *milanesa* has roots in Italy. After all, there's a common saying that Argentines are Italians who speak Spanish. The origin of the *milanesa* has been traced back to Milan and the *cotoletta alla milanesa.* In Argentina, the most common *milanesas* are made from *colita de cuadril,* or top-round sirloin in the US. Chicken comes in a close second, but you can also make these using veal or pork. The key is to butterfly the cuts, cover them with plastic wrap and then pound with a mallet until well tenderized. I recommend making these when you need to pound out pent up frustration or hostility. But don't overdo it; you want them about a ¼ inch thick. If you're on a health kick, you don't have to fry them; *milanesas* are much easier on the heart and cleanup time when baked in a hot oven. But when the craving sets in, there's nothing quite like a just-fried *milanesa.*

If you want a typical *milanesa* experience, squeeze lemon over the crispy hot delicacies and serve with creamy mashed potatoes, fries or an *ensalada mixta* of lettuce, tomato and onion. But if you want to go a bit fancy, eat a *milanesa napolitana,* topped with tomato salsa, ham and cheese. Or try it *a caballo*—on horseback—where a fried egg tops the delicious concoction.

And finally, the best part of making *milanesas* is making little breaded fried balls with the leftover egg mixture and breadcrumbs. Dorita always made them to spoil us. She'd pour just enough of the leftover breadcrumbs into the egg mixture and mix it well, making a paste that she formed into little balls. She sometimes even placed a small cube of fresh mozzarella inside and fried them in the heated oil. These golden delicacies are one of the tricks of the trade passed down from generation after generation of Argentine women.

3 pounds of thinly sliced **skillet steaks**, such as veal, thin top-round, braciole or sirloin

7 large **eggs**

1 cup **parsley**

5 cloves **garlic**, finely minced

2 teaspoons natural **sea salt**

1 teaspoon freshly ground **black pepper**

4 cups plain **breadcrumbs**

Vegetable oil for frying

Lemon wedges for garnish

Prepare the steak cutlets by trimming any fat. Cover each steak with a generous piece of plastic wrap and pound the steaks to just under a ¼ inch using a kitchen mallet.

Place the eggs in a shallow bowl or pan and whisk them together with the parsley, finely minced garlic and salt and pepper. Place the pounded steaks in the egg mixture, making sure to drench each one in the mixture. If they are too large, coat them well on all sides and gently fold them over. Cover with plastic wrap and place in the refrigerator, allowing the steaks to soak in the egg mixture for an hour.

Remove the steaks in the egg mixture from the refrigerator and allow to come to room temperature for 15 minutes.

Pour the breadcrumbs into another shallow pan. Place the egg mixture-drenched steaks into the pan with breadcrumbs, coating them well with the crumbs. Pat the steaks with your hands to make sure the breadcrumbs stick to each side.

Pour 2 fingers (2 tablespoons) of vegetable oil into a heavy skillet and place over medium heat. Once fully heated, carefully add one of the coated beef slices. Fry about three minutes on each side. Once the edges start to become golden, flip the steak and cook until golden brown and crispy. Drain steaks on paper towels to absorb the excess oil. Transfer to a towel-lined plate and repeat with remaining steaks. Serve immediately with lemon wedges.

Chapter 6

El que se quema con leche, ve una vaca y llora

He Who Burns Himself With Milk Sees a Cow and Cries

I have a culinary confession: I've never been much of a fan of pickled foods. I'll only eat actual pickles made from cucumbers, tucked into a Chick-fil-A spicy chicken sandwich—which I can't get enough of. Pickled red onions? On tacos, sure. But don't push it. Baby corn, on the other hand, I just can't swallow, no matter how hard I try. But like grilled *mollejas* (sweetbreads), one of my more unexpected gastronomic obsessions, I surprisingly can't get enough of *berenjena al escabeche,* or pickled eggplant. *Escabeche* is a traditional preservation technique widely used in Latin America and throughout Mediterranean regions. A tasty side dish that can be used as a delicious appetizer on its own or as a sandwich filling, it's a classic dish from Argentina that combines eggplant, crushed red pepper flakes, white vinegar and olive oil, making a dish that goes well with meats, cheeses and Argentine wine. And while I may not be an avid enthusiast, pickling does have its virtues. It rescues, or at least delays, past-prime vegetables from their usually doomed fate. If only a tablespoon or two of vinegar could do the same for a relationship once rot sets in.

* * *

It took all of two days for me to fall for Gastón, even after quickly dismissing him as an arrogant, *machista* ladies' man. From the moment I met him, I'd pegged him as the typical Latin Casanova Mom warned me about growing up. That made it all the harder to get a pulse on why the both of us seemed to like him so much.

As for Gastón, he'd already sized me up as the American princess he'd always imagined me to be from one bedside photograph. But it didn't faze me. For the first time ever I was more interested in being myself than pleasing a man. Because if there was anything I'd learned from Dorita and Mom—not to mention my own break-up—it's that women need other women more than we need men.

I awoke that first night at the ranch at four in the morning from what was supposed to be a quick *siesta*. After tossing and turning in bed, I got up, made myself a *café con leche* in the kitchen and headed outside, mug in hand, towards the next building over that held the administrative offices. It was a moonless night; darker than dark, which made me uneasy. Ever since my Gentleman Caller started sneaking up on me, I was skittish when I found myself alone in the pitch black. It wasn't so much the dark I was afraid of, but the thought of what was out there that I couldn't see. I quietly shuffled along the walkway, careful not to spill my mug of steaming milk, each step quicker and shakier than the previous, past the courtyard to the office. I kicked open the door and flipped on the lights, making sure to lock the door behind me.

The place was a disaster. Papers piled on the large desk spilled over onto the cement floor studded with bills, empty Oreo cookie packages, notepads with to-do lists and contracts—some branded with boot marks of passersby who simply ignored the mess and went on with their business. I was beginning to understand more and more why we were there. At that moment, I couldn't have thought any less of Gastón. I imagined my parents must have employed him out of respect for their good friends and his parents, Jorge Luis and Graciela.

I powered up the computer and waited for the slow dial-up internet to connect. It felt like forever since I'd had any contact with the real world, even though it had barely been three days. I couldn't wait to catch up with my friends and find out how Sonny was doing. Taylor had promised to take great care of her. But just as I clicked to open her email, I heard footsteps outside the door and the rattle of the doorknob. *Could it be him? My Gentleman Caller?* But from what I remembered, he never seemed to need material things of this world—a key, for instance, to make an entrance. The sun hadn't even begun to break. My heart started pounding and I looked to see where I could hide. Just as I heard a key in the lock, I grabbed the first thing I could find, a letter opener, and crawled under the desk. My heart was pounding in my throat—no one should be up at this hour. But as the door swung open, to my relief, I heard Gastón's beefy *Castellano*.

"*¿Hola?* Is someone in here?" he asked, closing the door behind him.

While I was relieved, sheer embarrassment settled in. What would he think of me now—clad in flannel pj's, hiding underneath his desk, dull letter opener in hand?

"It's just me, Gastón," I crawled out from under the desk. "I was just getting this letter opener I'd dropped."

"*Claro.* Of course you were. What are you doing up so early?" He was in the jeans he'd worn the day before and a white undershirt that had thinned out from years of use.

"I couldn't sleep and thought I'd catch up on my email. You?"

"You woke me up. My bedroom's next door. I heard the dial-up," he said, brushing his hair into place with his hand. "No one's ever in here. You startled me, that's all. But no worries. Around here we're usually up before the sun. *El caradura* of your Dad shamelessly calls like clockwork between four and five a.m. to have our morning meeting. It's forced me to become an early riser."

"Well, you may have scared the shit out of me, too."

"Yeah? What could a girl like you be scared of?"

"Hmm, out here in the middle of the night? Oh, I don't know. Wild animals? Ghosts?"

"Really?" he asked, holding back laughter. "If it makes you feel any better, we have visitors on the ranch *cada muerte de obispo,* once in a blue moon. If anything's going to sneak up on you, it would likely be a *cascabel*—those rattlers are the best at hide-n-seek. Or *el zorro de las pampas,* the fox that set up a den in the pasture next door. He's harmless, but they bring the pumas. We've had more sightings than usual since the fox made Santa Elena his home."

"Good to know, I think."

"Next time you get scared, there's a loaded shotgun hanging in the closet there. Last year the ranch caretaker, López, killed a puma who'd made our pastures his hunting ground. López was next door in his underwear when he shot the puma from his doorstep. Took just two bullets to take the cat down. We don't see them often. They're pretty good at staying away. But when there are sightings, the guns are always at arm's length, ready to go."

"I'm not sure that makes me feel any better. But noted. I wouldn't know how to even shoot one. I'm just going to get back to my emails if you don't need the computer."

Ducking down to clean up the papers thrown all over the floor, he mumbled, "I was planning to get to this before you and your brother came in later this morning."

"Really? Why bother? Now that I've seen the way you work, maybe we should do it together and try to get a system down to organize things."

"How do you know I don't have a system?" Gastón asked, pulling up a chair beside me. "So, what's the news from Pittsburgh? Anything exciting?"

I was half annoyed, but to my surprise, I began telling Gastón about my dog Sonny, my friends Taylor and Megan, how I had no desire to be at the ranch and finally, Tripp. I told him everything, unloading months of emotions onto him. I found myself telling him, a complete stranger, my life story. Why did the words flow so easily? I'd been tight-lipped for so long and was also acutely aware of the fact that I didn't know Gastón even existed before that summer, and in a couple of weeks I'd be back home and likely never see him again.

With no context to digest my story with, Gastón was an objective sounding board. After I told him I was done with men altogether—

that I didn't want to cook for a man anymore, that I didn't want to get dressed up for a man or wait around on a Saturday night for a man to finish up his golf game or whatever it was he did—Gastón finally added his two *centavos*.

"You know, when you autopsy a failed long-term relationship, memories, even bad ones, often grow sweeter with time. Being in a relationship is like riding a bike, or a horse. Once you fall—and it sounds like you fell hard—you have to get up, brush yourself off, and get back on again. Otherwise your ex wins. And you'll end up punishing yourself, and other men, for something he did."

Just as I was about to tell Gastón that I'd once spent a summer on a bike trip through Quebec and Vermont, where I clocked enough miles to last me a lifetime, the phone rang.

"And there he is." Gastón looked down at his watch. "Just after six. Your Dad must've slept in today. I have to take this. It'll be a while. You mind if I use the computer? We have to discuss the cattle inventory."

"It's all yours. I'm actually going back to bed for a couple of hours," I said, getting up. Before leaving, I turned back to thank Gastón. But he was already engulfed in conversation.

I managed to sneak back into the house, crawl under the sheets and fall into a deep sleep.

A couple hours later, I sat on the couch nursing my second *café con leche* while planning my day. Where would I even begin to make a dent in Gastón's office?

"What are you smiling about?" Oscar asked.

"Nothing. I'm not smiling." *Am I?*

Oscar shrugged his shoulders. "Whatever. I'm going to head over to the office. Gastón showed me how to pull the financials this morning. I want to see if I can make any sense of them."

Just then, I heard a knock on the shutter of the open window above the couch.

"*Buen día*," Gastón greeted me. "I'm going out, but I have office hours later this afternoon if you need another emergency therapy session."

I tried hiding my smile as I pushed aside the image of his full lips and bob of his Adam's apple from my mind.

Oscar and I spent the day in the office. He pulled reports, while I tried making sense of the piles of papers scattered on desktops and the floor.

"Stop cleaning up. Seriously," Oscar said. "Gastón probably has some sort of system here that makes sense to him."

"Maybe, but half of these bills are past due and don't even seem to be entered into Microsoft Money. You're pulling reports that most likely aren't accurate, since half of these bills and payroll reports haven't even been accounted for yet." It was like the blind leading the blind.

That night at dinner, Mom set the table for five. Gastón, smelling of soap and a clean shave, came in shortly after we sat down with Emilio, one of the veterinarians my parents would call on when Gastón's brother and the head veterinarian, Marco, was tending the herd at another ranch. La Santa Elena served as headquarters for a conglomeration of nine cattle ranches in all—most of them named for my family members. Don Alfredo and El Vasco, after my grandfathers, were close by just behind Santa Elena, while the other ranches, La Poupée, La Valentina, La Camila and La Josefina that collectively made up the part of the ranches known as La Santa María Dora, were several hours away and only accessible by dirt roads.

Gastón chose the seat next to mine, pulling his chair in until our knees met. I shifted in my chair, giving him some room, but his knee found mine again. Maribel and Cati, the caretakers, served tenderloin from an older cow that, coming to the end of her working life, had been slaughtered for our arrival. In the days to come, they would prepare the different cuts of the animal—the filet and rump, tongue *a la vinagreta* (Mom's favorite) and the innards, including the sweetbreads, kidneys and intestines, for our family meals. Meanwhile, I'd soon come to learn that most cattle ranchers didn't eat as well as I'd imagined, at least in our case. My parents saved the grass-fed steers and heifers they slaughtered between eighteen and twenty-four months old for market and ate the older cows of little value that could no longer bear calves. While our grass-fed beef was prized for its tenderness, marbling and mild flavor, the meat served on our table was intensely flavorful with a deeper beef taste, but also a little gamy with some chew to it. Mom always made sure it was cooked medium-rare, which is why I did a double take when Cati and Maribel served Gastón a tray of his very own cuts. In contrast to our thick pieces of tenderloin with pink centers, his tray held leathery, well-done filets that appeared almost shriveled. Gastón acted as if he didn't notice and obligingly served himself as he recounted the day's immunizations they'd administered at La Josefina.

"So you go out to the other ranches and help with the herds in addition to managing the ranch and the bookkeeping?" I asked.

Gastón looked at me with a glint of mischief in his eyes that hinted at some probable inappropriate joke he'd planned on making, but he merely answered, "I do everything and anything the day puts before me. Most often that includes several trips to different ranches to put out fires the *gauchos* come across, trips into town to go to the bank or get supplies and then, when the sun goes down, payroll and bookkeeping."

"Today we had to put down two German Shepherds at La Josefina," Emilio added. "Beautiful dogs. It was a shame, but it appears a puma left behind a steer he'd hunted, and the dogs, after getting a taste of the very herd they were trained to protect, began killing the cattle themselves. Here we were hunting puma, when it was our own dogs attacking the herd."

I shot Gastón a conciliatory look, motioning to the juicy filet that remained untouched on my plate to see if he'd like it. He slid his plate up so I could discreetly pass it along. I had no idea he wore so many hats, and here I was judging him on his office-keeping skills. He motioned to me to serve him another piece of the good filets from our side of the table. I was coming to understand that the cooks, Maribel and Cati, made it a point to serve different cuts of meat that corresponded to the status of the visitors dining with us. In Gastón's case, it seemed they were making sure he didn't forget that he too was one of the help. It always struck me as surreal that once we passed through the gates to La Santa Elena, we became instant rural aristocracy, when back home in Pittsburgh, we were just a normal family who cooked and served our own meals and loved finding the best "Maxx for the Minimum" deals at TJ Maxx.

I excused myself from the ranch talk at *sobremesa* and headed back over to the office to check my email, secretly hoping Gastón would follow, but he didn't. Then, just as I was powering off the computer, the door opened and Gastón walked in. My heart dropped as if I were seeing him for the very first time. *What the hell was wrong with me? Hadn't I sworn off men?* I suddenly realized how gorgeous he was—six-foot-three; lean; dark, silky, wavy hair that was more brown than black. Almond shaped golden-brown eyes with flecks of yellow and green that sat on high cheek bones. A prominent jaw that balanced out his significantly curved nose that had earned him the nickname *narigón*, or big nose, as a child. I didn't mind it and would soon come to learn other women didn't either.

Gastón brought a chair over, turning it around and straddling it. "The psychologist is in session." He winked at me. His calloused hands clutched the back of the chair as if he were on a roller coaster. He shimmied up close to me, once again doing this not-quite-touching thing that he did under the table at dinner. I didn't know if I was imagining the electricity between us.

"I see you cleaned up the office. Now I'm not going to know where anything is," Gastón said.

"So there's an order to your disorder?"

Gastón threw his head back, laughing. "You have me all figured out, don't you? I'm pretty much useless; I wander around all day *al pedo como teta de monja*, right?"

"Just like you had me figured out—*Princesa* Josefina?" I nudged Gastón's shoulder. "What does *al pedo como teta de monja* even mean?"

"You know, useless. Like a nun's tits? Spend a day with me, and you might just feel differently."

"Stop it. My *tía* Ángela is a nun." I looked at him sternly, swallowing my laughter. "She's one of the funniest women I know, by the way—definitely not your typical nun."

"C'mon. *No seas boluda*. It's just a saying." Gastón snickered. "And I've met your aunt. She came to something or other at my parents' house a couple of years ago. She's no ordinary sister, that's for sure. So, what's new with your friends in Pittsburgh? Any more Tripp sightings?"

We talked for hours that night about nothing and everything until Gastón finally got up around two a.m., telling me he had to get a couple of hours of sleep before my father's, like clockwork, early bird call.

"I'm beat, too. I'm going to bed." I stood up to go.

Putting his hand in the small of my back, Gastón walked me through the covered gallery to my bedroom door. He leaned against the wall, smirking. "So, you think you're ready to get back on the bike?" Then he kissed me on the cheek.

I didn't answer. I couldn't. Instead I slid into bed, once again giddy. I didn't know what was happening between us, but it seemed my heart had an agenda of its own. What was I thinking, falling for someone who lived in a different country?

The following morning before breakfast, I ran over to the office to see if Gastón was still in. I didn't know what I planned on saying. I just knew I couldn't wait to see him.

As luck had it, I ran into him coming out of his bedroom. With another woman. She was tall, with legs for days, a tiny waist, an ear-to-ear smile framed in generously plump lips and black curly hair down to her waist. And don't even get me started on the rest of her. It appeared Gastón, too, liked extra lemon with his *milanesas*.

"Josefina, morning. Perfect timing. We were just talking about you. This is Claudia," Gastón said.

"*Hola*," she said. "*Un gusto*. Gastón has told me a lot about you," Claudia said, cheek-kissing me hello. At least four inches taller than me, I felt short and clumsy by her side.

I wanted to turn around and run as fast as I could. But instead, I acted cool, cheek-kissing her back and mentioning that I too had heard a lot about her. Gastón shot me a look. *Really? When?*

With all of the talking we'd done the past two nights, it never once occurred to me to ask about Gastón's life, and definitely not whether he had a girlfriend. He certainly never gave me the impression he did. What was I getting myself into? I excused myself, turning down an invitation to have breakfast with them, reminding myself that this was God's way of saving me from yet another heartbreak. I couldn't believe I'd let my guard down this far. From the moment I met him, I knew better. Yet even after meeting Claudia, I couldn't help but wonder why Gastón was so interested in my bike-riding abilities, anyway.

I shook myself off and went about my business of trying to get the finances in order with Oscar for the rest of the morning. I avoided Gastón as much as possible, figuring I was safe until dinner time.

I wasn't. I almost choked on my shredded carrot, egg and parsley salad when Gastón and Claudia nonchalantly came to the house for lunch that afternoon. Mom stood up, hugging Claudia. Apparently they'd already met. *She could have warned me Gastón had a girlfriend. But then again, why would she?*

Once again, Gastón chose the seat next to mine, while Claudia sat across from him, next to Oscar, who had also noticed her perfectly firm lemons.

As we ate, Gastón did that not-quite-touching thing again he seemed to be so good at, his knee barely brushing mine. *Was I imagining it all? His girlfriend was just across the table.* As Cati and Maribel offered Mom, Oscar, Claudia and me *matambre*—Argentinian flank steak stuffed with hard-boiled eggs, bell peppers, a mixture of parsley, garlic and olive oil, cut into thin, round slices—they served Gastón his leathery sliced left-over filets from the day before. No one seemed to notice except me. Not even Claudia. I made sure not to share my *matambre*, leaving him to enjoy his gristly meal. I didn't have much of an appetite, but I polished off my plate, bite by bite, making sure he noticed just how much I was enjoying it. Gastón, meanwhile, kept trying to get my attention, but I made sure to direct it to Claudia, hanging on her every word.

I'd almost made it through the meal with my dignity intact when Gastón's brother Marco walked in during *sobremesa*. He'd been inseminating cattle at La Poupée for the past couple of days. After greeting Mom, Oscar and me with cheek kisses, Marco walked over to Claudia, who got up and embraced him tightly before taking his face in her hands and softly kissing his lips. As he took a seat beside her, Marco asked Claudia if she'd had a chance to meet Oscar and me.

"*Sí.* Gastón introduced me to everyone, *mi amor.* I was in good hands."

I could feel Gastón's eyes on me. I could even feel his smirk. But I didn't dare look his way, making sure not to give him the pleasure of seeing the sheer relief that washed over me. I poured myself a half-glass of Malbec that I topped off with the soda syphon and washed down my stewing emotions.

Meanwhile, Cati handed Marco a plate of the second-class meat reserved exclusively for the help. This time everyone took notice, especially Mom, who asked Cati what exactly she was serving Marco.

"*Doña* Poupée," Cati began, "We don't eat the steak medium-rare as you prefer. You've lived in the US too long to remember that Marco and Gastón prefer their meat like us, well-done."

But Mom wasn't buying it. Nor were Gastón and Marco.

"Actually Cati," Gastón began. "Our dad is a master griller. Since I can remember, he's served up the juiciest, most tender meat every Sunday. Call us spoiled, but we definitely prefer ours a bit more pink."

Mom shot Cati a look, and she immediately removed the tray of overcooked meat, marking an end to her attempt at serving segregated dishes. Meanwhile, I passed the tray of *matambre* to Marco, who happily served himself as I avoided eye contact with Gastón. I was embarrassed after not having given him a chance earlier to explain who Claudia was, but in that moment, I felt mostly relief that he wasn't with her.

Still, after the guests in the dining room dispersed and everyone went their separate ways, I escaped to the office, knowing the rest of the table, Gastón included, would retreat to their rooms awhile for the afternoon *siesta.* I needed to unload these new feelings on Taylor. Email was the closest thing to talking to her. We'd come up with the code name Larry for Gastón, just in case I accidentally left my Hotmail account up for all to read. I dumped my mixed emotions into an email—from the moment we met when I found him nothing more than an annoying Argentine *mujer-*

iego whose womanizing ways wouldn't work on me, to the night we talked all night about Tripp, to the dating advice he so readily offered up, to the smell of his Davidoff Cool Water aftershave that made my mind go places it shouldn't. And finally, to meeting Claudia and how relieved I was to learn they weren't dating. As I pressed send, Gastón appeared at the door, but instead of entering, he leaned against its frame, crossing his arms against his chest.

"So, Claudia, huh?" He smirked.

"What? I like her. She seems nice."

"Really?" Gastón said with that mischievous look in his eyes again. "That's all?"

"*Claro.* Really. Have they been going out for long?"

"You thought we spent the night together, didn't you?"

"What would it matter? It's none of my business."

"You don't think I would have mentioned her in our late-night talks? You think that little of me?"

"What was I supposed to think? You both came out of your room first thing in the morning. You were tucking in your shirt, for God's sake."

"If you'd stayed around to let me explain, I'd have told you that she arrived at dawn that morning on the overnight *coche cama* sleeper bus from Buenos Aires. She was coming to see Marco. He asked me to pick her up from the bus station since he wasn't getting in until this afternoon. Marco and I share a room. We both got back and fell asleep. Me on my bed. She on Marco's. That's all."

"Does it matter? You don't owe me an explanation."

"*¿No? No te importa un pepino* if I was with her or not? Just like that. Cool as a cucumber. You tell me. Does it or doesn't it matter?"

I didn't answer. I heard Oscar approaching on the outside gallery. "*Ché* Gastón, are we on for tonight?"

"*Sí.* I was just about to ask your sister here if she wanted to tag along. We're going into Suardi later to have some beers. Wanna come?"

* * *

That night, Gastón took Oscar and me to the only bar in town. Except for three other tables, the place was empty. It didn't matter though; it felt so good to get out. And while Oscar and Gastón did most of the talking, I loved following along their table-tennis banter. Each was quicker than the other. After a couple of Quilmes drafts, I had to pee. The place went still the very moment I got up to walk to the bathroom. Everyone turned my way, fixating their eyes on every step I took. When I got back to the table, I flashed my teeth, asking Gastón and Oscar if I had something in them.

I checked my shoes to make sure I wasn't dragging toilet paper. "Why's everyone looking at me?"

Gastón, beer halfway to his mouth, slowly shook his head and lowered the bottle. "Of course they're looking." He laughed. "Suardi's a small town. The internet might be slow, but the gossip's fast. They're all wondering who this new girl is and what she's doing at their local watering hole. They're asking themselves who in God's name your brother is, how I know the both of you, what you're doing here and how long you're staying. By the time you leave, they'll manage to find out everything from your last name to your shoe size to what it is you're running from."

That night, we spent hours at that table shooting the shit.

"*La noche está en pañales*, the night is young," Gastón said, motioning to the waitress to bring another round.

Under the table, Gastón inched forward. Our knees touched. This time I didn't move away. His way of barely touching me made me shudder with excitement.

When we got back to the ranch, Gastón and I headed back to the office, and Oscar went to bed.

"I'm just going to send a quick email to check on Sonny," I said.

"I'll walk with you," Gastón said, explaining to Oscar that he had to lock up.

We stayed up most of the night talking, leaning into each other and flirting. Gastón made me do tongue twister after Spanish tongue twister to teach me to roll my double *r*'s.

"You just need to *bajar un cambio* and the double *r*'s of *guitar-rrrrrrra* will come naturally," he said, raising his eyebrows.

That wasn't the first time a man had told me I needed to chill out. And in that moment, I really did. I didn't think it was possible for him to be so close and not actually touch me.

"So, I feel like you know everything about me. What about you? Now that we got Claudia out of the way, is there anyone in your life? Or was there at one point?"

Gastón lowered his head. His eyes were bloodshot, letting me know he was fighting sleep to get in a little more time together.

"Let's just say that I don't have, nor have I ever had, a Tripp in my life. Nothing worth writing home about, anyway."

"That's all? After everything I've told you?" Up close I could make out the tiny spiderweb lines around Gastón's eyes. They told stories about him, stories that could lull me into listening, whether or not he was ready or willing to share. Nearing thirty, Gastón's weathered eyes revealed that he was a man with real responsibilities, one I could suddenly see myself spending my life with. Up until then, it seemed I'd only dealt with boys my own age.

Gastón fixated his gaze on me, making sure I was listening. "Sure, I've had girlfriends. One for a little over a year. But I honestly don't carry any of them with me. There's nothing to tell. And since I've been here at the ranch, I really don't have time for a relationship. It's a full-time, seven-day-a-week job. Not to mention the fact that I'm often here alone on my down time. Speaking of, let's get some sleep. Your dad will be calling soon for our morning meeting. Let me walk you back to your room."

I got up, and as we started walking back along the open gallery, the dense cover of unfamiliar Southern Hemisphere stars blanketing the night sky inspired something in me, causing me to do something I hadn't planned, and certainly had never done before in my life. Grabbing Gastón's hands, I turned to face him and hugged him tightly underneath the moonlight.

I looked up at him, took a deep breath and quickly said what needed saying before I changed my mind.

"I know this might sound crazy, especially since we live worlds apart, but somehow, sometime in the past couple of days, something happened and I can't stop thinking about you. Am I imagining this thing that's happening between us?" I dug my face into his chest, waiting to see if he felt the same. I could feel his heartbeat but nothing else. He was silent. His arms, hung by his side, failed to hug me back.

Suddenly I was mortified. I had been brought up the Latina way: always taught to fiercely play up my femininity and intelligence, while sitting back and doing nothing as I waited to be pursued. *If it happened, it happened; if it didn't, it didn't.* I was raised to believe that men needed to feel like they had earned the affection of the woman they're with.

Gastón lowered his head. Once again, I focused on the tiny crow lines around his eyes. *What aren't they telling me?*

He grabbed my hands and mumbled under his breath something about me being the boss's daughter, and that while he'd love to see where this could go, he couldn't, wouldn't risk his job or our families' lifelong friendship. Then, kissing my hands, still in his, he said he hoped I understood.

I wanted to disappear at that very moment. Gastón didn't strike me as the type of man who worried about *should. How could I have read the situation so wrong?*

"I get it. *Dios mío.* Of course, what was I thinking? Forget I said anything at all. It must have been the Quilmes talking. Beer sometimes does that to me—makes me all sentimental," I said, half-smiling as I reassuringly patted his arm while briskly turning to go. "I've got it from here. Goodnight."

I could feel Gastón watching me as I walked back to my room, but I didn't dare turn around. I couldn't let him see the tears pooling in my eyes.

* * *

To my relief, several days passed before Gastón and I ran into each other again. It seemed we were avoiding one another. With my bruised ego, I was more than okay with that. Oscar and I spent our days in the office, recreating general ledgers as we got the financials and books in order. Afterwards, I'd stay late into the night, emailing with Taylor. One day, I went to the hairdresser with Mom. No matter where she was—Pittsburgh, Florida, even

Nowhere, Argentina—Mom had a standing Friday wash-and-style hair appointment with her faithful stylists, who she treated like family and longtime confidants. Her ability and utter mastery of small talk with everyone, from the receptionist to the manicurist, never ceased to amaze me. She talked their ears off, *hasta por los codos*. That Friday she was particularly interested in her hairdresser's blow-by-blow account of Gastón's latest sighting with an unknown woman the other night in the town bar. Little did she imagine I was the very woman she was talking about.

"The bartender said she's a smaller girl with long brown hair who spoke perfect Spanish, but with an accent he couldn't put his finger on. Definitely not from around here. But Gastón seemed smitten. All of the girls in town are dying to find out who she is. You know ever since he arrived last year, Gastón's the hottest catch in town. We don't get many transplants in these parts."

Mom laughed, "I can imagine. And let's be honest, not only is he cute but his personality is infectious. I've known him since he was a little boy, and I've always thought he's more than charming. Josie here's been spending quite a bit of time with him. Did he mention anything?" Mom asked, turning my way.

"*No. Nada*," I said, staring back at her in the mirror. "But he strikes me as someone who doesn't kiss and tell."

"*Claro*. I agree," Mom said. "I'll get to the bottom of this mystery girl the next time I see him. He'll be back from the cattle round up tomorrow."

"Oh, I'm sure we'll know sooner than later. Yesterday's story gets buried deep within our *pampas* for only so long. All it takes is one strong gust or a change in the wind to dislodge even the deepest of secrets."

I of course pretended to have no idea of who this mystery girl might be, going as far as to share the anecdote that I'd thought I caught Gastón red-handed coming out of his room with Claudia, who turned out to be his brother's girlfriend. We all got a good laugh out of that one, and I came to finally understand this was a town where everyone knew one another—who their family is, what they do, who their love interest of the moment is.

Those past days, I'd made myself at home in Gastón's office, taking advantage of the fact that he'd gone with the crew of *gauchos* to work at some of the adjacent ranches in preparation of the annual *yerra*. Once a year, La Santa Elena held a *yerra*, where young calves were *capados*, or castrated, so they would gain weight faster. The cattle round up between the adjacent ranches, Don Alfredo and El Vasco ("The Basque One," named after my late grandpa Caminos) and La Josefina had been going on for two days. The *gauchos* had been tirelessly working to separate the calves and mothers from the rest of the cows and bulls, driving them the several miles into the wire-fenced pen within La Santa Elena's main corral. The calves that were born well-endowed and showed good characteristics for reproduction were spared as future bulls. The bigger the balls, the better the bull.

The *yerra* was the absolute highlight of the year for the *gauchos*. Against hundreds of *terneros*, or calves, there were a mere seven *gauchos*, a second veterinarian, Marco and Gastón. This was when they had the opportunity to demonstrate their mastery with a lasso over a long weekend of hard work and camaraderie, followed by the traditional *fiesta* where the men gathered to slowly barbeque the *creadillas*, or the castrated testicles they'd harvested throughout the process. It's said that the *gauchos* roast and eat about twenty million calf testicles every year. Nothing goes to waste on the farm; it wouldn't be respectful to the animal. It's also rumored that eating calves' testicles increases a man's sexual prowess and performance.

The following day after lunch, Mom told Oscar and me to strap on our boots. "It's going to be a long afternoon."

Together, the three of us climbed up the corral's fence to watch the show while three of the *gauchos* worked to drive the calves away from their mothers into the chute of the main corral. There they bunched together, staring mournfully through the gate of their corral, sniffing the air and calling desperately for their moms. The very young calves, some still unsteady on their legs, were too stunned to do more than curl up in a corner. Meanwhile, in their holding pen on the other side of the fence, the mothers milled around, anxiously awaiting to be reunited with their calves. They moved continuously, following each other around and around. Only the bulls stood still. Like most males, they were oblivious to what was going on. Their paternal role, after all, was of short duration.

Meanwhile, the remaining men—Gastón included—rode into the clumps of calves, singling them out one by one. Each calf tried at all costs to escape them. Then the lassos began to whistle through the air, dropping softly just before running feet. *Snap!* I looked up to see Gastón leap off his horse and swiftly regain his balance as he tightened the loop he'd flung around the calf's legs. The calf shook itself free in time, skipping to safety—but not for long. Eventually, it would be lying in the dust with the others, all four feet trussed together, with a booted foot on its neck. Particularly feisty calves sometimes found themselves upside down with a *gaucho* sitting on each end. Gastón stood up, brushing off his jeans, and ran to mount his horse again. The men reveled in the action. I didn't know whether to keep looking or walk away, but as the rancher's daughter, I was supposed to appreciate the choreography. And who was I kidding? As Blanche Devereaux, the sassiest of the *Golden Girls'* core four, would say, it was a good excuse to shamelessly watch. I chuckled under my breath as my mind wandered back to a certain *Golden Girls* episode I'd seen years back, when Blanche shared her thoughts on fantasies in her best, ladylike southern drawl: "I mean, if she's gonna have fantasies, they oughta be the normal, healthy kind, like . . . sweaty Argentinian cowboys whippin' things while they ride naked on the back of Brahma bulls." Nothing like life imitating art—except for the naked part. But let's be honest, Gastón knew what he was doing—he might as well have been.

* * *

This went on all afternoon. I couldn't take my eyes off of Gastón, who instead of orchestrating from the sidelines, jumped right into the center of the action along with Marco, who called the shots from center ring. I watched his rounded biceps flex as he straddled the calves, pinning them down for Marco and the other *gauchos* to cut the testicles from their sac. This was a delicate operation, performed meticulously and without sentiment while the calves' nether parts were emptied of testicles that were then deposited into a bucket. Mom assured me it wasn't painful. "See Josie, the calves leap up and scamper back to the others as soon as it's over." Regardless, it was still painful to watch, especially after Gastón had so blatantly rejected me the other night.

Mom called Gastón over just as the sun began to sink. It was time for the *gauchos* to head over and begin to inventory the castrated calves before releasing them back into the open range to join their mothers. I was exhausted from watching. The whole thing was so foreign to me: Gastón, the methodical attacks on the now testicle-free calves, all of it. I leaned over the fence, laying my head against the top rung. *I've had enough.* I looked up, preparing to go inside, and noticed the V-neck of my shirt had fallen away from my chest slightly, showing off my sheer white bra. As I went to adjust it, I met Gastón's eyes from across the corral. He'd also noticed and looked at me with the same intensity from my dream weeks before back in Pittsburgh. The one where he was looking for me from across the driveway. *But why? He's the one who rejected me.* I hopped down from the fence and headed towards the house. I told Mom that I'd be skipping dinner that night. I planned to head straight to bed after showering. It was safer that way.

Back at home, ash and sparks swirled through the air outside my window late into the night as the *gauchos* sat around the open fire grilling the hundreds of testicles they'd accumulated throughout the day. They ate them straight from the grill, sandwiching them between fresh bread. I could hear Gastón's voice and his deep laugh as I laid in bed. It made me want to lose myself in the depths of his River Plate *Castellano.*

I managed to avoid Gastón for another day, but now that the *yerra* was done and over with, it was time to begin the audit, which meant I would have to sit in the office by his side for hours on end. Thank God Oscar was there to act as a buffer, especially since my mind kept going back to the *yerra.* I'd recall moments like the one when Gastón barely managed to flip over the tall fence to avoid total collision with a thousand-pound bull. Even being trampled by a hundred-pound calf was a dire thought. The *yerra* was the worst thing that could have happened; it only reinforced my feelings for Gastón.

Oscar, three years older than me, also seemed to have a man crush on Gastón. As I lay in bed, I could hear them talking late into the night, swigging beer and smoking cigarettes in the covered gallery outside my door.

The following day Dad arrived at the ranch, which meant he and Gastón would be away from La Santa Elena for a day or two visiting the other *estancias*. I threw myself into the audit and catching up on emails with friends in between. I wrote to Taylor letting her know I'd crashed and burned with Larry. She wrote back, congratulating me for getting back in the game. "Plus," she reminded me, "Don't discard Robert. He's still single." It was nice to hear, but it didn't spark anything in me.

A couple of evenings later, just as I was about to turn off the computer, Gastón appeared at the door. It was past midnight. He, Mom, Dad and Marco had just arrived from visiting the ranches of La Santa María Dora. My breath caught as the door opened and I saw him. I wasn't expecting them back until the following day.

"*Hola* Gastón. How was the trip? I wasn't expecting you so soon," I said, trying to slide past him in the doorway. I didn't give him a chance to answer. "Good? Okay, goodnight. I'm beat."

But Gastón, intent on talking, put out his arm, blocking me from passing. "*Ché*, you've been avoiding me for days." The musty aroma from his armpit smelled of hard work and lust.

"*¿Que?* What are you talking about? I'm not avoiding you. I'm just going to bed, that's all. We head back to Buenos Aires in a week. There's a lot I have to get through before then."

But Gastón wasn't buying it. He lowered his head and cupped my face in his hands, forcing me to look up at him. The distance between him and my five-foot-four frame was clumsily obvious, but his eyes commanded me to listen.

"I'm not letting you go until I can get this out. The other night I only held back because I was afraid of screwing things up; of losing my job if your parents found out that we were together. I've regretted it every second since," he said, slowly touching his lips to the top of my head, sending a shudder through my whole body. *A kiss on the head? Is he teasing me? I don't need him to take care of me. I need him to kiss me, forcefully, with the same ease and confidence he showed at the* yerra *the other day, pinning down calf after calf.*

I managed to duck from underneath Gastón's arm and escape his grip. "Don't worry about the other night. I honestly don't know what came over me. It's like I told you from the start: I came here for one reason, to do the audit." *Well, that and the* medialunas *with* dulce de leche.

As I turned to head back to my bedroom in the main house, I could hear my *abuela* Dorita's voice. "*El que se quema con leche, ve una vaca y llora.*" He who burns himself with milk sees a cow and cries. From then on, I'd be more careful by avoiding cows and Gastón altogether. This place messed me up. I wasn't sure who I was here. Was the ancestry I claimed enough? Was I Argentine aristocracy or a Yinzer *gringa*, visiting from her steel town home in Pittsburgh? It didn't matter. This would all be behind me when I got back home—out of sight, out of mind. I was counting on it.

I just need to get through the next week, I thought when I was suddenly met with two slanted, piercing honey colored eyes that appeared to be fixated on me. Startled, I jumped back. A *pampas* fox was standing right outside our home's covered gallery. Its determined posture and bushy tail told me that I'd caught it in the middle of a hunt; its entire body, from the rich, reddish fur covering its head and neck, to the black line running down its back, was pointed like an arrow—straight and tightly aimed. Its motive was more than evident. Gastón came up behind me, wrapping his arm around the small of my back. "Come on. He's harmless. But let me walk you to your room. You shouldn't be out here alone this time of night. You never know what's lurking in the shadows."

My thoughts exactly.

Meal by meal, my parents welcomed Gastón and Marco into the family. The following day, Cati and Maribel once again prepared Mom's favorite, *lengua a la vinagreta*, and reluctantly offered the same to Marco and Gastón. I pretended to eat my food as I moved it around the plate. My *Yanqui* ways kept me from being able to enjoy certain cuts of meat, like tongue or intestines. Eating them may have been part of my DNA, but it wasn't a part of my everyday upbringing back home. Gastón, on the other hand, served himself portion after portion, as if he hadn't eaten in days. It was almost as if he was nervously throwing it down. The fact that he chose to eat the cow's tongue only seemed to further enhance his already loquacious personality. As usual, he'd made a point to sit next to me. Underneath the table he caressed my knee. The more I tried to move away, the farther his hand traveled.

You could cut the tension between us with a knife. That afternoon, while most retired to their rooms for the afternoon *siesta*, I went to the office in hopes to get some work done. Gastón was sitting at the computer.

"Hey. I'm just going to grab a couple of papers and take them back to the house with me," I said, hoping to get in and out. But Gastón grabbed my arm and pulled me onto him, catching me by surprise. Before I knew it, I was straddling him, my hands flat against his chest. Gastón ran his hands through my hair, and grabbing the back of my neck, slowly touched my lips before he tenderly kissed me, closing the distance between us and leaving no more room for misunderstanding. My lips parted as I gasped in surprise. But Gastón only deepened his kiss, pulling me closer. His hands worked their way down my back, pressing my hips deeper into his. Overcome by emotion, I stopped for a moment and pulled back to catch my breath before lifting my hand to his face and returning his touch. My fingers outlined his lips before I leaned back in to kiss him. Minutes passed like this, hearts beating harder, our hands going everywhere.

Gastón's lingering, deep kiss engulfed my entire body, causing the past months and years to fall away. Tripp fell away. Pittsburgh fell away. A multitude of emotions and images ran through my mind, showing me the kind of lover he could be if I would only let him. I saw us walking hand in hand, growing old together. I saw the kind of future he could offer me. A future in *Castellano*. It was something I'd never imagined possible. A future that my *abuelo* Alfredo had in mind for me all along. A future I could only find in his Argentina. But my life was back in Pittsburgh—more than five thousand miles away.

When I finally pulled up for a breath, Gastón followed, his lips finding mine again. I was still trying to catch up, yet I couldn't get enough. I wanted every inch of Gastón, who broke the kiss only long enough to lock the office door. Like teenagers, we made out for hours. By the time he walked me back to my room that evening, my lips were sore. His taste lingered on them.

"See you at dinner." Gastón said as he kissed me, then pulled me away at arm's length to get my attention. "This is what I was afraid of, there's no going back now. From the moment I saw you get off that airplane, I knew I had to have you. And now the ranch will never be the same. I was fine on my own before you got here. But now that I know what I'm missing, it'll be unbearable once you're gone."

"Jesus, I wish you would have told me this before. We wasted all that time." I pictured Gastón all alone once I was gone. The isolation that swayed through the *pampas* surrounding the ranch was indeed palpable.

Our clandestine love affair continued throughout the rest of the week—caresses exchanged underneath the table, kisses stolen in the midnight hours in the office. During the day, we'd sit with Oscar, putting together budgets and inventory sheets. During the night, we'd meet in the office after everyone else had gone to bed. Gastón talked about the future while I began to dread going back home to Pittsburgh. Other than Sonny, I felt for the first time I had nothing to go home to. Like the *gauchos*, I felt I had my prized possessions right there with me: Mom. Gastón. Dorita, just hours away back in La Plata. But Pittsburgh was all I'd ever known. I kept trying to tell myself this was just a passing affair, one I'd always be able to look back at fondly. But with the exception of Robert, I didn't do temporary. It wasn't in my vocabulary.

My final night at the ranch, I heard a knock on the bedroom door that led to the home's outdoor covered gallery. Gastón had waited for my parents' lights to go out before coming to spend our final night together, bottle of Malbec in hand. We spent the night under the sheets, mostly holding one another. With goodbye looming over our heads, we talked for hours about anything and everything—our families, how we could possibly make this work, how Gastón ended up at the ranch in the first place.

"One call later from your dad and I was packing my bags. I came with no expectations. Marco being here was enough to convince me, *pero mierda*—I had no idea what I was getting myself into. I run around here half the time like a chicken with its head cut off. Your dad told me he needed a bookkeeper, but a week into the job, the administrator left, and somehow I ended up as bookkeeper and administrator all at once. I haven't caught my breath since."

"I can only imagine. My parents have boundless energy and expectations."

"I figured with them so far away most of the time, that it would be a pretty lax job. Then your dad's four a.m. daily calls hit me, along with your mom's hourly calls that start at nine a.m. where I basically have the same conversation over again."

"That's my parents for you. Their schedules are crazy. I imagine you think of my dad as your boss, but the ranches are a side venture for my parents. They're secondary to everything else they have going on. Take my dad. He's a doctor first, rancher second. He's usually out the door before sunrise, making his morning rounds at the hospital. We don't often see him until dinner around eight p.m. He fits the ranches in before and after. He and Mom are always on hyper drive, which means they aren't always on the same page. I swear, they both have more energy than anyone I know. Me included. I just feel like they're always pushing the envelope. When is enough, enough?"

Gastón shook his head. "Did Oscar tell you what happened at the rodeo auction in Rosario?"

Gastón and Oscar had recently car tripped with Mom and Dad to Rosario, the city my mom was born in, to attend a cattle auction. My parents planned to bid on bulls to fortify their *caba-ña* of purebred Hereford to beef up the cattle-breeding side of the Santa Elena.

"By the time the bidding had begun, we'd all separated. Oscar and I met up again in the stands when the prized Braford your parents had their eye on came up for bid. The bids came fast and steady, but as they slowed, it became apparent there were two very determined parties. That's when Oscar realized that your parents, from opposite ends of the arena, were bidding against one another, fighting over the same bull, driving up his price more and more. It was straight out of a movie," Gastón laughed.

I shook my head. "It's so telling on so many levels."

"How so?"

"Like I said, they're like the Energizer Bunny. Going, going, going. Imagine, they didn't even realize they were bidding against one another. They're the most competitive people I know. Especially with one another. It's actually entertaining to watch—sometimes."

"Oh, believe me. I've seen it. Marco and I keep score. They're quite a match."

"Right? How do you think they got where they are? But it worries me, too. I wish they'd slow down. Our lives are in the States, still they travel down here at least five or six times a year. Often alone because of their packed schedules. And it's not an easy trip. It takes more than thirteen hours to get here from Pittsburgh. I just feel like they've been chasing the American Dream for so long that they don't know when to call it quits. And as much as I hate to say it, they're getting older. We all are."

"Something I've noticed is that your dad gets all nostalgic every time he arrives, reminiscing about the good old days in La Plata. His eyes gloss over when he starts telling stories about my dad and him. But your *mamá* is definitely more *Yanqui*. She's always talking about the United States as if it's the best thing that ever happened to your family. That it gave your mom and dad opportunities they would have never had, had they stayed."

"That's probably true. But Mom loves Argentina too. Sometimes I think she chooses to forget everything she gave up to make a life there. It's what they wanted. She never looked back, but it wasn't as easy as she makes it out to be. Imagine, with everything she has back home, she's traveling here almost every other month. That speaks volumes."

"I'm sure she comes to see your *abuela* too."

"Definitely. Speaking of, just before the trip I found the craziest thing. Mom had me searching for our passports and I came across a folded piece of paper with her travel documents where she wrote down her first experiences of living in the United States. It was worn, and she had it stashed inside an expired passport of hers. She must have been about your age when she wrote it. Her words struck me so much. She wrote about Argentina with such longing. It's as if she wrote a eulogy to the home she'd never return to, locked it away, and then never looked back."

"What'd it say?"

I reached over Gastón and opened the nightstand drawer. "Don't ask me why, but I kept it. Somehow it held a glimpse into a part of Mom I never knew—it was like a window into her soul."

Grabbing the papers, I slowly unfolded them and began reading, stumbling over Mom's quick-handed cursive.

WAKE UP . . . Despierte. Muy a lo lejos se siente aqui a la Argentina—*Argentina feels worlds away from here—a country more or less far away and mostly unknown to mainstream North Americans. The news in the papers of my home are almost non-existent. Every once in a while, a headline will appear about a political assassination or other. But mostly it seems everyone I meet, generally speaking, thinks of Argentina as an underdeveloped country that is behind the times. Much more than it really is. I'm referring to the prevailing idea here in the US that they are much better off than Argentines. But even from here, my fellow Argentines have also drunk the Kool-Aid that they are much worse off than most Americans than they really are.*

There's no doubt that I could put together a long list of enviable aspects of living in the US—starting with its more stable economy. Nevertheless, more than one American would envy the basic comforts and lifestyle that Argentines enjoy on a daily basis. The simple pleasures that Americans—at least ninety percent of them—seem to be denied of, or at least choose to deny themselves of. For example, Argentines as compared to North Americans can . . .

1. Watch the same amount of TV—just not in color. But when watching here, its frowned upon to talk over the TV. We Argentines add our own color when watching;

2. Drive some forty percent less in less expensive cars (we don't have access to car loans or leases), and smaller in size, but the Americans seem to rely on their cars for every outing. Walking here in Pittsburgh is almost obsolete;

3. Generally eat much better for much less;

4. Participate in recreational activities that are mostly the same in quality and attraction. The middle class in Argentina can more easily participate in cultural activities that seemed reserved only for the upper class here in the States;

5. Dress much better than most Americans. Generally speaking, Argentina's blue-collar class dresses like only the wealthy dress here in the States.

Finally, while Americans have access to mortgages that allow them to purchase larger homes with larger lots than the typical Argentine, who must purchase a home in cash, the Argentines live every square inch of their homes much more. They open them up to their families on Sundays enjoying afternoon-long sobremesas, they open their doors for neighbors or friends who stop by. Here, most of the socializing is outside of the home. And even when a friend asks you to drop by, I've learned the hard way that you should call beforehand to schedule your drop in.

"Keep going," Gastón nudged. "I couldn't agree more. I don't know why anyone would ever want to leave Argentina. I certainly wouldn't. Your mom wrote that?"

He wouldn't leave was all I heard.

"It sounds more like your dad. You sure your mom wrote it?"

"Yes. It's her handwriting. Plus, I asked her about it. Mom seemed to be working something out in her own head as if she was trying to wake herself up from a fog. She was twenty-eight or twenty-nine tops—and had five kids under the age of eight in tow. Can you imagine?"

"What'd she say when you asked her?"

"She read the first couple of lines, then handed it back to me, as if she already knew the rest. She chalked it up to culture shock. But then she started telling me about her first year in the States. How her English wasn't as good as she'd counted on it being. How Dad was on call all the time. It made me realize Mom and Dorita really took on the brunt of the move. She also told me about the amazing things people did to help them. Like Millie Andreasen, their realtor at the time. I guess my mom and dad had problems getting their money out of Argentina when they first left. Turns out Millie lent them the money for the down payment on the house until Mom and Dad's bank transfer went through. I'm pretty sure it took weeks. Mom said Millie took one look at her and Dad with five small children and felt really compelled to help her. Growing up, Millie was like a step-grandma to us. She was always around and one of Mom's greatest shoulders to lean on. And then she told me about *Tía* Olga, a Peruvian who'd also just recently landed in Pittsburgh with five kids."

"A Peruvian aunt?"

"Not by blood, but she's always felt like one. Mom found a soul mate in Olga. Her husband was also a doctor who practically lived in the hospital those first years. So they formed a sisterhood where they helped raise one another's kids while they kept each other company."

"And taught one another English?"

"I imagine. Over vodka and tonics," I laughed, taking a sip of wine. "You know, I stayed with Olga for more than a month after our house burnt down. I was only six or so. Mom said she was the only one I would go with."

"Then she must mean a lot to you."

"Definitely. But as for the letter, I'd never seen that side of Mom. She was super *familiera*, she still is, and yet her and Dad's love and ambition gave them the courage to leave everything and start over from scratch. I don't think I'd have it in me. That's why I hold onto it."

"You know what they say about love," Gastón said with a smirk, handing me a drag of a Marlboro Light.

"No. Tell me. What do they say?"

"When it comes to relationships, the only thing that matters is that *you* love your girlfriend; it doesn't matter what your mom, your friends, your neighbors—and especially not your wife—think."

I hit Gastón playfully. He never ceased to surprise me with his humor. I realized, lying there in his arms, that one of the things I'd found so attractive about him—other than his quick wit and contagious storytelling ability—was that he lived for today. He wasn't chasing some sort of expectation of what he was supposed to be. Even at twenty-eight, he didn't seem at all worried about his career path nor his future, as much as he just wanted to be happy and content. Gastón told me that night, "Life is the journey; the everyday. It's not about the destination. At the end we all end up in the cemetery." He was the same on the outside as the inside. At least that's the impression he gave me. He didn't have a filter. Like many Argentines I'd met, he never self-censored. And he didn't—couldn't—care less what anyone else thought about him, which was a stark contrast to the *que dirán* or "what would they say" mentality back in the States. Maybe I was blinded by love . . . or lust.

"What are we going to do? I leave in just hours. I can't go back. Not yet. I just found you." I intertwined my legs in Gastón's. I couldn't go back to the way things were.

But Gastón didn't answer and just kissed me, slightly pushing me away, making it clear we wouldn't be sleeping together. That night at least. "I know this isn't goodbye. But we have to first figure out what it is."

Frustrated, I took a sip of Malbec. Why suddenly did Mr. *Rico Suavé* here need to take it slow? From what I gathered since meeting him, Gastón seemed to be the one to sleep-n-run with girls. My imminent departure in the morning gave him the perfect out. But he didn't take it. I put the wine to Gastón's lips. "Here. Sip from this and remember me."

Gastón took the glass, placed it on the table and flipped me over playfully, pinning me down underneath him. This certainly wasn't helping suppress my desire. "This isn't our last night together. It can't be. We're just getting started." He stared deep into my eyes. "Stay. You can't get on that plane Sunday night. Please tell me you're not?"

I closed my eyes. "I don't want to. I definitely have to leave tomorrow with my family for Buenos Aires. We're celebrating Dorita's birthday this weekend. The drive will give me time to figure out how to stay. I have to find the right words to convince my parents it was their idea." It would have been much easier if I actually knew what I was planning on doing.

"Stay. Promise you'll stay." Gastón kissed me tenderly.

"I'll do everything I can. But if I don't, will you visit me in Pittsburgh?"

"*Claro*. I promise. But first I need to get a passport."

Like Argentina's at once revered and loathed infamous First Lady, Evita Perón, so often said, "Time was my greatest enemy."

* * *

I fell asleep and awoke to an empty bed. Clothes were strewn everywhere, along with an empty wine bottle and overflowing ashtray—Gastón's untidiness seemed to be rubbing off on me. I looked around the room at the mess and realized I was falling in love with him. If I didn't find a way to stay, I'd never know where this might take us.

Later that morning as we prepared to leave, Gastón kissed my cheek as I turned to get in my parents' Land Rover to begin the eight-hour car ride home to our apartment in Buenos Aires. The goodbye was painful. With Mom, Dad and Oscar watching, we made sure to keep things light, as if our departure had no effect whatsoever on one another. The knot in my throat swelled up as I turned around and watched Gastón get smaller and smaller, finally losing him to the canopy of ancient Eucalyptus trees bidding us goodbye. I had a sinking feeling in my stomach. This couldn't be it, but the ball was in my court to decide the possibility of us. I had only two more days before our return flight to Pittsburgh to figure it out. Something told me if I left, I'd never return. That things would return to status quo, and life would move on, as would Gastón and I—separately.

The following day was my *abuela* Dorita's seventy-ninth birthday. To celebrate, we took her to the *parrilla* Los Años Locos (The Crazy Years BBQ Restaurant) on the Costanera Norte—the coastal corridor on Buenos Aires' northern riverside that runs alongside the world's widest river—the Río de la Plata. That evening at dinner, I must have been on my third glass of Malbec when, out of nowhere, I threw caution to the wind and announced to my family that I wouldn't be heading back to Pittsburgh with them. I told them that while the bulk of the audit was done, there were still a lot of loose ends I felt we needed to tie up. And then, I mustered the courage to finally tell them I'd be going back to the ranch to finish up and suggested I might even travel for a month or two in Argentina before returning home for the holidays. My parents were stunned. I was stunned. I hadn't planned any of this. It just happened. Dorita, on the other hand, was ecstatic. She took my face in her hands and kissed me all over, thanking *Dios* that her prayers had finally been answered—one of her *Yanqui* grandkids would be returning to Argentina to spend some real time with her.

"If only your *abuelo* Alfredo were here to see this," she said.

Something told me he was—he'd had a hand in this all along. I thought back to the dream I had earlier that summer, when Alfredo told me I needed to come back to Argentina. *That someone was waiting for me.*

Dad stirred in his seat. Who was he to argue with Dorita? And on her birthday of all evenings. "What about the office? You're telling us this two days before we go back? You can't just keep mindlessly living your life. You need to seriously start thinking about your career."

"I know, I know. But I've never felt more strongly about anything. And remember, Dad. You're the one who insisted I come in the first place."

"For a month."

"You don't have to remind me. But the distance has really helped me clear my head. I don't want to go back and fall back into the way things were. I need to experience it on my own for a while."

Dorita shuddered in delight as Mom looked at me suspiciously over the rim of her vodka and tonic with a twist of lime.

"This doesn't have anything to do with a man, does it?" Dad looked at me, once again trying to instill that Catholic guilt in the event I might be thinking of doing something I shouldn't.

"What man might that be? We've been in the middle of nowhere for the past four weeks."

Dorita saw where the conversation was going and jumped in. "Don't worry, I'll take care of her. If it makes you both feel better, I'll go back to the ranch with her so Josie's not alone." Dorita's words sealed the deal, at least with Mom. Plus, having Dorita at the ranch meant we'd be eating a lot better that week. Maribel and Cati always took a back seat to Dorita. Wherever she went, she reigned in the kitchen.

"Are you sure this is what you want? It seems so out of the blue," Mom questioned. She knew how heartbroken I'd been. But I could only imagine she was concerned I might go back home and slip into my old ways.

"I've never been more certain. I don't want to go back to Pittsburgh. Not yet, anyway."

Somehow I'd convinced them. Maybe it was the incessant partying they'd witnessed night after night or my looming depression that had finally lifted in the past month. Maybe they wanted me to experience the home they both loved so much. But they didn't push back. *Who were these people and what did they do with my parents?*

"Okay, but we'll be back for a visit just before the holidays. We'll celebrate your birthday in Argentina with Dorita, and then *si o sí* you'll be coming back home with us, Josie. *Capiche?*" Mom said.

Dad started saying something, but Mom, serving him another piece of steak, shot him a side glance.

I couldn't wait to call Gastón and tell him. But then it dawned on me: I didn't have the phone number for the ranch. It occurred to me that I was staying for a man I barely knew—I didn't even know how to reach him.

The following day, we made the forty-five-minute drive from Buenos Aires to La Plata for one last meal before my parents and Oscar headed to the airport to take the red-eye home to Pittsburgh. Gastón's parents had invited us over for an *asado*. It's what they did on Sundays, religiously. Jorge Luis, the masterful *asador* (grill master), started the meal off with whole, perfectly-cooked-until-tender artichokes that we dipped, leaf by leaf, into a dressing of extra-virgin olive oil, red wine vinegar, salt and pepper. As we ate our *entrada*, the chirping of the short ribs slow roasting on the tableside *parilla* reminded me to pace myself. I set my artichoke heart aside, asking my godmother, Graciela, where the bathroom was. I'd hollowed out the little hairs protecting the heart, saving the best for last. But when I got back to the table, it was gone.

"Don't tell me you ate it," I whispered half-jokingly to Mom under my breath so no one else would hear. "That's the best part. I was saving it for when I got back."

"I'm sorry, Josie. I thought you'd left it behind."

I patted her knee. She could have it. Giving Mom my heart was the least I could do, considering I hadn't been honest with her these past few weeks. We were normally so close. I was used to telling her everything—most everything, at least. But I knew that given the lifetime friendship she had with Gastón's mom, not to mention the fact that she and Dad were his boss, I couldn't tell her about me and Gastón until I knew where things stood. Sure, sparks were flying, but there was no use in sounding the alarm before the fire.

Just a whiff of the *mollejas al verdeo* (grilled sweetbreads served in a green onion and white wine sauce) being passed around the table made me quickly forget about my poached artichoke heart. Somehow, grilled sweetbreads—crispy on the outside with a creamy, tender interior—were among the few cuts of organ meat I'd been adventurous enough to try. When cooked well, they are the absolute star of the *asado*. It's the cow's thymus gland, but lucky for me, I didn't discover this until after trying them for the first time. What followed was an absolute feast of sorts: a variety of charred *achuras* (entrails), *chorizo* and *morcillas* (blood sausage). As we ate, the Malbec flowed freely. Finally, Jorge Luis began to go around the table, offering each guest cut after cut of *tira de asado* (long, thin strips of ribs), *vacío* (flank steak), *lomo* (tenderloin) and *entraña* (skirt steak), with my absolute favorite, *berenjenas al escabeche* (pickled eggplant), which, like *chimichurri*, is most always served as an accompaniment to grilled meats. The table went silent as we enjoyed our first taste of each cut. Dad raised his glass and summoned the obligatory round of tableside applause to recognize the grill master's talent that happens once all the guests have been served. "*¡Un aplauso para el asador!*"

Clad in his canvas apron, Jorge Luis graciously bowed as he placed *mignones* (bread rolls) on the meat-laden trays to soak up the juices. Mom caught my longing gaze and almost immediately passed me one.

At *sobremesa*, as we settled into *carne*-coma heaven, Graciela brought out crystal cordials she filled with a citrusy Limoncello. Its crisp aroma curled over the table, permeating all of our senses. As we sat slowly sipping it, we became giddy and let our guards down, like open books. Our parents began one-upping one another with their childhood stories. Graciela told the story of how Mom and Dad set her and Jorge Luis up at Mom's nineteenth birthday party at my *abuelo's* house. Dad told the story about the time he and Jorge Luis ran into the girls at the horse races, and how Mom and Graciela, trying to play it cool, pretended they didn't know who they were. This back and forth reminiscing went on for a while until Graciela asked Mom about the ranches, and how Gastón and Marco were working out. "Be honest," she said.

"Great," Mom said. "They're good boys." Always one to enjoy a good piece of gossip, Mom shared with the table that her hairdresser told her that talk around town was that Gastón had a new girl—someone from out of town with long, brown hair. "They were seen having a drink in a bar. Josie and I tried to pry it out of him, but no luck," Mom said, turning my way.

"That's right. He was mum about it when I asked him," I said, winking back at Mom. Oscar, meanwhile, hit me under the table.

"Ouch. What's up?" I said under my breath, kicking him back.

He'd finally put two and two together. Oscar whispered. "He's the reason you're staying."

Oblivious to our exchange, Gastón's younger sister, Soledad, chimed in, laughing. "What else is new? I'm sure she's his latest fling. I'm pretty sure Gastón was hanging out with his best friend's younger sister last time he was here in La Plata. By the time they figure out who this new girl is, he'll be onto the next."

Graciela seconded that. "Gastóncito can charm the pants off of any girl. That's for sure. My oldest has the heart of an artichoke—he's always scattering his leaves left and right—pursuing a different girl every weekend."

I almost choked on my Limoncello. *Not again. What have I gotten myself into?* I could have really used this information a day or two ago, before announcing to my family that I was staying. Mom had unknowingly stolen my artichoke heart earlier that day, and I couldn't risk Gastón doing the same. My heart was intact, barely, but like the artichoke, it was still surrounded by the rows of petals with tiny thorns guarding it since Tripp. I imagined Gastón knew how to get around these thorns. Thorns aren't a problem if handled carefully; they soften when cooked.

"Are you feeling okay, Josie?" Mom asked, noticing I'd suddenly become quiet.

"I'm just in a food-coma funk, that's all." But really I was more confused than ever. Was I just another conquest of Gastón's? He knew how fragile I was. I still planned on making one last trip back to the ranch to find out, but I wouldn't let him derail my new plans of staying in Argentina with Dorita.

To top things off, Mom's other childhood best friend, Rosa, who also happened to be Gastón's aunt on his dad's side, became suddenly fixated with me once Mom told her I'd be staying in Argentina for the next couple of months. She was intent on trying to set me up with her oldest son and Gastón's cousin, Santiago. I spent the rest of the *asado* making and skirting plans with poor Santiago, the recently graduated architect who wasn't even there to offer his own opinion. *I'm sorry, I can't date your son, Rosa, because I'm in love with your nephew and his cousin, Gastón, who I've just learned is a womanizing son-of-a-bitch. So, thank you, but no thank you. I'll pass on any men associated with the last name Oría. In fact, I'll pass on men altogether right now.*

We were among the last guests to leave that day. I helped Graciela clear the dishes. As I went to grab the cutting board Jorge Luis had used to make his garlic, parsley and oregano-laden *chimichurri* steak sauce, she stopped me. "Leave that right by the fire. I have to burn the garlic skins."

"I'll just throw them away."

"Listen up, *Nena*. Didn't your *abuela* teach you anything? You never throw away garlic skins. Burning them attracts wealth. I collect them in a bowl until there's enough to throw in a fire, and as they burn, you're supposed to recite, *"platita, platita, platita . . .* money, money, money."

"Hmm, that's a new one for me. I can't keep up with all of Argentina's culinary superstitions. How about this?" I gestured to an untouched plate setting. "Were you expecting someone else?"

I was quickly learning that Graciela was a superstitious one indeed. "No, Josie. You know what they say: if you sit thirteen people at a table, one will die before year's end. So, whenever we are thirteen, I make sure to set a table for my dearly departed father who passed almost twenty years ago."

"Another one I've never heard. It's very macabre."

Mom chimed in, "It's just a silly superstition. Just like hotels that skip the thirteenth floor. This thirteen-at-a-table one is tied back to the twelve plus one of *Jesús* and his Disciples at the Last Supper. We all know how that ended."

"Yes, but at least *Jesús* had the good fortune of rising from the dead three days later. I'm not sure we'd be so lucky, so I set the extra place for *Papi*. Just set the plate and silverware aside, and leave the crystal to me," Graciela said, collecting the wine and cordial goblets with a tray. One to never let a good thing go to waste, Graciela began polishing off the remains of Limoncello left behind at each place setting. Lucky for her, her father's Limoncello was untouched. The others, not so much. Then, as she sipped from mine, she suddenly paused.

Graciela's eyes locked on mine from across the table, revealing everything she didn't say. For a long moment she stared at me, reading me. Seeing all the hope and desire and fear I was feeling in that moment. A million crazy images raced through her head. Gastón playing footsies with me under the table, the two of us holding hands, his hand sliding up my thigh while he sipped his *café con leche* at the breakfast table, a kiss he stole behind a bathroom door, the reflection on the computer monitor screen of our arms interlocking, touching, grabbing. With that one sip Graciela quickly came to realize, clear as day, that my heart belonged to her first born. *Whose other secrets had she discovered that day?*

Graciela carefully put down the crystal cordial glass, cleared her throat and excused herself from the *quincho*—the covered outside dining area and home to their coveted *parilla*. She headed straight to the living room to make a phone call. As we began saying our goodbyes, I heard her from the other room. "Gastóncito, *hola*. It's *Mamá*. *Ella no*. Do you hear me, son? Not her. I mean it. You can have anyone you want. Anyone but her."

Berenjenas al escabeche (Pickled Eggplant)

Good for one asado, for saving vegetables from looming rot or for keeping in an air-tight container in the back of your fridge for months only to pull out when guests drop in, unannounced.

Escabeche is originally a Mediterranean marinade which has made its way into cuisines of several countries all over the world and has been altered in as many ways. It's a Latin mainstay and a specialty many Argentines always have in the fridge, ready to serve when needed. This eggplant is great for a crowd since it is made in advance and can sit in the fridge for several days, getting better each day. It adds a perfect punch to fattier grilled meats and makes a great side dish or appetizer served alongside a fresh baguette.

2 medium sized **eggplants**, washed

Coarse salt

1 cup **white vinegar**

½ cup **water**

¼ cup **olive oil**

¼ cup **vegetable** or **canola oil**

1 teaspoon **dried parsley**

1 teaspoon **dried oregano**

2 cloves **crushed garlic**

Crushed **red pepper** to taste

Salt to taste

Trim the ends off the eggplant. Cut in in half lengthwise, and then lay it flat side down and cut into ¼- to ½-inch slices. You can also slice the eggplant into rounds. Put the slices, layer upon layer, in a roasting pan. Sprinkle each layer with coarse salt and let sit for about an hour. (The salt draws out the bitterness and moisture from the eggplant.) Drain and rinse the eggplant. Put the eggplant, vinegar and water in a stock pot and bring to a boil. Lower the heat to a simmer and blanch the eggplant until it takes on a translucent look, about 10–15 minutes. Thicker eggplant slices will require more time; thin slices, slightly less. The eggplant should be flexible and chewy but not falling apart. Meanwhile, combine the remaining ingredients in a bowl. When the eggplant has cooked through, drain off half of the vinegar/water mixture and put the rest, along with the eggplant, in the bowl with the oil mixture. Mix well. Refrigerate until cold. Transfer to a tight-sealed container and refrigerate after each use for up to one month.

Chapter 7

Estás mandando fruta
Stop Talking Nonsense

Argentina is all about the *empanada*. You can't walk a block without encountering some sort of establishment that sells the coveted handheld pockets of love. *Empanada* filling options are endless: *carne* (ground beef), *carne cortada con cuchillo* (chopped steak), ham and cheese, cheese and onion, caprese (tomato, cheese and basil), *humita* (sweet corn-like mush), mushrooms and cheese, and vegetables (mostly swiss chard in a white sauce). Every region has trademarked their own emblematic *empanada*: the *salteña* from Salta, the *tucumana* from Tucumán, *la mendocina* from Mendoza and *las patagónicas* made from Patagonian lamb. But I'd learned from an early age that not all *empanadas* are created equal, and I only imagined how good Gastón's father's would be. If his *asado* skills were anything like he cooked, then we were in for a treat.

* * *

That evening, I'd gone to the Buenos Aires Ezeiza International Airport with my parents and Oscar to see them off. We were seated at a café just outside the security gate, waiting until it was time for them to board. After the all-day Sunday *asado* at the Orías, all Mom and I could manage to eat was a light dinner before saying our final goodbyes.

"Bring me a *sándwiche de miga doble with* ham, eggs, cheese and tomatoes and a *cortadito*."

"Mom," I interrupted, apologizing to the waiter. "Coffee at this hour? Don't you want to sleep on the plane?"

"I never do. I might as well enjoy one last *cafecito*."

I wouldn't know, I thought. Mom and Dad always traveled business class while we were back in coach. It was a perk they'd rightfully earned through the years, but one they understandably couldn't extend to all of us.

Usually reserved for *la merienda* at teatime, *sándwiches de miga* are consumed by the pound in Argentina. They're paper-thin and crustless, made from the kind of bread that's so soft it sticks to the roof of your mouth. The *miga*, or crumb, is lightly brushed with melted butter or mayonnaise (I choose to ignore this little fact) to keep the bread moist. The bread isn't like any found in the United States—it's bright white or light brown (if wheat) and very light—perfect for guilt-free consumption, or better put, for stuffing your face imperceptibly since the bread literally melts in your mouth. While Mom ordered a double-stack sandwich, I preferred mine toasted and ordered a single-layer ham and cheese *tostado* alongside a banana *licuado* (smoothie).

It was close to ten o'clock. I was planning on sleeping that night, so I opted for a smoothie over coffee. Oscar and Dad, with the excuse that it was their last supper in Argentina—for a while at least—ordered *milanesas* pounded so thin that they topped the length of a foot-long ruler, *al caballo*, with two fried eggs, a side of fries and a pint of Quilmes.

"Your Dad and I are giving you until your birthday to stay in Argentina. I'm coming back in December just before Christmas and you'll be coming home with me. What do you plan on doing until then? You might as well travel. I could call Luci in Mendoza and you could visit their *bodega*, Lagarde Winery. They have some of the oldest Malbec vines in all of Argentina. And you should definitely see your *tía* Solana in Mar del Plata. The salt from the ocean air will do you well; you're looking pale."

"I'm okay, Mom. Let me get my footing before you go making plans for me. Buenos Aires is a huge city. I want to take my time and experience it."

"I can only hold your job for so long. Once you've wrapped up the financials, give me a call so we can review." Dad's look said everything he didn't. I escaped to Aspen for a year after graduating college, I lost myself again after the breakup with Tripp and now I'd be romping around Argentina aimlessly trying to find myself. *Slap your picture on the side of a milk carton and let's get on with it already.*

Something told me Dad was wishing that he was the one staying behind. While he and Mom had been in the States at that point for more than twenty years, Argentina tugged at his heart strings. He'd left because the military government at the time clipped his wings and there was more potential for his medical career in the US. But Argentina kept calling him back. Dad was always reminiscing about the good old days in La Plata. And who was I kidding? At that moment, I couldn't help but agree with him. It was time for me to figure things out.

Now that everything with Gastón was up in the air, part of me wanted to board the plane with my family. For the past month I'd collected memories with him: lustful kisses pressed up against the office wall like teenagers making out in the stacks of a school library; tipsy late night tell-all gab sessions; under-the-table X-rated footsie encounters. I loved the way he listened to me as if I were the only person in the room. But I couldn't risk being hurt again. I didn't even know why I was so surprised about Gastón anyway. *Maybe I was overreacting?* I'd had him pegged from the beginning, but somehow his charm had gotten the best of me. Then again, that's what his mom said he did best.

I was stuck between a rock and a hard place. I was planning on heading back to La Santa Elena the following evening, leaving me no choice but to confront Gastón with this newfound knowledge his mom had so readily offered up to the table. Part of me wanted to run back to Pittsburgh. In time I'd come to forget him. But another part of me felt I'd only scratched the surface of my newfound Deep South alter ego, Josefina.

"We've asked your *abuela* to act as your chaperone to the ranch. Maribel and Cati have also stayed behind to cook your meals, so you're all set," Mom said, handing me two *cochecama* sleeper bus tickets for the following evening. "Gastón will be waiting for you and Dorita at the bus terminal on Tuesday morning."

"Mom, I'd rather you tell Maribel and Cati that they can leave. Honestly, I can't stand their cooking. I think they do it on purpose. Dorita can cook while we're there."

"No. They keep an eye on things for me and *Mamí's* getting older. She gets tired. She needs her 'Juanitas' in the kitchen to help her cut and clean up."

"*Bueno, chau hija,*" Dad said, kissing my cheek goodbye. "Let's go, Poupí."

"I'll miss you, JoJo." Mom hugged me tightly one last time before disappearing into the International Departures security gate. "And remember, be good. We've brought you up to be a lady," she added, giving me one last squeeze.

"I know, I know. Why buy the cow if you can get the milk for free? I've got it," I yelled after her sarcastically before turning to hug Oscar goodbye. "Love you. I'll miss you. And take care of Sonny. Don't overfeed her!" I pointed straight at Mom who I'd caught red-handed more than once feeding the dog filet mignon, Chinese food, pizza or whatever else was for dinner. At that point, Sonny was the only thing waiting for me back in Pittsburgh, aside from my friends, of course. But they'd always be there. They always had been.

* * *

It's incredible how your life can drastically change from one day to the next. Since arriving in Argentina, my world had been upended. Instead of heading into fall, spring had sprung. Being in a new country meant I had to once again learn to do the most basic of things, from scratch. As much as *Abuela* Dorita could help me figure out bus routes, where to buy my groceries and what places to avoid, Gastón was the one I'd planned on relying on to build my life there in a way that felt right; authentic; Argentine. Since meeting him, Gastón reminded me on more than one occasion that I was Argentine. Yet living in Argentina didn't come as naturally as I'd hoped. I didn't know where I fit in the land of my parents and *abuelos*. I turned heads back in Pittsburgh when I spoke *Castellano* with my parents, and I stuck out like a sore thumb in Argentina. I was fully neither, and not fully both.

I grabbed a taxi from Ezeiza back to my parents' Buenos Aires apartment. It was past eleven, and I sunk into the back seat, leaning my head against the cool window. It was a perfectly clear evening. Even stargazing was flipped upside down in Argentina. Mom, having spent the first twenty-nine years of her life in Argentina before immigrating to the United States, always said the stars were a lot different in the Southern Hemisphere. Take the Three Marys constellation, more commonly known as Orion's Belt. According to Argentine folklore, these three stars represent the Marys who, very early on Easter morning, visited the tomb of Jesus while carrying a broom, a thurible and an alabaster chalice to anoint his body. It's said they were the first who heard the announcement of Jesus's resurrection. Back in Pittsburgh, The Three Marys always appeared equidistantly, right side up, while in Argentina they looked to be upside down and were commonly referred to as the saucepan of Orion. The pan's handle is formed from the small group of stars below the belt called Orion's Sword, while the pan is outlined by the three belt stars, or The Three Marys.

"But are they really upside down?" Mom would say. "In Argentina we would say that they're upside down in Pittsburgh. It's all a matter of perspective, Josie."

Back in Pittsburgh, the saucepan reference didn't make any sense. Food would fall right out of it. That night, the skewed stars helped me understand in a most visceral way just how far I was from home.

Back in the taxi, the *tachero* attempted to engage in conversation. Like most Argentine taxi drivers, his main topic of concern was the latest political rife. But I made it clear I was in no mood to chat. First off, I didn't want him to notice I couldn't roll my double *r*'s. "Never draw attention to yourself by speaking English when traveling alone by taxi or bus," Mom reminded me over and over. And second, I knew absolutely nothing about Argentine current events, let alone politics.

Gastón totally disagreed with Mom. He'd told me the way to really get to know Argentina is to talk to strangers: cab drivers, waiters, the person standing next to you on the bus, the person ringing up your dry cleaning. That was his way. But I wasn't chatty like Gastón. A master in shooting-the-shit, he talked to anyone and everyone.

"Most times you'll forget the stranger you talk to. But sometimes, just sometimes, people have the most interesting things to say, if you're listening," he had told me during one of our nighttime conversations. That's what I'd loved most about Gastón: he was an uplifter, and he listened. I could learn a thing or two from him. But in that moment, the only thing I knew as I gazed out the car window into the night sky was that I really didn't know him. Not like I thought I did.

I was tempted to ask the *tachero* to take me to Dorita's house in La Plata, but that would have added another hour to the trip and Dorita would have been long asleep by the time I would arrive. I decided I'd see her soon enough.

As I called for the elevator to our family apartment in Buenos Aires, it seemed emptier than usual. I thought I'd enjoy my newfound freedom, but instead I already missed my family. I couldn't even allow myself to think about Gastón. How could I miss someone I'd never had?

Exhausted, I headed straight back to my bedroom and began undressing. That's when I heard the elevator door open and close from the foyer. Then came the clicking sound of the doorknob.

I must have forgotten something in the cab, I thought, shimmying my form-fitting Vitamina jeans back around my hips. I expected to find the *portero* waiting for me. We'd had the apartment for years and the doorman was like family, always bringing up our bags and groceries and asking about everyone back in Pittsburgh. But as I headed down the hallway towards the entry, it wasn't at all what I'd expected. *He* was there, clear as day. My silver-fox Gentleman Caller. Standing in the doorway, looking at me in that way he always did. As if he needed to tell me something. *But what?*

"¿Hola?" I yelled, grabbing a candlestick from the hallway credenza as I planned my next move. The way he always managed to sneak up on me made me skittish as hell. *Run to the kitchen and*

grab the direct dial phone to the doorman, or lock myself in my room?
I opted for the latter, hiding behind my door. *Dammit, no lock.*

"What do you want?" I yelled, cracking the door. "I'm not alone. The doorman is on his way up." My voice was shaky but firm, like a barely trembling custardy *flan*. The one thing that always seemed to keep my fear at bay when it came to my unexplained poltergeist was that he'd always seemed to vanish as quickly as he appeared.

I peeked my head out the door, and with one foot already in the foyer, my Gentleman Caller looked back at me and removed his cap as he graciously nodded his head. He tapped his wrist, devoid of a wristwatch, with two fingers, signaling for me to give it time—that things aren't always what they seem.

What? Who?

He never answered. *Did he even talk?* It happened so fast I couldn't even comprehend it. Once again, he bid me farewell before closing the door behind him. I waited but never heard the elevator doors open. *Was he still in the foyer?*

I ran to the kitchen and rang the doorman, wanting to see if he too had seen my Gentleman Caller. "The man on the elevator, can you stop him? He was in my apartment! I don't know how he got in. I might have accidentally left the door open," I gasped, thinking I had to check if the spare key we'd hidden behind the plant in the foyer was still there.

But the doorman seemed confused. "*Señorita* Josefina, you must be mistaken. The elevator has been parked in the lobby since you went upstairs half an hour ago. No one has entered or left your apartment since."

"*No puede ser,*" I snapped back, frustrated. *But of course, the elevator hadn't moved. He couldn't see him.* Still, I insisted. "He came in. I saw him with my own two eyes. He was older, in his seventies or so."

You'd think by now I'd be used to talking to this ghost who didn't talk back, not with spoken words, at least. What I couldn't understand was why he even bothered. Our encounters were sporadic and brief. They never seemed to go anywhere. It was almost as if he'd show himself to me every once in a while, just so I'd know he was there. He'd politely acknowledge my presence, and with the tip of his hat, vanish. Just like that. *What was the point?*

Moments later, the doorbell rang. It was the doorman. He'd come up to search the apartment. "I promised your *mamá* I'd keep a close eye on you."

We walked the entire place, opening closets and checking behind the curtains. We even checked the service hallway and elevator in the back. But it was clear no one was there but us. Before leaving, he promised to keep a close guard during the night. I climbed into my parents' king size bed after locking the bedroom door behind me. Their room had an en suite bathroom, which meant I wouldn't have to brave the hallway alone in the middle of the night. I didn't think I'd get much sleep that night, as I constantly popped my head up from under the covers, making sure the bedroom door was still closed. It seemed that in the city that never sleeps, not even the dead got a chance to rest. As for me, the roar and hum from the cars on Avenida Libertador lulled me into a restless sleep.

* * *

"*Hola,* Dori Bori." I kissed *Abuela* hello. "Are you ready for our trip? I hear they serve champagne and play movies on the bus."

I'd met Dorita the following evening at La Plata's bus terminal. As we sat sipping a *cafecito*, waiting to board the bus, I ventured to ask her whether she'd had any strange experiences in the apartment.

"What kind of experiences?" Dorita asked. "*¿Fantasmas,* Josefinita? You think you saw a ghost?"

I don't think I saw a ghost. I know I did. I've been seeing him for years now. With turn-of-the-century clothes and a hat, said no one.

"I once read in ¡*Hola!* magazine that when faced with a paranormal experience, you're supposed to tell the energy what year it is and that they don't belong there," Dorita said. "Did you try asking him to leave?"

Try? I did. I have. But he doesn't talk back. He tips his hat to me. He closes doors. He doesn't slam them, but he closes them. Politely. Apparently, he opens them too.

Dorita continued to tell me in her own way that I was probably just missing home. I shrugged her off. "Of course, *Abuela*. Come to think of it, I was super tired last night."

When it came time to board the bus, Dorita told me her son, my *tío* Álvaro, would be picking her up at the end of the week to take her to their beach house in Pinamar for my cousins' spring break. "He invited you to join us," she said as the bus driver loaded our bags into the luggage compartment.

Dorita and I settled into the *coche cama* bus, where the seats fully reclined. I barely slept that night, tossing and turning as I imagined what I would say to Gastón when I saw him. Part of me wanted to slap him, while another part of me wanted to grab and kiss him long and hard. My heart was pounding as we pulled into the bus terminal ten hours later. Endorphins shot through my veins. I was determined to play it cool. Not only for my sanity, but also because of Dorita.

But to my surprise, Marco, his brother, was waiting for us at the terminal.

"*Hola*. How are you? Gastón had to go to La Santa María Dora so he asked me to come," he said, planting cheek kisses here and there.

"Marco, *mi amor*. Look at you," Dorita grabbed his shoulders. His six-foot, five-inch frame towered over my five-foot *abuelita*. "I haven't seen you since you were a young boy. You're so grown up and handsome."

"*Gracias*, Dorita. *Muchas gracias*," Marco said, hiding his embarrassment behind a shy half-smile. I got the impression that unlike his older brother, Marco preferred to blend into the background. Still, everyone said his old Hollywood movie-star looks made him the better looking of the two oldest Oría boys. Marco was statuesque with broad shoulders, a tiny waist, dark brown, silky hair and a smile for days that seemed to show off more teeth than humanly possible. But it didn't matter. Gastón's personality had sealed the deal for me. Secretly, in some sort of masochistic way, I couldn't wait to see him. I was grateful we hadn't slept together before my suspicions of his womanizing ways were confirmed by his mom, of all people. Thinking about our last night together and the feel of his back under my fingertips left me with a ravenous curiosity about just what kind of lover he would be. But knowing what I knew, if I caved in a moment of weakness, I'd feel ill with regret afterward, like that self-loathing feeling after polishing off an entire bag of Cape Cod kettle-cooked potato chips. You know it's wrong, but you just can't stop.

As I reached for my bag, I felt the crushing weight of my previous heartbreaks pulling on my chest and shoulders. Here we were again. It seemed cruel that I could be so intimate with someone, spend an entire night with a person, go to sleep with him and awake thinking about him, only to know nothing about him— his telephone number, his whereabouts, what he did today or last week. *Was I talking about Tripp or Gastón? Both?*

"The *encargado* of the ranch discovered cattle missing early this morning, so they're thinking there are cattle poachers in the area. Larry—I mean, Gastón—went to file a police report," Marco explained as he winked at me.

I half-smiled back, biting my tongue as I muttered a curt, "Larry, huh?" Gastón had been reading my emails with Taylor all along. For someone who spoke so little English, he certainly had no trouble translating his code name. He'd known how I felt about him from the beginning. No wonder he was so full of himself.

As we entered the final leg of the canopied, century-old, eucalyptus-lined avenue leading to La Santa Elena, I spotted an older man up ahead standing at the gate. *It couldn't be. Did anyone else see him?* I thought as the Ford F-150 bounced down the packed-dirt driveway. "Who is that?" I asked, bracing myself against the dashboard.

"Opening the gate? It looks like López, the *encargado*. He's the caretaker. Cati's husband."

Phew. I was already dealing with the ghosts of boyfriends past and couldn't deal with any otherworldly visitors just then. "I didn't know Cati was his wife. She seems to be everywhere I turn when I'm in the house. It's as if she's spying on me all the time."

"Just *chusmeando*." Marco laughed. "She's always digging up gossip. The *gauchos* that work here swear she's your *mamá's* informant. Nothing else for her to do at the ranch, besides sunbathing in the nude."

"*¿¡Qué?!* Sunbathing *desnuda?* Does Poupée know?" Dorita asked, horrified but also somewhat intrigued.

"Who would have thought? Cati's short-cut, mousy brown hair and round, five-foot stature certainly don't give the impression of a show-girl alter ego!" I chimed in.

Marco, happy to have someone to talk to, kept laughing. "Last summer López built a wall around their small patio. We thought it was just for privacy, until one morning Gastón went looking for eggs. Their chickens lay more than they can eat. So we take a few here and there when they're not looking. That morning, Gastón jumped the wall and got much more than he'd bargained for. *Ooh,* Cati gave him a mouthful."

"*¿Y* López? Gastón must have been in trouble with him."

I loved that my seventy-eight-year-old grandma found the humor in all of this.

"Oh, he was caught red-handed, alright. And you know, there's some things you just can't unsee. López wanted to get him. But come to think about it, we're still not sure if he was more upset about the eggs or his wife."

"Comical. Probably a little bit of both. Now it makes perfect sense why Cati makes a point to serve you and Gastón separate trays of well-done shriveled, leathery beef." If Gastón had been there, he'd have somehow gotten away with comparing Cati's *limónes* to the trays of dried-up beef he'd become accustomed to being served.

Marco, on the other hand, much more reserved, left it at, "*¿Viste?* You noticed? Payback's a bitch," before waving thanks to López as he closed the gate behind our truck. "*Gracias, Viejo.*"

As we came to a stop by the house, Max, our faithful German Shephard, came barreling towards the car. Most people were afraid of him, but he was really just a big baby. Mom's baby. She had standing orders that meat be mixed into his dog food at all meals and that he receive a good bath and brushing at least once a week so his hair didn't become matted like most of the dogs on the ranch. Cati must have loved that. Even the dog was treated like royalty.

"Hey boy," I grabbed Max's ears, shaking his head. "Who's this you've got with you?" A brown lab puppy that couldn't have been older than three or four months was trying to keep up with him.

"That's Bacco. He's mine. Just about fifteen weeks old. But he'll catch up with Max soon enough," Marco said.

"Hello Bacco, sweet thing." I couldn't resist picking him up and rubbing his puppy belly. "I have a golden at home. Her name's Sonny. Short for *Sonrisa*. I know it's cheesy, but she's made me smile from the moment I laid eyes on her. She's just about two now and likes to bring me birds."

"Dead or alive?"

"Perfectly asphyxiated, unfortunately. I'm hoping she grows out of it."

"Gifts. You know, it's in their DNA. They were bred to retrieve. I'm counting on this guy to do the same. Well, hopefully with things that are already dead." Spoken like a true veterinarian. Marco grabbed Bacco and patted him on the head. "They're both great breeds. Loyal as hell."

"Definitely. Sonny's the thing back home I miss most."

"Well, I know Gastón would be happy to hear that. He was really bummed to miss you this morning. But he'll be back later tonight. And don't be too hard on Larry," Marco winked again. "From the moment you stepped onto this ranch, he hasn't been able to help himself."

"It seems he helps himself to whatever he wants. But thanks for the heads up. See you around."

Not sure what to make of my comment, Marco looked at me curiously. "Yep, *hasta luego*. I'm headed to La Camila in a bit for a few days. Gastón should be arriving tonight. He couldn't wait to see you."

It seemed Marco was in on our little secret, which struck me as odd since Gastón didn't seem to be one to kiss and tell.

Since our arrival, Dorita shadowed my every move. *Does she sense something is up?* She never once mentioned Gastón's name, but she certainly took this chaperoning thing seriously, sleeping in my bedroom, knitting across the desk from me while I worked in the office and eating breakfast, lunch and dinner with me. I, on the other hand, kept looking over my shoulder, waiting for the sound of Gastón's silver Volkswagen Gol to come barreling down the dirt driveway, leaving a trailing dust cloud that never seemed to catch up with him. For such a tall guy, his choice of car stumped me. Smaller than its American equivalent, the Volkswagen Golf, it was one of the smallest cars on the market.

"It gets the job done," Gastón had said.

But instead of seeing him whip around in his hatchback, I'd catch glimpses of Cati and Maribel lurking around corners, trying to see what I was up to. But no Gastón. It seemed almost intentional that he wasn't there. I wondered if our moms were in cahoots.

But finally, Gastón arrived the second night. Half asleep, I heard a knock on the bedroom door that led to the covered gallery outside. Engulfed in the latest royal family of Monaco scandal, Dorita asked "*¿Quien será a esta hora?* It's past eleven. Who could that be?"

"Josie. *Soy yo.* It's me. Are you awake?" Gastón whispered from the other side of the door.

I raced to drag myself out of bed, but Dorita beat me to it. Hers was the queen bed closest to the door. *¡Hola!* magazine in hand, Dorita cracked the door open. "Gastón, *hola.* Josefinita is sleeping. Is everything okay?"

"*Perdón*, Dorita. So sorry. I didn't mean to wake you."

I could tell by his voice he was taken aback. Gastón hadn't expected a gatekeeper, especially not my *abuela* Dorita.

"I promised Poupée that I'd check in on Josie when I arrived. I just got in. I'll see you both tomorrow."

"*Hasta mañana.* See you tomorrow," Dorita said, closing the door.

"Wait. Sorry, it's just . . . can you tell Josie *el psicólogo* will be here first thing in the morning. He has early morning office hours?"

"The psychologist? Josefina didn't mention anything about seeing a therapist. But I'll let her know." Closing the door behind her, Dorita turned, looking at me. "*¿Lo escuchaste?* Did you catch that? What's he talking about?"

"Don't worry, *Abuela.*" I didn't want to get into our inside joke of our first days together when I'd divulged my most intimate secrets to him, all at once.

I turned to face the wall. All I needed was for Dorita to spot the disappointment in my face. My heart dropped when I'd heard his velvety *Castellano*. I wanted more than anything to wrap myself up in it, but I knew my heart couldn't handle any more disappointment. "He's always making some sort of inappropriate joke or another. I have no idea what he's talking about. Oscar probably mentioned to him that I was depressed or crazy."

"It's okay *mi amor*. I understand if you're sad. Your *mamá* doesn't want to talk about Tripp because she thinks you're better off without him. But I understand your disappointment. Really, I do. All those years you waited for him."

"*Gracias, Abuela*. I appreciate that. I really do. Goodnight," I said, closing my eyes to try and relive the last night Gastón and I had held one another in that very bed. I imagined his foot nestled between my legs, caressing my calves as we caught up on years of not knowing one another—our childhoods, our dreams, our most ticklish spots.

The following morning, I could barely manage to drink my *café con leche* as I planned how I would handle Gastón.

Dorita noticed. "Why aren't you eating your *tostada*? Are you feeling okay? You tossed and turned all night long."

"I'm good. Just feeling restless thinking about everything I have to finish in just a few more days before we head back to Buenos Aires"

"I asked Cati to run to the market and get *pan de miga*. I'm making the egg salad *sándwiches* you love so much. Do you want singles or doubles?"

"Ooh. Now we're talking. Doubles. Extra celery and no *mayonesa*. You promise?" My aversion to mayo was one that had challenged both Dorita and Mom since I was a child. Especially since mayonnaise, like *dulce de leche*, is a major food group in Argentina. With pretty much any order of fries, hotdogs, chicken, *milanesa* or even salads, you'll find a serving of mayonnaise. My family loves it, too. My sister Camila would eat plain Hellmann's mayo sandwiches on toasted Town Talk bread with tomato slices. And if it wasn't mayonnaise, it was Mom's favorite—*salsa golf* or mayo with ketchup.

Dorita knew me all too well. She'd already planned on making the salad with *mendicream*—a take on our cream cheese.

Just as we were clearing the table, there was a knock at the door. "*¿Hola? Puedo pasar?*" He didn't wait for us to answer. Gastón came in, clad in his faded jeans and a worn out U2 Joshua Tree T-shirt with his hands tucked into his jean pockets.

"Dorita, *Hola*. It's been a while. Sorry about waking you up last night," he said kissing her hello as he stared over her shoulder straight at me.

"*Hola* Gastón. *¿Que tal?*" I asked, getting up to greet him. His just-out-of-the-shower smell was still new enough to arouse every inch of my body. I hoped no one noticed as I brushed a quick kiss on his cheek. He'd certainly noticed my indifference.

"How am I? Let's see, Josefina. Just fine, I think. Could be great, but that depends. *How are you?*"

"Would you like a coffee, Gastón?" Dorita asked. "I can't believe how big you and Marco are. Such handsome young men. How is your *abuela* Helsa? I haven't seen her in a while. I'll make sure to call her when I get back to La Plata."

"I'm already caffeinated. Thank you. And you know my *abuela*. Always the same. I swear she's made of wax—as are you. What is your secret?"

Dorita, falling victim to Gastón's charm, blushed. "*Gracias, hijo*. You should have seen your *abuela* and me when we were younger. We turned heads wherever we went."

Gastón chuckled in agreement, "Oh, I believe it. I've seen pictures." He grabbed a buttered *tostada*. "Do you mind?" Gastón helped himself to the jar of creamy raw honey. "Josefina, you didn't answer. How are you? Your parents told me you were coming back. I'm glad I'll have a couple more days of help getting the books in order." His hazel eyes didn't move from mine as he took a bite of his toast.

"I'm good. We're just here until the end of the week." Our conversation was forced and awkward. Gastón looked confused.

"Would you like to join us for *la merienda* this afternoon? Do you drink *mate*, tea or coffee?" Dorita asked. A faithful *meriendera herself*, halfway through her *café con leche*, she was already planning out her table for the afternoon tea she'd serve fresh off her *siesta*.

"I'd love to. Coffee. Black with sugar only is my preference. But I'll drink *mate* if that's the drink of choice."

"Coffee it is. Josefinita here likes *mate*, but she doesn't like sharing the straw with others, so I told her she'll have to enjoy it alone here, so no one gets offended when she doesn't pass it along."

"*Abuela*. Stop."

"Don't worry," Dorita patted my knee. "They don't drink *mate* in the States. Why would you feel comfortable passing your drink among a group of people if you don't do it back home?"

"*Claro*. It's like wine at church." Gastón seemed to always know what to say to make someone feel better "Who wants to drink it after dozens of mouths have grazed the chalice? When Jesus said, 'Drink this wine, it is my blood,' He didn't mention anything about also imbibing the spit of your entire congregation. You're telling me that the *toallita* the catechist uses after each person drinks cleans off all those germs? Nah. I always stop at the Host."

I bet he didn't even go to Mass. But that was beside the point.

"*Bueno*, I'll see you ladies later," Gastón said, then looked at me. "Josefina, did you have some time to go over some things with me in the office?"

"Maybe later. I'm not feeling so great this morning," I said, getting up. His expression went from hopeful to somber, which killed me, but I pretended not to notice the electricity between us. This whole playing it cool thing took a lot of work. I'd barely slept, thinking about the outfit I was going to wear. I'd decided on a short gray mini skirt with a casual white tee and my brown riding boots. Even if I wasn't going to be with him anymore, that didn't mean I was going to let Gastón down easily. I still wanted him to grovel. A little at least.

Minutes later, I heard Gastón and Dorita chitchatting away outside as I lay down on the couch in the living room. They were both talkers, especially when the smell of coffee curled over a table. I'd managed to doze off when Gastón found me. Outside the window, he'd pried open the shutters. "*La puta madre*, Josie. What's up with you? You just acted like you barely knew me."

I got up from the couch, pulling down my skirt. "We have to talk. But not now. Things have changed. I can't do this—I can't be another one of your conquests. I've heard all about them."

"What? From who? *Cortála*. Cut it out. *Estás mandando fruta*. Where's this coming from? Can we go somewhere and talk? You're not making any sense."

"I'm the one not making sense? What does 'I'm sending fruit' even mean?"

"It means you're talking nonsense. What'd I miss? Whatever it is, at least hear me out and give me a chance to explain."

"Clearly, we don't understand one another, Gastón. Or should I say *Larry*? We're done talking. I don't want Dorita to overhear us." I said, closing the shutters on him.

"That's it? So, our Royal Highness is back in full force?" he said, blocking me from closing the shutters. "It seems we're back to the first day we met. Cold as ice. And what about Larry? What are you talking about?"

He knew.

"Are you suddenly too good for me? Is that what's really going on? Just say it. *Vamos*, Josie." Gastón reached for my hand unsuccessfully. "Come on. I've been dying to see you. You have no idea."

Things weren't going as planned. I'd imagined myself nonchalantly telling Gastón I'd had second thoughts about being together. I didn't owe him any explanations. He knew from the start that my heart was fragile. But in that moment, I couldn't think of what to say next without sounding like a needy girl who'd been played. So I closed the shutters instead and walked away, but barely. My knees buckled the moment I got to my room. Enough had been said and had I stayed, my anger and frustration would have turned to tears. And I wouldn't give Gastón the pleasure of seeing me cry. That meant I cared. And God knows I did.

I didn't expect Gastón to show up for the *merienda* later that afternoon. But he did. Nothing seemed to faze him. Dorita had set the tea up outside on the covered gallery. It was a beautiful afternoon, with a crisp blue sky and sun that had warmed the Spanish terracotta tile underfoot. As usual, *Abuela* outdid herself. She had piles upon piles of *sándwiches de miga*, double-decker sandwiches, with a crunchy egg salad. The other sandwiches, *simples*, had a thin layer of cooked ham and cheese on wheat. Dorita also made her *rosquitos*, baked doughnuts that were more like a very dry baked biscuit formed into a rustic circle. She'd first started making them for us as kids from leftover dough from *tartas* and pies she'd make. We'd all fight over these *rosquitos*, even with an entire *tarta* in front of us to be eaten. Dorita finally got so fed up with our quarrelling that she started foregoing the *tarta* altogether to make *rosquitos*. Hers were similar to scones and the perfect consistency for dunking in coffee, tea or milk.

"*¿Que tal, chicas?* How goes it, girls?" Gastón asked, cheek-kissing the both of us.

I grabbed a *rosquito*, taking a huge bite of it. At least he came bearing gifts. He'd brought a tray full of *facturas*, a variety of popular mini pastries from the local *panadería*. They came in a variety of shapes and sizes and were filled with *dulce de leche*, *crema pastelera* custard and *dulce de membrillo* quince paste.

"*Gracias* Gastón. You shouldn't have. But I'm glad you did. These look delicious," Dorita said, inspecting the tray. Other than his philandering ways, Gastón's mom had brought him up right. It was considered bad taste to show up to an invitation for tea empty-handed. Did the chivalry come to him naturally or was it part of his mom's instruction? A part of his cultural making? *Or is it all an act? Is he one of those men that has a way of making you believe anything before a word comes out of his mouth, simply because of the way he is?*

"Josie?"

"I'm going to serve myself a tea, *Abuela*." I grabbed the tea pot, pouring myself a cup. As I reached for the milk, Dorita stopped me.

"Do you want to end up alone?"

"What? No. I mean, I guess not. Why?"

"You never put milk in your tea before the sugar, or you'll never get married," she scolded, passing me the *azucarera*.

I obliged. I wasn't taking any chances.

La merienda brought out the chatty side in Dorita. She grilled Gastón on everything from politics to questions about each of his five brothers and sisters. Gastón was just filling us in about his youngest sister, Belén, fourteen years his junior, when Dorita started eyeing the large plate of *facturas*, mulling over which to choose first. She reached for a *pañuelito de grasa* pastry in the form of a folded handkerchief filled with *dulce de leche*. "Josefinita, do you know that most of the *facturas* on this plate are named after political satires? That one over there, the long sweet pastry, is a *vigilante* or 'the watcher.'"

"Oh, so it's named after Cati, then?" I retorted.

"Touché, Josie," Gastón chimed in. "Then you have the *bombas* and *cañoncitos* over there, bombs and cannons filled with *dulce de leche*. They're both my favorites. Well, anything with *dulce de leche* is," Gastón said. "Apparently your granddaughter here likes salty more than sweet," pointing out the fact that I had downed half of the *sándwiches de miga*. I was eating my frustration. "So, Josefina, your *mamá* told me you'll be traveling around Argentina for the next couple of months. Where do you plan on going?"

"I don't have any plans yet. Maybe I'll just hang out with *Abuelita* here and explore Buenos Aires." I grabbed Dorita's hand, noticing her perfectly manicured nails. With everything she did, I'd never understood how she managed to keep them painted.

"We're planning on going to Pinamar in a couple of days," Dorita reminded me. "Your *tío* Álvaro is coming to take us to his beach house with the family the day after tomorrow."

"Really? Leaving so soon?" Gastón tried to reach for my leg under the table, but I'd made sure to move my chair just outside of his reach.

"Right. I guess that'll be my first trip. I'd like to see the coast and visit my *tía* Solana in Mar del Plata too."

"So, what made you decide to stay?" Gastón's targeted questioning was beginning to make me hot under the collar.

"Nothing to go home to, other than Sonny, of course. And I've never had the opportunity to spend any real time in Argentina. If I don't do it now, when will I ever?"

"But what about the audit?"

"He's right, Josefinita. Will you be able to wrap everything up before Saturday?" Dorita asked.

"I will. All of the financial reports are basically done," I said, not letting Dorita in on the fact that they'd been completed a couple of weeks before when Oscar and I were working together. Sure, there were a couple of loose ends left to tie up, but I was mostly using the audit as an excuse to come back to the ranch and spend time with Gastón. He knew that. His face said it all.

The table fell silent.

"*¿Y vos?* How about you, Gastón? Any plans to travel soon?" Dorita asked.

"Actually, yes. I'll be traveling to La Plata next weekend. I'm planning on stopping in Buenos Aires beforehand to check in on a friend. I hope she'll be there," He raised his left eyebrow my way.

"*¿Tu novia?* A girlfriend?" Nothing was off limits for Dorita, who was serving herself a second serving of *café con leche*.

"I don't know yet. It's still too soon to tell. But if I have a say, *sí, mi novia.*"

Just then Cati and Maribel showed up to clear the table. For once I was happy to see them coming around the bend.

I skipped dinner that night, faking a stomachache. I had only a day left with Gastón, and even though we weren't together per se, I was dreading leaving him. He was the reason I'd stayed. But I couldn't risk getting involved with a man who didn't know how to be faithful. *Been there, done that.* Here I was falling for a twenty-eight-year-old man who'd never had a serious girlfriend. There had to be a reason for that, and I didn't want to find out for myself.

The following morning Gastón burst in on breakfast. "*¡Buen provecho!* Please, carry on. Josie, sorry to bother you, but your Dad called. He needs me to take you to the bank so you can sign some papers for him."

"That's funny. He didn't mention anything to me. I'll call him."

"No need. He said it's urgent, but he left me with explicit instructions. We shouldn't be long, Dorita."

"Okay," I said, taking a last sip of my *café con leche*. "Let me get my things. I guess I'll need my passport for ID?"

"Nah, it's a small town. They'll know who you are."

"Okay. I'll be right out." I kissed Dorita goodbye before meeting Gastón outside. He was waiting in his Gol, ready to go. In the car, he reeked of cigarettes and a sleepless night. I'd forgotten just how fast Gastón drove, even on those dirt roads. "So, what exactly is it that I'm signing?"

For once Gastón was silent. This wasn't the man I'd come to know.

We drove in silence. The stench coming into the car let me know we were nearing the pig farm. "Gastón, talk to me. Where are we going?"

Gastón came to a stop at the only light heading into town and looked at me. "Not until you talk to me. What's going on? What changed?"

"Nothing. I just realized that this can never work. We live worlds apart."

"I don't get it. When your mom called to say you were coming back to wrap up the audit, I thought the universe was giving us a second chance. I'd never been happier. I hated that I wasn't able to pick you up from the bus station. Is that what this is about? Or is it about Larry? I'm sorry I read your emails, and I'm even more sorry Marco told you. He was just kidding around, but it was wrong of me. It's just that, from the moment I saw you get off that airplane, I've wanted to know everything about you."

"It's not about Larry. But we'd agreed not to tell anyone until we were ready. You could have warned me that you'd told Marco about us."

"He figured it out. I didn't tell him. He saw us coming out of the office late one night. He warned me not to mess around. Don't forget that both of us work for your parents. He just wanted to make sure I'd thought everything through. But what about you? *Mi mamá* called me after that *asado* you went to at my house. She knows about us."

I shifted uncomfortably in my seat. "I didn't tell her. In fact, she warned me about going out with you. Your sister Soledad, too. In so many words."

Frustrated, Gastón punched the steering wheel. "They did what?"

"They shared your womanizing ways at the table. What was it your mom compared you to? Oh yeah, the heart of an artichoke that goes spreading his leaves left and right. Imagine. I had to sit there listening to how you can charm the pants off most girls—apparently your latest conquest was your best friend's younger sister. Who's next?"

"They don't know what they're talking about. It's just that I rarely bring girls home."

"Right, because you upgrade women like cars? By the time you're done with one, you're already onto the next?"

"*No seas boluda.* Come on," he laid his hand on my leg. "So, how did my mom find out about us then?"

Annoyed, I shoved Gastón's hand away. "Ask her. It wasn't me. It's like she read my mind. And as if it wasn't bad enough that I had to sit through an hour-long *sobremesa* that centered around your womanizing ways, just hours after telling my parents I wasn't going back home, your *tía* Rosa was determined to set me up with your cousin Santiago once she heard I was staying in Argentina. Apparently, the joke's on me. I can't seem to get away from you Oría men."

"Santiago? What the hell. I'll kill him. *¿Te intentó levantar?* Did he put the moves on you?" Gastón asked as we entered the town of Suardi.

"What? No. He wasn't even there. It's your aunt who is intent on getting us together. But that's all you care about? You have no idea how I felt hearing everyone talk about you. It was like a stab in my gut. How could I have thought that we had something more than a fleeting thing? I decided to stay for you, but it turned out to be pointless. Anyway, now that I'm here I'm going to make the most of it. Can we go now?"

"I knew it! I knew you stayed for me. *Dios mío.* Thank God. I've been waiting for you to say those words, Josie. Don't you see? This is the chance of a lifetime," he said, downshifting gears. "Ranch life has been wearing on me. And then, out of nowhere, you came into my life. I can't lose you. My family doesn't know what they're talking about."

Just as I thought I believed him, I couldn't help but notice in my rearview mirror that a girl on a scooter was following us. "Do you know that girl behind us? She's been tailing us since we got into town."

Gastón looked back. "*Carajo*. Fuck. Not now. Give me a second," he said, pulling into a parking space in front of the bank. "I'll be right back."

The girl pulled in next to us. *You've got to be kidding me.* Her perfectly straight, long blond hair swept along her shoulders as she took off her helmet. She stared straight at me as she walked towards Gastón to meet him. She looked like the prettiest girls back home, except skinnier. Her shorts were so short they left nothing to the imagination. Nothing jiggled when she walked. Gastón shot me a piercing look as he cheek-kissed her hello.

It was ludicrous that I had a front-row seat to watch this go down. If anything, it only proved my point. I would have gotten out of the car, but I had nowhere to go. No way to get back to the ranch. I had to admit, though, I was enthralled. At least I got to see Gastón in action as he grabbed the young girl's arm, pulling her away from the car. From the looks of it, she didn't seem to like what he had to say, as she stormed away moments later, but not before shooting me a scathing look with her blue eyes.

Hey, don't look at me. I'm in the same boat as you.

"It's not what it looks like," Gastón said, climbing back into the car.

"Whatever it was, it looks like you took care of it." I reached for the door. "Well, are we going in?"

"Where?"

"To the bank?"

"No. I made that up so I could talk to you."

"Oh, that's funny. What exactly do you want me to say? At least I fell for someone worth stalking. Jesus, Gastón. Is she even eighteen?"

"Yes. I mean, I don't know. I think so. What does it matter? She's out there and I'm in here with you. I went out with her a couple of times when I first got to the ranch. She's been pulling this shit ever since. She's not you. I told her to leave me—to leave us—alone."

"Just take me back to the Santa Elena. Please. Don't make me ask you again. This is a joke."

Gastón turned on the ignition and headed back to the ranch. We drove in silence for a while until Gastón turned to me. "I can only imagine what you heard about me that day at my house. I know my reputation precedes me. I'm not proud of it. But I never cared. *Levantando minas*, picking up women, was just a game. But then you suddenly came into my life. I'm pretty sure you dropped from the sky, because I feel as if you're the angel I didn't know I was waiting for."

"Oh, give me a break, Gastón. Do these lines really work for you?"

"I mean it. You're probably thinking we barely know one another, but I've never felt like this before. I see us sharing dinners by candlelight, falling asleep watching a movie in bed, waking up in one another's arms in the morning. Having breakfast together. You're the first person I've ever wanted to hang around to see the next day. Why do you think I haven't slept with you? I don't want to screw things up. That's usually where things end for me." Gastón looked at me as he made a left at the pig farm.

I didn't look at him. I'd be a goner if I did. *Just look ahead, Josie. Keep your eye on the horizon.*

"Let me prove it to you. Now that you'll be in Argentina for the next couple of months, I'm going to do everything I can to see you as much as possible and convince you to stay here for good. With me by your side. I'll make the trip every weekend. Just know that if you stay, it will only be you and me. But what about you? I don't want to have to compete with the ghost of your ex-boyfriend. I don't want to compete with his memories. I'm giving you all of my heart. It's all I have to give you. It's everything I have to give you."

Why did everything sound sexier in *Castellano*? There he went doing it again—charming my pants off. It was getting harder and harder to say no to him.

"I don't know. I mean, Gastón, you have a stalker. And she's gorgeous. I just witnessed her firsthand."

"I knew her from before I met you. I haven't been with her in months. Are you going to let *her* keep us apart?"

"I don't know. I'm so confused. I can't think."

Gastón pulled over just after making the final right hand turn onto the driveway leading into the Santa Elena. I looked back.

The dust cloud trailing the car finally caught up to us and began slowly enveloping the car in a reddish-brown fog.

"Josie. *Mírame*. Look at me. My mom asked me to stay away from you. I told her it's too late. But I promised her I wouldn't hurt you. And I won't. Just give me a chance." Gastón grabbed my hand. "Please, let's do this."

I believed him.

I sat there for a second, and with my heart in my throat, barely managed to get out, "Okay. But you better not hurt me."

Gastón took my hands in his and our eyes locked. He started pulling me over the middle console, but straddling him in a mini skirt and riding boots wasn't easy. Once we got the steering wheel out of the way and I managed to squeeze my leg between the driver's-side door and Gastón's seat, he cradled my hips with his hands. Wrapping my arms around him, I almost couldn't breathe from the force of his desire. My fingers trembled as I began unbuttoning his shirt. I placed my hand on his heart.

"It's yours." He kissed me tenderly.

"Are you always this cheesy?"

"Cheesy? Like a block of *queso*?"

"You know—*cursi*. Sappy," I said, running my fingers through his hair.

"Ah, only with you," he deepened his kiss, pulling me into him even tighter until we heard a tap at the window.

Jumping over the console, I adjusted my skirt back down. "Who is that?" The dirt cloud had slowly begun to dissipate, and we could barely make out the silhouette of a man with his horse.

Gastón cranked the window as I grabbed a ledger book from his bag, acting as if we'd been reviewing numbers. Or something. "*Hola*."

"*¿Todo bien* Gastón? Do you need a jump? I was working the pasture over there and noticed you've been pulled over for a while." It was a *gaucho* from the ranch, thinking we had broken down.

"No. All good, *Viejo*. Thanks. We were just going over some numbers here. But we'll be on our way now. *Chau. Gracias.*"

The *gaucho* tipped his hat to us as we pulled away. Two things became at once apparent: we'd have to be much more careful if we were going to keep *us* under wraps, and traversing this new relationship in Spanglish would be much more challenging than we'd imagined. But whether by bike, car, bus or even horseback, we'd see where it took us.

That afternoon, as Dorita and I had our *merienda*, I let her know that I'd found some more things that needed taking care of. It would take me at least another week to wrap up the audit.

"*Pero,* Josie, Álvaro is coming to get us first thing in the morning. Do your parents know?"

"I'll call them tomorrow, Dori. Don't worry. You go on without me. I want to finish here, so I don't have to come back. I'll grab a *coche cama* back to Buenos Aires next week. I'll be back by the time you get home from the beach."

Gastón joined us for dinner that night. As usual, Cati served him his own leathery steak and we slipped right back into our under-the-table love affair.

The following morning, after kissing Dorita and Álvaro goodbye, I slipped a note under Gastón's door inviting him to dinner. Then I let Cati and Maribel know they could have the night off and turned the kitchen upside down trying to figure out what I could make him. I didn't have a car so I couldn't go to the market. I'd have to work with whatever we had, and that wasn't much. Tomatoes. A can of tuna. A block of parmesan cheese.

I ended up baking tomatoes stuffed with tuna mixed with sautéed onion, garlic, lemon and parsley, topped with a crunchy mix of breadcrumbs, garlic, basil, pepper, grated Parmesan and olive oil. Since it was just us, I'd planned to eat in the kitchen. No need to go to the trouble of setting the dining room table on the other side of the house. But Gastón had something else in mind. He showed up with a bottle of Malbec in one hand and a blanket in the other.

"I thought we could eat by the light of the stars," he said, pulling me into him. "I couldn't wait to see you." The force of his hug suspended me into the air.

"Are you sure no one will see us?" I asked.

"I know just the spot. It's tucked away out of sight by the pastures."

Gastón set up the picnic blanket outside in the yard and uncorked the wine while I plated the tomatoes. That's when I realized I'd accidentally left the lemon halves in the pan to cook alongside the stuffed tomatoes. The entire dish smelled and tasted of lemon. They were almost inedible. But there is something celebratory about a terrible meal, one you couldn't have made worse, that lingers in your memory with a lurid taste.

"Your *limón* with tuna is delicious," Gastón joked.

"I thought you liked extra lemon."

"Everything in moderation." Gastón grabbed one of the lemon halves and squeezed it over my mouth, kissing me.

"I can cook better than this. Let me have a do-over tomorrow night," I said, coming up for air. "Maybe you can drive me to the market to pick up a couple of things? We have some oranges back at the house. I'd love to bake you an orange cake with cream cheese frosting."

Baking was my specialty. As a girl, I spent hours on end in the kitchen with *Abuela* Dorita, baking anything and everything with whatever ingredients we had in the pantry.

"Now, who can pass up an offer like that? Why don't you let me cook for you and you can take care of dessert?" Gastón asked. Petals from the linden tree rained down on us, caressing our skin like snowflakes.

"What, you know how to cook something other than cow's testicles? Don't think I didn't see you after the *yerra* washing them down with wine."

"*Son deliciosos*. They taste just like chicken. Doesn't everything though? That's what I'll make you. Spatchcock grilled chicken. It's my dad's recipe."

We spent every evening together the following week. During the day we saw one another as much as possible. We ran errands. I sat in the office with Gastón, helping him pay bills and complete paperwork. We went horseback riding and I went with him when he visited the other ranches.

We went to La Josefina and drank *mate* with Angel, the caretaker, who invited us into his home. Argentines are so fanatic about their loose-leaf *yerba mate* drink that they carry it with them most anyplace they go. They have elaborate leather carrying cases for it and drink it anywhere and everywhere—in their homes, at work, on park benches, in cars on road trips. They carry a thermos of hot water to constantly refill the gourd from which the tea is drunk. *Mate* can be drunk any time of day, but the most important part of the tradition is that it's drunk communally. It's as much a social experience as it is a way to quench thirst. Friends gather in the late afternoon to *tomar*—drink—*mate*. Among them, the person who assumes the task of serving the *mate* is designated as the *cebador* who prepares the gourd with the dried, loose-leaf *mate*, and serves it to each person. He adds near-to-boiling water and takes the first slow, steady sip out of a metal straw with a sieve at the end called a *bombilla*, making sure the temperature is just right. The *cebador* then begins to pass around the *mate*, refilling it in between turns. That afternoon at La Josefina, Gastón assumed the task of *cebador*, and after taking the first sip, refilled it before passing it to me.

"*Gracias*." I handed the gourd back to Gastón after taking a sip.

"Are you done or just being polite?"

"Polite, I guess. Why?"

"Saying '*gracias*' to the *cebador* means you've had your fill and don't want anymore," Gastón explained, patting my knee under the table. "Stick with me and I'll make an Argentine out of you yet." That day Gastón taught me the true beauty behind the *mate*-drinking ritual. It was inclusive. The circle was always open to newcomers. No matter your status, there was always a standing invitation to join in.

Back at La Santa Elena, Gastón cooked dinner for me the remainder of the nights we spent together. Between the two of us, it was clear who commanded the kitchen. I couldn't help but think that *Abuela* Dorita would be enthralled to encounter a man who rivaled her culinary ways. Gaston's dad had taught his sons to cook. But their way of cooking was more primal—just wood, flames and meat: *Choripán* sausage sandwiches topped with *salsa criolla*—finely-sliced red bell peppers, tomatoes and onions combined with olive oil and white wine vinegar with a pinch of salt and pepper. Spatchcock chicken slow-cooked over live embers with a lemon-garlic sauce. Hamburger patties topped with fresh fried eggs he'd taken from López's private chicken coop. A boiled potato and egg salad with loads of raw garlic, parsley and olive oil was a favorite staple of his. *Riñones*, or kidneys, sautéed with green onions, garlic and white wine came in a close second. I didn't dare tell Gastón I didn't eat kidneys, and when I tried them I was surprised to find them delicious.

Gastón would sneak into my bedroom late at night and leave before the sun came up. We took things slow, but now I understood why. The way Gastón undressed me with his eyes made me, for the first time, feel like a woman.

Almost a week had passed since Dorita left, when one morning Gastón and I accidentally slept in. We were awoken by a knock on my bedroom door at a quarter to eight. I opened the door just a crack, hiding Gastón from view.

"*Buen día*, Cati."

"*Señorita* Josefina, sorry to wake you. But *el doctor Caminos* is looking for Gastón. Please let him know he needs to call him right away."

"I haven't seen him. But if I do, I'll make sure to let him know," I said, closing the door. I looked at Gastón. We'd been discovered. Soon my parents would find out, if they didn't already know. Gastón threw on his clothes and ran to the office. As I watched him go, I caught a glimpse of Cati and Maribel giggling from the kitchen window from across the covered gallery.

Shortly after, I received a call from Mom. "Josie, *hola*. How are things at the ranch? When do you plan on sending your father and me the reports you put together? I just got off the phone with your *tía* Solana. She's headed to Buenos Aires for the weekend to pick out some fabrics and wants to spend some time with you."

"But it's already the weekend."

"I know. We just spoke with Gastón and asked him to get you a ticket for tonight's bus ride back. Solana will meet you at the bus station in the morning. You'll have all day tomorrow and Sunday with her. And don't forget to send us the reports by email before you leave! Call me when you get in tomorrow. Love you." She hung up before I could get a word in. If Mom and Dad knew about me and Gastón, they hadn't let on. Yet, something told me they were at least suspicious. First Cati knocked on my bedroom door looking for Gastón, then, not even an hour later I was asked to pack my bags so I could spend the weekend with my aunt in Buenos Aires. Was it a coincidence, or was Marco right about Cati? Was she Mom's personal informer, after all? But if she'd snitched, why hadn't Mom said anything?

I spent the greater part of that day finalizing the financial analysis and projections I'd been promising Mom and Dad before Gastón drove me to the bus station in the evening. López had hitched a ride into town with him, so we never really got a chance to say a proper goodbye. As I cheek-kissed López, and then Gastón, he slipped a letter folded into a tiny rectangle into my hand. "I'll be traveling home next weekend. Maybe I'll see you around?"

Once settled on the bus, I turned on the overhead light and began reading his letter.

> *Josie:*
>
> *This isn't goodbye. Nothing of the sort. It's simply, "Chau. See you soon." Actually, I'll be seeing you in a couple of days tops because I plan on visiting you as soon as possible in Buenos Aires or La Plata. Wherever it is you land.*
>
> *I don't know how to begin to express my feelings for you. In these past two months since getting to know you, I've felt like never before. You've made me dream about a future together. I've never felt as close to anyone.*
>
> *After these past couple of days, I don't know how I'll live away from you. It makes me sad thinking that although I'll have you in Argentina for at least the next couple of months, I won't be able to kiss my girlfriend first thing in the morning. But we're so united already that I know we'll get past this. So, think of me, and often. When you look to the sky, to the stars, to the moon, remember me. I'll be here at the estancia, looking up at the same sky, and thinking about you. Waiting for you. That way we'll be together, always. And don't forget that I gave you all of my heart. I just ask you keep it beating. If you're happy, then my heart, now yours, will always feel alive.*
>
> *Bueno, mi reina, my queen. (Quite an upgrade from Princesa Josefina.) This is a melancholic love letter at best. But now that*

our lives came together so quickly, I know we'll find a way to always stay together. Keep this letter always. In it, I leave you my eternal love. Read it when you're feeling lonely, and you'll know that someone loves you more than anything in this world.

Remember always: you're the most important for someone. Never feel small. Especially since you now have two hearts. Yours and mine—que te lo regalé el día que te conocí—that I gave you the day we first met.

A million besos. I love you, Gastón

I was smiling ear to ear as I folded the letter and placed it back in my bag. Gastón never ceased to surprise me. I'd never received such a romantic letter. I could get used to this dating in Spanish thing. As promised, Gastón came into town to visit the following weekend. We headed to his parents' home to eat *empanadas*.

On our way from Buenos Aires to La Plata, Gastón looked at me from behind the wheel. "They know about us. I had to tell them. *Mamá* kept insisting she knew. I couldn't lie to her. Now that they know, you're part of the family. They'll take care of you while I'm away at the ranch."

"You don't think your mom will tell mine?" I asked.

"No. But I think she's hoping you'll tell her soon enough."

When we arrived, Jorge Luis was sitting at a wood table, assembling knife-cut beef *empanadas*. I'd grown up watching Dorita make them with ground beef but had never witnessed anyone go to the trouble of hand-cutting pound after pound of sirloin into tiny cubes to make *empanada* filling. The table was so large it sat at least twenty in his outdoor kitchen dedicated for all things *asado*.

"These *empanadas* are typical of *el Norte Argentino*, the northern Salta region," Jorge Luis explained. Either way, they were a labor of love. That day, Gastón and his dad elevated the *empanada* to a new art form. Their *masa* consisted of a simple blend of lard or butter (or both), flour, salt and water. As I sipped my Quilmes beer, I was entranced with the way Gastón's strong hands—the same hands that lassoed and took down hundred-pound calves—swiftly made the most delicate *repulgue* (crimped edge) that rivaled only Dorita's. Lucky for me, he seemed to have inherited the Argentine gene for nimble fingers that could—among other things—effortlessly create an immaculate border that locked the filling in, keeping it from seeping out while the *empanadas* baked.

That evening, Gastón's parents welcomed me into their family. His dad made it a point to cook alongside his son that day to make me feel at home. But given the history between our families, we all treaded slowly. Each of us around that table knew what would happen if impatience got the best of us. Now that they knew our secret and were conspiring to help Gastón and me freely see one another to explore our new transcontinental relationship, Jorge Luis and Graciela—my parents' oldest friends—were co-conspirators. We'd each end up taking the heat. And no food was worth a scalding rooftop mouth burn—not even *empanadas*.

Still, that first-bite anticipation of waiting for the molten-hot *empanadas* to cool was at once the best and most agonizing feeling. In that bite was a multitude of emotions—new beginnings, eagerness, hope, boldness, affirmation, trust and confidence. My jaw locked in delight, relishing in the perfectly seasoned chunks of steak married with hardboiled egg, green olives and loads of spicy green onion. I don't know if the *empanadas* that night were just that good or if it was thanks to new-love euphoria, but I didn't even mind the raisins hiding in my handheld hot pocket. And that was a big deal, because up until that point, I'd never met a raisin-laden *empanada* that I didn't dissect until I'd removed each and every one of the golden buggers before devouring the rest. It was one of my few childhood culinary aversions that Dorita had absolutely no patience for.

I gave Gastón a *God, that's good* look.

"I know," he mouthed back, subtly motioning that I had a bit of cumin and paprika-infused juice dribbling down my chin. I was beginning to understand why Gastón relished food and wine. Suddenly I couldn't wait for dinner to be over.

As we lingered at *sobremesa*, Graciela and Jorge Luis jokingly let me know I'd passed their *empanada* test.

"*Test*?"

"It's like *Doña* Petroña once put it. You know her, right?" Jorge Luis asked, eating the last remains of the *ensalada mixta* directly from the salad bowl. "She's to Argentina what Julia Child is to the US."

"*Claro.* Of course. Dorita and Mom have her cookbook."

"Well, once on her cooking show *Buenas tardes, mucho gusto* she announced that any guest who dared to eat an *empanada* with a fork and knife at her table would never, ever again be invited back. Instead, *empanadas* are to be kissed, long and hard, to keep the juices from going all over the place."

I can't say I wasn't relieved. I never had eaten an *empanada* with a knife, but I certainly didn't know that was a tableside requisite among these parts.

Graciela leaned over the table and whispered to me, "You know *ahijadita mía*, you're the first girl he's brought home in years. So, will you be joining us tomorrow for our Sunday *asado*?"

"*Claro.* Of course! I wouldn't miss it. Could you pass me *la jarrra de agua* so I can refill my water glass?" I made sure to trill my double *r*'s a second longer than usual to make sure Gastón heard me from across the table. He subtly smiled, nodding his head in recognition. I was exactly where I wanted to be in that moment. Things were slowly coming together for Gastón and me. Thanks to the Orías, I found myself gaining a new appetite for life. To paraphrase Julia Child, who once said of her first years in France, "I felt myself opening like a flower."

Empanadas al cuchillo
(Knife-Cut Beef Handheld Turnovers)

MAKES 60 EMPANADAS, *to be kissed long and hard. As a general rule of thumb: one or two empanadas are a snack; three or more a meal.*

There are several things you need to know about *empanadas* before diving in chin first. There's nothing quite as bad as enduring a mouthful of rooftop-burn. First, you need to start your filling at least a day ahead of time, so the mixture can fully cool and congeal. This mixture is refrigerated for at least 3 hours or overnight before adding the hard-boiled eggs. (Truth be told, I often add them when the filling is hot. Both ways render a delicious filling.) Second, store-bought *tapas* (pastry discs) make just as good *empanadas* as those made with homemade dough— that is assuming you use the right ones. My grandma Dorita used to make her own *tapas* when she would come to the States, but only because she couldn't find them anywhere. She wasn't a masochist. She knew when and how to take a kitchen shortcut when warranted. I've included a recipe for *tapas*, but I promise you it's just not worth the hassle. You can find *empanada tapas* in your local Latin American grocer or purchase online. There are many different varieties of the refrigerated dough discs: *hojaldre* (puff pastry), *para freir* (for frying) or *criollas* (a drier dough that mimics homemade). I'm faithful to the *La Salteña* brand and only use their *criollas* (sometimes also packaged as "*sequitas*"). The *empanada* filling in itself is juicy, and the drier dough consistency soaks up the juices, creating a crispier finish. I stay away from the puff pastry *tapas*, as I find they render a very greasy *empanada*. Goya Foods has an *empanada tapa* readily available in my hometown of Pittsburgh, but they render a very bready, thick *empanada*. Not my cup of tea, but some prefer a bread-heavy handheld. There are also different sizes of *tapas*: *copetín* (bite-sized), the square-shaped *pastelitos* for sweet fillings such as *dulce de membrillo* (quince paste) and the regular size. You'll want the latter for this recipe.

Third and possibly most important—the great raisin debate. Not everyone likes them. I spent most of my childhood avoiding Dorita's evil stare as I picked them out, one by one, from each *empanada* that crossed my path. She had no patience for it. That made two of us. Out of respect for her and Jorge Luis, I've included them in the recipe below, but heartily suggest omitting them. Gastón would agree.

Finally, onto the edging. A leak-proof seal is essential to mastering the *empanada*. Dorita always said a perfect *repulgue* should have 16 to 19 crimps to make the perfect crescent shape. Good luck with that! But remember, practice makes perfect. I have discovered that there is a *repulgue* gene that must be recessive. Gastón, Dorita and Graciela all have it. Me, not so much. But fret not. *Empanadas* freeze easily. I assemble five dozen at a time and freeze them, uncooked, for up to four months. Placing them in the oven frozen tends to keep the juices from seeping out of amateur *repulgues* such as my own.

There's one last thing: no matter how hard I've tried, I never get the filling-to-*tapa* ratio right. It's likely you won't either, especially if you're following this recipe. Neither did Dorita, nor Mom nor Jorge Luis. Most Argentines reserve the remaining filling for *pastel de carne* or *pastel de papa*, more commonly known as shepherd's pie. Just consider it the recipe that keeps on giving.

DOUGH

4 cups **water**

3 tablespoons **salt**

7 tablespoons **pork fat**, or high-quality lard cut into pieces

12 to 13 cups all-purpose **flour**

2 raw **eggs**, lightly beaten

Or 4 20-piece packages of La Salteña Tapas Criollas

FILLING

10 large **eggs**, boiled and peeled

¾ cup pitted **green olives**

3.5 pounds **top-round sirloin**

4 ⅓ cups **scallions**, white and green parts, chopped

17 ounces (2 ⅓ cups) **vegetable shortening** (I prefer Spectrum Natural Organic All Vegetable Shortening)

5 cups yellow **onion**, chopped

5 heaping tablespoons Spanish **paprika** (pimenton dulce)

Salt to taste

1 heaping tablespoon **cumin**

2 heaping tablespoons crushed **red pepper flakes** (non-spicy)

1 tablespoon **cayenne pepper** (adjust accordingly to your heat preference)

½ cup **raisins** (optional)

Make the dough. Place water and salt in a small saucepan and bring to boil over high heat. Add the pork fat and stir until it melts. Transfer to a large wide bowl. Allow to cool to room temperature.

Gradually add 5 ½ to 6 cups of the flour, mixing with your hands, until the dough forms a ball. Generously sprinkle flour on a work surface to prevent dough from sticking. Knead the dough, adding more flour until it will not absorb any more. The dough should be on the drier side. Divide the dough into quarters and form into four discs, wrapping them in plastic. Refrigerate and chill for at least 1 hour or up to 24 hours.

Make the filling. Boil the eggs 12–15 minutes. Remove from water and allow to cool. Peel and cut into slices. Set aside.

Cut the pitted green olives lengthwise into three or four slivers, depending on the size of the olives.

Trim the fat and nerves from the sirloin. Slice lengthwise into strips, and then line up the strips, and slice into 1-centimeter cubes or chunks. Be careful not to mince the meat too finely, as this should be a rustic chop.

Wash and slice the scallions 1 centimeter thick. Set aside in a bowl.

Heat the shortening in a large skillet with high sides over medium-high heat. Add the yellow onions and cook, stirring until softened and translucent, about 5–7 minutes. Add the paprika, salt, cumin, red pepper flakes and cayenne pepper, stirring well to combine. Add the cubed beef, stirring to combine. Add the olives and raisins (optional). Once the beef has a nice golden sear, remove the filling from the heat. You do not want to overcook the meat, as it will finish cooking with the empanada. Carefully stir the scallions into the filling, making sure not to break up their form. Continue to carefully stir the filling every 10–15 minutes until cool. Cover and chill the filling completely, at least 3 hours (preferably overnight) in the refrigerator.

Form *tapas* if you are not using store-bought discs. Cut one of the dough discs in half, keeping the other half covered in plastic until ready to use. With a rolling pin, roll the dough onto a generously floured work surface into a rectangle about ⅛-inch thick. You can also use a pasta machine to do this. Using a biscuit cutter or water glass, cut the dough into 3½-inch circles. You should be able to get 6 circles per batch. Transfer the circles to a floured baking sheet and cover with plastic wrap. Repeat with the remaining dough.

Assemble the *empanadas*. Stir the eggs into the cooled filling. Place 2 heaping tablespoons of the filling in the center of each *empanada*. The technique to master in this recipe is to hold the open *empanada* with one hand while using the other hand to crimp the outer edge to seal it, as well as adding a decorative braid. The less dexterous among us should use a fork for this. With your finger, wet the circumference of the disc with water to create a seal-tight edge. Fold the bottom of the dough to meet the top of the disc, encasing the filling and forming a half moon, and press the edges together well. Make ½-inch edges by pressing the rims between your fingers to create a rope along the edges. The *empanadas* can sit uncovered at room temperature for 20 minutes before baking or can be refrigerated for up to 1 hour before baking.

Preheat the oven to 490°F. Line three baking sheets with parchment paper. Place the *empanadas* on the prepared pans and brush them with the egg wash, if using. Bake them for 28–30 minutes, until their bottoms are golden (rotate the pans in the oven halfway through baking, back to front and top to bottom, to ensure that all of the *empanadas* bake evenly). Transfer the *empanadas* to a cooling rack; let them cool for 3–5 minutes before serving.

Cook's note: To freeze, set assembled, uncooked *empanadas* in a single layer on a baking sheet and freeze until solid. When solid, transfer to freezer tight zip-top bags and freeze for up to 4 months. To cook, place on a parchment-lined baking sheet, brush with an egg wash and place directly into preheated oven.

Chapter 8

Sacramentos, bolas de fraile y suspiros de monja
Sacraments, Friar's Balls and Nun's Sighs

"What's for dinner, Mom? *¿Que vamos a cenar?*" Is there any question more hated by moms than this? In a house with six children constantly calling this out to you on a seemingly well-timed rotation from the minute they walk through the front door? As if you have nothing else to do with your day. Those five words are undoubtedly a setup for most any home cook. There is no right answer, given most everyday meals don't come with a hundred percent approval rating. Growing up, on days Mom found herself unprepared and had clearly had enough—God bless her—she narrowed her response to the following: "*Caca.*" That was a telltale sign to stop where you are, shut your mouth, back up slowly and steer clear until dinnertime or summoned. Unless your hormones had you feeling extra sassy that day and you dared ask—"Will that shit come on a stick or will it be neatly tucked away and baked into a golden-crusted *tarta*?"

Not all *tarta* is created equally. Argentines will put just about anything between two pie crusts and call it a day: butternut squash and ricotta, ham and cheese with *morrones*, eggs, corn or tuna. Name any ingredient and there's probably a layered *tarta* it calls home. But Argentina's Eastertime tart, *tarta pascualina*, is the crowned queen among them. Traditionally eaten during Lent and Easter, this savory pie is immensely popular in Argentina and eaten year-round, despite its moniker. From her envious filling—sautéed swiss chard, onion, ricotta, *pâté de foie* and hard-boiled eggs—to her double-decker flakey pie crusts, she's *la Madre María de tartas*. Our Mother Mary of savory pies. A testament to how the simplest of ingredients can be combined to create the most unforgettable first bite—one that can fortify you with the strength to rise up, dust off your pants and move on.

* * *

What at first seemed like a fleeting romance forged over *milanesas*, Malbec and under-the-table rompings at *sobremesa* was intensifying. But no matter the plans we made, life continued to throw curveballs, testing us in more ways than one. The largest I'd experienced thus far had brought us together in the tiny town of Suardi. It's like they say: you don't find love, it finds you. Neither of us saw it coming, and now we couldn't imagine our lives if it hadn't. But while Argentine food culture was very much a part of our love affair, we'd soon discover that food was only half of the story. Because while *sobremesa* fostered connections that reached far beyond our wildest expectations, it could just as easily break them up if neglected.

"You're going to have to tell them sooner or later," Gastón said on the other line of the phone. "Cati and Maribel are *mas pesadas que collar de melones*. They're becoming more and more annoying. Everywhere I go, they're giggling here and there or whispering about us behind closed doors. I'm not sure what they're up to, but it's only a matter of time before it gets back to your parents. And if your *mamá* doesn't hear it from them, she'll find out from the town hairdresser next time she's in Suardi."

I had told Gastón I wanted to first get a job before telling my parents, so they couldn't force me to go home. With the looming deadline of the holidays before us, Gastón held up his part of the bargain by faithfully making the eight-hour car trip to visit me in Buenos Aires each weekend. During the week, I spent most of my days in La Plata with Dorita. We'd snuggle in her bed with our coffees and watch her favorite *novelas* as we decided what to make for lunch that day. Then I'd go around the block to the neighborhood *verdulería* for the day's vegetables, stop at the *carnicería* to buy whatever cut of meat or chicken we'd planned on making and then hit the *kiosko* just around the corner from Dorita's house to buy the latest gossip magazines—*¡Hola!, Caras, Gente, Para Ti*—and two *alfajores*: one for Dorita, one for me. *Alfajores* are to Argentines what chocolate chip cookies are to Americans or macarons are to the French. It's the national cookie made of two soft, crumbly biscuits sandwiched with *dulce de leche*, chocolate or regional jams.

Most Spanish words beginning with "*al*" have Arabic roots, and this cookie is no exception. Its origin can be traced back to the Moorish occupation of Andalusia, Spain, and the great Mediterranean culinary traditions. There are countless versions of *alfajores*; each Argentine province puts its own stamp on them, claiming to have the best ones. My all-time favorite are Havanna's seventy percent cacao puro *alfajores* with *dulce de leche*. Mom and Dorita were more partial to the Italian meringue ones, also with *dulce de leche*. Dorita and I would eat them with coffee most days at the *merienda* around four thirty as we flipped through our magazines, catching up on the latest who's-who and monarchy antics.

Some days, when I was feeling more adventurous, I'd jump on a bus to Buenos Aires and explore the city and its iconic neighborhoods—La Boca's brightly painted ghetto, San Telmo's cobblestone streets, Palermo Soho's bohemian boutiques or Caballito's sprawling parks. When I needed a taste of home, I'd order potato skins at TGI Fridays in Puerto Madero, overlooking Rio de la Plata's riverbank as I devoured the tour guide books that told me where to go next.

The more I immersed myself in Argentina's capital city, the clearer it became that Evita Perón's dying words, "I will return, and I will be millions," proved more prophetic than ever. It was as if she'd never left, even after succumbing to ovarian cancer at the age of thirty-three. Some say it's no coincidence Jesus and *Santa* Evita walked this earth the same amount of years. They both lived short lives and became even more famous in death. So much so, Evita was officially proclaimed by Congress to be the "Spiritual Leader of the Nation" as she lay on her deathbed, slowly and horrifically succumbing—against her will—into her inevitable immortality. Sainted or not, there was no eternal rest for Argentina's most celebrated First Lady. Evita's unappeased ghost was most everywhere I turned—her face-adorned memorabilia sold in flea market stalls; her graffitied name and likeness decorated military green walls; her portrait hung in government offices. Not to mention the statues, monuments and buildings built in her honor.

Even more intriguing was Argentina's fascination with pies and politics. I came across a handful of preferred haunts for both activists and foodies—restaurants devoted entirely to former, three-time president General Juan Domingo Perón and his second wife, María Eva Duarte de Perón, that served to nourish (possibly even overstuff) the immortal spirit that's become Evita. Inside, they served up indulgent comfort food favorites like *pastel de carne* (shepherd's pie) with sides of socialist anthems blaring from the speakers, makeshift altars to Evita and "ode to the working class" artwork displayed on walls. Cocktail menus included concoctions named after *los descamisados*, the "shirtless" working class, served in "power to the people" pint glasses—there was no room for dainty, bourgeois glassware in these types of establishments.

Dorita made it clear on more than one occasion that not all Argentines fancied this form of Peronist Chic mix of earnest politics with pop-culture cuisine. Sure, they served up tasty fare, but while Evita had been adored by millions, she was loathed and despised in equal measure by anti-Peronists who sought to restore democracy. One of the most controversial and influential women in the Western world, to her admirers Evita was a saintlike defender of the poor; to her critics, she was a two-cent actress born out of wedlock into poverty who'd slept her way to the top only to become an irresponsible spender out for personal glory. But Evita's haters didn't derail her. In fact, they added fuel to her fire and gave her an inordinate delight in sticking it to them. In one of Evita's more fiery speeches to the Peronist masses, she shouted into her microphone, "There are some oligarchs who make me want to bite them just as one crunches into a carrot or a radish." Either way, no matter who she was—Evita the good, Evita the bad—she lives on, even in death. I felt her presence all over Buenos Aires and beyond.

* * *

Back in La Plata, weekends were reserved for Gastón. I found myself running out of excuses to give Dorita as to where I was going and with whom. As much as I hated keeping our relationship from her, I couldn't share it with Dorita. Not yet. She pledged allegiance to my mom—as she should. When in town, Gastón and I spent most of our time together poolside at his parents' home in Gonnet, right outside of La Plata. Every once in a while, we took a drive. We'd go north of Buenos Aires to El Tigre in the Paraná River delta, and one time we took a day trip over to Uruguay by ferry to explore Colonia's historic streetscapes. Sometimes we just drove.

I told Gastón about the car accident when I was sixteen, and I didn't talk about that with anyone. I told him that I almost killed my *abuelo* Alfredo and brother Oscar. I left out the part about the stranger who mysteriously disappeared after pulling me from the wreckage, holding my hand until help arrived.

"I mean, what was I thinking? I'd had my license for a day or two, tops. And all of a sudden jumping over the front seat to grab the wheel of the Suburban doing seventy-five down the highway seemed like a good idea?"

"Why beat yourself up about it? You have to let it go."

"It's just that ever since, I've felt like we were given a second chance for a reason. That there's a reason we got out alive. And now I can't seem to figure out what that is."

"*Tranqui.* Relax, Josie. We'll figure it out together. But from now on, let me do the driving."

That's when Gastón asked me to stay. I told him I was planning on it. That meant I had to start looking for a job. I told Gastón how I'd almost followed a career in healthcare but wasn't so sure I wanted to do that anymore. I'd taken a bunch of marketing classes at Duke, so maybe I'd try something new. I began putting a resumé together to look for a job so I could consider the option of staying. For more than a while. For Gastón.

Each Sunday as we said our goodbyes, Gastón would slip me a love letter reminding me why I'd once again entered into a long-distance relationship in a foreign country. While each letter was poetic in its own right, Gastón ended each with his trademark sign-off, "this letter *vale por felicidad . . .* is good for happiness," followed by another offering of an organ or two. By the time Thanksgiving rolled around, he'd entrusted me with his heart, his pancreas, both of his kidneys and his thyroid. I didn't dare tell him I didn't like organ meat.

That Thanksgiving was the first I'd ever spent far from home. To my surprise, Gastón had come into town earlier than usual and asked if I'd like to have dinner with his family. That evening, we arrived at the Orías' outdoor covered *quincho* to find a table filled with some of my Thanksgiving favorites—*pavo* (turkey) roasted with oranges and herbs, stuffed with a *ciruela pasa* (prune) and sage stuffing and *puré mixto de calabaza y papa* (mashed potatoes mixed with butternut squash) and a spinach and walnut salad.

I hadn't planned on celebrating Thanksgiving that year, but Jorge Luis concocted the surprise to make me feel less homesick, putting his own twist on traditional recipes. He'd rubbed butter mixed with herbs and *dulce de leche* between the skin and the bird and all along its cavity. The meat was delicate and moist and the skin was extra crispy. That night, as we lingered around the table after *Sangsgivin'* dinner, as Gastón's parents pronounced it, Graciela presented me with a *servilletero de cuernito*, a napkin holder made of antler. And with that simple gesture, the Orías let me know that I would always have a seat at their family table.

I'd recently spent most of my days standing hours upon hours in line at different government agencies so that I could reestablish my Argentine citizenship and begin the process of looking for a job. I'd contemplate Evita Perón's favored hairstyles captured in portraits—her signature chignon bun tied at her nape took the prize—as I came to realize Argentines did lines better than anyone. They were used to it—I wasn't. In America we didn't do much waiting.

With just three weeks until my twenty-fifth birthday, I'd begun leaving my resumé with family friends, at neighborhood stores and community boards at the US Embassy and US Chamber of Commerce. I applied for anything to do with marketing and communications. I knew it would be a long shot, but I had two things most Argentines didn't: English as my first language and dual citizenship and passports.

Two days before Mom's arrival, I got a call from the chamber of commerce. "Standard & Poor's International is seeking an English-speaking person to fill their marketing position. Are you interested in interviewing?"

"Interested? Of course, I am. Sorry, what company was that again? Standard and . . . ?"

At the moment, it seemed the universe was on our side, cheering on Gastón and me. At the time I'd never heard of the global rating company, but with less than a week to go until my return flight to the States, I was sure as hell going to show up for the interview. It was the only one I'd gotten.

Gastón called me later that evening to ask how it went. At that point, we needed a Hail Mary to keep me in the country. "So, *¿cómo te fue?*"

"Nerve-racking. The managing partners, Diana and Viviana, are two badass women. One more than the other. You can tell they don't take crap from anyone. They were in their twenties when they co-founded Risk Analysis SA, one of Argentina's first local rating agencies. Standard & Poor's bought them out three years ago, leaving them to run the Argentine office. Anyway, I kept messing up and would *tutear* them. I couldn't keep my *vos* and *usted* straight. Which makes me nervous." To *tutear* someone meant you had a close relationship with the person you addressed, while the *usted* was used when you were supposed to be a bit more formal, or when you had to address your listener with some kind of respect.

"Did you tell them growing up you spoke Spanish mostly at home?"

"I did. But then they suggested we continue on with the interview in English, and things took a turn for the better."

"So what happened at the rest of the interview?"

"One of the partners, Diana, seemed ready to give me an offer right then and there. But Viviana, not so much. She thinks my Spanish could be better. I told them I just needed a chance to prove myself. That between a good auto-correct on my computer and Spanish-English dictionary, I could write professional press releases. God knows I wrote enough Spanish lit papers back in college. Plus, my English is good. Fluent."

"*Mierda*," Gastón laughed. "Shit. *Se ve que no tenés abuela.*"

"What do you mean? I do have a grandma. *Abuela* Dorita."

Gastón laughed. "It's an expression—'I see you don't have a grandma.' We use it when someone gets full of themselves. When you chuck modesty altogether and toot your own horn. You know *abuelas*, bragging on their grandkids all the time."

"I hope I didn't get too far ahead of myself. I know I can do the job. And it's a really good one. If things are going to work between us, I need something of my own. I can't rely on you all the time. We don't even live in the same city." I knew Gastón was a force, and if I didn't get my act together I'd get swept up in his life. It had already happened once before. I refused to be "Tripped up" again.

Later that afternoon, Viviana's assistant called to offer me the position. "Viviana would like you to start Wednesday, January 6 at the latest." She spoke in a matter-of-fact tone that let me know nobody left Viviana waiting. "Oh, and she asked that you brush up on your Spanish as much as possible before then."

From that moment, things moved at lightning speed. After accepting the job offer, Gastón was my first call. My parents were second in line. I needed to forewarn them I wouldn't be traveling back to the States with them. I'd been dreading having the much-anticipated talk about Gastón, but both took the news much better than expected. Dad said he'd had a hunch from the moment he left me at the ranch at the end of September. He joked he hoped it didn't affect the audit, but mostly he wanted to talk about the job offer with Standard & Poor's. "*Mi hija*, working on Wall Street. How'd that happen?"

Lucky in love. Destiny. A ghost or two. I didn't bother clarifying that I'd be working in a subsidiary office halfway across the world from the credit-rating agency's New York headquarters. Dad was never one to dole out praise easily, so I took what I could get.

Mom was surprised, or at least pretended to be. I kept asking her if Cati hadn't spilled the beans. I was sure she had. But Mom said that Dad was the only person who'd mentioned something about us once or twice—and she assured him it was just in his head. I wasn't sure I believed her, but Mom genuinely seemed excited too—already imagining who among our sisters or her band of *chicas* she'd call first to share the news with. I'd already prepped my sister Laura, whom I'd been confiding in since the very beginning, to play dumb when Mom told her.

"Did Graciela know?" Mom grilled me.

"Not until recently. Gastón took me to their house for Thanksgiving. She and Jorge Luis put two and two together. Are you sure you didn't do the same?"

But Mom insisted otherwise. The two of us spent hours on the phone planning out the following weeks. She'd fly directly to the ranch before spending my birthday with me in Buenos Aires. Then we'd head back to Miami for the holidays. I could fly to Pittsburgh right after New Year's Eve to pack up my things. "What about Sonny? I can't ask Taylor to adopt her."

Mom had it covered. She'd fly Sonny down to Miami Beach to live in Florida. "Sonny's family. She'll stay with your Dad and me."

This I couldn't believe. After all, Sonny had been the cause of major contention between Dad and me a couple years back when I brought her back from Aspen with me. That argument took a good year to run its course. Slowly Dad came to love Sonny, and she immediately returned his affection once he began sharing slice after slice of hard salami with her. And now with her move to Miami, she was headed into the lap of luxury where she'd enjoy Bayside adult swims in my parents' saltwater pool, followed by three meals a day that mirrored whatever my parents were eating.

What shocked me even more was that Mom insisted on Gastón spending New Year's with us in Miami. "If you're willing to leave everything for him, it seems only right he sees where you come from. Plus, he can help you pack your things back in Pittsburgh. He should meet your friends, get to know that side of you.

And, Josie, if things with Gastón don't work out, you always have Standard & Poor's. That's a resumé builder right there."

Days later, I blew out my twenty-fifth birthday candles with Mom, Gastón and my oldest cousin on Mom's side, Paulina, in Buenos Aires at the formal and elegant French restaurant, Au Bec Fin, which occupied all three floors of what was once an aristocratic home in the 1920s. Mom chose the restaurant. It had been a favorite dining spot of my Francophile *abuelo* Alfredo's since the early '80s. As I savored my prawn mousse bite-by-bite in the private second-floor dining room, I imagined what it would have been like to live inside the restored mansion with the prestigious Recoleta address during Argentina's Belle Époque era.

Two years younger than me, Paulina was the only one of us still sober by the time *sobremesa* rolled along that evening. I'd invited her to make sure Mom didn't have the opportunity to steer the conversation towards me and Gastón. We weren't in any position to answer questions we couldn't even answer for ourselves.

Dinner had gone off without a hitch up until that point. As usual, Gastón was his cool-as-can-be, chatterbox self. Mom, on the other hand, was nursing her third vodka and tonic with lime as the plates were being cleared. She rarely enjoyed more than two. By the time she finished her drink, nostalgia came in and pulled up a seat beside her. Mom began reminiscing about her childhood in the Mendoza wine valley. *Abuelo* Alfredo had made his career in the large petroleum company YPF and they were living in executive housing tucked into the foothills of the Andes mountains. Mom was just ten or eleven when the military attempted its first coup against Perón's populist government. One night, after the revolutionary militants attempted to take their neighborhood, they fled.

"Your grandfather put Dorita, Álvaro and me in the back of our car. He handed our driver, *Mamá* and me loaded pistols, and told us, 'Shoot first if they stop you.' We were all crying. I didn't know if we'd ever see my father again. But things calmed down. The coup failed. That time. But when we went back as a family the following week, the house, along with most of the neighborhood, had been burnt down."

"I never knew that story. I'm sorry, Mom." I placed my hand over hers. With regular swings between the left and right extremes of Argentina's political pendulum, I'd learned from an early age to never voice your opinion on Argentine politics or religion. Argentines generally don't take well to foreigners' opinions on these matters, unless you can demonstrate exceptional knowledge of Argentine social, cultural and economic news.

Gastón had a thorough understanding of Argentina's current events, probably because he talked to every cab driver and waiter that crossed his path. "I'm pretty sure YPF had already moved *Mamá's* family back to La Plata by then," Gastón said, remembering that our grandfathers had met at YPF years before.

"So now I can't understand why my youngest daughter wants to come back," Mom said. "To a turbulent past we escaped. Dictatorships. Populist governments. An unrelenting military. Political unrest. Daily protests. So many it's hard to even know what they're protesting anymore. Still, people march, closing highways, making it impossible to get around the city. And nothing changes. Just another day in Argentina. And I haven't even mentioned the 150 percent yearly inflation rate that her dad and I worked so hard to take her away from." As the evening went on, Mom made it clear that my dating Gastón and deciding to live in Argentina was like a slap in her face.

Paulina and I stayed mum as we sipped our *cafecitos.* Like Jorge Luis Borges, the famous Argentine author and poet, once said, "Don't talk unless you can improve the silence."

But as usual, Gastón knew just what to say. Putting his hand on Mom's shoulder, he joked, "Poupée, neither Josie nor I have a dime to our name. We don't have anything to lose." With that, some of the tension cleared. Gastón always seemed to be able to make Mom laugh, even in the most awkward of moments.

"All I have to say, Gastóncito, is you better learn English. Who knows when the next economic crash will happen? After growing up in the States, let me tell you, Josie's not used to riding them out." And with that, Mom raised her glass, offering a toast, "To Josie and Gastón." She turned to me. "He's a gem, by the way. Finally, my dear, you've met your match. Better yet, someone who'll put up with you."

What's that supposed to mean?

I was slowly beginning to understand and respect the complexities of the woman I'd called Mom all my life. Full of mystery and contradictions, she had a love-hate relationship with a country she was unable to live in, with a European-influenced yet Latin society she was unable to live without. It was familiar territory for most Argentines: economic crisis triggered by mounting deficits and debt, and political instability with sharp swings between governments of the right and left. In that climate it was hard to see what lay ahead, let alone make plans. Yet it was home. It always would be.

Gastón and I rang in that new year with my family in Miami Beach. Everyone seemed to embrace our relationship, especially my brothers and sisters. They each immediately fell for Gastón's quick wit—when they could understand him. I repeatedly had to remind him that we grew up speaking our parents' and grandparents' generation of *Castellano*. We didn't have his contemporary Argentine slang down.

Just before the stroke of midnight, Mom passed out overflowing goblets of apple *sidra*, by far the most popular carbonated alcoholic drink among Argentines during Christmas and New Year's. She also had champagne for those who preferred a drier bubbly, along with small cups of *las doce uvas de la suerte*, a Latin tradition that consists of eating twelve grapes of luck, one with each clock bell strike at midnight, to welcome the new year. According to tradition, eating the grapes in this manner leads to a year of good luck and prosperity. Rare is the Argentine who risks tempting fate by skipping the grapes, one for each month of the new year. If the grape is sweet, it's said that that particular month will be a good one. If it's sour, take note: a rough month is up ahead. Logistically speaking, eating twelve grapes in a minute is challenging to say the least, leaving little time to chew and swallow, much less savor. Still, that year I couldn't help but notice that my first three or four grapes were terribly sour.

The following day Gastón and I made a whirlwind two-day trip to Pittsburgh to pack up my things and catch up with friends. Taylor picked us up from the airport, hugging us both at the same time. "Larry!" She cheek-kissed Gastón. "We finally meet. I feel like I know you already from Josie's emails. And you brought back our girl."

Gastón hugged her back, laughing. He also met Megan and Robert, among others. I was afraid it might be awkward being around Robert, but we easily slipped right back into our friendship. He and Gastón also hit it off. While Gastón didn't speak a lick of English, he somehow carried on conversations with each of them. Before we knew it, we were headed back to the airport. We said our goodbyes to one another the following day in Miami. After a brief layover, Gastón was headed back to Argentina. His trip back would take him through Panama and Bolivia before arriving in Córdoba, while I was flying the red-eye to Buenos Aires later that evening.

"Call me the minute you arrive in Buenos Aires," Gastón said.

"When will I see you?" I asked, holding him tight.

"Probably in a couple of weeks. I've been away for almost two. I'll need to work the next few weekends to catch up on things."

"I have an uneasy feeling in the pit of my stomach. I don't want to make this move without you. It's like I'm moving to be with you, but you're not going to be there. I'll be alone the first day of my job and the days after. I don't even know if I can do it. I sold myself as this strong, determined woman, and I'm scared as hell. I've never even written a press release in English, let alone in Spanish." *Come to think of it, I'd never even held a position in marketing. I may have oversold myself just a bit during that hours-long interview.*

"You're going to do great. And if you get tired or can't find the right words in Spanish, talk to them in English. They did find you at the American Chamber of Commerce. And I'll call my sister Soledad to pick you up on the weekend, so you can relax by the pool with my family. Take your *abuela*, too. We've got this. *Chau.*" He looked back and yelled, "*Te quiero tanto que no se cuanto.*" I love you so much, even *I* don't know how much. To this day Gastón says this all the time. He knew I was moving for him, and him alone.

Back at the house, it was apparent something was eating at Mom from the moment I walked in. That night at dinner, Mom started off the conversation commenting on my new job—

among other things. "Your dad and I feel you can't pass up the opportunity to live in Buenos Aires and work for a company like Standard & Poor's. You know, it's not a nine-to-five position. I'm sure you've realized that by now. It could be the start of a promising career. Why don't you cool things down with Gastón for the time being and focus on your new job? Make your own friends and life."

It took me a couple of seconds to digest Mom's words. *What was she talking about?* "What's this all about? Of course I know the job's going to be super demanding. They made it clear in the interview. But I'm moving for Gastón. I just left him at the airport earlier this morning. You invite him into our home and make him feel like family, and then all of a sudden want me to dump him just as we are about to begin our lives together. Just like that?"

"Of course not. I love Gastón like a son. I've just been thinking that he's not even in the same city. Why tie yourself down?"

"Really, Mom? Where's this coming from? What's made you change your tune? Before we went to Pittsburgh you were super supportive of our relationship." While I wanted to tell Mom off, I bit back an angry retort. I could hear *Abuela* Dorita in my head reminding me, "Josefinita, *el enojo es un mal consejero.*" Anger is a bad advisor. Instead I stabbed my pasta with a fork, twirling my linguine unapologetically. Had Mom forgotten why I was moving to Argentina?

Mom pushed her plate away and looked me in the eye. "I didn't want to say anything. Not yet, anyway. But more cattle have gone missing. Over the past six months, cattle have disappeared from several ranches. At first we thought it was poachers, or even puma hunting them, but there's simply too many. Some of the *gauchos* have suggested that this started happening soon after Gastón took over as administrator. You know, there's a black market for cattle. It's an easy way to pocket money on the side."

I painfully put my fork down. I'd hoped to finish my beefy linguine before excusing myself to go to the airport. Mom made her rich brown meat sauce with a flat iron steak that she cooked low and slow for the better part of the day, alongside dried plums that broke down into a thick, sweet, fruity syrup that enveloped the beef. Who knew when I'd get another chance to enjoy Mom's home cooking? Still, I didn't know how to begin to react to Mom's accusations, but then it occurred to me—Cati. This had her name written all over it.

"Mom, does this have anything to do with Cati? Since that first day I saw her serving Gastón second class cuts of beef I quickly came to realize she had it in for him."

But Mom skirted the question. "All I'm saying is that your relationship with Gastón could put our own personal business in jeopardy."

"Since when? Please, answer the question. Did Cati tell you this? You know she's a vengeful person. She looks at Gastón and Marco as the 'help.' My dating Gastón doesn't fare well with her plot to remind him of this—each and every chance she gets. I won't let her fabricate this story, not at Gastón's expense."

But Mom insisted I cool things down with Gastón until my parents could look into things further. In a couple of hours I would be boarding a plane to move halfway across the world to be with the man I loved, and my parents were all of a sudden asking me to put the brakes on our relationship? *To hell with sobremesa.* I shoved my chair with enough force to jar the table.

"Josephine, sit down," Mom said. "We have an hour before we leave for the airport. Let's talk this out."

But I was done talking. Fifteen minutes later, I was in the back of a Yellow Cab headed towards the Miami International Airport. I'd skipped *sobremesa* altogether, and aside from Mom shouting from the doorway as I got in the taxi—"Make other living arrangements when you arrive. If you can't do this one thing we're asking, you're no longer welcome in our apartment!"—I said goodbye to no one.

"Just remember you and Dad are the ones who sent me to Argentina in the first place. Be careful what you ask for!" I slammed the door shut and told the driver to go.

I arrived in Buenos Aires the following morning, exhausted. As I sat waiting for my luggage, I thought about my *abuelo* Alfredo. Where was he when I needed him, now? From the moment he'd appeared at my bedside that summer, assuring me my heart was in the palms of his hands, things I'd never dreamed possible began happening. It was as if he'd understood all along that I was stuck between two worlds—Pittsburgh and Argentina—and the only way to fix it was to bring me home, back to his Argentina, to Gastón. He and Dorita had a hand in playing matchmaker to Gastón's parents. Now it was time to bring things full circle and play cupid between Gastón and me. But just as it seemed everything was finally coming together, my parents yanked the tablecloth from under me.

I didn't understand why Mom was suddenly saying these things. It wasn't like her. She loved Gastón. She didn't have to say so; it was obvious from day after day of *sobremesas* we'd shared together at the ranch. He was a gentleman, and she loved that about him. He could match Mom in conversation on any current event, no matter where it was happening in the world. He made Mom laugh like a schoolgirl. He listened. He could talk Mom down from the ledge when she got upset about one thing or another at the ranch. She, too, was lighter around Gastón. There was peace in his love. Peace like I'd never felt before. It came at the perfect time.

Still, my life was slowly turning into a shit show. In just two days, I'd be starting a new job, in a new country, in a different language, and now I had to find a place to live on top of that.

At least I still had Dorita.

* * *

The one thing I didn't have after landing in Argentina was my luggage.

After submitting a lost baggage claim, I grabbed a taxi to Dorita's home in La Plata. Mom must have called her, because she'd been waiting for me with a just-out-of-the-oven, steaming *tarta pascualina*. Dorita's was inches thick and contained just a touch of *pâté de foie* to ground its earthy parts and add a depth of flavor. Chock full of onions, swiss chard and—after a stint in the oven—eggs that hard boil and bake right into the pie, it was just what I needed to regain my footing. *Tarta pascualina* is likened to Argentina's resurrection pie—its "Eastertime tart." Italian immigrants who voyaged to South America to gamble on a new life brought the recipe for this tasty and filling pie. Its origins lie specifically in the region of Liguria, Italy, where the dish can be traced back to the sixteenth century. The traditional recipe calls for thirty-three layers of phyllo pastry, representing the number of years of Christ's life—*Evita's too.*

"What now, Josefinita?" Dorita asked at *sobremesa*, refilling our glasses with a nice, cold Torrontés Argentine white wine.

"I don't know. I start my job the day after tomorrow. Can I stay here until I figure things out? I haven't even had a chance to talk to Gastón. He's probably worried I haven't called."

"Of course you can. But you know it's at least an hour commute both ways to Buenos Aires."

"I know. But what other choice do I have?"

"You could call your *mamá.* You know one call is all it will take."

"I can't. I can't do what she's asking of me. Once I get my first paycheck I can look into renting a small apartment in Buenos Aires."

"You're always welcome here. But, about Gastón, maybe you should wait a day or two to settle in before calling. Your *mamá* told me everything. How you got up from the table and left for Argentina without so much as a goodbye."

"Of course I did. You don't know the rumor spreading at the ranch. And Mom seems to believe it—or is at least entertaining it."

"That some of the *gauchos* suggested Gastón might be the one stealing cattle? Why don't you give your parents some time to look into this before continuing on with him?"

"Oh. So she told you. Come on, Dori. You know Gastón—he wouldn't dare. This has Cati written all over it. She's been after Gastón and I from the get-go."

"But why would Cati make up something like that? Why would she go around saying Gastón's stealing?"

Just like a childhood game of telephone, or in Argentina, *teléfono descompuesto*, in just a matter of hours the story had gone from cattle going missing under Gastón's watch to him stealing. It was like the Argentine slang-language tango, *Cambalache,* says: *el que no afana, es un gil.* He who doesn't steal, is a fool. "I don't know, *Abuela.* For her own personal gain? To prove her worth to Mom so she keeps her around? She strikes me as someone who steps on others to get ahead. Cati's extremely calculated. When I was at the ranch she was always spying on me. I've no idea why. Just like I never understood why she serves Gastón and his brother separate cuts of meat from the rest of the table. To spite them, I imagine. But she's got some sort of agenda. And for some reason, Mom's protecting her. If she reveals her source, Cati might stop being her eyes and ears. You know what they say, while the cat's away, the mice will play."

Dorita shook her head. Other than the separate cuts of beef oddity, she didn't seem to agree with me. "Gastón's a good man. And he comes from an even better family. Just remember, plums don't become prunes in a day. It takes time. But they're worth the wait. Let's keep this between us for now. The truth will soon come out. And we certainly don't want this getting to Gastón or his family."

We sat at the table for a long while in silence. "Is there anymore *tarta*?"

"*Si. Como que no.*" Dorita went to the kitchen to get me another wedge of pie. She held my right hand as I ate with my left. "You know, Josefinita, your Mom has always spoiled you. She's just worried, that's all. Something tells me she's having trouble reconciling the fact that her youngest daughter is moving back to the very place she worked so hard to take her from."

I sat listening as Dorita told me about the first years after Mom and Dad moved to the States in 1974.

"You were barely six months old. Poupecita was just twenty-nine, with five young children under eight years old. We landed in Pittsburgh on June 30. As long as I live, I'll never forget that date. *Presidente* Perón died the following morning—July 1. I can still picture the *New York Times* headline—'Perón dead at 78; wife takes over a divided nation.' I had to dig way into the paper to read the article. That day Argentina—and the Americas—got its first female president—Isabelita. Perón's third wife served as both First Lady and vice president during his third term in office. His untimely death left her to inherit the presidency at just forty-three years old."

"It's funny how few people know her name, compared to Evita. She was overthrown soon after, right? I learned about this at Duke."

"It's true. Evita never held a political seat, but she was very powerful—even more so in death. Her ghost continues to haunt Argentina's political corridors. As for Isabelita, she was ousted soon after. And unlike Evita, most forgot her. Or wanted to. Perón's passing set the ball rolling for another military takeover in 1976. But my point is that your parents took you from all of this uncertainty in search of a better life. I tried to help them every way I could, like doing the cooking and watching you all while your mom went to her English lessons. Your father was always at the hospital working. If he wasn't, he was on call. If I wasn't there for your mom, she would have been alone. It was a huge strain on all of us." A faraway look came over Dorita. "And don't even get me started on Pittsburgh winters. That was something none of us were prepared for."

I sighed. "Mom never talks about the hardship. She only talks about America, the land of opportunity. How they never would have been able to achieve what they have back home in Argentina."

"It's true. The government at the time wouldn't have allowed it. They had taken over the hospitals and placed their own men at the top. Your father wasn't allowed to practice medicine the way he wanted. They didn't even allow doctors like him to perform catheterizations. They clipped your Dad's wings, and he was born to fly. To soar. Everything you have now, it came at a price. Your *mamá* and *papá* had to leave their home. Their friends. Their family. An Argentina they loved."

"I get that, *Abuela*, but Mom followed her dreams with the man she loved. I'm doing the same. Mom and I aren't that different after all."

"You are a lot more like your *mamá* than you know. Not everyone can leave everything behind to follow their dreams. It takes blind faith. The difference is your mom didn't follow your dad. They went together. In your case, you're following Gastón. And that's hard for your mom. She's mentally struggling with everything she went through to move her young family to the US, only to see you choose to live in the very country she took you from to secure a better future. She thinks Argentina will get in the way of the life she wishes for you. Only time will tell." Dorita looked at my plate. "Here, have another piece of *tarta*."

I did. It fed me the courage to make Argentina my new home and, with the help of Dorita's stories, melted away the seething anger I'd been feeling for Mom since I'd left Miami the day before. It gave me pause. It was my own resurrection pie.

Dorita set me up in the back room just off the dining room, where Alfredo slept during the last years of his life. The closets were still packed with his clothes, shoes, hats, faded photos and his faithful smoking pipe that Dorita had always detested. Yet she never had the heart to get rid of it. That afternoon, as I plummeted into my *siesta*, I felt Alfredo's presence as if he'd been sitting on the side of my bed, watching me sleep.

* * *

The airline delivered my bags the following morning. But as I un-packed, I discovered that while the bags' top layers were intact, just as I'd packed them, the rest of the luggage had been filled with old stuffed animals and newspapers. Everything was gone— my clothes, my great-grandma Josefina's ring that I was gifted on my twenty-first birthday, my shoes, my undergarments, my books and purses. After a closer look, I realized the black Tumi luggage that my parents had given me as a college graduation gift had been swapped out for cheaper black baggage. I was literally start-ing over from scratch. I'd drained my bank account before leaving Pittsburgh, all $783 of it. It had to last me until I received my first paycheck at the end of the month. I could buy a couple of basics to mix and match and a pair of black heels. It would have to do.

I called Graciela in a panic. She picked up me and Dorita and took us to *el centro* in downtown La Plata so I could pick up a couple of outfits to get me through my first week of work. Graciela, always the faithful godmother, chipped in for a pair of heels. *Did Graciela know that people at the ranch were accusing her son of stealing?* I wondered, mortified. I missed Gastón more than ever.

My first few weeks at Standard & Poor's were traumatizing. From the hour-long, standing-room-only bus commute to the huge learning curve to speaking Spanish professionally to the ten- to twelve-hour workdays, I was exhausted. For lunch, we'd always order from the skyscraper's first floor restaurant. Waiters clad in tuxedos would deliver our meals to the thirty-third floor with cloth napkins and real silverware. All fifteen or so of us broke as a team in the conference room, eating together almost daily, post-lunch *sobremesa* included. No one ate at their desk, except for Viviana, who most days ate her daily meal of *lomito al plato*, tenderloin topped with a slice of beefsteak tomato, in the privacy of her own office. I was grateful for that.

I was terrified of Viviana at first. When she was around, I had to be on all of the time—sharp as a whip. It was exhausting, pretending like that. But in the safe confines of the large conference room where I ate among analysts, assistants and the HR team, my brain would simply go into standby mode. I'd drift off into space as I picked at my go-to dish—lentils baked in a butternut squash boat, topped with loads of melted cheese, garlic and chopped parsley.

"Josefina, earth to Josefina." My colleagues would jokingly shake my shoulder, summoning me back to the lunch table.

For weeks, having arrived back home at Dorita's close to nine p.m. most evenings, I'd skip *sobremesa* altogether, swapping it for a good hour or two of mindless English-language TV on the Sony Channel back in my bedroom. *Friends. The Nanny. Saved by the Bell.* It didn't matter what was on or how old the sitcom. All that mattered was that it was in English and didn't require any thinking on my behalf. Sometimes I'd crawl into bed with Dorita, who'd catch me up on her melodramatic Spanish *telenovelas*.

It was all so exhausting. What had I been thinking, moving to Argentina and working for an American company? What happened to the daily *siesta* I was so looking forward to?

Weeks passed before Gastón had an open window to come visit. We spent the weekend at his parents' house, but since I'd moved in with Dorita, we rarely, if ever, had the opportunity to be alone. Added to that was Gastón's conflict with my parents, who were also his bosses. He was desperately trying to get to the bottom of the missing cattle. Not to mention my stress at Standard & Poor's. By the time we ended our days together, we mostly found ourselves fighting sleep more than fighting to keep our hands off one another.

One afternoon, Gastón and I found ourselves alone, poolside, while his family slept *la siesta*. "So, when were you planning on telling me about the rumors swirling around La Santa Elena? Your parents didn't mention anything?" Gastón asked, serving me a *mate*. "López told Marco what they're saying, that I've been stealing cattle. They've been running me ragged, sending me most weekends to one ranch or another."

"I didn't want to hurt your feelings," I said between sips. "I'm surprised we didn't see this coming. I just know Cati's behind it. She's the one accusing you of stealing. Not Mom. She merely said some *gauchos* suggested the cattle have gone missing on your watch. Her words keep getting inflated. That's why I didn't tell you."

"Something tells me it's Cati, too. She's had her eye on Marco and me since we first set foot at La Santa Elena. She can't stand that her husband López doesn't have a seat at your parents table—and we do. He's been there much longer than us. But that's not our fault—it's of his own making."

"I agree. You know anyone's welcome, as long as they claim their place. I'm sure Mom or Dad invited him once or twice—at least. Cati's setting you up. But how can we prove it?"

"I'm on it. Give it time. So tell me, this whole rumor mill has nothing to do with you living at your *abuela's* house?"

"It has everything to do with it. But I'm walking on eggshells lately. You know Dorita, she believes anything Mom says. I'm just trying to keep the peace until I figure out my next steps. I can't even rent a place in Buenos Aires. I looked into it, and I don't have any credit established yet."

"Let me help. We can rent a place in my name. Or even better, why don't you stay here with my parents for a while? It would cut your commute by twenty minutes each way."

"Thanks, but I have to figure this out on my own. Your parents don't know what's going on, do they?"

"Of course they do. But don't worry. They won't say a thing."

"No. I'm done. We need to put a stop to this absurdity. You need to leave the ranch. We barely get to see one another as is.

I moved for you, but you're not here. And most nights it's almost impossible for me to even get you on the phone."

Gastón was torn. He didn't have another job lined up. He also knew leaving just like that wouldn't be the right thing to do. He respected my parents too much to leave without any sort of notice. He also didn't want to abandon his brother Marco, who'd be left to live alone at the ranch. "You don't know just how lonely it is there, Josie. We get through it because we have one another. If I leave now, it wouldn't be fair to him. I'd be leaving him to clean up my mess. Our mess."

"I don't see how else we can make this work." I handed the *mate* gourd back to Gastón. "*Gracias.*" *I was done.*

Weeks passed before Gastón and I saw one another again. The honeymoon period was over. Thinking, conversing, drafting emails and writing letters and press releases in Spanish took me twice as long. Between the Saturdays I'd spend in the office playing catch up on work and Gastón's unpredictable travel schedule, we saw one another just once or twice a month. To top it off, more cattle continued to go missing. Something had to give.

Still, the days passed and I slowly began carving out my own life in the city. One Saturday towards the end of February, I unknowingly walked right into the *Carnaval de Buenos Aires*, an annual event that takes place on the streets at the end of February. I was walking on *Avenida Corrientes* from the bus stop to the office, when all of a sudden, passersby were doused with buckets of water poured liberally from jokesters in apartments above. Surprisingly, most people were good-natured and began dispersing, drenched but laughing. I was lucky to be spared—barely. Later that day, over a couple of Quilmes beers with work friends, I learned that water bombs and *carnaval* went hand in hand.

Before I knew it, colorful, intricately decorated chocolate eggs began appearing in shop windows, each one bigger and more beautiful than the next. *Semana Santa,* or Holy Week, was right around the corner. Gastón and I would finally have five days to ourselves. I envisioned us traveling four hours south to the shore or renting a hotel room in Buenos Aires to have some mindless downtime together, ideally in a hotel that had cable with English channels. But Gastón had other plans in mind for us. He wanted to spend the long Easter weekend with his friends at a cabin in the mountains in Córdoba. It meant less travel for him and would give me a chance to explore Córdoba's legendary foothills. I was hesitant to go, but he had recently traveled all the way to Miami and Pittsburgh for me. I'd later found out that that was Gastón's first time out of the country, with the exception of a trip to Rio de Janeiro with his family as a child. How could I refuse him?

"Okay, but you have to promise me we'll visit La Cumbrecita tucked in the hills outside of Córdoba. Everyone at work keeps telling me it's the cutest little German town with the best teahouses. Apparently, we have to try their *raspberry empanadas* that taste like homemade Pop-Tarts."

"Like what? A Pop-Tart?"

"You don't know what a Pop-Tart is, do you?" *Of course he didn't.*

* * *

La Cumbrecita, complete with its fairytale wood-beamed Alpine cottages, hand-painted decorations and flower boxes overflowing with red blooms, didn't fail to deliver. Neither did the picturesque views and raspberry *empanadas*, which were way better than any Pop-Tart I'd ever tasted. But the rest of the long weekend fell short. I felt terribly out of place. We were with Gastón's best friends, but I couldn't seem to find common ground with the women. From the moment we got there, it seemed the men went one way and the women another. Except for the Easter lamb the men planned on grilling, the women mostly gathered in the kitchen preparing dinner, swapping stories and stealing sips of wine, but I couldn't seem to infiltrate their circle. What I really needed was something to occupy me so I could naturally ease into their conversations. One of the women who'd just finished her residency in gynecology finally engaged me in conversation as she chopped butter lettuce for an *ensalada mixta*, complete with sliced onion and tomato wedges.

"How do you get together with friends back home, Josie? What do you all do for dinner? Meet up at your neighborhood

McDonald's before hitting the bars?" She glanced around, laughing with the rest of the women, before turning her attention back to the salad.

I was so taken aback, I didn't even know how to respond. I'm sure they saw what I wasn't saying written all over my face. *If you'd just hand me a knife, I'll show you the woman my grandma and mom brought me up to be.* Extremely offended by her sheer ignorance and the utter disdain some Argentines seemed to have for *Yanquis* like me, I was tempted to shoot some ignorant questions right back at her. *Now that we're on the topic, why do you Argentines insist on eating so late at night? Personally, I find it's making me gain weight. Or how are so many Argentine women so damn skinny when you all appear to live off of red meat, carbs, caffeine and sugar? Not to mention the Malbec.* Food staples in Argentina are *medialunas*, pasta, *ñoqui* (gnocchi), *bistecs, dulce de leche, helado* (gelato), *choripán* and copious quantities of Malbec. Yet, no exaggeration, my US size four jeans were the equivalent to a size large in Argentina (and, honestly, that was with me sucking in and jumping up and down to try to button them).

I took a sip of wine and got up to leave the room. "I actually prefer Burger King to Mickey D's. The BK Big Fish Sandwich is my Friday night go-to. My *abuela* Dorita got me hooked on it." (I'd always loved that my *abuela*, a homemaker in every sense of the word, who had cooked from scratch almost every one of the meals she and my grandpa had shared over the past fifty-plus years, couldn't resist a BK fried fish sandwich with tartar sauce and lettuce on a sesame seed bun.) I grabbed an uncorked bottle of Malbec and wine opener. "Now if you ladies will excuse me, the trip seems to be catching up with me. I think I'm going to skip dinner tonight." I left the room before I could read any of their faces.

Gastón later came to convince me to join them at the table. "What happened? The girls said you seemed off. Rambling something about someone named Mickey D."

I rolled my eyes. Of course my sarcasm fell on deaf ears. "I need some downtime. They're lovely. I'm sure it's me. I'm just not feeling myself, at all. I haven't in weeks. Right now, all I need is this book I'm reading and this bottle of Malbec."

"That's all you need?" Gastón regarded me with a raised eyebrow. "Apparently."

As he went to leave, Gastón turned to ask if I was on my period. I was. Her Royal *Princesa* was. "But don't you dare blame this on hormones," I said to him. "I've been begging you for an entire weekend to ourselves." Other than the fact that my period had put a hamper on our plans to finally sleep together, after all of these months and miles traveled, we'd barely had a moment alone. I would make sure to be on my best behavior the rest of the weekend, but the tension between me and Gastón was slowly mounting.

On Easter Sunday, Gastón and I cut *sobremesa* short. He left me at the bus terminal to catch my *coche cama* bus back to Buenos Aires before starting his four-hour trip back to La Santa Elena. There was no letter this time. As he kissed me goodbye, he didn't entrust any more of his organs to me. Instead he said, "Let's try to see each other next weekend so we can reset."

"Reset? That'll do it? You have no idea how hard this move's been on me without you. Finally, we get five days together and you ignore me completely, leaving me to hang out with a group of women I've met maybe once." I crossed my arms over my chest. "But this isn't about them. In time I know we'd bond. It's about us."

"I wanted you to get to know my friends. Is that so bad?" Gastón threw up his hands in frustration.

"No. Not if we'd done it together. Instead you throw me in a room with a bunch of women who've known each other for years while you were off with the boys. What is this boy-girl thing, anyway?" I didn't give him a chance to respond. "And given how long we've been apart, I don't understand why we didn't carve time out to be alone. It's been almost four months since I moved. For you. When are you going to tell my parents you're leaving? Are you? Are you looking for jobs in Buenos Aires or La Plata?" Again, I didn't give him a chance to respond. I kissed him goodbye and boarded the double-decker bus.

Unfortunately it wasn't only our heated goodbye that left me feeling uneasy; my seat on the upper deck seemed to sway back and forth during the bumpy ride. I finally drifted off only to be jarred awake as the bus came to an immediate stop. Outside my window was sheer commotion. A two-trailer cattle truck had collided with a jackknifed big rig, spilling frantic, wayward cows all over the highway, along with bovine limbs and decapitated carcasses. The sheer chaos of the cryptic scene was all too much of a reminder that I was feeling out of control—at work, with my parents, with Gastón. Our trip was delayed for hours, which meant I'd have to head straight into work from the bus terminal. It was not the best way to end my first *Semana Santa* in Argentina.

Later that week, one night at *sobremesa*, Dorita informed me she'd be returning to Miami Beach with Mom after her upcoming visit to the ranches, which meant I'd soon be homeless, again. I hadn't spoken with my parents in nearly four months, and it was time to rally the courage to do so. I no longer cared what they were saying about Gastón back at La Santa Elena. That was his problem to deal with. He elected to continue his employment on the ranch, which meant it was up to him, and him alone, to solve.

* * *

Mom and I slid back into our mother-daughter relationship the moment she arrived in La Plata. We did as us Caminos do and brushed our grievances under the table linens Mom collected throughout her travels. Even though I tried to broach the subject a couple of times, Mom made it clear there was no need to continue to hash it out or dissect leftover crumbs. There would be no explanations. Sorry didn't come easy in my family, for me included. I left it as simply as I could. "He's the man I'm going to marry, Mom."

Mom took a sip of Chardonnay, looking at me over the rim of her glass. "I know. I knew from the moment you told me you were dating. He's the man for you. I see that now," she said in an uncharacteristically soft, resigned tone. "But before believing it, I needed to know that you were willing to see it through."

"So you did know? Cati told you, didn't she?"

Mom skirted the question altogether. "Come, come with me."

After having heard the entirety of my belongings had been stolen in the move, Mom had begun collecting work clothes and suits during her weekly TJ Maxx runs. She showed up with a suitcase full for me and announced that I was welcome to move back into the apartment. She and Dad decided that as long as I paid for the utilities, I could stay as long as needed, on one condition: that I didn't have any men there. She didn't say Gastón's name, but she didn't have to.

The following weekend I moved out of Dorita's place, kissing her goodbye and wishing her a safe trip to the States. We'd come to really enjoy one another's company, from eating breakfast each morning to falling asleep together. She knew how in love with Gastón I was. And while she was ecstatic that he was Argentine and had brought me back home to her, Dorita was torn between her excitement and the rift it had caused with my parents.

Meanwhile, Dad's younger sister, my *tía* Ángela, phoned me my first night back at the apartment. After losing her twin sister, Lucia, to meningitis at just sixteen, Ángela decided to devote her life to the church and, against my grandparents' wishes, entered the sisterhood. But Ángela defied all preconceived notions of how a nun should behave. She wore street clothes and loved food—eating *and* cooking it. And like many, Ángela had to fight back temptations to overindulge in it. She cooked for her fellow sisters on Fridays and Sundays, often choosing a fish dinner or *milanesas*. She loved to ride her bike around La Plata and was a fiercely competitive chess player. She taught kindergarteners her winning chess moves, but wore her heart on her sleeve, allowing those who needed a win to claim it, free and clear. Up until I met Gastón, she was the funniest person I knew.

That day, Ángela told me that Dad had called her to see if she could check on my every move once in a while, making sure Gastón didn't come to the apartment.

"Now Josie, you know I'm rooting for you and Gastón, but I can't lie to your father," she said to me over the phone one day. "I've taken an oath, and my older brother is depending on me to keep you celibate." She laughed into the receiver. "So, I want you to speak to every person who works in your apartment building. Even the boy who washes cars on weekends. Get them on your side. Have Gastón charm their pants off. Explain to them that you're relying on their discretion when it comes to sharing with your parents who comes in and out of the apartment. And whatever you do, don't tell me anything. ¿*Capiche*?"

"*Claro, Tía.* I hear you loud and clear. Thanks for the heads up."

"Great. Now that we have that out of the way, tell me everything about Gastón, and don't leave anything out. I've always prayed that one of you girls would come back to us."

I told Ángela most everything. How Gastón was the first man I ever felt I could be exactly myself with—on the good days, the ugly days and everything in between. There was no pretending. No covering up a mood. That he penned me love letters every week. *Up until recently.* That he was passionate and had no tolerance for gossip. That he went to Mass with me on Sundays, even though I knew he didn't usually go and didn't want to. I told Ángela that he drove me to the cemetery to visit *Abuelo* Alfredo's grave. That he'd wait, patiently, as I sat there telling my grandpa this and that about my move to Argentina. I told her how he loved to cook. That Gastón always made sure to serve me first and reserved the best cut of meat or most generous portion for me. That he opened my car door every time. No man had ever done that for me, except maybe for prom. That other than Dad, he was the best storyteller I'd ever known. He could work a room like no one I'd ever met, talking enough for the two of us. He read papers from all over the world late at night and then again at breakfast. He opened my eyes to a new way of thinking. And I loved that about him.

"Oh, and he's funny, *Tía*," I added. "Really quick on his feet. Sometimes I can't believe the things that come out of his mouth. He makes me laugh like no one ever has." I made sure to leave out the part that Gastón would be arriving the following day to spend the weekend with me in Buenos Aires.

It had been almost two weeks since Gastón and I had last seen one another. Things still seemed tense since our trip to Córdoba. I couldn't help but feel he wasn't empathetic about how overwhelmed I'd felt those past months. And I simply couldn't understand why he continued to work at the ranch when he knew the rumors swirling around—lies that were created by some of the staff for the sole purpose of breaking us up.

That Sunday, after an *asado* at Gastón's parents' home, we planned on having loose-leaf *mate* with his friends before heading back to Buenos Aires for a night full of romance.

Things between us seemed to be getting back to normal as we pulled into the local Walmart to pick up a tray of *facturas*, although Gastón seemed more and more stressed about work, my parents and Santa Elena. Then out of nowhere, the conversation went from the brand of *yerba mate* we planned on buying to the fact that Mom hadn't once mentioned our relationship while she was at the ranch.

"I don't need you to fight my battles," he said. "But I need to know you're on my side."

"Fight your battles? Let's not forget my parents kicked me to the curb these past four months because I fought for us. Not you. Not me. Us. In a different country." And that's when I gave him the ultimatum: the ranch or me. Make a choice.

Plus, I'd found myself becoming more and more insecure and began obsessively questioning why we hadn't consummated our relationship. I had at first found his desire to take things slow endearing, but now I mistook it as him not being attracted to me. *Where was this womanizer who sowed his leaves left and right that I was warned so profusely about? Was he just a tease who, as they say in Argentina,* "Calienta la pava pero no ceba los mates"—*prepares the* mate *but doesn't drink from it? Were his needs somehow being met elsewhere?*

My insecurities got the best of me. "What, Gastón? Am I not as attractive as the Argentine women you're so used to conquering? Is that it?"

"When *carajo* are you going to realize that *you are Argentine*, Josie?! Hell, we were born in the same hospital down the street!" He walked ahead of me as we left the store. Instead of opening my car door as usual, Gastón grabbed the tray of *facturas* from my hand and headed directly to the driver side and got into the car. His long legs ate the distance in just a couple of steps.

I stood, stunned. *That's unlike him.* So was what happened next. Gastón started the car and took off without me, leaving me stranded at the Walmart. I waited in the parking lot for ten minutes, John

Travolta's "Stranded at the Drive-In" from *Grease* playing in my head. I was sure he was bluffing. But he wasn't. Gastón never came back. I went back into the store and bought myself another dozen *facturas,* all of them spilling with *dulce de leche,* and flagged down a cab to take me back to Buenos Aires.

Seventy pesos and an hour later, I arrived at the apartment. I'd managed to down a half-dozen brazen pastries during that cab ride home—*cañoncitos* (little cannons) puff-pastry cones filled with *dulce de leche,* profiteroles *bombas* (bombs) also filled with *dulce de leche, vigilantes* in the shape of police batons filled with pastry cream, *sacramentos* (sacraments) pillows filled with what else but *dulce de leche, crema pastelera* and *dulce de leche*-laden sugar-topped fritters called *bolas de fraile* (friar's balls) or, in honor of *Tía* Ángela, *suspiros de monja* (nun's sighs). I'd recently learned that *bolas de fraile* and *suspiros de monja* were one in the same—their names interchangeable for a nun's full-frontal gasps and sighs upon coming face to face with a cloaked brother's balls, in all of their naked glory. Edible therapy at its best.

Ridden with Catholic guilt, I threw the remaining *facturas* away as I entered the apartment. It was awful to be forced to fight in a second language. I'd lost my edge in Spanish. Never in my life had I been left in a parking lot of any sort, let alone an hour away from home. Not to mention in a foreign country. And Gastón thought *I* had a bad temper? Talk about the pot calling the kettle black!

Weeks passed. Gastón didn't call, and neither did I. Instead, I spent my time getting lost among Buenos Aires' graceful homes, colonial buildings with turn-of-the-century French and Spanish styles dispersed among high-rises flanking treelined boulevards, regal avenues and narrow streets. I visited the city's fountains and parks, from the Japanese Gardens to the Bosque de Palermo, patterned after Paris's Bois de Boulogne, complete with riding stables, a boat pond, gardens, tennis courts and seemingly endless paths. I visited museum after museum, followed by handfuls of unpretentious eating halls with white tablecloths that each claimed to have the best *milanesas* in town. On Sundays I dedicated my hours to visiting the city's various outdoor markets in search of artisanal treasures, from the Feria de San Telmo to the artisanal fair in Palermo viejo to the Feria de Recoleta. There were too many to hit all at once.

One Sunday, after checking out the fair, I made my way through the labyrinthine Recoleta Cemetery next door that held no less than 6,400 graves. In the heart of Buenos Aires, La Recoleta is built as if it's a city within itself, with main walkways splitting into smaller arterial paths that lead visitors around city blocks lined with grandiose mausoleums in every state of repair and disrepair, some resembling Gothic chapels, others Greek temples, fairytale grottoes and elegant little houses. One in particular stuck out at me, a huge pantheon smack dab in the center of the cemetery that was home to Luis Federico Leloir, a doctor and biochemist who became the first Spanish-speaking scientist to win the Nobel Prize in Chemistry. Still, according to Mom, inventing *salsa golf*—Argentina's ubiquitous dipping sauce that Mom religiously ate with *palmitos*—was among Leloir's greatest accomplishments.

As I walked among this place where the dead far outnumbered the living, one thing was clear—drama lived on. And not just about La Recoleta's most sought after resident—Evita Perón. Her embalmed corpse took an unpredictably strange journey that reads almost fictional before being laid to rest among Argentina's elite. Upon her death, Evita's body was laid in state in her former office for two years, until a military coup deposed her husband, leaving her remains to the whims of a new government. A military decree ordered Evita's body to be done away with, in the hopes the Argentine people would forget her. Evita disappeared from the world for sixteen years before it was revealed that she'd been secretly buried in Milan, Italy under a false name. Her damaged corpse, exhumed in 1971, flew to Spain where it spent a few years in exiled General Juan Perón's dining room. Apparently her former husband wanted to make sure Evita always had a place at his table. When Perón and his third wife Isabelita returned to Argentina to become president—again—and vice president, respectively, Evita's body stayed behind in Spain until Perón died in office in 1974. Isabelita, newly crowned president of the Republic of Argentina, had Evita flown back to Argentina to be with her dead husband. Only then did the Argentine government finally place Evita alongside her family in La Recoleta, a full twenty-two years after her passing. Evita lives on, more than sixteen feet underground, in a crypt fortified like a nuclear bunker, so that no one should ever again be able to disturb the remains of Argentina's mythical First Lady. Body or no body, the personal notes jammed into the door of Evita's tomb, alongside fresh bouquets of roses and carnations, were testimony that the Argentine people never forgot her. They never will.

Who needed TV—this place was a real-life telenovela. I came across the tomb of Rufina Cambaceres, who was laid to rest at just nineteen in a mausoleum adorned with a marble statue of her walking out of its door. Rufina's mother had her hand purposefully sculpted around the door's latch so the young girl never felt trapped again. Story has it, Rufina suffered from a type of epilepsy that could render her unconscious for hours at a time. On an evening in 1902, while preparing to go to the Teatro Colón with her mother, Rufina had a seizure. Many hours later, not one, but two doctors confirmed she had finally died. Rufina was laid to rest in La Recoleta. That's when the true nightmare began. She woke up. Scratching and clawing inside her tomb for days, she was discovered too late by the groundskeeper who'd noticed her coffin was out of place. The cemetery staff discovered her tortured body having endured a living entombment. Rufina had died twice.

Like its walking paths, La Recoleta's ghost stories went on and on—among them the ghost of a caretaker who never left, his keys still rattling as daylight succumbs to dusk. Luz María García Velloso, daughter of the playwright Enrique García Velloso, who died from leukemia at the age of fifteen in 1925, is another popular resident. While her tomb was decorated with a statue of a young girl restfully sleeping on her bed, Luz María apparently frequented the corner of Vicente López and Azcuénaga (where the cemetery is located) dressed in a beautiful white gown. Each night she'd seduce one lucky young man with her beautiful looks and long, blonde locks. Legend has it the young men often invited her for a walk or a coffee before enjoying a night of romance. After meeting them, the lady in white, as they called her, would say she felt cold, and the men would kindly offer her their coats. She'd then accidentally spill something on the coat and promise to return it the next time they met. When the men arrived at her home to retrieve it, they were informed by her mother that Luz María had died long ago. They'd run to the cemetery to see if it was true and find her tomb there along with the stained coat. The men realized then that they'd been with a ghost. It's said, to this day, local *porteños* living in Buenos Aires' capital city avoid picking up girls at that very street corner. Talk about death imitating art.

Another weekend, after deciding to rejoin the living, I found myself window shopping on Calle Florida, Buenos Aires' open-air pedestrian mall, when the cookbook *Repostería Argentina* called out to me from behind El Ateneo bookstore's display case. I took it home and started baking up a storm—from a *dulce de leche pionono* sponge roll, to a cappuccino cheesecake, to molding elaborate chocolate ribbons.

I left my most valiant attempt for last, the elaborate *corona de reina*—a stunning banana cream ice box pie named after the Queen's crown, due to its form and majesty. I was certain that Dorita had taught me everything I needed to know to take it on. I meticulously followed the recipe, step by step: I pressed the chilled shortcrust pastry dough evenly onto the bottom and sides of the springform pan; baked it in a 350°F pre-heated oven for ten minutes; removed the pan from the oven and with the back of a fork pressed the sides of the tender dough upwards, creating a "queen's crown." After returning the pan to the oven for another five minutes, I repeated the same steps another two times. As the crust rested, I creamed the bananas until smooth, and carefully folded the purée with fresh whipped cream. Hours later, after turning out the filling into the crust and patiently allowing it to set in the freezer, I carefully unmolded the deep-dish crown in all its majestic glory. Yet, just as I thought I was out of the woods, successfully completing the precarious transfer between the springform pan to the pie plate, the *tarta* settled and the crown cracked. Even after the most careful handling, it didn't turn out as the shiny cookbook photo promised.

I knew a thing or two about broken promises. I'd thought I was—in his own words—Gastón's *reina. How could we be over? Just like that?* I got vanilla ice cream out of the freezer and topped my crumbly crust with a generous scoop, because—let's be honest—even bad pie is good.

* * *

Like Gastón, the city of Buenos Aires had gotten under my skin and seeped into my soul. If I couldn't be with him, a day spent wandering the city streets came second best. It was my chance to finally get to know it; to get to know myself. I decided if things didn't work out between us, I'd stay anyway. Living there had awoken something in me I didn't want to let go. Not yet. Still, I couldn't believe Gastón hadn't called. He was the one who left me stranded at the Walmart. I wouldn't, couldn't, be the first to reach out.

Even though we were nearing the tail end of April, Buenos Aires was experiencing a random four-day streak of miserable high temps and humidity. The air was thick and sticky. Summer was giving fall push back. By the fifth day, the whole Río de La Plata seemed to be evaporated in an intense blanket of fog. I'd decided to walk the twenty blocks home from the office that evening. As I walked, I couldn't help but sense I was being followed. The hairs on the back of my neck told me so. But I didn't notice anything or anyone out of the ordinary whenever I'd quickly look over my shoulder. Still, I couldn't shake the feeling and turned into a hair salon I'd been eyeing for weeks now. I was tired of my hair sticking to the back of my neck.

"Cut it all off," I told the girl behind my chair. "Like a pixie cut. You know, like the actresses Mia Farrow or Winona Ryder?"

The problem was, I looked nothing like either. Neither did my jaw line or hair. I found out it was much thicker and not so easy to rock a short cut. The hairdresser tried talking me out of it, suggesting I go halfway with a chin-length bob, but I was suddenly in need of a drastic hair exorcism. I don't know if I'd felt I'd been hiding behind my locks, but cutting my hair was an important step in cutting away the past. It was part of me becoming more comfortable with who I was at the time. The hairdresser braided my hair before cutting off more than a foot of strands in one fell swoop. Now that it was short, my hair seemed two shades darker. As the hairdresser styled it, I didn't feel one way or another about it. I was almost numb and it was simply something I needed to do. I left the salon that evening lighter, a different person.

The final ten or so blocks home, I felt the stare of every man I passed on the back of my neck. I'd never realized how vulnerable short hair could make a person feel. It exposed things previously hidden: the port wine stain on the back of my hairline, the freckles across my shoulders, my American accent. I got home and, after convincing the doorman that it was me, uncorked a bottle of San Felipe red wine that I drank for dinner in front of the TV, watching reruns of *Friends*. I missed my hair already. It was all I could do to keep myself from calling Gastón. Instead I called my parents. After telling them I'd chopped my locks, Dad shared a pantyhose hack he'd used back in the day in medical school to slick back his short, thick black hair. So before heading to bed, I wrapped a control top pantyhose turban around my head to tame my new cut.

I was looking forward to sleeping in the following day, a Saturday. My ten-hour workdays were catching up with me. But a noise coming from the kitchen awoke me. No one else was supposed to be in the apartment.

I grabbed a high heel shoe, wishing I had my mom's handy kitchen axe, and slowly headed towards the clanking that sounded like pots banging. Heart racing, I imagined it might be my Gentleman Caller. But he didn't usually make such a ruckus. Still, I was pretty sure it was him who'd been following me the previous evening, even if I hadn't spotted him. Always the gentleman, he'd allowed me to have my hair cut in peace. But now, given the chance, I'd finally confront him.

As I peeked around the kitchen doorway, I froze.

There he was.

Gastón.

He was wearing his faded Levi's that sat snugly across his narrow hips and a clean, white T-shirt that clung to his broad shoulders. Fresh and confident. Wielding a spatula in front of the stovetop. The smell of eggs wafting over the kitchen reassured me that all was good again. *How'd he even get in?* I made a mental note to talk to the doormen. Gastón must have charmed his way up through the back-delivery door. Of course he did. Like his mom had said, "He could charm the pants off of anyone." Good thing I wasn't wearing any.

"Gastón? What are you doing?"

He turned to hug me. "*Mi amor*, did I wake you? I wanted to surprise you with breakfast in bed. I convinced Carlos downstairs to let me in through the service door in the back."

"Of course you did."

He put his hands on my shoulders and gave me a good look over with a quizzical look on his face. "What's this on your head?" He snapped the pantyhose against the back of my neck.

I'd completely forgotten I'd gone to bed with it on and ripped it off. I must've looked ridiculous. "I cut my hair."

"I see that. All of it. Who are you and what have you done with my *novia*?" The look on his face said it all. *Is this you or a pre-pubescent version of your younger brother Federico?*

"Girlfriend?" I asked, patting my hair in place, making sure nothing was sticking up. For a moment I'd almost forgotten I'd gotten it cut in the first place. *What was I thinking?* "I'm here, but I'm not so sure about the *novia* part anymore."

Gastón pulled me close to him, smoothing out my hair. "I love it. I love you. *Te quiero*. The hair's totally unexpected. But so what? It suits you."

"*You're* totally unexpected. You never called."

"Neither did you."

"I didn't hightail it out of Walmart without you."

Gastón frowned. "I know. What can I say to make things better? I'm so sorry. I know that doesn't cut it. I just got so angry I couldn't think straight. I needed to be alone to sort it out. We were on fast-forward. I had to hit the pause button to figure out how to get us off the collision course. But I can't explain it. I got a sudden urgency to see you yesterday. I felt as if you needed me more than ever."

I leaned back and looked at him. It was true, I'd had what seemed like a manic moment when I'd entered the hair salon. It's as if he felt that I'd decided to move on from my past—with or without him. "That's strange. Yesterday I finally decided I had to move on. I wasn't going to allow myself to get stuck—again." I brushed back my hair, signaling my drastic new hairstyle.

"It was the strangest thing, but I couldn't go another minute without seeing you. Even stranger, we lost Bacco yesterday."

"Bacco? Marco's lab? No." Tears gathered at the corner of my eyes. "I'm so sorry. What happened?"

"*Pobre*. He was just a pup. That son of a bitch López ran him over with this truck. He laughed nervously, saying it was an accident. But I don't think it was. He didn't even stop. Little Bacco died instantly. Marco was crushed."

"What are we going to do about Cati and López? They're poisonous."

"Nothing. We're done with them—I told them myself that I was on to them, that our families went way back and that I wouldn't let anything or anyone get between us. They got the point, loud and clear. After we buried Bacco, I jumped in the car and started driving to you. I'll never leave again. I promise. It's just that . . ."

"Just what?"

"You drive me fucking crazy. I can't live without you, but I also can't put up with you. We're going to have to figure this out."

I planted my face into Gastón's chest, wrapping my arms tightly around him. He smelled of soap and tobacco. Wearing only an old T-shirt and underwear, my legs started to give out from under me. Suddenly I felt weak, like I hadn't eaten in days. The bottle of wine I'd had for dinner the night before may have had something to do with it. "What are we going to do?"

Gastón cupped my cheek. "I'm going to keep you." His arms engulfed my entire body, as if it was the very oxygen he needed to breathe.

"I started thinking we might be over. I don't even know how to fight in Spanish, let alone make love in it."

"What are you talking about, Federico? I mean Josie?" Gastón's hazel eyes twinkled with mischief. "Yes, you do. In fact, you're quite good at fighting in Spanish. What's it your dad calls you? Little mean Josephine?" he joked, stroking the dimple in my right cheek that surfaced each time I smiled or laughed.

"So, breakfast in bed . . . what are we having?" I peeked over his shoulder.

"Now that you're up, instead of the breakfast in bed that you *Yanquis* love so much, how about a twist on your tradition? Breakfast then bed? That way we save ourselves the crumbs, the spills and the unseen drips."

"Can we reverse the order?"

He looked at me seriously. "We'll need our strength."

Gastón was making slow-cooked cheesy eggs scrambled with American cheese and a side of avocado, smashed with lemon juice, salt and pepper. He cooked the eggs over low heat with plenty of butter and cheese, stirring constantly until the mixture formed small, delicate curds bound in a velvety sauce.

"How'd you know I like cheesy scrambled eggs with avocado?"

"You told me once a while back. That your *mamá* cooks them nice and slow so they stay creamy. That you're a tough critic when it comes to scrambled eggs," he said, spooning them onto two slices of toasted white Bimbo sandwich bread.

"Mom is the queen of scrambled eggs. She makes them all the time." I took a bite. *God. His are even better than hers.* But I'd never dare tell Mom. I'd never tasted eggs so extravagantly creamy and rich. The fresh burst of citrusy avocado mash on top cut their richness perfectly. "You know, eggs for breakfast is utterly American. Most Argentines would be appalled."

"Not me," he said, taking a bite. "You know, when an Argentine makes you eggs before noon, it means they really love you." Gastón put down his fork. "I called your parents last night."

"Oh, yeah? Is Dad still calling you at four a.m.?"

"Of course he is. But we didn't talk about the ranch. We talked about you. About us."

"What?" I put down my fork. "Dear God. What made you do that?"

"I grabbed the ranch cell phone and called them from the car last night. Your mom and I spoke for over an hour. I talked to your dad, too, and let them both know that I was giving my three months' notice, that while I hated leaving my brother and the opportunity of running their ranches, I'd found the woman of my dreams who left everything for me. So it was time I did the same for her. I also told them I'd never stolen a cent from them, and if they were ever able to prove otherwise, I would stay away from you forever."

I just about choked on my eggs. "You know they never thought you were behind any of that?"

"I know. But I needed to set the record straight. With everyone."

"Wow. I need a moment." We both did. We sat in silence until I was able to gather my thoughts. "That was a mouthful. I honestly don't know what to say. I figured things with them would just blow over. It was getting better. You know, my first day back in Argentina, Dorita told me at *sobremesa* that plums don't become prunes in a day. That they take time, and they're worth the wait. We have time on our side."

"I couldn't take it anymore. I had to clear the air with your parents. Otherwise, the tension between us wouldn't go away. Plus, I don't like prunes."

"Prunes, huh? I thought you liked everything. I've never seen you turn anything down."

"Love plums. Hate prunes. And soup. It's for sick people."

Gastón leaned over the table to kiss me.

I broke away. "Maybe they were waiting for you to make a move. Maybe my parents needed to see you meet me halfway. Otherwise, why the change of heart? I talked to them last night, too. They were in a really good mood. No wonder Dad was so concerned about my hair. But they didn't mention anything about your call."

"I asked them to wait until we talked."

"But what will you do? Do you have any idea?"

"My dad and I have been talking about me joining him at Distribuidora Tolosa. He needs help with collections and managing the larger general contractor accounts."

"Is that what you want to do?"

SACRAMENTOS, BOLAS DE FRAILE Y SUSPIROS DE MONJA

"I want to be near you. I'm open to anything that will help me do that. And plus, it would give me a chance to reconnect to *Papá*. For us to get closer." Gastón grabbed my chair from underneath the table, pulling me in closer. His fingers slowly moved up my thighs. "I saved the best for last. Then there's the part when your Mom and Dad said *yes*."

"Yes? Yes to what?"

"To giving me their blessing to ask you to marry me." His smile, one edge higher than the other, was slow and sexy and filled with so many promises. All of which I believed he would keep, or at least do his best trying.

"But we haven't talked in weeks! And now you're talking marriage? Let's just savor where we are and not be in a hurry. You're the one who said we were on fast-forward."

"I did. But I'm okay with it. We just needed to be on the same page as your parents. It was getting between us."

"I agree. It's just sometimes I think things got so complicated between us because they moved too fast. Can we start with living in the same city? I can't wait for us to be in Buenos Aires together. To come home and have dinner together each night. To explore the city at night and on weekends. There's a new Broadway show on Corrientes I'd love to see—*Mi Bella Dama*—*My Fair Lady*. I've fallen in love all over again with this city."

Gastón's thick brows drew together. "You don't want to marry me?" His thumbs hooked the sides of my Caro Cuore cotton bikini underwear as if he was preparing for my answer.

I put my hands on his, squeezing them. They were calloused but comforting. Sliding my hips out from under his grip, I stood up and snatched the last bite of creamy eggs with *palta* on his plate before throwing my arms around him and settling into his lap. I loved how soft his T-shirt felt, like he'd washed it thousands of times. "You already know the answer. Come on, *Larry*." I tugged on his chin. "You've known from the beginning. Do you even have to ask? I just don't want to rush into things."

"I think it's too late for that." Gastón wound his arms around me. My stomach jumped nervously as he leaned over and, taking my thighs in his hands, began teasing me as he shook them, singing the popular but naughty *Ravana Flan* jingle that played over and over on TV commercials:

> ♪ *Si se mueve (if it jiggles) . . . flan flan*
> *. . . si se mueve (if it jiggles) . . . flan flan*
> *. . . es Ravana (it's Ravana), el más rico flaaaaan*
> *(the tastiest flan of all) . . .* ♪

"Stop," I slapped his hands away, laughing. For the first time in my life I wasn't self-conscious about my body with a man. If he liked *flan*, I could serve it up by the jiggly spoonful.

"Wait here," Gastón said, lifting me off him before quickly returning with a plate holding an avocado, lemon, salt and pepper and two spoons. "Open it," he said, handing me the avocado.

It was already split in two. Inside, Gastón had replaced the avocado pit with the white, metal twist-tie from the Bimbo sandwich bread bag.

"Your parents said yes. What about you? Can you put up with me for the rest of your life?" Gastón asked, wrapping the twist tie around my left ring finger.

"Are you asking me to marry you for real?" I was baffled. *Why was I asking so many questions? Shut up and say yes.*

"It's like you said: do I even have to ask?" Gastón looked into my eyes. "In these past months together, I've felt every emotion possible: love, hope, exhilaration, and at times you've made me so fucking mad that I had to leave you stranded in a Walmart parking lot. You drive me crazy . . . for better and for worse. For the first time in my life I can't stop thinking about starting the rest of my life with someone. You even got me to start donating my organs, something I'd never even considered before meeting you. I've already given you my heart. It's all yours. Now, with this twist-tie, I give you my stomach—that is, if I haven't already given it to you. I can't remember at this point. But if you say yes, feed it well. And remember, to thrive, it requires *asado* at least once a week."

Our eyes locked. For a moment, I had no words.

"Is that a yes?"

"Yes, of course," I wrapped my arms around him tight. "Yes! But on one condition."

"What's that?"

"That we move back to the States. Not now. Not forever. But before we start a family. I want you to know the rest of me. If we never live there, you'll never fully know me. All of me. Plus, I have to see my dog Sonny. I miss her terribly."

"If I have to move to be with you, then the answer's yes. I'll do whatever it takes for us to be together."

"Okay, and one more thing: *asado* is the one thing I don't do. I can never figure out if the meat is done without cutting into it. And I know for you Argentine men that's sacrilege."

"It's all in the touch. You just have to know how to gently finger grilled beef." Gastón placed his index finger over my mouth, slowly, barely outlining my lips. "And the sensation should be the same as when you touch this point here between your lips and nose." His finger landed on my cupid's bow, lightly pulsating it. "*Esto es jugoso*. This is rare." He traced my mouth again, stopping on the indentation just below my lip and above my chin. "*Esto es a punto*. This is medium. And this here," his finger slowly pushed down on the tip of my nose, "*Esto es bien hecho*. This is well-done." My entire body tingled. "But skilled grill masters generally stay in this area." Gastón slowly kissed me.

Caught up in my own personal *asado* lesson, I'd almost forgotten to breathe. "How about you take care of the grill, while I take care of the rest?"

"Deal. By the way, who's Neiman Marcus? Your mom said you can't live without him."

"Oh God. The things that come out of her mouth. She's just trying to scare you off."

"She said I should know what I'm getting myself into. She also insisted you'd want an engagement ring. Is that right? You know, we don't use them here."

"I did grow up with the fairytale of a man kneeling before me, surprising me with a beautiful promise ring. But this'll do," I played with my twist tie wrapping my ring finger.

Gastón drew me into his arms, scooped me up and took me to the bedroom. I held onto his flexed bicep. He whispered into my ear, "*Mi casa es tu casa*."

"This is my parents' place."

"I mean I'm your home. And you're mine. There's no more 'back in Pittsburgh' or 'here in Argentina we do it this way.' There's just us. From now on, we're home."

Gastón laid me onto the bed. My toes curled in anticipation as I felt the force of his weight descend upon me. I pulled him in even closer. "Don't stop."

"Not this time. Not ever again."

There he was. There we were. Together in Spanglish. Finally.

* * *

Later that year, on my twenty-sixth birthday, Gastón asked me to marry him. Again. American style. We were at our favorite restaurant, La Parolaccia Del Mare in Puerto Madero. I ordered the black squid ravioli *neri* stuffed with salmon in a light cream sauce sprinkled with caviar. As I took my first bite, three violinists appeared at our table, playing Luis Miguel's *Bolero*, "*Por Debajo de la Mesa*" ("Underneath the Table"). It told the story of the way we fell in love. It was our song.

Caught up in the moment, I was oblivious to what was going on until our waiter, dressed in a pristinely pressed white shirt and black pants, brought an ice bucket with a bottle of chilled Chandon champagne. Gastón leaned into me, scooting his chair closer to mine until our feet touched and our legs tucked into one another. Underneath the table, he took my hands, intertwining his fingers in mine. He slowly slipped a diamond engagement ring on my left ring finger, whispering softly, "Josefina Ursula Caminos, will you marry me?"

I did. Five months later, on May 24, 2000, we were pronounced *Señor* and *Señora* Oría in a civil registry office in City Bell, Argentina. While our church date wasn't until later in October, we secretly wed in Argentina to begin Gastón's INS immigration papers. Word on the street was that Argentina was headed full throttle towards an economic collapse. That's when we decided it might be a good time to consider moving back to the States.

I'd gotten a job offer in Miami as the online financial editor with the Argentine financial tech company Dineronet.com that started the first of July. With just a month and a half notice, the only option to enter the US with Gastón's papers intact was to marry. I told Mom and Dad they didn't need to bother to come to the ceremony. That it wasn't our real wedding. But they surprised me and showed up like clockwork a couple of days before.

"The thing is, Josie." Mom kissed and hugged me hello. "It may not be in front of God, but *this is the real wedding*. The one that counts. Once you say, 'I do,' there's no turning back. And I'm not going to miss my baby girl getting married. Even in front of a justice of the peace. Now, grab your coat. We're going shopping for a wedding dress."

Who am I to say no?

Our Argentine wedding celebration was perfect. Just the way we wanted. We invited thirty of our closest family members to Oliva restaurant on Camino Centenario and drank copious amounts of wine as we lunched on *milanesas* with lots of lemon—the first meal Gastón and I had ever shared together at a roadside Esso gas station. *Sobremesa* was even better, as our parents, a little boozy, shared their childhood memories of growing up together, spilling secrets parents don't usually divulge to their children until they're adults themselves.

Toast after toast was made. I looked down at the end of the table and saw our grandmothers, Dorita and Helsa, sitting together, engulfed in some sort of juicy conversation. Mom, Dad, Jorge Luis and Graciela were on the other side, reminiscing. Laughing. One-upping one another with stories. Gastón and I were in the middle of these two generations and on the cusp of starting our new life together—one that would make up the third generation of the Caminos-Oría story.

As we made our way back to the apartment in Buenos Aires that evening, bellies and souls full, Dad looked at Mom as the elevator doors opened onto our foyer. "Poupi, where is Gastón sleeping? Since, like Josie said, this wasn't the real wedding, they should wait until the church ceremony to sleep in the same room."

"Don't worry. I made up Federico's room in the back." Mom answered.

Gastón and I looked at one another, laughing under our breaths. There we stood. Husband and wife. In the middle of an immigration process, preparing to pack our things to make a transcontinental life together in Miami. All that, and Dad was concerned we needed to sleep in separate rooms. But we didn't care. We'd come this far. We could wait another five months before pushing our beds together. The following day we headed to La Santa Elena for our fake honeymoon with my parents. It was where we fell in love and the ideal place to start our first day as Mr. and Mrs.

Mom made sure to call ahead and ask Cati and Maribel to set an extra place at the table. "And, Cati," Mom said over the phone as she winked at me, "Have a young *novillo* slaughtered so you can prepare the finest cuts of meat—medium rare—for the newest member of the family, our son-in-law, Gastón."

* * *

Five months later, on October 28, 2000, Gastón and I said "I do" all over again in front of a hundred and fifty or so family and friends in Miami Beach's St. Patrick Catholic Church. Dad and I pulled up in a white Rolls Royce Phantom as the sun was putting herself to bed. Dad got out and rounded the car before opening my door. Clad in black tails, he crouched down, extending his hand to help me from the car. As I put mine in his, he stopped and looked around. Then, without taking his eyes off mine, he whispered, "*Hija*, I can get right back in that car with you if you're not one hundred percent sure. And we can ride off into the sunset."

Never mind I am already Mrs. Oría on paper. But I appreciated Dad's fatherly sentiment. It meant the world to me. Because of him, I'd escaped my life in Pittsburgh at twenty-four and returned to the home I never knew: Argentina. What I didn't know at the time was that I wasn't fleeing my life but running towards it, into the arms of the man I was meant to share it with.

Arm in arm, Dad and I climbed St. Patrick's sweeping steps towards the towering entry doors. They'd been closed to make sure we made a grand entrance. A wave of raw emotion swept over me as we stood anxiously awaiting to enter. There was no one else there but us, as far as I could tell. But in the instant my sister and matron of honor, Laura, swept open the doors, a blur of movement flashed to my left near the top of the stair railing, just under the lamppost.

I could see all I needed from the corner of my eye: a figure standing by the stair's edge. He was some thirty feet away, close enough for me to notice his silver beard and herringbone cap. He stood there with his hands tucked away in his pockets, a posture strikingly familiar to my Gentleman Caller's. *Had I willed him there?* I knew I wasn't imagining him. I could feel him. I could sense him as plainly as the beating of my heart.

"You ready, Josie?" Laura asked, holding her bouquet in front of her growing eight-month pregnant belly.

Dad gave my arm a squeeze. "You know, you're the only one of your sisters who didn't cry as I was about to give her away."

I squeezed him back. "I'm happy, Dad. Really happy. I've never been more sure of anything."

Dad adjusted his square-rimmed glasses. "Then *vamos, hija.* Let's not keep Gastón waiting any longer."

I looked back one last time from behind my wedding veil just before entering the church. My Gentleman Caller dropped his gaze and nodded, motioning for me to head in. "*Bendiciones, Josefina.*" He silently gave me his blessing.

Reverend Alberto Cutie, known as *Padre* Oprah to fans of his television program and bestselling book, *Real Life, Real Love*, officiated the ceremony. The congregation loved this man. Nine years later, the charismatic Cuban-American priest left the Catholic Church after the Spanish-language magazine, *TV Notas*, scooped photos of him kissing a woman on the beach. Mom was the first to see the salacious images on CNN as she sat in the kitchen one morning eating *palmitos* straight from the jar. From that moment on, she always joked our marriage was obsolete.

Now, twenty years later, Gastón and I still celebrate both anniversaries.

One in *Castellano*. One in English.

Both in Spanglish.

Tarta pascualina (Spinach and Egg Easter Pie)

SERVES 7. *But go ahead and double the recipe if you're so down in the dumps the only place you can go is up.*

Tarta pascualina is traditionally associated with the Easter holiday for several reasons. First and foremost, it's a meatless Friday favorite during Lent since most versions are vegetarian. But true to our carnivorous ways, my family, as many do in Argentina, incorporates a can of *pâté* to add an extra depth of flavor to the filling. When she didn't have *pâté* on hand, *Abuela* Dorita would substitute with two beef bouillon cubes. Feel free to omit both altogether if you've given up meat or simply don't prefer it. In addition, the thirty-three layers of phyllo dough required in the original, age-old recipe are representative of the passion of Christ. Not all *pascualina* recipes require phyllo dough. I personally prefer a drier short-crust pastry instead. In fact, I often take a shortcut and use pre-made *La Salteña* tarta shells.

Feel free to modify this recipe as you see fit, or according to the ingredients you have in the fridge at the time. You can substitute the Swiss chard for spinach if that's your preference. Some also add red peppers. The cheeses can vary as well. Some add mozzarella in addition to parmesan and ricotta. Finally, the cooking mode varies from one recipe to the other. In some recipes, like my version below, the eggs are placed raw into wells in the stuffing, and they bake together with the rest of the preparation. In others, the eggs are hard-boiled before cooking.

DOUGH

2 cups **water**

1½ tablespoons **salt**

3½ tablespoons **pork fat**, or high-quality lard cut into pieces

6 to 7 cups all-purpose **flour**

1 raw **egg yolk**, lightly beaten with water

Or 2 prepared **pastry sheets** for double-crust pie (top and bottom)

FILLING

3 tablespoons **unsalted butter**

2 tablespoons extra-virgin **olive oil**

3 large **onions**, chopped

3 cloves **garlic**

4 large bunches **Swiss chard**

3.5 ounces *pâté de foie*

2½ cups freshly grated **Parmesan**

1 cup whole milk **ricotta cheese**

Salt and freshly ground **black pepper** to taste

Freshly ground **nutmeg**

9 **eggs**

Make the dough. Place water and salt in a small saucepan and bring to boil over high heat. Add the pork fat and stir until it melts. Transfer to a large wide bowl. Allow to cool to room temperature.

Gradually add 5 ½ to 6 cups of the flour, mixing with your hands, until the dough forms a ball. Generously sprinkle flour on a work surface to prevent dough from sticking. Knead the dough, adding more flour until it will not absorb any more. The dough should be on the drier side. Divide the dough in thirds and form into three discs, wrapping them in plastic. Refrigerate and chill for at least 1 hour or up to 24 hours.

Make the filling. Melt 2 tablespoons butter with the olive oil in a large skillet over medium-low heat. Add onions and sauté slowly until soft and translucent, about 15 minutes. Add garlic for last couple of minutes, making sure not to burn. Transfer to a large bowl. Set aside.

Trim bottoms of Swiss chard and carefully wash. Trim stems from the leaves and roughly chop. Reserve the leaves and the chopped stems separately.

Bring a large pot of water to boil. Blanch the chard stems in boiling water for 2–3 minutes, until tender. Add the leaves and blanch one more minute until wilted. Drain in a colander. Squeeze the chard dry. Roughly chop the stems and leaves together, squeezing again in a clean cheese cloth to remove the water.

Combine chard with the sautéed onions and garlic, mixing well. Beat in 2 eggs, one at a time. Stir in pâte, Parmesan and ricotta. Season well with salt, pepper and nutmeg. Cover with plastic wrap and set aside in refrigerator.

Put the pie together. Preheat oven to 375°F. Grease a round cookie sheet or shallow baking pan. Roll one dough round into a circle to the length of the pan. Brush lightly with olive oil. Roll out the second piece of dough and lay it over the first so that the bottom of the pan is lined with two layers. Press the dough into the bottom corners of the pan all the way around.

Spoon the chard filling evenly over the dough, smoothing it with a spatula. Make seven equally spaced wells in the filling and carefully add an egg to each.

Roll out the third dough round and lay over top of the filling (or use strips to cover in a crisscross pattern). Pleat the dough all the way around to seal completely. Decorate the top with trimmings if desired. In a bowl, beat the egg yolk with a splash of water. Brush the beaten egg over the top of the tart.

Place the tart on a rimmed baking sheet and bake for 35–40 minutes, until the top is golden brown. Let cool to room temperature before serving.

Part Three

LAS PAMPAS
AND THE PRAIRIE

Chapter 9

Dios aprieta pero no ahorca
God Tests Our Hearts
But He Doesn't Choke Them

buela Dorita once told me that Hippocrates, the father of medicine, recommended lentils to keep a man virile into old age. They were considered an aphrodisiac that ensured the birth of sons. Today, lentils can be found in almost any Argentine pantry. They've been a food staple since biblical times when Esau traded his inheritance to his younger brother Jacob for a bowl of lentil soup with a side of bread. I can only imagine how good that stew must have smelled for Esau to chuck it all—his firstborn birthright that carried along with it his family name, titles and wealth. Seems like a tasty trade, but a bad bargain. That's how worthy these little brown gems of a legume are. Rich, warm and filling, lentils also harbor medicinal virtues.

Lentils formed a pivotal part of Dorita's kitchen rituals. Even to this day, the smell of them simmering on the stovetop reminds me of her cooking. Her *guiso de lentejas* stew, slow cooked with dry *chorizo seco*, was a warm blanket on a cold winter's night. But Dorita didn't let the weather keep her away from them year-round. During warmer months, she'd lighten them up vegetarian style, always cooking *al dente*, until just tender, and serving them cold.

Abuela taught me to make lentils as a twenty-six-year-old newlywed at my parents' home in Miami. Which, *Doña* Petrona style, meant no recipe.

"Josefinita, sauté the onions with a little bit of garlic, then add the lentils, some water or stock, a bay leaf, a pinch of this, a dash of that, cover and simmer slowly—and, *ya está*. There you have it. And remember to give them time. They're better the next day."

* * *

As a wedding present, Dorita and my oldest sister Valentina gave Gastón and me a MacKenzie-Childs Wittika blue pedestal cake stand with whimsical animal charms hanging from drop beads, along with a compilation of tried and true recipes in a spanking new edition of the cookbook *El Gran Libro de Doña Petrona*.

The book is one of Argentina's top three literary bestsellers, along with the Holy Bible and *El Gaucho Martín Fierro*. Mom always said the cookbook was a rite of passage for Argentine women. At least one was gifted at every wedding. But like Bibles tucked away in hotel nightstand drawers, most sat unopened in the back of bookshelves or pantries, always at the ready to offer moral support, just in case. Working mothers today rarely read them. Still, you can find at least one *Doña* Petrona cookbook in most every Argentine kitchen.

Ironically, one of the secrets to Petrona's success was that she was ahead of her time: she recognized the role of working mothers in her books. More and more women were breaking out of their generational confines, and, mostly for economic reasons, leaving the home to work. She gave these women tips on how to manage their working days while keeping their husbands happy. She offered time-honored tips on running a home smoothly. Still, during her lifetime, *Doña* continued to see the *ama de casa* as her target audience, since it was presumed that, as a professional housewife, she was the one feeding her family.

Doña Petrona died at the age of ninety-six of a heart attack at her home in Olivos in the outskirts of Buenos Aires. Her loyal, long-serving friend Juanita was by her bedside. It's rumored that Petrona credited her good health and longevity to a generous nightly drink of Scotch, along with a cigar she'd smoke at home after each taping of her cooking show. Today, nearly thirty years since her death, Petrona's cookbook is in its 103rd edition.

The version Dorita gave me was the seventy-eighth. Inside the cover, Dorita penned the note in her swirly cursive, "Feed him well, Josefinita. *Con todo nuestro cariño, Abuela* Dorita y Valentina."

"I love it. It's perfect." I hugged them both. Dorita and Valentina knew that Gastón and I would eventually fall into our respective places at home and in the kitchen. Gastón, the cook. Me, the baker. Both one another's "Juanitas."

* * *

As newlyweds, Gastón and I managed to slip away from Argentina just ahead of disaster. While my transatlantic hauntings had seemed to wind down, the ghosts of crises past continued to plague Argentina. We arrived in Miami just in time to avoid the disastrous effects of the *corralito* of 2001—the economic corralling of all Argentine bank accounts. Like placing animals in cages, the corralling restricted the withdrawal of funds in order to stop a bank run that threatened to collapse the nation's financial system.

My in-laws were among the millions of Argentines who lost lifetimes worth of work. The *corralito* claimed their longtime family business Distribuidora Tolosa, which was where Gastón had been working since leaving the ranches, up until we moved to Miami. It forced them to start over from scratch. Us too. While Gastón and I managed to get the little savings we had out of Argentina, trouble followed.

Stateside, the bursting of the dot-com bubble triggered the folding of Dineronet.com, the financial tech company that had lured me away from Standard & Poor's. When they offered me the position, I couldn't turn down the salary and competitive benefits package, especially since I knew I'd be the only one of us working until Gastón's green card came through. We were told it could take up to a year for him to get his social security number.

The timing couldn't have been worse. Five months into my job, Dineronet folded, just two days after we'd signed our lives away to a thirty-year mortgage on our first home. We never did get a chance to live in it. The check for our down payment hadn't even cleared as I watched the real estate agent nail another "for sale" sign in the front yard.

Always the protective older sister, Valentina came to our rescue. An established executive saleswoman, she got a small business loan of $30,000 that she gave to me and Gastón to pay the mortgage until it sold. We didn't have to ask. She offered, and she never pressured us to make a payment. She made them for us for fourteen months until the house finally sold. We paid her back, but I've never forgotten that.

As for my parents, they invited me, Gastón and Sonny to live with them until we figured things out. Gastón and I began to regret that we hadn't booked a return ticket to Argentina, where at least we would have had a place to ourselves.

I began questioning whether leaving Standard & Poor's was the right move. I'd begun to carve a career for myself there and hated to admit it, but Viviana Zocco had been an incredible mentor as my boss. It wasn't often that the chance to work directly with a woman of her caliber came along. I started wondering whether we would have been able to ride out the economic crisis after all, and whether my job at Standard & Poor's would have remained intact.

Then there was the whole INS fiasco. Gastón's immigration papers took more than a year to come through, leaving him unable to work for the first year and a half we were stateside.

"*Estoy más al pedo que cenicero de moto,*" Gastón complained one day. He'd been passing time honing his English language and cooking skills.

"What's wrong?"

"I'm feeling about as useful as an ashtray on a motorcycle." Gastón didn't know what to do with himself now that he wasn't working. He'd dusted off and read just about every cookbook lining the shelves of Mom's Miami Beach kitchen.

"I don't know. That Chicken Marbella recipe you made from the *Silver Palate* cookbook last night might just be worth unemployment. Who would've known that capers, olives and prunes were the trifecta of briny-sweet magic that's good enough to drink?"

"It was good. Wasn't it? And I don't even like prunes."

While I'd never been better fed, fear began to sink in. There we were: me, twenty-six. Gastón, thirty-one. Both unemployed and living with my parents. At least we'd been able to push our beds together in my childhood room. But just as my mind started wondering, *Abuela* Dorita would set me straight. "In life, your most driving forces aren't often the best of memories. As much as it's tempting to turn back the hands of time, never regret your decisions, no matter where they've led you."

As usual, Dorita's words rang true. I brushed myself off and made a pact with my parents. They'd pay for night school if I got a day job. Soon after my newfound unemployment, I was accepted to the University of Miami's Master's in Communications program. During the day, I worked writing for the online portal of the local Fox News station from six a.m. to two p.m. Then, most weeknights I'd head down to Coral Gables for class from three to ten p.m. Gastón and I barely saw one another for those first months. Once his green card finally came through, he got a job as a credit analyst with GBM, a Latin American subsidiary of IBM.

* * *

Miami had always seemed like the ideal place for me and Gastón to land. I'd always dreamed of living by the water, and I had gotten used to seeing it every day in Buenos Aires. While not directly on the ocean, Buenos Aires borders the widest river in the world, the Río de la Plata, which some consider a marginal sea of the Atlantic. And it seemed only natural that Gastón would have a better chance of acclimating to a city like Miami, where a large part of the population was Spanish-speaking. His accounting degree didn't transfer to the States, which made it much more difficult for him to begin his job search. He considered going back to school for his CPA, but after drawn out conversations at *sobremesa*, he finally admitted he didn't like accounting. But even after landing a job at GBM as a credit analyst, it became clear that Gastón felt less and less at home in Miami. It wasn't his place.

The kitchen was the one place Gastón felt most like himself. He stayed true to his Sunday *asado* tradition, rain or shine. He couldn't find the same cuts of beef and organ meat as back home, but he'd begun experimenting with new cuts and dishes, creating new transcontinental traditions of his own.

Meanwhile, my Gentleman Caller, having gotten the message that three's company in a marriage, had all but disappeared. Two and a half years into living in Miami and after graduating from my master's program, we once again packed our bags in search of a new home. Mom begged us to stay. She thought eventually we'd find our place in Miami. But Gastón had already made plans to work as a mortgage officer with my brother Oscar at his company.

This time we were headed back to the city of black and gold, where, as they say in Pittsburgh, the *Stillers,* Pirates and Penguins play, and where you're never too far away from *Ahrn* City Beer, Heinz ketchup, pierogies, dippy eggs, chipped chopped ham, *sammiches* and salads dressed in fries, or burnt almond torte cake.

Aside from the chance to reunite with my childhood friends, I wasn't so convinced that returning to Pittsburgh was the right move. After living in Miami and Buenos Aires, it felt small and landlocked. But who was I to deny Gastón a chance at finding a job that made him feel fulfilled? As Dad always said, it's a lot easier to be someone in a small town or city. That was Pittsburgh for you: a mid-sized city with a small, hometown feel. And that was more important than ever. Gastón seemed to be losing himself. I'd taken him away from the very home that made me fall in love with him. It was up to me to set things right, but I wasn't sure I could.

"Let me get this straight. You're telling me that 'jeet jet?' means 'Did you eat yet?'" Gastón asked at the first *sobremesa* we shared in our new home.

We'd been back up north for three months, and Gastón was finally starting to understand Pittsburgh slang. "Yup. It means exactly that. You aren't the only one around here with a thick accent. Like you and your friends back in Argentina, Burghers have a dialect of their own."

"And 'worsh rag'?"

"That's the towel you use to wash your body off."

"How about 'jagoff'? Someone called me that the other day when I," Gastón mimed air quotes, *"cut them off."*

"It's the Yinzer version of your '*boludo*.'" I pinched Gastón's cheek. "If you cut the guy off, which I can't imagine you did, you can take it as a hard 'jerk.' Like *boludo*, its meaning changes depending on its delivery or inflection."

Soon enough, Gastón got the hang of Pittsburghese and was even able to recite by heart the iconic Century III Chevrolet jingle that for nearly three decades had been stuck in the heads of anyone who watched local TV—*"Century III Chevrolet, Lebanon Church Road, Pittsburgh . . . minutes from the mall."*

Hours away from Argentina, Gastón unrelentingly daydreamed about moving back. I'd told him over and over that I'd go back in a heartbeat if he found a job or opportunity we couldn't pass up, but he never did. He seemed happier in Pittsburgh, but still, Gastón wasn't all there. He'd put on a brave face and rip his jokes, but like *sobremesa*, they often didn't translate. He was much funnier in *Castellano*. More and more, Gastón seemed faraway, like he was just going through the motions. Still, life and the varying shades of gray that hung low between Pittsburgh's hills and valleys moved onward, and soon enough we found ourselves knee-deep in careers as we desperately sought to start a family of our own, but that also came with its challenges.

I was twenty-nine when I became a mom. I'd been working as the public relations manager at the Pittsburgh Cultural Trust for just over a year when our golden-locked firstborn, Lucas, was born. He was a challenge from the beginning. It took Gastón and me more than two years to get pregnant. Then, soon after our first appointment with a fertility specialist, we somehow did without any outside intervention. Or, as Mom would often correct me, *I* got pregnant.

"There's no 'we' when it comes to giving birth," she'd remind me. She had a point. There certainly was no "we" when it came to the toxemia that landed me on bed rest thirty-three weeks into the pregnancy. That's when I had the ultrasound that changed everything. During one of my weekly scans, the technologist looked at me and Gastón, asking if we'd like to know the sex.

"It's a girl. They told us a while back. We've already named her Isabella." One of our friends, who also happened to be an obstetrician, had scanned me at twenty weeks during our last trip to Argentina.

The ultrasound technician stared at me with a blank face. "I'd hold off on painting the nursery pink. Do you see this here?" She pointed to two legs, spread wide open. "Your son is sending you a message loud and clear. That package there in the middle says it all."

Gastón and I looked at one another, relieved that we'd painted the nursery shades of baby blue and celadon green. We'd always known we wanted at least three or four children, so we made sure to pick neutral colors. Still, while I was relieved to be spared the surprise of finding out that the baby we were expecting was actually a boy during the stress of labor and delivery, I couldn't help but feel a momentary stint of sadness for the girl we weren't having. For the past twelve weeks, I'd been imagining the daughter we'd soon welcome into this world. That feeling passed soon enough, as an image of Lucas sucking his thumb popped up on the overhead ultrasound monitor. All that mattered was that he was healthy and that I could carry him to term with my mounting toxemia-induced high blood pressure.

Doctors induced me four weeks later after determining that Lucas' lungs had fully developed. After a grueling fourteen-hour labor and delivery, Lucas came into this world on a late August evening. Gastón and I were thrilled. We'd never felt such elation, and I'd never felt such exhaustion.

The following morning when the labor and delivery nurse entered the room asking how many bowel movements Lucas had had during the night, I lay silent, deferring the question to Gastón. He looked back at me, shrugging. It hadn't occurred to either of us to change his diaper. With so few firsts that come in life as adults, those first moments of parenthood were truly unforgettable.

Mom and Dad were both there for the delivery. Dad, true to his generation of men who didn't believe it was their place to witness the intimate details of childbirth, waited outside in the hallway until he was certain my legs were closed and nicely tucked away under hospital sheets before coming in.

"Lucas Gastón Oría. *Hola.* I'm your grandfather."

"He looks just like you, Dad. Don't you think?"

"Of course you'd say that. The ugly ones always look like me."
Dad laughed. "You know what they say. *Yerba mala nunca muere.*
The bad weeds never die. They keep coming back." He wasn't too
off the mark. During delivery, the doctor had to help Lucas through
the birth canal with vacuum suction. As a result, he was born with
a bald, cone head that temporarily made him look like a wrinkled,
tiny old man.

"Poupi." Dad looked at Mom. "Did you notice his time of birth?"

"*Claro.* How couldn't I? 8:25 p.m." Mom squeezed Lucas' tiny
foot. "The same time that Eva Perón entered immortality."

"What is it with 8:25 p.m.?" I asked, intrigued.

"That exact time was beaten into our heads as kids," Dad said.
"I was thirteen when Evita died. Like Jesus, she was just thirty-three
when she sat down to her last supper. Years after her death, until
Perón was overthrown in '55, Argentina's national evening news
was interrupted every single night for an important announcement.
'It is 8:25 p.m., the time when Eva Perón entered immortality.' For
as long as your Mom and I live, we'll never forget."

Clearly. Argentines didn't. They didn't cry for Evita; she never left them. Fifty-some years later, her presence still lived on in
Buenos Aires, its surroundings and my West Penn Hospital labor
and delivery room some 5,300 miles away.

The following six months with Lucas were a blur. He was extremely colicky and cried most afternoons from four p.m. to eleven
at night or so until he was finally so exhausted that he couldn't muster another tear. This continued until Dorita came to visit. One late
winter Sunday afternoon she sat on my couch, imploring me to go
shower while she watched Lucas. I was walking around the kitch-
en, bouncing him up and down as he screamed bloody murder.

"*Abuela*, I can't. It's his witching hour. Can't you see?"

But Mom, sitting beside Dorita, insisted and took him from
me. An hour later I came downstairs, my hair freshly washed and
blow-dried. I didn't hear anything, other than Mom and Dorita
quietly chatting as they sat having their teatime *merienda*.

"What's going on? Did you drug him? How'd you get him to
sleep? It's only five," I said, peeking into Lucas' bassinet. There he
was, sleeping like an angel. On his stomach.

"*No lo molestes*. Leave him alone, Josie. Come make yourself a tea. Or are you drinking *mate*?" Mom said, shooing me away from the baby.

Since leaving Argentina, I'd become an avid loose-leaf *mate* drinker. The teatime ritual grounded me, always reminding me of the home that tugged at me and Gastón, beckoning us home.

"Mom, the pediatrician told me babies can't sleep on their tummies until they're one. It's in all of the baby books." I said sternly, yet quietly enough to make sure not to wake Lucas.

"Don't look at me. *Mamí* put him down that way. And you know what they say: never, ever wake a sleeping baby."

Dorita kept her eyes down and sipped her *café con leche*. "Since when can a doctor or book teach you how to mother? It's instinctual. Every baby's different."

The next day, I threw my baby books out. Lucas continued to sleep on his stomach, and Gastón and I finally got some sleep, just in time for me to start my new job back at Dad's tristate diagnostic medical testing center. He needed a finance manager who could also do marketing, among other things. He also offered me a ten-hour, four-day work week that allowed me to spend more time with Lucas at home. I couldn't pass up the offer.

Gastón and I were just settling into parenthood when we got the news that I was pregnant with our second child. It came as a shock to all of us. Lucas was just eight months old. I'd gotten pregnant before I'd even had a chance to have a period. I'd always heard there was a slight possibility of getting pregnant while breastfeeding, but I never thought it would happen to us, especially since it took us so long to conceive Lucas. Once I wrapped my head around it, I told Gastón I was sure that our daughter Isabella, the one we'd expected with so much anticipation, was on her way. But she wasn't.

From his surprise conception to his precipitous arrival five weeks before his due date, Mateo was in a hurry from the beginning. I'd awoken one late January morning, nearing the end of my pregnancy but still with over a month to go, convinced I was coming down with something. I'd showered and gotten dressed to go to the office. It was payroll day and I was training the new bookkeeper. I had to be there, otherwise a hundred or so employees wouldn't receive their bi-weekly checks. But within the hour, I was doubled over in pain. Gastón and I almost didn't make it to the hospital before Mateo made his appearance. To this day I remember the ice-cold chill of scissors against my skin as a labor and delivery nurse cut my pants while Mateo was making his way into this world. I'd barely made it from the wheelchair to the hospital bed when I felt him in between my legs.

"The baby's crowning. We'll have to do without stirrups," another nurse said, instructing Gastón to hold back my other leg with all of his might. Scared to push without an epidural, I fought back with all of mine.

"I need drugs! I never even did Lamaze!" I glared at Gastón.

We always looked forward to our weekly Lamaze classes when I was pregnant with Lucas, even though we never managed to sit through an entire session. Every time we'd try to, Gastón and I would begin to get on one another's nerves, so we'd skip out during break time and head to Tessaro's just down the street for hardwood-grilled, no frills, no fuss cheeseburgers. Juicy on the inside with a sweet, smoky crust on the outside, the patties hit the spot every time, even making us forget what we'd been bickering about in the first place. "I was never planning on having a natural childbirth anyway, *Gordo*," I'd confess at our weekly Lamaze *sobremesas*. "Are you going to eat those pickles?"

I never did get that epidural I was asking for. My OB entered the room just in time to catch Mateo. To this day, I'm not proud of our first mother-son interaction. As the doctor laid a crying Mateo on my chest and asked Gastón if he'd like to cut the cord, I repeatedly barked, "Get him off me!" *Talk about ruining the moment. Another first botched.*

In that moment, I was in so much pain that I felt myself levitating over my own body. The doctor scooped Mateo up as she instructed one of the nurses to give me a Stadol cocktail through my IV. It calmed me down almost immediately, and I got my much-needed do-over and properly welcomed our eight-pound, fourteen-ounce baby boy with large, dark almond eyes and a full head of spikey black hair. Gastón kissed the both of us, wiping away the tears pooling in his eyes.

From that moment on, Mateo was a dream compared to his colicky older brother, whose inconsolable crying fits kept us up night after night for seven straight months. But Mateo came with his own challenges. We'd just made plans to spend the holidays that year with Gastón's family in Argentina, when Mateo, on the heels of his six-month checkup, began running a fever that quickly took a turn for the worse.

At a sick visit that morning, our pediatrician reassured us that it was probably just a common reaction to his vaccines. It was only after my persistence that he gave us an order for bloodwork to run a culture. At the hospital laboratory, the phlebotomist tried drawing blood two times in one arm without luck. Mateo was squirming on my lap as she tried his second arm. I held him down against his will, but still, she couldn't find a vein suitable enough. That's when another phlebotomist, who, after a fourth failed attempt to draw blood, said, "Your son is very dehydrated. If I were you, I'd take him back to his doctor. He doesn't look good at all."

We did. And again, his pediatrician sent us away. "Get some fluids in him and try again tomorrow. For now, just try to keep him comfortable. He just had vaccines a couple of days ago. This is a normal reaction."

What happened next wasn't. Later that afternoon I was called out of a meeting at the office for an urgent call. I'll never forget the panic in my sister Laura's voice when I picked up the phone.

"It's Mateo. He's worse. He's like a ragdoll in my arms. Super lethargic. I think you need to take him to the doctor. Now!" Laura had four kids of her own, so I trusted her maternal instincts. She lived up the street from us at the time and was first on my in-case-of-emergency call tree I'd taped to the refrigerator for our babysitter.

Gastón met me back at the house within the hour. After seeing Mateo, we headed straight to Dad's office to see if his staff could draw his blood. As I cradled Mateo in the back seat, I could feel his heart racing against my body. The beat echoed in my heart and filled the silence all the way to the office.

Used to routine blood draws on the elderly at nursing homes, Dad's phlebotomists almost never missed a stick. But after another round of failed attempts with Mateo, one of them called in my dad as a last resort. Dad was finally able to get blood through Mateo's groin as Gastón and I fought to hold his little body still against the examination table. But Dad wasn't convinced it was enough to get a culture. That's when he ordered an EKG to check Mateo's heart. The test confirmed what Dad had suspected all along: his heart was racing over two hundred beats per minute. One to never lose his cool, Dad called our pediatrician right away to let him know his grandson was tachycardic, dehydrated and in desperate need of medical attention. But the pediatrician put him in his place, reminding him that while Dad was a cardiologist, he wasn't used to treating children.

"Doctor, you of all people should know a faster heart rate is common in kids with a fever. Tell your daughter we'll see her son again in the morning if he's still not feeling well tomorrow."

Dad hung up, and after taking one more listen to Mateo's chest, told us to head to the ER. Mateo declined further during the half-hour drive to Children's Hospital. After several failed attempts to breastfeed him, I held my own breath trying to listen for his as I scanned the length of his body with breathless anxiety, trying to reassure myself that his chest was still rising and falling. "Drive faster, Gastón!"

Gastón drove straight through the last light standing between us and the hospital. For once his mad Argentine driving skills paid off.

"He won't wake up!" I cried into my cellphone to the ER staff. "We'll be there in a minute." I threw my phone down and willed Mateo to cry or show any signs of a fight. Dad had also phoned ahead to give the attending ER doctor a rundown of his grandson's symptoms. As we pulled into the emergency drop-off, four or five men and women in white lab coats surrounded the car. I opened the back door and Mateo's almost lifeless body was snatched from my arms as another doctor began taking his vitals with his stethoscope. Immediately a cacophony of high-pitched voices ricocheted around the hospital entrance.

"He's going into shock. Get a heel stick. If you can't get blood, try the head. Call in the surgical team in case we need a central line."

Mateo was whisked away beyond closed doors. Gastón and I stood off to the side, staring at one another, terrified and dumbstruck.

"Are you baby Oría's parents?" a woman in SpongeBob scrubs asked minutes later as we sat in the waiting room. "Please come with me."

She took us into a private room and let us know that a team of surgical doctors had been called to the ER to insert a central line into Mateo so they could administer the fluids he desperately needed. "We tried to get blood to send to the lab so we can determine what infection your son's fighting, but he's so dehydrated his veins kept collapsing. They're doing everything possible to stabilize him."

"I need to see him," My throat went thick as I swallowed past the knot. "Please, just let me hold my son's hand while he's getting these tests. He's probably so scared."

"I'm afraid that's not possible. I'm not sure you realize just how sick your son is. He's lost consciousness. You'd only be in the way. We'll let you know as soon as there's news."

Over the next several hours, doctors of various specialties came out to the waiting room, updating us on Mateo's vitals and reassuring us he was stable. Gastón and I sat holding hands among a sea of worried parents and grandparents. They were all strangers, yet we were all connected in some way, experiencing the same panic and worry. Some worse than others. Our blank stares said it all.

When I wasn't praying rounds of Hail Marys and Our Fathers, the "what-ifs" and "could-have-beens" began playing games with my head. *What if we'd listened to our pediatrician and let Mateo sleep it off? Would he have ever awoken? How could I have gone into work in the first place? Where was my mother's intuition? We could lose him.*

The attending physician broke my trance. He came out to let us know that Mateo had been stabilized and we could finally see him. Gastón and I silently followed the physician to the back of the pediatric intensive care unit (PICU), walking past countless hospital cribs and beds tucked away behind sterile white curtains, each with sick children and worried families of their own, until we got to Mateo. He was hooked up to all sorts of machines and monitors with tubes, alarms and display panels. The noise and fluorescent lights were almost too much to take in at once.

The following two days, I sat vigil at Mateo's bedside in the PICU while Gastón and Mom took turns taking care of Lucas and hospital shifts. Mom also took care of Mateo's pediatrician, firing him on the spot the moment he appeared for rounds the following morning. She also tried to convince me to leave the PICU for a meal or a shower, but except for bathroom breaks and to pump my engorged breasts, I refused to leave his side. Mateo needed to see my face when he woke up in that strange place. While the hospital staff assured us that he was stable for the time being, I couldn't believe it until I saw it with my own eyes. I needed to see him show signs of a fight, see him cry or smile his ear-to-ear grin.

But for close to two days, he did nothing but sleep, sometimes twisting and turning in what seemed like agony. Meanwhile, we continued to get no answers. Blood cultures came back contaminated and inconclusive. The staff drew more blood and changed his antibiotics. Except for the incessant beeping of the machines monitoring Mateo's IV, blood pressure and heart rate, not a sound came from his crib.

For the most part, I'd been able to fight off sleep. My Hail Marys played like a broken record in my head. The worry had all but dried up my milk. It's like the tango says, *el cambalache . . . el que no llora, no mama*; the baby that doesn't cry, doesn't get nursed. Gastón insisted we take turns spending the night in the hospital, but I refused his offers.

Then, in the still of the early morning after Mateo's second night in the PICU, I awoke to *coos* and *ahs*. I'd dozed off for a couple of hours and was struggling to come to, when I noticed the shadow of a man standing next to the hospital crib. Mateo was sitting up and had grabbed a hold of the man's finger with his fist.

Middle of the night checkups were the norm in intensive care, so I assumed it was a technologist or nurse coming to check his vitals or take more blood. But when I finally got my bearings and jumped up to say hello to my little man, I noticed his visitor was clad in street clothes.

The visitor's eyes met mine from the other side of the caged crib. *I know those eyes. I know that closely trimmed silver beard.* The man gently released his finger from Mateo's grip and, looking straight at me, bid me hello and goodbye with a subtle tip of his herringbone cap before turning to leave. He was back. My Gentleman Caller was the first to greet Mateo from his two-day slumber.

Still trying to get my bearings, I slid my hand through the crib's steel bars, grabbing hold of Mateo's hand as I thanked God that my son had awakened. As soon as he noticed me, Mateo stuck out his arms and began crying. He wanted me to pick him up. I wanted to, but Mateo was connected to too many wires. I wanted to call after the man, but I'd barely had a second to react before he was gone.

"*Matu, mi amor, Mami's* here, baby boy. It's going to be okay." He curled his fingers around mine.

The on-call nurse came in. "Look who's finally awake! This is a good sign, Mom. A very good sign," she said, lowering a side of the crib so she could listen to Mateo's heart through her stethoscope.

Finally able to take a full breath, I stepped out of the PICU and called Gastón. "He's awake, *Gordo*. Our Matu's awake." As I walked back towards Mateo's crib, my eyes kept flicking from side to side, unconsciously scanning the hospital hallway for any sign of my Gentleman Caller.

Mateo was transferred to a regular hospital room later that afternoon. The following three days, as I'd walk down the hallway to grab a cup of coffee or splash my face with water to freshen up, a feeling of unease would come over me. I'd stop whatever I was doing after catching a glimpse of movement from the corner of my eye. But more often than not, when I turned around, there wouldn't be anyone or anything there to explain it, other than a nurse or doctor on a mission. I decided I was either going crazy or just needed some sleep.

Later that day, since Mateo was stable, Mom and Gastón convinced me to join them in the hospital cafeteria for a teatime *merienda*. As I sipped my Lipton tea with lemon juice from a packet, I told them all about my paranormal encounter.

"There was a man at Mateo's crib side the morning he woke up. Mateo was holding his hand. He was so comfortable with him.

It was the strangest thing. It was as if Mateo knew him. I'm almost certain it's the same man I kept seeing over and over, who I first saw with Tripp. I haven't seen him since our wedding in Miami. But he's back."

"He was at the wedding?" Gastón said. "You never mentioned that." Gastón looked at Mom, as if they were both deciding who could best handle the situation. Best handle me.

"That's beside the point. He was there this morning. Out of nowhere. You know how tough it is to get past those PICU doors."

Gastón grabbed my hand. I'd told him about my Gentleman Caller on several occasions, and while he never outright said he didn't believe me, he always thought I had been exaggerating. "You need to get some rest, *Gordi*. Why don't you go home for a while and freshen up." Since giving birth to Mateo, I never managed to lose the last remnants of baby weight. Unfortunately, *'flaca'* was short-lived—a fleeting nickname Gastón had given me based on first impressions, but like my yo-yoing jean size, it never stuck.

I refused. I wasn't leaving that hospital without my son.

"The man was probably there for someone else. He was probably just walking by and heard Mateo," Mom said. "Maybe he wanted to let you sleep."

"No. He clearly pushed back our privacy curtains to get to Mateo. People don't do that in the PICU. He was older, Mom. Like a grandfather. And had the same silver beard as the man who pops in and out of my life. I wanted to thank him for being there when Mateo woke up, but he disappeared before I had the chance."

"It was probably a nurse's aide. I can see the wheels spinning in your head." Mom took a sip of her coffee. "You've always had such an imagination, ever since you were a little girl."

But I knew better. He was back, at least for the moment. Mateo was now the third witness to encounter my Gentleman Caller. But what good were eyewitnesses if none of them could corroborate my story? Sonny was the second to see him. She'd fanned him with her tail at the dog park while he sat petting her on a warm summer day, just weeks before I traveled to Argentina and met Gastón. My latest eyewitness, Mateo, even seemed amused by him. But he'd only recently begun saying *mamá*. I couldn't very well ask him, "Son, do you see what I see?" And almost a decade had passed since Tripp and I saw my Gentleman Caller for the first time at my parents' home in Fox Chapel. Through the years Tripp and I spoke here and there after running into one another, but never about our ghost. Who knew if he'd even remember him?

Mateo was discharged three days later. We never did get a concise diagnosis, but like the car accident when I was a teenager, we'd managed to stay ahead of tragedy. But that didn't mean it didn't have a lasting impact. His week-long hospital stay taught me that terrible, unexpected tragedies could happen at any time, to anyone, and there was nothing we could do to prevent them. It made me thankful that we were able to walk out of that hospital that day in one piece. There were those who wouldn't be as fortunate. It also reminded me to always listen to mother's intuition. It taught me to savor the little moments, the shades of gray that happened when we were going about life on autopilot, between the black and white revelations.

Not even a month had passed since his discharge when Mateo once again landed in the ER, this time with a life-threatening asthma attack that came out of nowhere.

"You don't understand," I explained to the attending physician. "Our son doesn't have asthma. He's never so much as wheezed." But, evidently, he did. Whether it was a result of his recent mysterious illness or something he was born with that was just now presenting itself, we'd never know. But in that moment, and after a handful of ER visits that fall, we'd learned that the faintest sign of a runny nose or sneeze meant we had just minutes to get him to the hospital before a full-on attack came on. In the moments in between, Gastón and I met with pulmonologists, allergists and even homeopaths to get to the bottom of the health challenges that had robbed Mateo of his thigh rolls, emptied his deep cheek dimples and left Gastón and I void of any sort of peace of mind. Work, family dinners and our *sobremesas* all fell to the wayside.

As the holidays quickly approached, I began second-guessing our trip to Argentina. Few things frightened me more than overnight, transcontinental flights. Add in a baby prone to asthma attacks that went from zero to full throttle in minutes, and I'd suddenly feel a full-blown panic attack coming on. I'd picked my thumbs raw by the time I gathered the courage to tell Gastón.

"I think we should cancel our trip. It's too risky with Mateo."

"What? It's all figured out. *Estas buscándole la quinta pata al gato.* Don't overcomplicate things, Josie. My sister said she has everything under control. She has the nebulizer and the prednisone. Belén's going to travel with us."

Gastón's youngest sister, Belén, had recently passed her medical board exams as a pediatrician and had assured us she'd personally see to Mateo while we were there.

"We still need to get there. What if something happens on the way to Buenos Aires? We'll be in-flight for nine hours straight with a toddler and baby on our laps. It's too much. Maybe next year."

"The doctor prescribed the prednisone in case he has an attack on the plane. It's you who doesn't understand. I need to go home. It's been too long."

"*Home?* I thought this was home? If I'm not mistaken, Gastón, your name's on the mortgage, right there next to mine."

* * *

Weeks later, back in his hometown of La Plata, Gastón was back to his old carefree self. I could see it in his face. The moment we stepped off the plane, we were both relieved to have avoided a mile-high asthma attack. But Gastón's relief went beyond that. The years seemed to melt away from the frown lines that had begun to burrow in his brow from the moment we moved to the States. To Gastón, those five years passed by in a blur. He felt like he was an extra in his own life, that living in the US wasn't *his* story, and aside from the time he dedicated to being a father and husband, he thought about one thing and one thing only—how to move his family back home to Argentina.

We spent a *feliz* and uneventful *Navidad* in La Plata. Belén had held up her part of the bargain, overseeing Mateo's daily scheduled nebulizer treatments and meds. Gastón and I welcomed her help and took a breather, sleeping off our exhaustion poolside and visiting with a select group of family and friends, among them my *tía* Ángela. We'd set aside an afternoon for *la merienda* at her congregation.

From the moment we arrived, Gastón and I felt enveloped in love from Ángela's sisters who crowded around us, showering us with kisses and affection, holding their arms out to Lucas and Mateo. They asked about our lives and hung on to our every last word. Many of the nuns remembered Mom, who in her early twenties had been a music teacher at their Catholic school, and couldn't get over our likeness. The mere fact that I was Mom's daughter and *Tía* Ángela's faraway *Yanqui* niece who they'd heard so much about instantly made us family among this sorority of aging women, most of whom had shrunk below my shoulders.

Except for *Tía* Ángela. In her mid-fifties, she towered over all of the women with her full head of silver, short wavy hair that chased her playful smile as she greeted us. I'd always loved that my aunt, the nun who'd devoted herself to God and serving others, lived life as if she didn't have a care in the world.

To this day, that afternoon warms my heart. As we gathered around their dining room table, steam curled around the room carrying the smell of coffee and hot milk, melting away all formalities. The door opened to succulent, raw conversation.

"Gastón, how are you adjusting to the States?" *Tía* Ángela handed him a coffee just the way he liked it. Black, with loads of sugar.

Gastón's yellowish hazel eyes glossed over as he spoke of how much he missed Argentina.

"He's the one who wanted to move back to Pittsburgh," I said defensively. "I wanted to stay by the water in Miami Beach. We could have spoken Spanish everywhere we went, even at work. But Gastón didn't feel at home there. He said if he was going to live in the States, he might as well experience the real deal. I moved for him and look where it got us. Nowhere. Now he doesn't feel at home in Pittsburgh either. I can't win." I shook my head, frustrated.

"This is home, Josie. Argentina. We met here."

"Then find a reason to come back. I have way greater earning potential in the States. Find a job that makes sense for our family and I'll follow you. But until then, snap out of it. I've always said I would come back."

"*Chicos*," *Tía* Ángela offered us a tray of *libritos de grasa* with layers of folded puff pastry that resembled the pages of hand-held Bibles. "*Dios aprieta pero no ahorca.* God tests our hearts, but he doesn't choke them. Unfortunately, we tend to do that ourselves. Think of everything you both went through to be together. Family fights. International moves. Leaving everything behind. You've come this far. And now you have two kids to think of. When the bones are good, a house doesn't fall. No matter where it is."

"*Tenés razon.* You're right," Gastón grabbed two buttery *libritos*, one for him and one for Mateo to suck on, before squeezing my knee in agreement under the table.

Ángela and her fellow sisters listened to our confessions, offering up their own unfiltered opinions as they sipped on coffee, tea and *Coca Diet*. Gastón and I had somehow found the words for the pent-up feelings and frustrations we hadn't been able to verbalize until then. The boys were young enough to be oblivious to what we were saying. Lucas, two and a half, sat on my lap sipping his *submarino,* a mug of warm milk with a submerged chocolate bar, and Mateo teetered around the table among our legs, grasping at knees and the table's edge to keep upright.

Close to celebrating his first birthday, Mateo had recently begun walking. While the steroids he took for his asthma kept him underweight, they also gave him a round, full-moon face that was flanked with silky black curls.

Barely able to see over the table, Mateo blindly grasped at anything he could get his hands on—plates full of *facturas* and half-drunk mugs of coffee. I kept moving them just out of his reach, but like most determined babies, his persistence paid off. Mateo finally managed to grab a hold of a buttery *sacramento* oval-shaped pastry and began licking the sugar off. We didn't pay any attention to it until Mateo dropped it, coughing. I noticed that a flakey piece of the *sacramento* pastry had broken off and hysterically jumped into action, flipping Mateo over my legs and hitting his back to dislodge the bread from his throat. The room went silent, except for Mateo, who started crying hysterically and flailing his arms to escape my grasp.

"Josie, put him down. He's fine." Gastón stood up and grabbed Mateo from my arms. His look told me I was making it worse, and he was right. I'd overreacted, but that's how I was wired. Like Mateo's attacks, I went from zero to sixty in a matter of seconds.

Ángela, noting the panic in my eyes, patted the chair next to her. "Come, Josefinita. Your *café con leche* is getting cold."

As I settled down, the conversation progressed to our struggles with Mateo's debilitating asthma that seemed to have come out of nowhere.

"*Nena*, sweetie, take this." A sister grabbed my hand and placed in it a medal she'd just removed from around her neck. "For you. The medal is of Our Lady of the Rosary of San Nicolás. I dreamt with her last night. Our Blessed Mother told me I must pass her along. I wasn't sure to who or where, but now it's clear as day."

"*Gracias*. But I couldn't accept this. She's so beautiful." I thought of the few things my aunt, who had relinquished all material goods and wealth when she'd entered the sisterhood, had kept for herself.

"I insist." She batted away my hand. "Do you know the story behind the medal? It was made to commemorate the day the Virgin first appeared to a housewife named Gladys Quiroga de Motta. She was a mother and *abuela* who had no formal education or knowledge of the Bible. Yet the Virgin Mary chose her to deliver her messages. The first apparition occurred on the 25th of September in 1983 in San Nicolás, a small city north of Buenos Aires."

"September 25? That's my *abuela* Dorita's birthday."

"Even more reason for you to have this medal, then." The nun took it, hanging it around my neck. "Your *abuela's* birthday is now commemorated as the feast of Our Lady of the Rosary of San Nicolás. They say Gladys was thinking about the approaching spring weather when she noticed her rosary beads glowing like molten steel. Then, as she knelt to pray in her bedroom, *La Virgen María* appeared in front of her. Radiant and beautiful in a blue gown and veil, her whole figure glowed with light. In her arms was baby Jesus and a rosary. Mary only smiled at Gladys, never speaking. And then as suddenly as she had appeared, she vanished."

Just like my Gentleman Caller. Like Mary, his supernatural apparitions are silent, short and sweet.

"Josefinita," Ángela chimed in as she stirred Sweet'N Low into her mug of *café con leche*. "Mary also made an apparition to Gladys on the 17th of November that same year. Isn't that your *mami's* birthday?"

"*Sí*. It is." I looked at the image of Mary holding baby Jesus. It was more than a coincidence. A shudder of hope ran through me.

"Apparitions on both your mom and *abuela's* birthdays. It must be a sign, *Gordita*," Gastón gave me a tongue-in-cheek look as he took a bite of a *dulce de leche*-filled *suspiro de monja factura*, named after a nun's exacerbated sighs. "My wife here believes in all sorts of signs and spirits. Even ghosts."

"Don't mind him," I said to the group of women. "This coming from the boy who, growing up, used to attend both Sunday Masses just so he could kiss the girls he liked during the Rite of Peace before Communion." I grabbed a friar's ball filled with pastry cream, giving Gastón the side eye before directing my attention back to the sister. "What happened next?"

"Mary continued to appear to Gladys on and off for six years. Her medal is said to bring miracles to those that believe. Place her under Mateo's mattress and pray to her to heal him," the sister said, patting Mateo's head. "The congregation will pray for him as well."

"The medal answered a pregnant mother's desperate prayers with the miracle healing of her seven-year-old son on his deathbed," another sister added. "The boy's paralysis went away, and an egg-shaped brain tumor shrank away to nothing over three weeks. He'd been given his last rites and first communion before he was miraculously healed."

* * *

That teatime with *Tía* Ángela and her fellow sisters filled me up like a steaming dish of sacrilegious comfort food in the most sacred of places. In that room, there was no clear line between religion, food and the *sobremesa* that followed. Our plates were full of contradictions and pointed blasphemous metaphors: fat-laden, sugary "sacraments," "friar's testicles" in pastry form bursting with *dulce de leche*, sweet buns named after a nun's conflicted sighs provoked by a carnal encounter with fellow clergy. Sometimes it didn't hurt for certain terms to get lost in translation, but that day we felt more than understood. The message the nuns served up came across loud and clear. We felt the support of the entire congregation lifting our family of four up in faith and love.

As I climbed into the taxi that evening, waving goodbye to *Tía* Ángela and her fellow sisters, I was certain they would remember Mateo in the weeks and months to come with genuine concern and prayer as they gathered tableside. Just as blasphemy and gastronomy had long gone hand in hand, so did our daily bread and godliness, no matter its form or delivery. That afternoon, I'd come to understand and respect sisterhood on a whole new level.

"Who needs *abuelas* when those women have our backs?" Gastón kissed me. "You have the medal? It couldn't hurt to put it under Mateo's mattress."

Of course it couldn't. Divine apparitions on both Dorita and Mom's birthday? It was a lifeline—the sign I'd been looking for.

* * *

The following morning, we jumped on an Aerolíneas Argentinas flight and headed south with the boys, Belén and Jorge Luis to Villa La Angostura, a small mountain village in the Lakes District of Argentina's Patagonia. Graciela and the rest of Gastón's family would catch up with us in time to ring in 2006.

After losing his company, Jorge Luis decided to follow his lifelong Patagonian dreams and purchased Cabañas del Arbol, a small group of log cabins for tourists. As a young boy, Gastón's family spent a month each summer camping on the shores of the many Patagonian lakes. During that time, fly-fishing was the line that tied the father and sons together. In the midst of his economic downfall, Jorge Luis heard the bumbling rivers and still, mirror-like lake waters from his earlier years calling out to him.

The water's currents tugged at him night and day until finally, Jorge Luis decided that if he had to pick up the pieces and start over again in his mid-sixties, he'd make the best of it, hoping the fish would rise up to meet him. I'm not sure my mother-in-law Graciela agreed, but that's her story to tell.

Along with San Martín de los Andes, Villa La Angostura bookended the scenic Camino de los Siete Lagos, or the panoramic section of Patagonia's Route 234's Seven Lakes Road that travels through the Lanin and Nahuel Huapi National Parks past lakes, forests, snow-capped mountains and streams. Just twenty-six miles from the Chilean border, the town seemed right out of a fairy tale; garden gnomes, goblins and the Patagonian version of the Loch Ness monster, Nahuelito, included.

Tucked between the northwest shore of Lake Nahuel Huapi and Lake Correntoso, Villa La Angostura was famous among fishing fanatics, including my father-in-law. Among its main attractions were the emerald green waters of the *villa's* River Correntoso that ran downstream from Correntoso Lake to Nahuel Huapi. Running between 650 and 980 feet in length (depending on the height of the lakes), the river's said to be among the shortest in the world. What it lacks in size, the river more than makes up for in the abundance of large trout it dumps into the mouth of the Nahuel Huapi Lake.

Our first morning in town, Gastón promised me fresh trout for lunch as we made the half-hour walk from the cabins to the ice-cold Correntoso river. I watched from the pedestrian bridge above as Gastón put on his waders at the river's bank, tied his fly and carefully waded out into the clear, waist-high turbulent water. It had been years since I'd seen Gastón cast a fly fish rod, drawing artful, tight figure-eight loops that whipped back and forth, whistling each way to a four-count syncopated rhythm— back on one, pause on two, forward on three, back again on four.

As I leaned over the footbridge's wooden rail, my mind wandered back to the day I fell in love with Gastón at the ranch's *yerra* all those years ago. That day I stood leaning over the wooden railing of the *corralito* animal enclosure, watching Gastón tackle calf after calf with his bare hands. I'd never witnessed such extremes of masculinity, from the brutal to the beautiful to the poetic to the forceful. From the looks of it, Gastón was also lost in thought. Alone on that bridge in the half-light of the canyon, the river's waters spoke to me.

I'd taken Gastón away from the very place that made me fall in love with him. I'd made my bed. Now I had to lie in it.

"*Gorda*, you ready to go? Nothing's biting," Gastón yelled up at me from the river down below, taking off his wide-brimmed angler's hat. Past noon, the sun had begun to warm up the day, finally taking its place high in the sky.

"Sure. I'll meet you down there!" I turned, and to my surprise, a man was standing next to me. I hadn't noticed him until then. I smiled, stopping to take off my jacket and tie it around my waist. He grabbed the lip of his cap, nodding his head hello back with the ghost of a smile. I turned to go. Then stopped. Feeling his eyes on me, the now familiar sensation of the hairs on my neck and arms sprung up with anticipation. I did a double take. He was back. My Gentleman Caller. Pain and sadness were etched into the lines around the corners of his eyes, signs of a hard life. As usual, he was overdressed for the height of summer in his tweed cap, trousers and zipped-up windbreaker. I got lost in the moment and was rendered speechless.

"*Gorda*, are you coming?" Gastón yelled from down below.

I turned to go. As I looked back, my Gentleman Caller closed his dark eyes, took his cap off, and placing it against his chest, slightly cocked his head goodbye. The high sun fell on his platinum silver hair and beard like a spotlight that made him appear almost celestial. As I neared the end of the footbridge, I mustered the courage to go back and talk to him.

I turned around, but he was gone. *Was it the river down below that had been speaking to me? Or my Gentleman Caller?*

"Babes, did you see that man on the footbridge?" I asked Gastón.

"Who? I didn't notice anyone but you. But I was scanning the river for fish most of the time. Why?"

"No worries. I swear I saw him again. My Gentleman Caller. But forget it. No bites?" Conversations about my Gentleman Caller with Gastón often went nowhere. He was hungry and wanted to head home.

"*Nada*. Not even a nibble. But I promised you *trucha* for lunch. Shall we?" Gastón wrapped his icy fingers around my waist. "So now he's in Argentina too? He followed us down here to the end of the world?"

I didn't answer. Instead I started rubbing his hands in mine. "You're freezing," I said. "But what will we eat? I thought you didn't catch anything."

"I didn't. But *Papá* told me just the place to take you in town."

"I thought they were expecting us for lunch."

"I told them not to wait for us."

"Belén's been watching the kids all morning. We need to check on Mateo. It's almost time for his treatment."

"Josie, it's taken care of. I already cleared it with her. C'mon. Supposedly, this place has the best trout ravioli in town."

Jorge Luis wasn't lying. Gastón took me to Los Pioneros Parrilla Patagónica steakhouse. I ate the most delicious Patagonian trout ravioli in a light cream sauce tinged with just enough saffron to allow the delicately flavored, soft, pink flesh to speak for itself. Gastón opted for smoked trout *empanadas* followed by *chivito al palo*, or Patagonian goat stretched across an iron cross and cooked vertically over an open fire, allowing the goat to cook evenly while the fat drips off to continuously baste the meat.

"Goat?" I asked. "I thought we'd agreed to take a break from the obnoxious amounts of meat we've been eating since we got here." In the week we'd been there, I'd already eaten my favorite, *matambrito de cerdo,* pork flank steak drizzled in lemon juice, at least a handful of times—not to mention the other cuts of beef that followed.

"We did." My aggressively non-vegan husband dipped a forkful of goat into *pebre*, a sauce similar to *chimichurri* made with onions, tomatoes, herbs, garlic, olive oil, chilies and red wine. "That's why I ordered *chivito* instead of the *ojo de bife* rib-eye special."

I shook my head, laughing. "Just like Aunt Voula in *My Big Fat Greek Wedding* when she said, 'What do you mean he don't eat no meat? That's okay, I make lamb.'"

Back at my in-laws' cabins, I took advantage of the fact that the Orías' kitchen was unusually available. Graciela hadn't yet arrived, and Jorge Luis and Gastón split their time between tending to guests and fly-fishing escapades. After putting the boys down for their afternoon *siesta*, I set out to make some meatless dishes for dinner and lunch the following day.

I made *acelga* with *alubias,* greens-n-beans loaded with hand-fuls of swiss chard and cannellini beans floating in a velvety broth made of humble ingredients that together made a big impact. Oil-packed anchovy filets that disintegrated when sautéed with thyme and garlic added a flavorful umami base; beans added a starchy creaminess; and parmesan and butter added richness. I finished off the soup with fresh lemon juice that balanced out the flavors, waking up the one-pot meal of maritime goodness. All I needed was a good loaf of crusty bread from the *panadería* and dinner that night was taken care of. Through the years, Gastón had become accustomed to eating soup as a meal. Sometimes. *De vez en cuando.* But not all soups made the cut.

I also prepared a large pot of *lentejas* for the following day, sautéing brown lentils with onion, garlic, jalapeño, red pepper and cubed carrots before submerging them in chicken broth to slowly cook until just *al dente.* Sweet on meat, I knew both Jorge Luis and Gastón would miss the Spanish-style *chorizo colorado* and starchy potato common in a typical Argentine *guiso de len-tejas* stew, so I planned on serving them room-temperature with a spicy *picadillo* of raw garlic, lemon zest and chopped flat-leaf Italian parsley topped off with fried, crispy shallots. Like most *guisos* and stews, both the greens-n-beans and lentils would taste better the next day, just in time for the rest of Gastón's fam-ily to arrive.

That following morning, Gastón, Belén and I decided to take the boys on the tourist catamaran to visit the magical Parque Na-cional Los Arrayanes, the world's only ancient myrtle forest with trees over five hundred years old. When seen from the Nahuel Hua-pi lake, the *bosque* didn't look much different from the surrounding forest. But the moment we stepped off the boat and found ourselves underneath the enchanted woodland's canopy, its magic enveloped us. We were instantly blown away by the intense cinnamon col-or of the hundreds of contorted corkscrew trunks. Their white spots made it appear that at any moment the trees could morph into white-spotted dear and run away, and the sunlight illuminated the canopy's glossy green foliage and dainty white blossoms like a French Impressionist painting.

A profound sense of déjà vu came over me as Lucas let go of my hand and ran ahead, petting the trees, almost distrustfully at first, as if they were animals. Their bark had the same kind of softness as human skin, but it was cold to the touch and peeled off easily, leaving white spots behind. Mother Nature was in charge of dressing the trunks again and again.

I've been here, I thought. More than once. That's when I remembered that my parents and grandparents brought me and my siblings to this very spot when we visited the city of San Carlos de Bariloche when I was young. I couldn't have been older than ten. But there was something else. I remembered these trees calling to me before. Now, they were once again beckoning. Calling for something. I stopped and surveyed my surroundings, relishing the quiet. I didn't want to leave. For the first time in months, Mateo was breathing easily and didn't seem to need his regularly scheduled breathing treatments.

"Babes, how would you feel about letting Belén take the boys back on the catamaran while we walk back? It's a seven-mile hike through the Quetrihué Peninsula back to town. I'd love to get lost in these woods for a while."

"That's almost twelve kilometers—more than a while," Gastón said, looking at Belén.

"*Vayan*, go," Belén said. "I've got the *chicos*."

"It says here in the pamphlet it takes about three hours to hike back," I said. "We can work up a sweat for all the Malbec we're planning on drinking at lunch."

"Speak for yourself. I'm dreaming of an ice-cold Quilmes." Gastón reluctantly took me up on my offer.

We walked in silence for most of the way, taking in the forest and occasional lake views that appeared in breaks in the foliage. I still couldn't quite put my finger on the sense of déjà vu that had come over me, until a large, red-beaked, black-and-white Magellanic woodpecker got our attention. Nothing breaks the silence of hiking in the woods like the urgent, rapid-fire toc-toc-toc percussion of a woodpecker's rapping. We stopped and looked up into the sea of branches above us in search of the avian culprit. Said to be among the largest in all of the Americas, this particular woodpecker is found only in the Patagonian forests of southern Argentina and Chile.

"What do you think she's trying to tell us? We'll have to look up the symbolism of a knocking woodpecker when we get back to the cabins."

Gastón laughed, grabbing my hand. "So now Woody Woodpecker's your latest spirit animal?"

"Maybe. You never know." I punched his shoulder playfully.

"I'm sure it's a sign." His eyes rolled back facetiously. "I don't know what it means, *Gordita*. The only thing I do know—other than my calves are killing me—is that I finally feel at home."

"I know you do. If you want to move back to Argentina, we have to find the way to make it happen. Ideally before the boys start elementary school."

"No. I mean right now. Here. With you. You're my home. Wherever we are together is home. I feel like we've found our way back to one another."

I wrapped my arms around Gastón. "Me too. You know, this feeling has been driving me crazy all morning. But now I know what it was. That last summer I spent in Pittsburgh before meeting you, I went on a run with Sonny in Fox Chapel. The strangest thing happened that day. Sonny got away from me. She'd been chasing white-tailed deer that hid from tree to tree, and before I knew it, she was well into the forest trails. The trees, the deer and their flashes of white tail, Sonny . . . they all seemed to be playing tricks on me that day. I couldn't tell one from another. Eventually, they all merged into one and I felt as if I'd been transported to this very place! A place I'd only visited once as a girl and barely remembered. But that day I felt Argentina calling me home. I came, and there you were, waiting for me. You were the home I'd been looking for. I just didn't know it."

"I did. From the moment I saw you get off that plane."

"But how do we keep it like this? How do we keep remembering?" *He'll remind you*, something whispered inside of me. And all at once I had the strange impression that we weren't alone—that my Gentleman Caller was there in those woods with us.

* * *

The hike took exactly three hours. Back at his parents' cabins, Gastón and I sat down to lunch with the intense satisfaction of completing a seven-mile trek. As I sipped my Malbec, I watched intently as my ever-discerning father-in-law, who more often than not found flaws in most dishes, tried the lentils. My eyes followed each movement as he took a bite, chewed decisively, and swallowed.

"Carrots instead of *papa*? That's an interesting choice. I guess they're lighter than potato." Jorge Luis swirled his spoon around the bowl, dissecting its ingredients. "I have to say, I love the addition of these crispy shallots. I don't even miss the *chorizo colorado*."

"*Gracias*, Jorge. That means a lot coming from you."

"*Mmm. Está delicioso*. Perfect for this warmer weather," Graciela chimed in. Unlike her husband, she'd never met a dish she didn't like. The act of someone else cooking for her was enough to make any plate delicious.

Jorge Luis took another bite and, wiping his cleanly trimmed, salt-and-pepper gray mustache with his napkin, looked at Gastón. "Josefina can cook. I could tell after eating her greens-n-beans and now her lentils." He winked at me. "She knows how to combine her ingredients."

"*Mi gordita*? Definitely." Gastón grabbed my knee under the table. "The only thing about Josie is that she never makes the same dish twice. She'll start cooking without making sure she has all of the ingredients she needs and ends up improvising with whatever's in the pantry or fridge. Drives me crazy," he said, half-jokingly.

"You know, *hijo*, I have to disagree with you. Cooking is an unspoken language that only those who do it over and over again understand. Recipes are a lot like the rivers and lakes surrounding us. They're never the same."

I raised my eyebrows at Gastón and nodded in agreement. He squeezed my knee as if to say, "We'll settle this later," full well knowing he'd never live this one down.

Gastón and I took our playful squabble back to our two-room cabin. After laying the boys down for their nap, I jumped in the shower to wash off the morning's hike. As I emerged from the bathroom, Gastón grabbed me from behind, unwrapping my towel. The lentils had gone to his head.

"Shhh. The kids are sleeping. What if they wake up?"

Gastón wound his arms around me, putting his finger to my lips. He kissed me passionately. "One quick *siesterito*." The Argentine *siesta* with benefits.

I pulled back, hesitantly, staring at him with half-closed eyes. "The boys. We can't. Not here," I whispered in his ear. Still, I ached for the man I'd fallen in love with at the ranch all those years ago. He was back. And he wanted me, too.

His face inched even closer. "We'll just have to be quiet." My abdominal muscles jumped nervously as he pulled me down to the floor on top of him. Gastón grabbed hold of my hips, slowly guiding them back and forth with the swiftness and resolve of a seasoned angler: *back on one, pause on two, forward on three, back again on four*. I placed my hands on his broad chest, arching my back with pleasure, when Graciela suddenly walked into the bedroom holding a pile of just washed towels. Time froze. We all froze. I instinctively wrapped my arms around my bare breasts and collapsed onto Gastón for cover.

"Don't mind me. *Sigan no más*. Carry on." Graciela adjusted her signature round John Lennon eyeglass frames that, from sheer shock, had slid down the bridge of her nose. She calmly placed the towels on the bed before leaving. The bed where her two grandchildren were sleeping.

"*Gracias, Vieja*," Gastón said from underneath me.

I slapped him. *Really? You're thanking her? At a time like this?* I didn't know whether to laugh or cry as I stood up to get dressed.

"Where are you going?" Gastón grabbed my hand, pulling me back down. "We're not done yet," he said, reversing our position.

"Your mom just walked in on us naked, having sex on the floor next to our two babies. You can't make this shit up. And you want to finish? I don't think so. I can't ever face her again."

But I did. It took copious amounts of a crisp Sauvignon Blanc at dinner that evening to make me forget our salacious run-in with my mother-in-law. Jorge Luis had lured me to the table with freshly caught rainbow trout he'd pulled out of the Lago Espejo Chico just hours earlier. As its name suggests, the lake's turquoise, glacial waters were so quiet they offered up picture-perfect reflections of the surrounding trees and mountain ranges with mirror-like precision.

Jorge Luis butterflied the ruby red-fleshed trout and cooked it in a cast iron skillet over an open flame *à la manteca negra*, a subtle brown butter sauce perfumed with tarragon. By the time I wiped my plate clean with crusty bread and settled back into my chair, I'd managed to convince myself that my and Gastón's indiscretion would become just another of the many secrets buried underneath the timeless Patagonian river rocks that surrounded us.

I was wrong. At *sobremesa*, Jorge Luis smiled cunningly and offered up a *brindis*, raising his glass. "To Gastón and Josefina. *¡Sigan no más!* Carry on." He patted his son's back, as if to say, *that's my boy*.

The table erupted in laughter as Gastón's parents, brothers and sisters all clinked their glasses in harmony, yelling, "*¡Sigan no más!*" The joke was on us.

Nicolás Amancio Oría, our third son, was born almost nine months to the day afterwards, dripping in mischief. Gastón and I named Nico after Our Lady of the Rosary of San Nicolás, who we're certain helped Mateo overcome his debilitating asthma and Gastón and me find our way back home to one another.

Lentejas (Lentils)

SERVES 7. *Or one couple in search of a son with enough personality for two.*

In Italy, it's believed lentils should be among the first meal you eat for the new year to ensure fortune and prosperity. I don't need much of a reason to eat them—I love lentils in soups, salads, on avocado and egg Ezequiel toast. In the winter months, I add Spanish *chorizo* and up the quantity of broth to create a hardy stew. But if you do, make sure to use a traditional dry *chorizo* known as *chorizo seco*. You can either follow the recipe or improvise with what's in your pantry—that's how versatile lentils can be.

LENTILS

2 tablespoons extra-virgin **olive oil**

1 large **Spanish onion**, finely chopped

4 **shishito peppers**, deseeded and finely chopped (or 1 medium jalapeño, deseeded and finely chopped)

1 large **red pepper** or 2 smaller red peppers, finely chopped

3 **garlic cloves**, finely chopped

2 **carrots**, cubed

1 pound brown or green **lentils**

4 ½ cups low-sodium **chicken broth** or vegetable broth (adjust accordingly to just cover the lentils)

1 **bay leaf**

Salt and cracked **black pepper** to taste

PICADILLO

2 **garlic cloves**, chopped finely

Zest of 1 large **lemon**

Handful of flat-leaf **Italian parsley**, chopped

CRISPY SHALLOTS

1 ½ tablespoons extra-virgin **olive oil**

5 **shallots**, peeled and sliced into thin rings

Sauté onion in tablespoon of olive oil with a pinch of salt over medium-low heat until translucent, about 7–10 minutes. Add shishito peppers (or jalapeño) and red pepper, cooking another 5 minutes until soft. Add garlic, carrots and lentils. Sauté another minute or two, fully coating the lentils.

Add broth and bay leaf and bring to a boil. Once boiling, lower heat to medium-low and cover. Simmer for 20 minutes. Uncover and continue to simmer an additional 7–10 minutes, until just tender. Remove from heat and allow lentils to cool, uncovered, to absorb the remainder of the liquid. Add salt and cracked black pepper to taste.

Meanwhile, make the *picadillo*. Finely chop garlic with a pinch of salt. Transfer to a small bowl, mixing together with lemon zest and parsley until well combined. Set aside.

Fry the shallots. In a saucepan, heat olive oil over medium-low heat until hot, but not smoking. Add the shallots and cook, stirring infrequently to allow them to caramelize, until medium brown and crispy. Remove the pan from heat and set aside.

Once the lentils are cool to the touch, remove the bay leaf, discard, and mix in the *picadillo*. Serve room temperature, sprinkled with crispy shallots.

Chapter 10

Donde comen dos, comen tres
Where Two Eat, There's Always Room For Three

nlike most ravioli, which strive for more of a balance between dough and filling, *sorrentinos* resemble a large, round bowler hat that are unabashedly plump and overstuffed, typically with ham and cheese or a variety of cheeses or ground meat cuts. They'd always been one of my and Dorita's favorites. Second only, perhaps, to Argentina's passion for red meat, its fascination for stuffed and fresh pastas made perfect sense. After all, Italian is the largest ethnic origin of modern Argentines. My *abuelo* Alfredo's mom, Hermenegilda Agustina Barberis, was among the thousands of Italians who flooded Buenos Aires at the turn of the twentieth century, moving from Morozzo in the Italian region of Piedmont to Santa Fé, Argentina when she was just eleven.

The Italian tradition is unmistakable in Argentine food and wine culture, as well as the Argentine way of talking. Our son Mateo had inherited the latter. Once he started talking as a toddler in his signature sing-song rhythmic way, Gastón baptized him "*El Tanito*" since it was clear Mateo leaned towards his ancestral Italian roots.

Incidentally, there's nothing in *Italia* quite like *sorrentinos*, making them a wholly Argentine invention assembled almost entirely from the suitcases and memories of second-generation Italian immigrants. They were created in the 1930s in the Buenos

Aires restaurant Sorrento, where a creative chef from Mar del Plata—a resort city on Argentina's Atlantic coast—gave life to this passion. No matter where they were from, *sorrentinos* were an undisputed local delicacy. Your choice of sauce also added another dimension to the dish. Oftentimes, Argentine restaurants offered a selection of pastas and a separate list of sauces to choose from, allowing patrons to mix and match. Dorita always chose the *mixta:* a mix of *crema de leche* and *concasé de tomates,* a quick, fresh tomato sauce with garlic, basil and olive oil. Regardless of their preparation, *sorrentinos* are a larger breed that stand apart from their brethren ravioli family, making women—this one at least—gaga for them when pregnancy cravings hit.

* * *

Our son Nico arrived days before Halloween 2006. I went directly to the hospital after Lucas and Mateo's preschool Halloween parade. Graciela had come for his birth and would be staying two months to help out with the kids. Between work and three boys under the age of four, I wouldn't have been able to survive without her. From the moment we laid eyes on Nico, it was clear he was just like Gastón, in looks and character. He kept us on our toes from day one, exuding joy and a personality big enough for two. My mom knew it too. While he was still in diapers, she coined him *Nico Pico y su amigo*—his friend—*Federico.* It suited him perfectly.

Still, even with Graciela's help, Nico's arrival didn't come without its own challenges. Just as Mateo's health was stabilizing and we were settling into managing our family of five, the housing market fell, causing a mortgage crisis that led Gastón to lose his job and my brother Oscar his company.

In Argentina there's a saying that the stork delivers every child with a loaf of bread under his arm. Ours seemed to have dropped it along the way. Money got tight, so when he was just three weeks old, I kissed Nico and the boys goodbye and returned to work. By that time, I'd been promoted from director of finance to chief financial officer and was responsible for more than one hundred employees and eighty diagnostic testing offices throughout Ohio, Pennsylvania and West Virginia. I worked fifty-hour weeks, pumping breast milk during my lunch hour and right before returning home.

Things between Gastón and me were tense, and I felt I'd been robbed of time at home to bond with our newborn, but we didn't have a choice. It took almost a year for Gastón to find another job, this time as a credit analyst in the coatings division of Pittsburgh Plate Glass Co., also known as PPG. It wasn't his dream job, but it was a job. And that's all that mattered when we had three young boys to feed and a mortgage to pay.

Then, just as our family life began to stabilize, I found myself throwing up in Target. I'd stopped at the store to pick up diapers on my way home from the office, when suddenly an uncontrollable wave of nausea came over me. I'd barely made it to the public restroom before unpacking my lunch from earlier.

I started counting the days since my last period as I washed my hands. I left that restroom and bought a pregnancy test. It was in that Target I discovered I was expecting our fourth child. I didn't bother to call Gastón. Instead I drove home in silence, wondering how we'd manage our jobs with four young children under five. Now that Gastón was working, we'd have to find more reliable childcare. I'd have to call Graciela. I seemed to be monopolizing all her time, but my mom wasn't available. For visits and to spoil the kids, yes. But Mom and Dad traveled all the time. Between Pittsburgh, Miami, Argentina and the occasional trip to Europe, they were rarely in one place for very long.

As I turned into our driveway, it dawned on me: *Isabella*. She's on her way. Finally we'd have the daughter we'd fallen in love with when I was pregnant with Lucas and thought he was a girl for all those months.

I ran into the house and showed Gastón the pregnancy test. He swept me up into his arms, then picked up each of the boys, twirling them around. "We're having a baby!" We'd figure it out. We always did.

Mom, on the other hand, wasn't so happy. We got into a monumental fight when I finally told her we were expecting. I didn't choose the best time to tell her. She'd called me, elated, one day a month or so after Gastón and I found out, bursting at the seams to share the latest news.

"Josie, Valentina is getting married. Save the date: March 2008 in Buenos Aires. We're all traveling." Valentina had moved to Argentina the year prior; I wasn't the only Caminos girl our mother country tugged at.

I sat at my desk in silence. I was happy for my oldest sister who always took care of me like a second mom. But I was also sad because I'd miss it. I'd miss seeing my dear sister, who was rounding forty, say "I do." My due date was mid-March 2008. There was no way I'd be able to travel, especially not internationally.

"Josie, did you hear me? Your sister's getting married!" Mom shouted.

"I did. That's incredible. I have to call her. I want to hear everything! But I won't be able to be there."

"Don't be ridiculous! If you need help with the tickets, you know your father and I will help you."

"That's not it," my voice cracked.

"Then what is? Why would you even consider missing your sister's wedding?"

"I'm pregnant. We just found out a couple of weeks ago. We've been letting it set in before sharing the news. The baby's due mid-March next year. I won't be able to travel."

Now it was her turn to be silent. "Mom?"

"Si, *hija*?"

"Do you have anything to say? Congratulations, perhaps?"

"What were you thinking? After all the pressure you and Gastón have been under. She's not coming, you know."

"Who?"

"The girl you're looking for. You just keep trying. You and Gastón make boys. Don't you realize that? The chances of you having a girl goes down with each child you have."

"There's still a chance. Plus, we weren't looking to get pregnant. It just happened."

"You'd think by now you'd know how not to. Don't you realize how selfish you are? Your sister is finally getting married, and you won't be there."

"Really? You're acting as if I did this on purpose. How was I supposed to know that Valentina was planning on getting married? She never said a word to me. I knew her relationship was going well, but I couldn't have known he was about to pop the question."

"That's just it, Josephine Ursula Caminos. Always thinking about yourself. About what you want. Did you ever stop to think about your three boys? If you keep having children, it will affect them all financially. You've spread yourself too thin, especially with your time. You'll run yourself ragged."

"You're one to talk. You and Dad had six kids."

"Those were different times. I had *Mami* helping me. And your father had a very good paying job. Today things are entirely different. How can you be the breadwinner and mom of four children at the same time? Plus, I always tell your father we should have stopped after three or four kids."

"Thanks, Mom. You do realize I'm number five?" Another call beeped in. I was done with the conversation. "I have to take this. I'll talk to you later." I didn't wait for her to respond and hung up.

Mom called back. I didn't answer.

My sister Camila called me later that afternoon. "Josie, Mom's been trying to reach you. She's flying to Argentina and wants to talk to you before she goes. I have her in the car with me. We're on our way to the airport."

"I don't want to talk to her."

"She told me about the baby. Congratulations, I'm so happy for you and Gastón!"

"Thanks. Mom wasn't. Isn't. I have no desire to talk to her."

"Just say a quick goodbye. What if her plane goes down?"

I heard Mom yell, "Cami!" in the background. *Don't jinx it.*

"I'm just saying. You'd never forgive yourself. You'd always remember the last words you said to her were fighting words."

"Fine. Put her on."

She did.

"Josie, *hola*. I'm on the way to the airport. I'll be in Buenos Aires and the ranches the next four weeks. I didn't want to get on that plane without telling you what a good mother you are. I'm very happy for you. And we'll welcome this new grandchild with open arms." It was as close to a sorry as I'd get.

"Thanks, I guess. Have a good trip. I'm going to call Valentina tonight."

"Take care of yourself. How's the vomiting?"

"Back with a vengeance, like the other pregnancies. But I'm managing it."

"Okay. Good. Make sure you always have crackers on you. Call me if you need anything."

"I will. Have a safe trip. *Chau*. Love you." I imagined Mom was already plotting the baby stores she'd hit in Buenos Aires, an excuse to shop for a good cause.

"Wait," Mom spoke again. "Promise me this is the last baby, at least for a while. You can't keep looking for a daughter. Your *tío* Álvaro called me just a little bit ago to ask when I get in. I told him you were expecting and he told me to tell you it's a boy. You know he always knows—he hasn't been wrong yet."

I sighed in resignation. "I guess I shouldn't be surprised. But, Mom, don't worry. When I finally do have my girl, I'm going to name her after you."

"*Ay*, Josie. Always so *impertinente*."

"Do you prefer Beatriz or Poupée? Which is more fitting?"

Mom didn't answer. She didn't think having a girl was in the cards for me. "Goodbye, *mi amor*. Take care of yourself and give Gastón and the boys a kiss. I'll call you from the ranch."

* * *

Three months later, Gastón and I found out we were having another boy. We'd decided to meet at the ultrasound clinic since we both planned to return to work right after. I put on a brave face, but Gastón could see I was fighting back tears. When we got outside, he took me in his arms as I searched desperately for my keys.

"You okay? Let's go to lunch and celebrate. I still have time."

"I really don't feel like it. I have a crazy afternoon. I'd rather get back so I can get home earlier tonight." I opened my car door.

"Josie, wait. We're going to have the girl. Somehow or another. She'll come. We just have to be patient."

I looked at Gastón from behind the wheel, nodding in agreement. But I didn't believe it, and something told me he didn't, either. "I don't know why I'm surprised. *Tío* Álvaro called it weeks ago. We make boys." That much was clear. Male sperm swam faster, making their way to their prize quicker. And God knows patience had never been one of my stronger virtues. Still, Gastón didn't want me to lose hope. He knew how desperate I was to have a baby girl. It's not that I didn't want another boy, I just loved the idea of hour-long phone calls and window shopping with my adult daughter, like I'd done with Mom over the years. So I climbed into my Jeep and cried the entire way back to the office. Then, after parking, I wiped away my tears, freshened up my makeup and emerged from the car ecstatic that I'd soon be the mom of four boys. I couldn't wait to meet him.

Ignacio José, or Nacho as we call him, arrived the following spring on March 19, St. Joseph's day. That night Gastón made one of my favorite dishes, Chicken Riesling, a one-pot meal of fall-off-the-bone chicken thighs braised with leeks, shallots, little red potatoes with their skins on and large chunks of carrots bobbing in a steaming pool of dry Riesling, finished off with a squeeze of lemon and splash of cream. Gastón first came across the recipe in an issue of the now dearly departed *Gourmet* magazine. At home our kids only know the recipe as *Pollo* or Chicken *a la Nacho,* after he arrived unannounced just hours after that night's *sobremesa.* I was sopping up the very last bits of the earthy Riesling sauce on my plate with a piece of crusty Ciabatta when my first contraction hit. At first, I thought it was my stomach warning me that I'd once again eaten too much, until the pains kept coming, quicker and stronger.

Graciela wasn't able to come for the birth, so she sent Belén in her place. Belén had just finished her fellowship and was taking a month off before starting her full-time job as a pediatrician. Mom jumped on a plane back to Pittsburgh after Valentina's wedding to help those first weeks. And when it was time for Belén to leave, Graciela replaced her, staying the entirety of the three months her visa allowed.

We were sad to see Graciela go, but this time Gastón and I were prepared to juggle the four boys on our own. We became homebodies and lived in our own little world. It was the only way we could manage the kids, our careers and most importantly, our marriage. Until Argentina came knocking. Once again.

* * *

Nacho hadn't yet celebrated his first birthday when I had what I now chock up to a mid-life crisis. I was in my mid-thirties. By that point I had a successful seven-year career in healthcare, a good marriage and four beautiful young boys. Still, I secretly harbored a nagging feeling that had begun keeping me up most nights, an inner voice akin to that of Francis Mallmann, the Argentine born-and-bred celebrity chef, author and restauranteur most known for his Patagonian open-fire style of cooking. When asked about man's worst enemies, Mallmann answered, "Fear. And routine. They paralyze us. They're the worst enemies we have." Both showed up at my door unannounced, like my Gentleman Caller so often had. I found myself unprepared to fight back.

I'd often pace the upstairs hallway in our home around three a.m. looking for some sort of message or sign. I couldn't find the words to explain to Gastón what I'd been feeling, except that I felt like a hamster in a wheel running in circles, going nowhere. I'd often find myself worrying that tomorrow would look the same as today. *Was that so bad, after all?* My sister Camila was in the process of rebuilding her life after a painful and unexpected divorce. She never wanted to be part of a statistic. She never wanted that to happen. My friend Taylor continued to put on a brave face after her fifth miscarriage. And Megan, mom to two young girls, had recently successfully completed her last round of radiation in her own private battle with cancer. But routine had set in, and I'd lost interest in my career. For years I was the only woman at our directors' meetings, and I came to realize I'd come as far as I could go in my current position. It was up to me, and me alone, to rewrite my story. It would take me the greater part of a decade to plot my next move, but it was time I put pen to paper.

My Gentleman Caller helped me realize this. At least two years had passed since we'd last met. That was until one night, I found myself alone in the still of my bedroom when he appeared, clad in his usual outdoor cap and khaki windbreaker, at my bedroom doorway. Gastón was in the nursery down the hall putting Nacho down for the night, and I'd been fighting sleep as I lay reading a book. My eyes kept closing, but then I'd catch myself and force them open to try to finish the chapter. Suddenly, something caught the corner of my eye.

"Babes, is that you? Is Nacho asleep?" I turned to look at the door. It wasn't Gastón. It was my Gentleman Caller, leaning against the doorway, his cap in his hands as he looked at me with a compassionate smile. I felt my pulse throbbing in my throat, but I was rendered speechless and paralyzed. I was watching the scene unfold, but I didn't feel like I was an active participant. *Was I dreaming?*

My Gentleman Caller didn't enter the bedroom. Instead, he stood there, looking at me with dark eyes. He didn't utter a word, yet I heard him loud and clear. "You grew up watching your *abuela* in the kitchen. Go back to your childhood. The answer you're searching for is there, deep inside of you. Find it. Make it." I awoke the following morning tasting boiling milk and sugar in the air. I was more confused than ever, and yet things suddenly made sense. For some innate reason I didn't yet understand, I had to make *dulce de leche*. In some form or another, this one ingredient was a mainstay in most every Argentine's childhood, like peanut butter and jelly in the States. But even more.

From as far back as I could remember, I'd start each day with Lincoln shortbread biscuits slathered with *dulce de leche* during our holiday trips to Argentina. My seventh birthday particularly stood out in my memory. I'd spent it on the red-eye from Miami to Buenos Aires, but I knew Dorita was waiting for me with a special homemade birthday cake. That year she surprised me with the most magical Barbie doll cake I'd ever seen. Her sweeping ballroom-length skirt was made of *Abuela's* prized *torta de nuez* walnut cake, coiffed in alternating ruffles of *dulce de leche* and glossy meringue. She was a dream to behold—so beautiful that I didn't want anyone to eat her. I blew out the candles and instinctively grabbed the cake and ran, tripping over my feet. The cake and I both landed on Dorita's wood-planked dining room floor— me in one piece, the cake not so much.

That same trip, my *abuelo* Alfredo showed me his Argentina. Unbeknownst to me, my parents and Dorita had left me with Alfredo for the weekend while they traveled south to the Patagonia with my older brothers and sisters. As I awoke that Saturday morning, Alfredo tucked a newspaper under his arm. "Josefina, get dressed. Today I am going to show you *mi Argentina*." He grabbed my hand and we walked several blocks to his home-away-from-home when Dorita was away—La Confitería Paris. There it stood on the corner of Seventh and Forty-Ninth Streets in downtown La Plata, its glass walls showcasing every variety of *pastelería* imaginable. As is typical in Argentine cafés, the place was bustling with locals who'd come for a meal as well as those waiting in line to pick up *facturas* for the afternoon *merienda*.

We entered and found a cozy table for two that our waiter dressed with all sorts of delicacies—coffee, sugar cubes, linen napkins, a shot of sparkling mineral water and a little plate of *alfajores,* bite-sized sandwich cookies with *dulce de leche* centers. We shared the most delicious basket of fresh *medialunas*. Some of the croissants were sweet, some savory, some stuffed with *dulce de leche. Abuelo* had several *cortaditos*, espressos cut with milk, as he read his paper alongside me, while I sat in comfortable silence, sipping my *submarino* hot chocolate as I took it all in—the generations of *Platenses* (people from La Plata) who'd come together to discuss everything politics and the day's news to impeccably dressed men requesting window-seat tables to watch the beautiful women passing by. It's then I began to understand that silence too can be communion—that the one who says the least may just be the one who holds the answer.

I can't tell you how long the both of us sat at that table, but that *sobremesa* has stayed with me for a lifetime. Looking back, I realized how difficult it would be to recreate that kind of alchemy. But I'd be damned if I wasn't going to try.

* * *

I awoke the next morning more determined than ever to learn to make *Abuela* Dorita's *dulce de leche*. The idea came out of left field. Even after the hundreds of desserts I'd baked in my lifetime, I'd never once been tempted to attempt to make *dulce de leche*—not until my Gentleman Caller's visit the night before. Like most weekdays, I barely had a second to spare to kiss Gastón, feed Sonny, feed the boys, get them (and myself) dressed, drop them at preschool and make it to work before nine. As I said my usual good morning to Gastón, I added, "Babes, can you pick up some whole milk at the market? Make sure it's organic. And grab a couple of gallons."

Gastón looked at me, puzzled. "*Gordita, sos un aparato.* You know we can't afford organic." With four boys that went through a gallon of milk a day, he had a point. "I picked up milk yesterday. What are you up to?"

"I need more. I'm planning on making Dorita's *dulce de leche* tonight. I'm going to call her and ask for the recipe."

Silence from Gastón. Just a slight nod and look that screamed, *ay Dios, here she goes again with one of her projects.*

I didn't know what I was thinking, asking Dorita for step-by-step instructions. She'd taught me everything I knew in the kitchen, but never allowed me to write down one single thing. Her cooking depended on the day and it changed with the weather, the way she was dressed or the side of the bed she'd woken up on. She cooked to the beat of her own drum, measuring in *dedos*—one or two fingers of milk, Abuela?—*pizcas* and *puñados.*

Dorita was half asleep when she answered my call. "*Abuela,*" I said, notepad in hand. "*Buen día.* Did I wake you?

"Josie. *Hola, mi amor.* No, I was just getting up. How are you?"

"I'm good. Thanks for asking. I'm actually calling because I need your *dulce de leche* recipe." I myself was still trying to catch up with this newfound conviction that had come to me during the night.

"*Dulce de leche?* But why? Can't you find any in Pittsburgh? I'm sure your *mami* could send you some from Miami."

"I know. But I want to make it myself. The *dulce de leche* you fed us when we were younger."

"*No lo hagas*, Josie. Milk is very fickle. You have to tend to the pot for hours, and to be honest, I don't know if you have that sort of patience or time."

But I insisted, and reluctantly and impatiently, she began reciting the *dulce de leche* process by heart, in true Dorita fashion, without any detail as to measurements or cooking times. Reluctant because she wanted to spare me the despair and frustration of ending up with a pot of scalded milk after stirring it for two hours straight. Impatient because I kept asking for details she wasn't able to provide.

I cross-examined her. "But *Abuela*, what temperature do I boil the milk to? Should I get a candy thermometer?"

"Why would you? You do realize it's not candy? It's a preserve."

"I know, but at what point am I supposed to add the sugar? And how large of a teacup should I use to measure it? Do I add it all at once?"

"It depends on the milk and the amount of fat it has. That changes from animal to animal and the time of year. Once you get a feel for the milk, the rest will come to you. Sometimes you'll need more sugar, sometimes less."

Really, Abuela? *As if that's what I need to hear.* I hung up the phone with what seemed liked half of a recipe. I'd have to work on filling in the blanks by trial and error.

That evening after tucking the kids into bed, I began experimenting with pot after pot of scalded milk. I went through at least five gallons that first weekend, and on the third day, finally came up with a lumpy, golden spread that was edible, but more of a syrup in consistency. I was slowly coming to understand exactly what it was Dorita had tried to tell me. *Stir constantly until either you feel your arm is going to fall off or you're on the verge of screaming uncontrollably. Also, it's wise to have someone you adore talking to you in the kitchen while you're making it. Or, if you've truly mastered the art of keeping a telephone under your chin without it falling to the floor, a call with a good friend always makes the time go faster.*

The art of preserving milk could rob you of a good three or four hours, no matter the result. It was time consuming at best, but I didn't care; I was committed to getting it right. Besides, stirring the pot late into the night beat my restless nights and actually rendered me tired.

Gastón soon realized he could either fight my insanity or join me on my culinary quest to conquer the milk. He chose the latter. Most nights, we began taking turns stirring the pot. I secretly thought he wanted to see if he could make it better than me. But that was okay, because I needed his help. We'd uncork a bottle of Malbec and settle into the kitchen, meticulously charting temperatures, amounts and color, while the other sipped and stirred.

One night, after cleaning yet another scalded pot of milk, I looked at Gastón with a sudden realization. "Why don't we look up the recipe in *Doña* Petrona's cookbook? Dorita and Valentina gave us one for our wedding. I'm pretty sure it's on the shelf in the back of the pantry."

"*Buena idea.* It couldn't hurt." Gastón went to get it. "This is brand new. It's spine isn't even cracked. Have you ever even opened it?" he asked, handing me the book.

"Once or twice. I like having it around—you know, just in case. Here it is. *Dulce de leche.* Page 764."

"What's it say?"

I rambled off the ingredients. "Three liters of whole milk. One vanilla bean. Eight hundred grams of super fine sugar. One-half teaspoon of sodium bicarbonate."

"What temperature does she say to boil it to?"

"She doesn't. She only says to boil the milk until it begins to take on color and thicken."

"For how long?"

"No mention of that either. She also offers no particular order when adding the ingredients. And while she talks about a plate test to check whether the *dulce de leche* is ready, there's still no mention of cooking times or temperatures." *Of course there wasn't.* Like Dorita, *Doña* Petrona was of the generation of women who learned to cook by watching parents or grandparents in the kitchen. They were taught using approximations and interchangeable ingredients. Through osmosis, they learned to improvise.

Noting my frustration, Gastón put down his milk-laden wooden spoon and hugged me. "You know, Josie, *Doña* Petrona's career didn't take off until her late thirties. I think she was thirty-seven or thirty-eight when her first cookbook was published."

"She beat Julia Child. I think Julia was in her late forties when *Mastering the Art of French Cooking* was first published."

"I know you think you're too old to start over. But you're not happy at the office. Why don't you leave? Is that what all of this *dulce de leche* craziness is about? What are you waiting for? You know I'll support you either way."

Life was so easy before we had kids. We could just reinvent ourselves on a whim. But now we had four boys to think about. I had to put them first. "The boys are still young, *mi amor.* I can't leave my job. I've put too much time in. It's too risky. We have a mortgage to make each month. Now get back to stirring. The milk's acting up."

"Then what's this all about?"

"I honestly don't know. I just feel a need to make this *dulce de leche*. I can't explain it. Why or what's next, I have no idea, but something tells me this is the first step."

"First step towards what?" My whims weren't new to Gastón, still he looked at me in a way only he could. He knew me better than anyone in this world—that I had a tendency to jump into things without thinking them through. And that sometimes got me—us—into trouble.

"I haven't figured that part out yet." I didn't bother telling Gastón that my Gentleman Caller had given me the idea weeks before during a quick, unannounced bedtime visit. Or that maybe he wasn't the only one missing Argentina.

That was enough of an explanation to keep Gastón stirring. He'd married me for the good, the bad and the crazy, too.

* * *

After a month or so of working late into the night with Gastón, we finally made it: old school *dulce de leche*. The real deal. But just when we thought we'd figured it out, we'd create a batch that didn't turn out. We'd wonder what we did differently, tasting it over and over. And then it turned out again, and again, and then even better. Our pots of scalded milk were behind us—mostly.

There was still the occasional batch that would turn on us because we'd get distracted with the kids or something or other.

Then there was the week or so when I'd wake up and find a feathery frost covering the *dulce de leche* that formed from the salty tears I'd shed after our Sonny girl suddenly left us. Easy on the eyes, the brittle crystals were a reminder that angels were all around us. Hard on the tongue, they sprouted straight from the heartache I'd experienced that busy morning I found Sonny peacefully asleep at the base of our stairs. Since moving into our home some six years before, she'd faithfully waited to greet me there each morning, wagging her tail enthusiastically. I'd never experienced an unconditional love like hers. Some mornings I'd be too busy to even pay attention to her—barely patting her head with a swift hello. But she'd always come back—just as excited to see me as the day before. But that particular morning, she was still. Lucas, barely five, saw the sheer terror in my eyes when I couldn't wake her up, and began desperately shaking her himself.

"Sonny, wake up! Wake up! *Mami*, why won't she wake up? Call *Papi* at work," Lucas pleaded with me. "He'll be able to help her." The tears Lucas shed that morning robbed him of the innocence that protects children from growing up too quickly. Childhood— that blissful kingdom where nobody dies and your parents are superheroes who can fix all—is the first precious thing that death steals from a child. And there was nothing Gastón nor I could do about it. At fourteen, Sonny had lived a good, long life. Still, we were devastated by our first and only girl's unannounced departure.

Dorita was turning ninety that year on September 25, and my entire family was planning on traveling to Argentina to celebrate. That gave me six months, give or take, to perfect her *dulce de leche*. We were well on our way. Wanting to honor Dorita's legacy, I came up with a cockamamie idea to slap her face on jars of homemade *dulce de leche* to share with family and friends as party favors. It would be my gift to her.

I spent that summer leading up to Dorita's birthday tweaking the recipe. Then it occurred to me, why stop at party favors? Why not try to sell her *dulce de leche* nationwide? That's when I signed up as a guest vendor at local farmers markets to sample variations of *dulce de leche* and do some blind taste-testing of my own, mostly to get feedback on taste, texture and uses. People in the States didn't eat like Argentines, and vice versa. I'd have to tailor it to work for North American palates and eating habits. The response I got from friends and strangers alike was overwhelming. They loved it. Many bought several jars at once. They didn't know what they'd been missing and couldn't believe it tasted nothing like the caramel disguised as *dulce de leche* in the States.

They wanted more, even though they couldn't pronounce it. Most called it "*dolce,*" but it didn't matter. The Italian spin on the name was fitting. It hit me that *dulce de leche* was a global taste-bud doppelganger for the chocolate hazelnut spread, Nutella, which Italians ate like Argentines ate *dulce de leche*. Both could be spread on virtually anything and used as a complementary ingredient in recipes throughout the day, starting at the breakfast table. It got me thinking, what if I could somehow do for *dulce de leche* what the Ferrero Company did for their infamous chocolate hazelnut spread? Back in the day, it was an Italian specialty food item relegated to international grocery aisles or specific to Italian markets. But now it commanded a higher devotion as a mainstream ingredient that could be found on most grocery shopping lists. Ferrero's founders left no stone unturned as they worked to acculturate their spread globally. Where hard work, ingenious marketing and diligence weren't enough, they turned to faith, installing statues of the Madonna of Lourdes to watch over Ferrero factories around the globe. I somehow had that same blind faith and conviction and seriously began considering giving it a go with *dulce de leche*. Slowly but surely, I believed with time I could get it into local markets. I didn't have a choice. I couldn't get it out of my head. I lived and breathed the golden milk jam.

Come September, we'd prepared a batch of seventy jars for Dorita's birthday. I dressed the caps in embroidered doilies, sent a dozen to each of my brothers and sisters, and between all of us we buried them in our suitcases packed for Argentina. I couldn't wait for Dorita to try it.

* * *

Landing in Buenos Aires' Ezeiza airport that fall of 2009 felt surreal. It was the first time Gastón and I had been back to Argentina with all four boys. More than three years had passed since that last trip with Lucas and Mateo, who were now five and four years old. It felt great to finally be back. Somehow, Mom miraculously managed to get all of us—my five siblings and me—along with her thirteen grandchildren, to travel to Argentina to honor *Abuela*. Never one to miss an excuse to throw a party, Mom planned a beautiful daytime luncheon at the equestrian Club Hípico in El Bosque, the city's tree-lined forest neighborhood. We weren't certain whether Dorita would actually attend, as she was often bedridden due to her advancing age and a progressive syndrome that mimicked Parkinson's disease. But either way, we would celebrate her.

The following morning Gastón drove me to visit my *abuelo* Alfredo's gravesite at the cemetery. Pitbull's "I Know You Want Me (Calle Ocho)" *rrrrrrumba* blared on the radio. I sang along, totally exaggerating my double-*r* trill, my feet moving to the rhythmic beat. But while Pitbull's catchy tune made my tongue feel relaxed and loose, showing off its duly accomplished Latin swagger, my hands gripped the armrests of the seat as if my life depended on it. Even after all those years, driving in Argentina still managed to unnerve me. I was convinced the country was void of traffic rules other than the fastest cars ruled the right of way, the most aggressive drivers were deemed the safe ones and the hesitant and slow got pinned to the inside lanes.

I'd promised Dorita I'd take her to visit *Abuelo* at the Cementerio Campenario Garden of Peace—Alfredo's resting place for the last thirteen years. But when I arrived at her home earlier that morning, Dorita was quietly having breakfast in bed, still clad in her ankle-length blue silk pajamas. As usual, her platinum hair was perfectly styled, but she insisted she wasn't up to going out. Her mind was made up; she would rest so she could attend her birthday party the following day. I told her I'd go to the cemetery myself.

"Tell your *abuelo* I'll be seeing him soon," Dorita said.

"Not yet, *Abuela*. Not yet!" I shot back at her.

In the car, Gastón was three-fourths of the way around the Rotonda Gutiérrez, the untamed, two-lane traffic circle navigated by thousands who commuted daily from the suburbs of La Plata to Buenos Aires. Gastón and I must have made the trip hundreds of times when we were dating. Locals knew the traffic circle as the Alpargatas Roundabout, after the long-standing textile factory that sat just off the circle and made, among other things, Argentina's everyman's shoe, the *alpargata*. The *gauchos* were the first to make the distinctive canvas shoe popular. In their travels throughout Patagonia, the Pampas and the Andes, *gauchos* walked on foot and rode on horseback, always wearing the comfy *calzado*. Its affordable price tag also helped boost the shoe's popularity. Then, in 2006, the *alpargata* gained international fame when TOMS Shoes gave Argentina's traditional peasant footwear a pricey makeover, baptizing it in the States as the must-have casual shoe for a cause.

"Drop me off there, on the corner, Babes. I don't want you to be late to your *asado*."

"Don't be ridiculous, I'll walk you in. Remember the last time? It took you over an hour to find Alfredo's grave."

"*Gordo*, I mean it, drop me at the corner," I placed my hand on Gastón's as he downshifted the clutch in the center console. "I want to pick up some flowers over there." I pointed at the flower kiosk. "Across the circle from the Alpargatas factory." I looked down and suddenly felt embarrassed to be wearing my sixty-dollar TOMS, when just across the street they were making the originals that sold for less than ten dollars a pair.

Gastón feigned resignation and hastily pulled over, raising his fist outside the window to the car behind us who almost rear-ended us as Gastón suddenly, without warning, exited the traffic circle from the inside left-hand lane.

"*¡Boludo!* Jagoff! Didn't he see me crossing over?" Gastón looked at me, his penetrating honey-brown eyes appearing almost golden against his loosely trimmed dark, silky hair that in the past years had begun to slowly recede from his forehead.

"Are you sure you don't want me to go with you? I can catch up with my friends a little later. They'll be there all day."

We both knew Gastón couldn't wait to get to his friend's house in City Bell, where, in the early morning hours, his childhood friends had begun preparing the smoldering embers for their long anticipated *asado*. From our first meal together, I loved the way Gastón ate. I noticed he hadn't had his usual toast with butter and *dulce de leche* that morning along with his customary quadruple-shot espresso. Surely he was saving his appetite for what was to come. *Asado*, after all, was Gastón's religion. They would ceremoniously feast on *a parrillada como Dios manda* and serve up a barbeque spread fit for the gods along with a side of *¡ché boludo!*—friendly banter—with a spoonful of *chimichurri*.

Gastón always said you could judge someone's character by the *chimichurri* they served at an *asado*. In Argentina, each family had their own tried and true recipe, usually passed down from previous generations. To be considered authentic, *chimichurri* had to include the basics—*salmuera* (a fancy word for water boiled with salt), red wine vinegar, extra-virgin olive oil, garlic cloves, crushed red-pepper flakes and loads of oregano and parsley. The rest was up to the *asador's* own preferences and closely guarded family traditions. God forbid you bought it in the supermarket, or even worse—served *chimichurri* smeared over the just-grilled meat! That was sacrilegious. Each person, by the Grace of God, had a right to dress his steak any way he wanted. *Chimichurri* belonged in a bowl with a spoon, and should be passed around for each person to do with as they pleased.

I leaned over and planted a kiss on Gastón's stubbly cheek. "*Chau*. Enjoy your friends. I'll see you back at your mom's later tonight?"

Who was I kidding? It was clear that between the two o'clock afternoon *asado*, *sobremesa* and the rounds of *mate* they'd pass among each other while catching up on the past couple of years since they'd last seen one another, I wouldn't see Gastón until tomorrow. While he'd stayed true to his Sunday *asado* routine back home, in Argentina, a backyard barbeque not only referred to the beef, but to the whole folklore surrounding the preparation of the fire, the ways to ash-roast the varying beef cuts and, most importantly, the company at *sobremesa*—the part that was missing in Pittsburgh. After all, the table talk would run well into dinner time, until one or the other would finally offer up a "*¿Ché*, hey, how about we put together a *picada?*"—repurposing the *asado's* leftovers onto a charcuterie board that would buy them another three or four tableside hours. And with that, the *asador* would no doubt grab his knife and begin to slice the leftover *chorizo* and charred roasted red peppers, arranging them on a fresh cutting board into bite-sized pieces, while another would go into the kitchen and grab potato chips, peanuts, black olives, a can of *paté* and a wedge of *queso pategrás*, an Argentine cheese that resembles Dutch gouda. Baguettes picked up earlier that morning at the local *panadería* would be tossed in the middle of the table, with cold liters of *Quilmes* beer uncapped and poured. The friends would settle into their chairs, relaxed now that they had an excuse to reminisce about their boyhood antics well into the night. Drunk on stories and memories, the conversation would peak and wrap up with plans being made for another *asado*, this time with the wives and children, before Gastón headed back home to Pittsburgh.

I was getting out of the car when Gastón's long fingers wrapped gently around my arm, getting my attention. "*Ché, Mamá* told me she can watch the kids all day. Take your time."

"I will. And don't forget I need you to drive me to the equestrian club tomorrow morning. I'm meeting my family to set up for Dorita's party and need to take the party favors. They're still in the suitcase we brought."

"How could I forget? Only my *Gordita* would think to smuggle in seventy jars of *dulce de leche* from the States to Argentina. You do know there are whole aisles in the grocery stores here dedicated to the stuff?"

"Of course, but it's not Dorita's *dulce de leche*."

"That's why I love you. Crazy, but loyal."

"*Te quiero,* too." I shut the car door and Gastón drove off, relegating a passing Fiat 600 back into the left-hand lane.

* * *

I was secretly relieved to finally be alone. Since we'd left Pittsburgh to begin the red-eye trip to Miami and on to Buenos Aires, I hadn't had a moment to myself. From passing Nacho between our laps during the thirteen-hour trip, to seeing to every need of his three older brothers, to catching up with Gastón's family, we hadn't even stopped for a breath. It was just before noon. I'd have at least an hour to catch up with *Abuelo* before heading back to *La Plata* to have lunch with Dorita.

As I stepped through the unassuming gray cobblestone gates standing at the cemetery entrance, it seemed not a single soul was there. Off in the distance, I could hear the roar of traffic, but within the confines of the cemetery, all was quiet. To conserve the natural surroundings, cars weren't allowed past the cemetery chapel. Entering the hushed resting grounds seemed to silence the ten thousand things and four little boys constantly clamoring for my attention. I took out my grandfather's plot card, wrapped in his obituary that I'd cut out of the *Pittsburgh Post-Gazette* so many years ago:

> *ALFREDO FELIPE GERMAIN Passed away Mon., Aug. 5, 1996, after a long illness in Miami Beach, FL at the age of 80; he is survived by his loving and devoted wife Dora Fernandez Germain; Mr. Germain was a retired Civil Engineer and Operational Director of the Argentine Petroleum Co., YPF. He was a member of the Jockey Club of La Plata. He was loved and well respected among his family, colleagues and numerous friends in Pittsburgh, PA, Buenos Aires and La Plata, Argentina.*

My older sister, Camila, had been the first to learn of Alfredo's passing. As a newlywed, she was temporarily living at my parents' home on North Bay Road, just down the street from Mt. Sinai Hospital in Miami Beach. She'd been at the hospital all morning with Mom and Dorita. Mom had somehow convinced my *abuela* to leave the hospital to grab a bite for lunch. Dorita was reluctant as it meant varying her routine—for more than a year she would arrive like clockwork every morning when visiting hours began and never leave Alfredo's side until they were over—but that day Mom lured her away with the promise of a Burger King big fish sandwich. Dorita couldn't resist.

Camila, on the other hand, who since a young girl craved mostly salad and crunchy vegetables, always avoided drive-thru fodder. She chose to get a quick shower at home before grabbing a bite and returning to the hospital. Camila had just turned on the water and begun undressing when, out of nowhere, a large blackbird flew up to the small bathroom window overlooking the Miami skyline across Biscayne Bay. The bird was desperate, frantically cawing, cooing and clicking its beak against the glass. It got Camila's attention right away.

"No, *Abuelo*! Not now! *ALFREDO!*" Camila yelled as she frantically pulled on her shorts, flew down the stairs and out the door, her curly long brown hair trailing behind her.

She ran the two blocks to the hospital, scorching the soles of her bare feet as they pounded the scalding pavement. The afternoon August sun had turned North Bay Road into an oven, causing Camila's tears to envelope her in a smoky fog that rose up off the asphalt and carried her the rest of the way to the hospital. Up above, Camila could make out the hazy outline of the blackbird that seemed to be escorting her to Alfredo, its black feathers transforming into various shades of blue as he flew away into the blinding sunlight.

I was just twenty-two when I got the phone call we all dread. "He waited until we left the room, Josie," Camila cried into the phone, choking back tears. "He's gone."

* * *

Back in the cemetery, I looked again at the plot card, realizing Alfredo's grave was just ahead, right off the brick-lined path. While no one was in sight, I couldn't help but feel I wasn't walking alone. I turned around to see if someone was following me, half expecting to find my Gentleman Caller. Today, of all places, the company of my mysterious companion would actually make sense. But no one was there.

As I looked around the cemetery park, rows and rows of identical, modest, flat, rectangular marble stones lay flush with the grass, marking the landscape for acres in every direction. Neither fake flowers nor epitaphs were permitted on the markers, adding to the likeness of each grave. *What a shame,* I thought. I liked to read the epitaphs. They were like bite-sized *hors d'oeuvres* that provided a snippet of one's life story—or at least the story we hoped to be remembered by. *What would mine be?* I wondered.

The walking paths were lined with *tilos*, Linden trees, whose flower blossoms create a common tea used mostly to relax; *plátanos*, not a banana tree, but an indigenous form of maple; and towering ancient *araucaria* conifers commonly referred to as the monkey puzzle tree, were reassuringly protective, forming a canopy over the walkway. Yet I still found myself walking a little faster, turning every once in a while to make sure I wasn't being followed.

Argentina had just celebrated *el día de la primavera* to mark the beginning of spring three days before. And while there was still a chill in the air, the trees and plants seemed to be begging to awaken from a long winter's nap, bursting with anticipation as they prepared to unfurl their yearly offerings. The *tilo* trees would soon form buds that within weeks would bloom, forming inconspicuous dangles of creamy yellow star-shaped flowers beneath their pale green branches. Its blossoms seemed to announce their presence by exhaling the sweetest scent—a blend of honey and lemon peel—that was far-reaching throughout the city of La Plata.

When I finally came across *Abuelo*'s resting place, I grabbed a jacket from my bag and spread it across the lawn to sit upon. I took off my shoes and sat down, feeling the crisp dew on the grass between my toes.

I laid my hand on the cool gravestone. "*Alfreducci,* I'm here. It's been too long, I know. But I'm finally back." As we sat catching up, I ran my fingers along the black lettering etched in the marble, tracing the names and dates listed. I'd visited my grandfather's grave before, but on this particular day, as I sat talking to Alfredo about my four boys, Dorita's ninetieth and my promise that I would raise my sons to know *his* Argentina, I noticed something that stopped me dead in my tracks. My fingers, tracing the names and dates etched in the gravestone in front of me, willed me to take a closer look. My grandfather was buried alongside my great-grandmother and namesake, Josefina. Dorita's mom. Her name was etched in the marble just above Alfredo's. My fingers stumbled across my great-grandmother's date of death for the first time ever—September 25, 1969. How could I have never noticed the coincidence of that date? The following day, Dorita's ninetieth birthday, would also mark the fortieth anniversary of her own mother's death.

Mom, who'd always spoken of her *abuela* Josefina with such reverie, never mentioned this. Considering Mom was the one who discovered her lifeless body, it surprised me that she failed to mention it happened on Dorita's fiftieth birthday. *Did she forget? Block it out?* Just the thought of it haunted me. Why did no one speak of this in my family? Why, now, was I just discovering it on my own?

"*Abuelito, me tengo que ir.* I have to go," I said, sliding on my TOMS. "I'm having lunch with Dorita. We have to make sure she makes it to her party tomorrow. You know Dori. One moment she's excited, and the next she doesn't want to hear anything about it and says she's not going. She sends her love, by the way. But I'm afraid you'll have to wait a while longer to see her. We're not ready to let her go. We lost you. We can't lose her too." I was conscious of everything I'd left out: that Dorita's declining health scared me and that I was doing anything I could to hold onto her.

As I turned to go, a breeze picked up, carrying the soapy scent of orange blossom, lime basil and mandarin followed by a hint of musk, reminiscent of the 4711 Eau de Cologne Alfredo religiously splashed on his cheeks and neck each morning after shaving and carefully trimming his white mustache.

"*Te quiero, Abuelito.* I love you always."

I took in the etchings of the gravestone one last time before leaving. The names and dates sent a profound ripple of sadness through my body that would continue to haunt me for months to come. Then, as I went to leave, my neck began to stiffen, sending a tingling sensation throughout my body. Once again, I felt an eerie feeling, as if someone's unwanted gaze was upon me, watching me, but as I quickly spun around, no one was there.

I'd asked the caretaker to call me a *remis*—a pre-Uber sort of private taxi that employed drivers with their own personal cars—for 12:30 p.m. It was right on time; I was the one running late. I walked past the cemetery's weathered stone chapel on my way out. Its A-line pitched roof was reminiscent of a classic but modern mountain cabin. I glanced in and saw the altar clad in a white cloth and freshly cut flowers, set against a floor-to-ceiling wall of glass windows that overlooked the lawn containing Alfredo's gravesite. The pinpricks on the back of my neck heightened.

This time my uneasiness was justified. My Gentleman Caller was leaning against the altar, standing just under the large wooden crucifix that adorned the glass backdrop overlooking the landscape. *He'd been watching me all along. What does he want?* He was staring back at me from inside the chapel. His elbows were propped on top of the altar, his hands neatly folded in front of him, holding what seemed to be his hat. He looked out of place in the priest's usual standing spot. Our eyes met, and he subtly nodded and motioned to me. To do what, I didn't know.

Just then I heard the caretaker off in the distance calling my name. My car was waiting. I ran through the cemetery's large wood entry gates in search of my ride. I wondered if maybe my Gentleman Caller had once been buried there.

As we zoomed off, I couldn't shake the feeling that he was still watching me. I turned to look through the back window. No one was there.

* * *

Earlier that morning, I'd asked Dorita what she wanted for lunch.

"*Nada.*" she answered curtly.

I'd planned on taking her to Restaurant Abruzzese, a traditional Italian staple in La Plata since 1945, but Dorita refused to get dressed and leave her bedroom. If I couldn't get her to the restaurant, I'd take the restaurant to her. I called in an order of *sorrentinos* with overstuffed ham, cheese and walnut ravioli.

As I arrived at Dorita's house after the cemetery, I found *Abuela* sitting at her dining room table. No matter the guest or time of day, Dorita always laid out a freshly ironed tablecloth each time she intended to share a meal with someone. The table was set beautifully, with a freshly pressed white linen cloth and matching napkins, multi-color, hand-cut crystal wine goblets and her faithful Delft blue-and-white china.

Marta, her live-in nurse, couldn't have been taller than four feet. She always tied back her silky black hair studded with silver highlights into a gloriously thick braid at the nape of her neck. That morning she'd helped Dorita shower, brush her hair and put on a beautiful blouse. She'd recently finished painting Dorita's nails their usual nude color as she sat at the table waiting for me.

"*Perdón, Abuela.* Sorry I'm late. As usual, there was a line out the door at Abruzzese."

"*¿Y tu mamá?*" Dorita asked.

"Mom said to eat without her. She's still running some errands for your big *fiesta* tomorrow, so she'll be here a little later."

I ran into the kitchen and handed Marta the bag filled with cartons of *sorrentinos*, kissing and hugging her. "*Gracias,* Marta. How you get her to come out of her bedroom, I'll never know. But thank you."

Marta knew *Abuela* would later regret not having lunch with me, with the little opportunities we had to see each other. "*De nada,* Josefina. It's nothing."

"There's more than enough here. Make yourself a plate." I left the kitchen to join Dorita at the table. As Marta brought us our beautifully plated and arranged *sorrentinos* with *salsa mixta,* she soon followed with a bottle of Malbec to make spritzers: half a glass of wine mixed with *agua con gas* or seltzer water.

"*Mmm,* Josefinita," *Abuela* said as she took her first bite. And with each subsequent one, strokes of color began to return to her cheeks. The *sorrentinos* had, as I'd hoped, managed to revive Dorita's loquacious spirit and bring back the chatty *Abuela charlatana* I'd always been accustomed to, filled with stories and questions. We ate to our fill as we talked about Gastón and the kids, my job and my recent obsession with preserving milk into *dulce de leche.* I promised Dorita that I'd come by the following morning so she could try the homemade batch I'd made for her birthday.

Marta came in and retrieved the plates, commenting on how delicious the *sorrentinos* were as she offered tea and coffee.

"I'd love a tea *de tilo.* The same for Dorita."

As we sat sipping our tea, *Abuela* finally mustered the courage to ask me about my visit with *Abuelo.* I could tell she didn't like to bring up the subject; after all it was a grave reminder of the loss of the great loves of her life—her mom and husband. I told her about our talk and the fresh flowers I'd left on the headstone.

"I brought you some, too. I'll place a couple there in a vase by Alfredo's picture after lunch."

Since his passing, Dorita had set up an altar of sorts commemorating Alfredo that included her favorite portrait of him, along with a white candle that burned from morning to sundown and an icon of Mary, our Lady of Luján, considered the Patroness of Argentina, Paraguay and Uruguay. *Once I have a* dulce de leche *factory of my own, I'll erect her statue to watch over it,* I decided.

Now that Dorita had broken the ice about the cemetery, I began to apologize over and over that I never knew she'd lost her mom on her birthday. "*Abuela*, why didn't you tell me? Mom named me after her. Still, I know so little about her."

But at the mention of it, Dorita simply grabbed my hand, and with a sad smile told me it was just too painful of a memory that she preferred not to burden me with. "You remind me so much of *Mamá*. Since you were a little girl, I sometimes had to do a double take when you'd be off playing by yourself. Always talking to yourself. I couldn't help but think that she was visiting you, telling you *paso por paso*, step by step, how to make your Holly Hobby cakes."

"I certainly had my share of imaginary friends, that's for sure. *Pero Abuela*, tell me about her. Why won't you tell me about the day she died?"

Mom burst through the front door at that very moment, saving Dorita momentarily from enduring any more of my questions. Always the resourceful shopper, she was carrying bags of outfits she'd picked out for Dorita to choose from for the party.

"Sorry I'm late, *Mami*."

What else was new? Mom was always late. Like a good Argentine, she was faithful to the tradition of disregarding the virtue of punctuality altogether.

Dorita's eyes lit up at the sight of her. She called for Marta, asking her to heat up another plate of *sorrentinos* for Mom. "Sit down, Poupecita," she said patting the chair next to her. "*Donde comen dos, comen tres.*" Where two eat, there's always room for one more.

"What are we talking about, *chicas*?"

Marta set down a plate in front of her.

"*Mmm, que rico.* These are delicious," Mom said, digging in.

"I went to the cemetery to see *Abuelo* today, Mom."

"*Que bueno*, Josie. How's *Papí* doing? Was his grave in good shape? Does it seem like they're taking care of it?"

"Yes, of course, beautifully. I left some fresh flowers. But I've been trying at all costs to have Dorita tell me about great-*Abuela* Josefina. When I was there, I noticed that she died on Dorita's birthday. How could you not have mentioned it? Why don't we ever talk about these sorts of things?"

"It was a terribly sad day." Mom looked at Dorita.

Dorita sat silent, fiddling with her wine glass. It was clear that she intended to file away the subject of her mom's passing on her birthday, just as she did with the other untouchable subjects she didn't wish to discuss: the death of her only sister who died as a young girl; the stillbirth of nearly full-term twin babies she lost to hydramnios, a condition in which excess amniotic fluid accumulates during pregnancy; her dad, whose name she never spoke aloud after he failed to come home one day, and every day thereafter, when Dorita was just a girl. Mom never met her *abuelo*, yet she once told me that while Dorita never spoke of her father, she did, after years of prodding, divulge his name: Antonio. It was the first and last time she heard Dorita say it aloud. Dorita's silence was impenetrable. She was of the generation that kept their ghosts to themselves.

"Come on, *Abuela*. I'm sitting here in front of you as a mom to four boys of my own now. I'm all grown up, and yet I know so little of your own family's life stories to pass on to them one day."

"*Mamí*, Josie has a point. If you don't want to talk about *Abuela* Josefina, how about you tell us about your dad, my *abuelo*? Now, on the eve of your ninetieth birthday, I'd love to finally know something about the grandfather I never met."

"*Basta*. Enough." *Abuela* said softly, jumping out of her chair like *leche hervida*, boiling milk.

"But *Abuela*, I can't get that date out of my head. It's eating at me that your mom died on your birthday. We're family. I never met Josefina, but she's a part of me. She's a part of us."

Mom, who was sitting across from me, stepped on my foot under the table. She knew when enough was enough. She'd once explained to me as a girl that Dorita was of the generation who preferred to cordon off their most painful memories, rather than continue to breathe life into them by sharing them over and over.

Dorita slowly settled back into her chair. At that moment, she drank the last sip of Malbec pooling at the bottom of her glass, asking Mom to serve her a splash more. She took a deep breath and grabbed my hand. "Your great-grandmother Josefina didn't die on my birthday. It was merely the day she took her final breath. Your poor *mami* was the one who found her in the rocking chair."

"That must have been extremely painful for both of you."

"It was, which is why I choose to forget."

But she didn't. Some things you never can. "And your dad? What happened to him?"

Dorita took another sip of wine. She lowered her glass and stared into the distance. "It was an especially warm spring day, the last time I saw him. I was just a girl. I remember *Papá* grabbed his coat and favorite cap before kissing us goodbye. In those days it was illegal for a man to appear in public without a coat, even on days that the heat was unbearable."

"Really? How strange. What happened if you were caught in public without a coat?"

"You received a fine. Something like five *pesos*. That was a lot of money back then. *Papá* grabbed his jacket and cap that day, kissed *Mamá* goodbye on the cheek and turned just before walking out the door to nod goodbye to my brother and me. That was the last time I saw him. I can't tell you what I don't know. What I can tell you is that *Mamí* was left to raise us alone. And by then she'd already had enough heartbreak to last her a lifetime. She buried my older sister, María Josefa, the day she unexpectedly took her last breath when she was just a girl, barely twelve herself. Later, *Mamí* had to bury my brother Felipe too, who left us just as he was becoming a man. Our family of five became a party of two."

Dorita continued. "My father wasn't there to walk me down the aisle when I married your *abuelo* Alfredo. His absence killed *Mamí*. First, he took *Mamí's* dignity, then her heart, but not before he robbed her of her hopes and dreams. He left us all, but *Mamí* had to carry on and raise us. Alone. The not knowing took *Mamí's* leg, and then, finally, her last breath."

Dorita took another long drink of Malbec. *So much loss in one lifetime.* It's one thing to lose somebody. It's another to be left. The epiphany of Dorita's desertion almost brought me to tears. So many things about my *abuela* suddenly made sense in that moment. We'd never come to know what really happened to Dorita's father, Antonio. And if she did know, Dorita wouldn't tell us. She was a vault, and I respected that.

"Oh *Abuela*, I'm sorry," I said, sitting up. I'd come to understand Dorita's silence. She was taught to censor herself as a child. She and her mom kept smiling because that meant everything was okay. When you are so afraid of saying something you shouldn't, you begin to not say anything at all. It created a certain mentality; you begin to leave a lifetime of things left unsaid.

It was at that *sobremesa* I came to realize my *abuelo* Alfredo didn't just marry Dorita, but her mother Josefina as well, and in return he took on the responsibility as a young newlywed for caring for them both. In return, those two glorious women confined themselves to the kitchen from morning to evening with their mad skills, and nurtured him with their daily concoctions that they prepared using *puñados,* handfuls; *dedos,* fingers; *pizcas*, pinches and *poquitos*, little bits. The kitchen was their battleground where they waged and silently transcended their family battles and losses; their pots, pans, kitchen knives, shears, meat mallets, whisks and wooden spoons were their arsenal.

Dad and Mom relived this same story. For as far back as I could remember, Dad embraced Dorita with open arms. In marrying Mom, he took Dorita's hands as well. She fed him well, but always made sure to not overstep in Mom and Dad's marriage. Dad did the same. He never got involved in Mom and Dorita's mother-daughter relationship. But it was clear that Dad would take care of Dorita until the end of her days, without question. That was one thing I truly admired in him.

"What about you, Josie?" Mom asked. "What secrets are you keeping?"

"Secrets? None that I can think of. Why?"

"Well, Iggy's more than a year old now."

"Mom, it's Nacho. Not Iggy."

"He's my little Iggy Pop. What's wrong with that? You know the kids are going to make fun of him at school when he gets older with a name like Nacho in the States."

"Have you ever seen Iggy Pop, Mom? I don't think he's who you think he is."

"Ay, Josie. Of course." Mom shoved me off. "As I was saying, *Nacho* is more than a year old now. This is about the time you always seem to get pregnant with your next. You're not, are you?"

"What?"

"Pregnant? Or planning on getting pregnant?"

"Of course not! Where is this coming from? I can barely handle the four, let alone think of having another."

"It's just that your father and I are concerned you're going to keep trying until you get your girl. And what if she doesn't come? Are you just going to keep having babies?"

"Like I said, I'm not pregnant. But remember I promised you that if I ever end up having a girl, I'll name her after you. Deal?"

"Josephine Caminos Oría. Promise me you're going to stop. You have enough on your plate as is between your demanding job and the boys. And now, on top of everything, you're thinking of starting a full time *dulce de leche* venture on the side? I love your ambition, but you're juggling a lot of balls. One mishap and it can all fall."

"I know. I'm aware. I'm taking a lot of risks. But I can't keep working at Dad's company forever. I don't have a future there. I can't explain it, but I have a feeling about the *dulce de leche*."

"What about it?" Mom asked.

"That it's going to lead me somewhere. That I'm supposed to make it and introduce authentic *dulce de leche* back home. North Americans still don't understand Argentines' obsession with it. They don't know how to use it, because they haven't tried the real thing. I can't help but think it will open the door to a new career. But don't worry. I'm naming the *dulce de leche* company after Dorita. But the girl, she's all yours. I'm naming her after you."

"What girl? Something tells me she'll arrive when pigs fly."

Dorita, the more compassionate of the two, cupped my hand in solidarity.

"Maybe, Mom. But you never did tell me, do you prefer I name her Beatriz or Poupée?"

"*Ay*, Josie. Stop kidding around." Mom pushed her chair back from the table and got up. "*A otra cosa mariposa.* Moving on, *Mami*," she said, shaking off her frustration. "Tomorrow we celebrate life. Ninety years of it. Ninety years of you. Should we see what you're going to wear?"

"*Gracias, hija.* You're always thinking of me," Dorita said under her breath. She was more than ready for her afternoon *siesta*. She squeezed my hand. "If I'm going to turn ninety, I might as well look good doing so."

Mom turned to me. "I picked a little something up for you, too." She handed me a book, *Pasión por el Dulce de Leche* by Miriam Becker. On its cover was the picture of a classic five-layer *Rogel* cake made of delicious layers of sweet puff pastry sandwiched together with *dulce de leche*.

"Thanks, Mom. I love it. I can't wait to bake my way through it."

"Open it up."

I did. On the inside cover, Mom had written me a heartfelt note in her barely legible cursive handwriting:

Dear Josie:

Dulce de leche is your passion! I want to wish you from the bottom of my heart wonderful luck with La Dorita. You deserve it. I'm very proud of you and will be a silent supporter of your company. Congratulations to Gastón! He is a gem. And the forceful partner!

Love always, Mom

Bs. As. September 2009
p.s. Please keep this as a good luck token. BGC

"I love it. Thanks for the support, Mom," I said, kissing her cheek.

"I mean it. And if you'll have me, I'd like to be a silent partner and help in my own little way. What do you say? Equal shares between the three of us? You and Gastón do the work, and we'll split the cost three ways. No one has to know. It'll be our secret. I can't wait to see where it takes us."

"Yes. Of course. That's an offer I can't refuse! But why?"

"Because I want to make sure *Mami* lives on forever. I'll never be able to thank her for everything she did to help me raise you and your brothers and sisters. This is my little way of helping to make sure she's always around. And if anyone can make it happen, it's you. La Dorita will be our baby."

Dorita held up her hand. "*Oyen.* Listen here, *chicas.* La Dorita this, *dulce de leche* that. I keep hearing about my *dulce de leche*, but I haven't tried it yet. You'll need my seal of approval first before I give you my name. It's one of the few things I have left."

The next morning of Dorita's ninetieth birthday, I had breakfast with her. It was in that very same breakfast room where she'd so often fed me as a child that Dorita took the first bite of the *dulce de leche* I'd made for her. Her eyes grew big. Decades had passed since she'd made her own. She spread it generously over her whole wheat toast. "*Es tal cual como lo hacía yo. Gracias,* Josie. It's just like old times. Thank you for reminding me."

It occurred to me then and there, sitting at Dorita's table, that food is so much more than sustenance. It's the feel of a place. It's the essence of a person. It's something language can't get to. It's memories tucked away deep inside of all of us, reminding us who we are. It's remembrances in the making.

"What about your mom? Do you think Josefina would have approved?"

Dorita stirred her *café con leche* pensively. Her eyes welled with tears. "*Claro. Mami* taught me how to make *dulce de leche.* And now I've passed it down to you. It was hers, and it was mine. Now it's yours. But who will you pass it onto?"

"The world, *Abuela.* My fellow *Yanquis.* To anyone that needs or craves it. Even if they don't know it yet."

Dorita took another bite of her toast. And with that one taste, we were both transported back thirty years, enjoying Lincoln biscuits smothered with *dulce de leche.* Except this time the table was turned—and it was me feeding my grandmother. On her ninetieth birthday and the fortieth anniversary of her mother Josefina's untimely death.

Ham and Cheese *sorrentinos* (Bowler Hat Ravioli)

SERVES 7. *Unless you're a part of our family, where we typically count on six or seven* sorrentinos *per person—give or take.*

If you are keen on making your own fresh pasta, I would suggest investing in a *sorrentino* mold in order to create this ravioli's characteristic bowler hat shape. I, on the other hand, shy away altogether from making fresh pasta, with the exception of *ñoqui* or zoodles (zucchini noodles). Many years ago, I learned the trick of substituting wonton wraps for fresh pasta sheets, and I've been making ravioli this way ever since. For *sorrentinos,* I use a mix of wonton wraps and their larger big brother, egg roll wraps, to unabashedly stuff these plump pasta pockets into their characteristic bowler hat shape. Both wraps are readily available in most grocery stores. This combination creates quite a bit of excess leftover dough. I like to cut the remainders into strips and flash fry them in hot vegetable oil. Once crisp, I drain them on a towel and set aside to throw on salad for another meal. This semi-homemade version is not the same as the traditional *sorrentino,* which has firmer dough, but it's just as tasty, on the lighter side and, more importantly, half the work. These *sorrentinos* pair well with a simple tomato or a luscious cream sauce, or as presented below, *mixta,* a mix of both.

FILLING

2 tablespoons **olive oil**

2 ¼ cup chopped **shallots**

2 ½ cups whole milk **ricotta cheese**

12 ounces uncured **maple & honey ham**

¼ teaspoon **white pepper**

¼ teaspoon **nutmeg**

¾ cup **parsley**

3 cups shredded, low moisture, whole milk **mozzarella**

RAVIOLI

35 **wonton wraps** (1 12-ounce package)

35 **egg roll wraps** (2 1-pound packages)

3 **egg whites**, beaten to blend

WALNUT CREAM SAUCE

1 tablespoon **olive oil**

½ cup **walnuts**, chopped

2 large **shallots**, finely chopped

1 cup dry, crisp **white wine**

2 cups **heavy cream**

½ cup flat-leaf **parsley**, chopped

Pinch of freshly ground **nutmeg**

Salt and **black pepper** to taste

SALSA ROSA

1 tablespoon **olive oil**

1 medium-size **Spanish onion**

2 large or 3 medium **tomatoes**
(1½ pounds)

4 **garlic cloves**

3 tablespoons **unsalted butter**

1 bunch fresh **basil**

SPECIAL EQUIPMENT

Food processor

Heat oil in heavy small skillet over medium heat. Mix in shallots. Cover and cook 5–7 minutes until translucent. Transfer shallots to food processor bowl and allow to cool. Add ricotta, ham, pepper, nutmeg and parsley and pulse just until pureed, careful not to overmix. Add shredded mozzarella and stir into mixture with a spoon, making sure not to purée the mozzarella. Transfer to bowl, cover with plastic wrap and refrigerate for 30 minutes to an hour. The ravioli is easier to assemble when the filling is cold.

Place one wonton wrap on work surface; brush with egg white. Mound 1 rounded tablespoon filling in center of 1 wrap. Place one egg roll wrap on work surface; brush with egg white. Drape egg roll wrap over filling, egg white side facing down. Using your fingertips, carefully create pleats, removing all of the air, and press around edges and filling to seal. Cut the edges with a round cookie or ravioli cutter to mimic the *sorrentino's* round shape—being careful not to compromise the seal. Repeat with remaining wraps, egg white and filling, forming a total of 35 ravioli. Place ravioli in single layer on parchment paper. Cover with a slightly damp cheese cloth, then plastic wrap, and refrigerate. You can do this up to 6 hours ahead.

Make the walnut cream sauce. In a large pan, heat ½ teaspoon oil in heavy, large skillet over medium heat. Add the walnuts and sauté, stirring often, until fragrant and beginning to darken in color, about 3 minutes. Be careful not to burn. Remove and set aside onto serving plate using a slotted spoon. Add remaining oil in skillet and add shallots and a pinch of salt; sauté 5–7 minutes until translucent. Pour in wine and bring to a boil. Boil until the liquid has reduced by half, about 3 minutes. Add cream and lightly boil, stirring frequently. Add the sautéed walnuts and allow to simmer for 3–4 minutes. Season to taste with freshly ground nutmeg, salt and pepper.

Make the salsa rosa. Heat oil in heavy large skillet over medium heat. Add onion and sauté 5–7 minutes until translucent. Add the garlic and stir frequently, sautéing for 1 minute. Add the tomatoes and butter. Cover and simmer 12 minutes to blend flavors. Transfer mixture to a high-speed blender. Add the basil leaves and pulse until smoothly pureed. Return to saucepan and season to taste with salt and pepper.

Bring a large pot of salted water to a boil. Add the ravioli in 3 batches and cook until they rise to the surface and pasta is tender, about 3 minutes. Gently remove using a slotted spoon and transfer ravioli to skillet with walnut cream sauce. Toss gently to coat so ravioli do not stick together.

Spoon walnut cream sauce onto 6 plates, creating a circle. Outline the same with the salsa rosa. Top each with 5 ravioli. Adorn ravioli with a drizzle of the salsa rosa. Garnish with chopped parsley.

Chapter 11

Es pan comido
Piece of Cake

Vitel toné is the darling of all home cooks during Argentina's summertime Christmas season days. Mom's favorite, it's an odd mix of cold eye of round disguised in a tuna and anchovy sauce studded with capers that's as satisfying as a good tuna sandwich. Like *sobremesa*, *vitel toné* is devoid of any English translation. It's a stark reminder that there will always be a part of us, and a collective part of our world, that simply doesn't translate, especially when life knocks you off your feet, suddenly turning your world upside down. Since my car accident at sixteen, I'd managed to stay ahead of tragedy, for the most part. But since then, I'd secretly harbored a crippling fear of death. Not so much of my own but of those I loved most in this world. That is, until my thirty-sixth birthday in December of 2009, three months after Dorita's ninetieth. That's when everything changed.

* * *

After our trip to Argentina, I was busy trying to sell our *dulce de leche* in local markets while holding down my day job. I'd been fortunate enough to meet a buyer for our local Whole Foods Market at a farmer's market that previous summer, and after our first formal meeting he shook my hand and told me they'd be placing their first order by Thanksgiving. They asked if I could have my jars ready to get on their shelves by then, including the label and required nutritional analysis breakdown. At the time, I didn't know what all that entailed, but I agreed. We'd make it happen.

Somehow, we did. Things just fell into place and I delivered our first order of twenty-four jars the week before Thanksgiving.

"So, tell me about the in-store demonstration. Did people like the *dulce de leche*?" Mom daintily bobbed her herbal tea bag in her cup. Satisfied her brew was the right strength, she dangled the dripping tea bag over the cup and squeezed it against her spoon before raising her barely-there blonde eyebrows questioningly at me. "Do you think Whole Foods will place another order?" Mom's hazel eyes looked exceptionally light that afternoon under the fluorescent lighting in our booth at our neighborhood King's Restaurant. We'd just finished eating Western omelets with a side of rye and home fries. Mom had called me at the office that morning and asked me to meet her there for lunch after she was done with her life insurance exam. She'd passed with flying colors. "They said I'm healthy as an ox." With Dorita's deteriorating health, I was counting on it.

"The demo went well. But it's crazy how many people had never heard of *dulce de leche*. They can't even pronounce it. It seemed so easy in Argentina."

"Of course it did. It's part of our everyday fabric. But if we were in Argentina, you'd never be able to compete with the other brands. Here you can introduce Americans to the real thing. No one said it would be easy."

"*Claro.* I know. At first, people thought it was caramel or apple butter. But once they tried it, most loved it. Whole Foods ordered five more cases for the week before Christmas. I have to deliver them tomorrow."

"Oh, good. Let me know when you do."

"I've actually been meaning to talk to you about that, Mom. You have to stop snatching it all up. We need to give others a chance to buy it. That's the only way we can really test the market."

"Josephine Ursula Caminos. I don't know what you might be getting at."

"The manager told me they keep stocking the shelves for our demos, but that a short blonde woman with a thick accent keeps rolling into the store as soon as they get a delivery and buying them all up. Any idea who that might be?"

"Okay. *Bueno.* I'm leaving soon anyhow for Miami. Speaking of Miami, I'd like to celebrate your birthday before I leave. Let's do dinner on Saturday and then I'll have the whole family over to celebrate for lunch on Sunday. You mentioned something about a Japanese Steakhouse?"

"Lucas has been begging to go to Ichiban so he can see them set the Hibachi grill on fire. Testosterone and live-fire-cooking are slowly taking over my life. He's only six, but he's just like his dad. Give him an open flame and juicy steak and all's good in his world."

That afternoon at *sobremesa*, Mom promised she'd stay away from Whole Foods, until after the holidays, at least. As we ordered our second round of tea, I couldn't stop the tears from pooling in my eyes.

"I'm stuck, Mom. I feel like I'm going full throttle to nowhere." The majority of my discontent spawned from close to a decade of working at my father's medical diagnostic company, which was a path I had taken in order to support my family and possibly earn Dad's acceptance in the process. But it wasn't my destiny. My sleepless nights told me so. I knew I had to leave, but how could I risk my children's livelihood by following my own desires?

Mom sat intently listening, assuring me I was doing a good job as both a mother and provider.

"You know, Dad's thinking of retiring. If anyone deserves to, its him. He told me he's considering selling the company to his associate."

"He's been talking about it. You know your dad—he'll never retire. But it'll give him more time to oversee the ranches and travel. There's still so many places we dream of visiting. We're planning a three week trip to China next spring. As for his associate, *ya me enteré.* He mentioned it to me just yesterday. But it's still up in the air. Nothing's set in stone, and he'll see to it that you're taken care of. I think your father agreed he'd stay on for at least two more years to oversee the transition. I thought they'd offered you the same? You've made your place in that company."

"They did. They offered for me to stay on indefinitely. But still, it's left me thinking, *what's next*? If the company sells, it would go in a different direction—one I don't think I want to lead."

"I'm sorry you feel that way, but why?"

"I wish I knew. I feel like I'm at a crossroads and have to choose between the safe route—staying—or stepping out on my own and trying something new. I keep thinking I'm too young to be complacent. I want more. Is that wrong of me?"

"No," Mom sipped her tea. "Not at all. But you have to think of your family."

"I know. I'm not going anywhere, at least for now. I've worked far too many years and am way too vested in the company to walk away from it all, just like that." But I also knew that if this sale didn't go through, there would be another. I'd reached my potential with the company. It was up to me to make a move. My unhappiness was a beckoning call that told me my life was veering off course.

Mom knew it too and looked up at me as she paid our break-fast tab. "Stick with the *dulce de leche*. See it through. Even if it takes years. Something tells me it might just be your plan B. *Poco a poco*, you need to start setting your own table."

* * *

The elation of getting our *dulce* onto Whole Foods' shelves car-ried us into my birthday week, just before Christmas. Even though Mom had become a certified snowbird once my youngest brother, Federico, went off to Boston College—Dad only flew down to Flor-ida on weekends—she always made sure to celebrate my birthday in Pittsburgh before heading south. My sister Valentina was flying in from Buenos Aires with her husband and two-year-old daughter to spend Christmas and New Year's with my parents. Mom couldn't wait to have her only Argentine-born granddaughter with her for an entire three weeks.

That Saturday, my entire family—minus Valentina and Ca-mila—got together at Ichiban to celebrate my birthday. Mom had rented the back room to fit us all—Mom and Dad, Gastón, the kids and I all gathered with Oscar and Laura's families, along with my younger brother Federico. At *sobremesa*, we shut the doors to the room as Laura's husband took out his guitar. My family serenaded me with all sorts of *feliz cumpleaños* and happy birthdays before my three nieces got up to sing Taylor Swift's "Love Story." Their brother and my godson, Daniel, led them on guitar. It was an unforgettable night, etched in my heart and on my taste buds forever.

Mom called me early the following morning. I looked out the window to find a blistery mix of snow and freezing rain. There was at least half a foot of fresh snow on the ground and roads. She asked if I was going to Mass.

"Mom, even God grants us a couple of snow days in our lifetime. I'm not taking my kids out in this mess."

Still, Mom insisted that she needed to go to church. "It's Advent, Josie. Please pick me up. I don't have all-wheel drive. Then we can all get together at the house for a late lunch. I leave tomorrow for Miami. I want to see you and the kids before I go."

Who was I to turn her down after the birthday celebration she'd thrown me the night before? I left the boys with Gastón, who was notably happy to skip, and the two of us headed out to brave the icy roads. There couldn't have been more than ten of us in the pews at eleven a.m. Mass, but there we were. Like good Catholics, we'd made it.

During Mass, Mom sat holding my hand throughout the entire sermon. As far back as I could remember, her small fingernails were always perfectly polished in one of two colors that you could always find in her purse: Revlon's "Wine with Everything" and Chanel Le Vernis' "Ruby Slipper." It had always amazed me that her nails looked good with the loads of diapers she'd changed in her lifetime, the meals she'd made us over and over that we loved, the incessant spreadsheets she'd managed and checks she'd written for their companies, the *carinitos* she gave us each night, tickling the small curves of our backs and arms so we'd fall asleep. At the first sign of a chip or smudge, she'd grab her polish and paint right over it until her topcoat became so thick that she'd have to start over. As mom to six children, she'd learned this coping mechanism early on.

With age, my hands were starting to look like hers, minus the beautifully polished nails part. I did everything to try not to bite mine.

As we entered the grocery store afterwards, Mom stopped me in my tracks. She told me she needed me to know how good of a mother she thought I was. "Don't ever forget that." Mom placed her hand over mine as I went to grab a buggy. She seemed to be feeling extremely nostalgic that morning since she wouldn't be spending the holidays with the rest of us in Pittsburgh. Mom hated when the family was separated, especially at Christmas.

Back at Mom's, we were immediately met with the rich scent of olive oil, onions, garlic, laurel, parsley and roasted tomatoes when we walked into the kitchen. Gastón and the boys were there, along with Laura and Oscar's families. Federico, still a bachelor, joined us too. Dad was doing rounds at the hospital, but he'd make it home in time for lunch. Laura had a pot of sauce simmering on the stove for the spaghetti and *albóndigas* she was making. We uncorked a couple bottles of Cabernet Sauvignon and Malbec as we watched my sister roll the meatballs and fry them, one by one, before submerging them into the steaming pot of velvety sauce. We all crowded into the kitchen. It smelled like home.

"You okay, Mom? You seem tired." I took a sip of my Malbec.

"Great, *hija*. We couldn't have asked for a cozier Sunday to celebrate your birthday. Again."

"You know Graciela says its bad luck to celebrate before the actual day. What's that refrain she always says, Babes?"

Gastón wrapped his arms around me. "'You're celebrated all day long, but never before.' *Mamá* and her superstitions."

"That's it. Apparently if you can't celebrate on your actual day, you're supposed to wait until after."

"But look at how lucky you are. Since you've been little you've often had more than one party. One here and one in Argentina. Now you get two in Pittsburgh. What else could you ask for? Next you're going to tell me it's bad luck that we're celebrating on the thirteenth."

"Well, it is December 13, Mom. You said it, not me. Lucky for you, seven and thirteen are my favorite numbers."

That afternoon, after lunch, Mom excused herself from *sobremesa* unusually early. It wasn't like her at all.

"I just need to lie down for a short *siesta*," Mom said. "Don't leave," she looked at me. "I'll be back out in a bit."

"*Poupi*, mi amor, sit back down," Dad said. "Don't tell me you're getting old on me," he joked.

But Mom shot him a coy glance back as if to say, *I just turned sixty-four. What does that make you?* All jokes aside, there was a sad surrender in her eyes I hadn't been able to put my finger on. I'd noticed it more than once that day, and now again as she left the table and headed back to her bedroom.

Most of my family started leaving after a couple of hours had passed. Gastón and I stayed, considering I was the guest of honor and Mom had asked me to. Then, just as we began packing up to go, too, Mom called me from behind her bedroom door. She was in the back of her walk-in closet, sprawled out on the floor in front of her safe, sorting through boxes and boxes of jewelry.

"Oh good, Josie. Come, sit with me." Mom patted the carpet beside her. "I'm going through my jewelry deciding which of you girls gets what. I want to make sure there are no misunderstandings once I'm gone."

"Where exactly are you planning on going? Why are you doing this now? We were all waiting for you to come back to the table. Let's go to the kitchen and have a *café con leche*. We can do this another time."

But Mom kept sorting her jewelry and held up a strikingly beautiful quartz stone with bands of yellow and golden brown throughout. "This tiger eye gemstone set is for Valentina. It matches her personality. Are you writing this down? I need you to remember," she grabbed a set of golden bangles she thought would be perfect for my three nieces. "Josie, are you paying attention? Grab a pad and pencil and start getting this down."

"No. I'm not doing this with you right now. The boys are waiting for us. We're supposed to be celebrating my birthday. Is there something you're not telling me?"

"No. I'm leaving tomorrow for Miami and won't be back in Pittsburgh for several months. I just want to make sure that you girls clearly know my wishes. That's all."

"This is ridiculous." I peeled myself off the floor, wiping the carpet fibers from my pants. "You and Dad are young and healthy. You just passed your life insurance exam." I gathered the jewelry boxes to return to the safe. "We can do this when you get back in the spring."

But Mom kept separating the jewelry sets. Her eyes were downcast, lashes dark against her high set cheekbones. "Your father's going to outlive me, I know it. I want you girls to separate my belongings that I intend to pass on."

"Mom, stop it. Please. You can't say things like that. I'm going to make you a coffee. Come out and have a piece of cake with us before we leave."

We left shortly afterwards, bellies full of chocolate fudge cake and coffee, but not before Mom gave me my birthday gift: a light-blue tablecloth with a hand-embroidered, white flower border. "I picked it up in Uruguay. Make sure you handwash it, and remember what we talked about the other day." Mom looked at me with the same intensity from earlier that day in the market. "It's time you set your own table."

I nodded in agreement, hugging her thanks. I was sure Mom was about to make some comment or other about my tendency to use our family's heirloom linen cloths straight out of the dryer. Freshly starched and pressed tablecloths weren't my thing. I didn't have the patience to iron them perfectly like Mom. But she didn't say anything. Instead, she kissed me goodbye, and after wishing me a happy upcoming birthday and Christmas, she asked me to pray for her.

"Always, Mom." I hugged her back. "But what exactly am I praying for?"

Mom didn't answer. Instead she looked wistfully at me and held me extra tight before kissing me goodbye one last time.

* * *

Mom and I normally talked every day, sometimes several times a day, but I hadn't heard from her in several days since she left for Miami that morning after my early birthday *sobremesa*. It was unlike her to not call back, even after leaving several messages.

Valentina, who'd finally arrived from Argentina, told me that Mom was sick in bed.

"She just got her flu shot the other day in Pittsburgh." I explained to Valentina. "I wonder if it made her sick."

I was glad Valentina was there to keep an eye on her. I finally got her on the phone the day before my birthday, just for a moment. "It's just a stomach bug, Josie. I'll call you tomorrow," she reassured me before quickly hanging up.

The following morning, for the first time in thirty-six years, Mom didn't wake me up for my birthday. She'd always made it a point to be the first to greet her children on their special day, calling before seven a.m. to serenade you in her thick Spanish accent. Finally, I managed to get her on the phone after calling during my lunch break at the office. "Mom, I haven't heard from you. How are you feeling? You forgot my birthday."

I remember Mom mumbling something back to me. I think it was an apology, but I couldn't quite make out what she was saying. But before I could continue on with the conversation, her housekeeper, Luz, grabbed the phone, rambling in her Colombian Spanish that Mom wasn't feeling well and that she'd call me back later.

I tried to get some work done, but my thoughts were all over the place. Suddenly, a peregrine falcon flew right up to my windowsill and sat there looking straight at me, its black eyes so intense they almost knocked me off my chair. I got up from my desk to get a closer look and the falcon continued to stare, watching me cross the room. It was almost as if he had a message for me.

Once I got up close and crouched down to get a better look at him, he flew away. That's when I saw him. My Gentleman Caller, standing next to my car. His silver hair and beard gave him away. He caught my gaze, tipped his hat and motioned for me to come down. It was time I finally got to the bottom of his hauntings. I grabbed my purse and keys and ran outside.

By the time I got to the car, he wasn't there. The parking lot was empty. Not a soul around.

I tried to convince myself it was probably just an older patient who mistook his car for mine. But it wasn't. In my heart of hearts, I knew it was him. *But why?* I had the feeling he was there to beckon me home. So, I went on my way, wondering what he knew that I didn't.

That night at my real birthday dinner, Gastón surprised me with a homemade meal. We'd recently celebrated our ninth wedding anniversary. With each year, Gastón's cooking got better and better, while my jeans got tighter and tighter. Gastón made one of my favorites, steak and eggs benedict—perfectly cooked filet mignon topped with a fried green tomato and poached egg bathed in hollandaise sauce. Like a cozy sweater, this ultimate grown-up comfort food went perfectly with December's shorter days and thirty-degree highs. But the night of that thirty-sixth birthday, my nerves had stripped me of my appetite. I knew something was wrong—I just didn't know what. The air that day had changed—for the worse. It was anyone's guess what was coming. Like my *abuelo* Caminos, I feared I already knew. I looked up at the crooked picture hanging on the wall of a carefree, newlywed Mom on her honeymoon in Brazil—her long blonde hair tucked away in a flowing silk scarf—and saw broccoli cheddar casseroles gratinéed with French fried onions in my immediate future. *Was I overreacting?* I knew what was coming, I just couldn't stomach it.

Gastón looked up at me over the readers he'd finally broken down and bought earlier that year after turning forty. From across the table he raised his half-drunk glass of Henry Lagarde Malbec, a plump, violet wine whose aroma of ripe red fruits could instantly transport you to Argentina's wine-country region of Mendoza. Tucked up against the foothills of the Andes mountains, Mendoza was also the place Mom called home for part of her childhood.

"Don't worry. Your mom's going to be okay. *Vamos*, Josie. Valentina's there. She's taking good care of her." Gastón got up and moved Nacho's highchair aside to sit down beside me. He looked me right in the eyes to make sure I was listening, but his gaze just made me feel panicked. "What did she say when you last spoke?"

"She'd been trying to get Mom to the doctor since yesterday, but Mom refused, saying she didn't want to miss a minute of their visit. Valentina called an ambulance a couple of hours ago. Mom started slurring her words after throwing up what looked like ground coffee beans. She said Mom's barely eaten for the past couple of days, so she couldn't imagine what it was. The paramedics told her they thought Mom likely just needed IV fluids, but when Valentina met the ambulance at the hospital, the paramedics said Mom lost consciousness during the ride and rushed her into the ER. She hasn't seen her yet and they're working on her now. This waiting is killing me." I looked down, noticing my fork was trembling. Swallowing another bite of Gastón's beefy eggs benedict proved almost impossible. "I'm scared, Gastón."

"Don't be. I'm here with you. And she's where she needs to be." Gastón squeezed my knee under the table.

"I know. I'm trying to convince myself it's just a bad virus. And, on top of everything, I saw him again."

"Who, *mi amor*?"

"My Gentleman Caller. His visit has been haunting me all day. He only seems to show up just as something's about to happen. I can't shake this feeling. My mind keeps going where it shouldn't. Something's not right."

Gastón knew it too. He didn't need to say so; I saw it in his eyes.

The family and I were all in constant contact. We'd been told Mom likely had a bad strain of influenza that was causing a raging fever. We all hoped she'd be discharged before Christmas. Dad, who was still in Pittsburgh trying to see as many patients as possible before the holiday break, had assured us all that he'd booked the first available flight to Miami first thing the following morning to be by Mom's side as she recovered.

Meanwhile, Gastón was determined to salvage the few hours left of my birthday. He and the boys surprised me with a *Chocotorta* they'd made earlier that day. *Chocotorta* is a no-oven-mitts required, childhood favorite icebox cake made of layers of chocolate wafers or biscuits, cream cheese and *dulce de leche*. It's a requisite at Argentine dessert tables, like chocolate chip cookies and Jell-O salads in the States. While Gastón loved to cook, desserts and baking weren't his thing; they were mine. Which made this one all the more special.

My mood suddenly felt lighter as Lucas, Mateo and Nico proudly brought the cake to the table, singing *feliz cumpleaños* off-key. I took Nacho, just eighteen months at the time, out of the highchair and placed him on my lap. But just as the kids and I were about to blow out the candles, the phone rang. It was Dad. He'd just gotten off the phone with the ER doctor on call. His voice cracked.

"*Hija*, we have to fly out tonight. Your mom's in the fight of her life."

A flood of fear washed over me as I hung up the receiver, filling my head with a numbing dull noise. I couldn't breathe. That moment became suspended in time. I picked up the phone, frantically dialing *Tía* Ángela's number. We needed all the prayers we could get.

"Josefina, *feliz cumpleaños*. I was just saying at *sobremesa* that I'd been meaning to call you all day."

"Gracias, *Tía*, but it's *Mamá*," I choked on my tears. I couldn't get the words out.

"What is it? Take a deep breath. Is she okay?"

"She's really sick. She's in the hospital and the doctors don't know if she's going to make it."

Through the silence I could hear Ángela digesting my words. But before I knew it, Dad was at my front door. "*Me tengo que ir. Papá's* here. We're flying to Miami tonight to see her. Please pray."

"*Vayan no más.* Go. We were just headed to bed. I'm going to hurry and gather the entire congregation to pray," *Tía* Ángela assured me. "We'll do whatever it takes. Even if we pray all night."

* * *

I didn't want to leave. Outside, Dad was frantically honking the horn, pleading with me to hurry. But the boys were crying and didn't understand why we didn't have time to blow out my candles. It took everything in me to kiss them and Gastón goodbye. I'd never been so scared in my life. It was just before midnight when Dad, Laura, Oscar and I boarded the plane to Miami. There weren't any remaining flights, so Dad called on some of his connections and chartered a private jet to get us there as quickly as possible.

"Hurry," Valentina pleaded over the phone. She was waiting for us at Miami's Mt. Sinai Hospital. "Get here as soon as you can. I don't know if she's going to hold on much longer."

"We're on our way," Dad said, trying to calm her down.

As I stepped onto the plane, I paused, looking back at my younger brother Federico. He was standing on the tarmac with a stoic face. We hadn't been able to convince him to come with us. I tried explaining to him that if something happened to Mom, he may never forgive himself for not saying goodbye. But his mind was made up. He'd stay behind and hold down the fort at Dad's company. Somehow, I think he felt that as long as he didn't board that plane, this too would pass like a fleeting dream.

As I took my seat next to Dad, I laid my forehead against the cold airplane window, closed my eyes and started praying the Hail Mary on repeat. But I couldn't seem to remember the words. Never mind I must have said the prayer thousands of times throughout my lifetime.

Dad grabbed my hand. He didn't tell me it was going to be okay. He couldn't. But with a half hour until midnight, he wished me a happy birthday. "*Feliz cumpleaños hija.* How was your day? Did I already wish you a happy birthday? I don't think so."

"Thanks, Dad." As I stared out into the endless midnight blue sky, my mind went back to *Abuela* Dorita's ninetieth birthday trip that past September. I saw myself at *Abuelo* Alfredo's grave, tracing the date of my great-grandma Josefina's death with my fingertips—September 25, 1969. The same day as Dorita's birthday. The memory of that day had haunted me ever since, and I finally understood why. Mom would never see my kids grow up. It was in that moment I knew our family history would repeat itself.

That two and a half-hour plane ride to Miami seemed to last forever. Halfway into the trip, I switched prayers. *Please Lord, send me a sign that Mom's going to be okay.* Moments later, three shooting stars appeared in the dead of the night—one right after the other. It wasn't the sign I'd wanted, but it was the sign I'd asked for—the three *Marías* showing Mom home.

We arrived at Mom's bedside around three a.m. She was being kept alive by machines, but something told me Mom was no longer there. I stroked her hair and, ducking down by her side, whispered in her ear, "We're here, *Mami.* We came as fast as we could." I kissed her cheek. It was cold; so cold. I choked back my tears. "*Mami,* if you have anything left, please fight. We can't live without you. I can't live without you. But if you don't, then go in peace. Either way, just know I love you *siempre* and forever." My knees buckled as I retreated to an armchair behind her bed. I was so scared, I couldn't breathe. Dad and Laura, on the other hand, managed to keep their cool as they sat on either side of her bed, holding her hand and talking as if she was going to make it. But God had different plans.

Dad, Valentina, Camila, Oscar, Laura and I sat with Mom another three hours, marking time with the digital beeps of the monitors until one of the machine's alarms alerted us that Mom had taken her final breath. I looked up at the monitor. Flatline.

In that moment, a team of doctors and nurses rushed into the room. One of them ushered us out as the others frantically surrounded Mom's bed, trying to resuscitate her. Fluorescent lighting, antiseptic smells and drawn, anxious faces filled my head at once. *Save her. Do more.*

But I knew. She'd already left. Mom was no longer in the body the doctors worked on for more than forty-five minutes, attempting to revive her. As we sat helpless in the waiting room, I was suddenly five again, sitting on the stone wall in front of our house on Churchill Road, before the fire. We were waiting for the school bus. I'd recently started kindergarten at Shafer Elementary. I liked it but hated leaving Mom—my separation anxiety was palpable. It felt as if each time I stepped on that bus, I would never see her again. Mom was sitting next to me when she glanced at her watch, then looked at me, brushing my stick-straight bangs from my eyes. She knew I was feeling anxious.

"I forgot your lunch box, *mi amorcito*, I'll be right back." Mom kissed me, running inside. I looked back at her with my brown, round eyes. *Don't leave me! Mom, don't leave me! Ever!* Seconds later, the yellow school bus came barreling up the road, flashing its lights as it came to a stop. *Wait. No. Mom's not back. I can't leave without her. I can't live without my mom.* The bus doors hissed as they opened, beckoning me in. I looked back at the house. *Where are you, Mom?*

"Coming, sweetie?" the bus driver asked. "We don't have all day now." I got up slowly. Reluctantly. Stepping onto the bus, I picked the first empty seat, scooting in and pressing my forehead against the window. Tears rolled down my face as I looked back. Mom emerged from the house in her blue terrycloth robe. Her blonde, short hair bobbed up and down as she ran towards the bus, waving my Wonder Woman lunch box. She was so pretty. I'd always thought she was the prettiest of all my friends' moms. Coming to terms she'd missed the bus, Mom stopped, blowing me kisses, as we drove away. She got smaller and smaller until she was a mere speck. Until she was out of sight. But never out of mind.

Tears flooded the waiting room linoleum floor as we sat silently, listening to the doctor tell us they'd done everything they could. There were no words. I'd only seen Dad that vulnerable once before, when his own father died. He crumbled back into his seat, covering his face with his hands. We could go in and say goodbye, the doctor said.

We did, surrounding Mom on all sides of the bed. Touching her. Stroking her still-warm cheeks. Kissing her. Telling her we loved her. Camila had called Monsignor Senior from St. Patrick's Church to give Mom her last rites. He hadn't made it in time. But he still prayed over Mom, assuring us it still counted. Monsignor prayed over us too, asking that we'd find peace. Before leaving he turned and asked that we let Mom go, in due time. That it was important we allowed her soul to go in peace. That she wouldn't be able to if she felt us needing her, holding her back.

When the nurses finally came in to let us know that it was time to take Mom to the hospital morgue, Camila asked for one more minute. I laid my head against Mom's chest.

As I desperately searched the room for some sort of explanation, my eyes landed on the whiteboard. "Beatriz Germain Caminos. Date of Death: 12/18/2009. Time of Death: 07:36 a.m."

Meanwhile, Camila pulled out a pair of nail scissors from her purse and began clipping small strands of Mom's platinum blonde hair. It was the only part of her we could take with us. Camila placed them in four biohazard specimen transport plastic bags she'd found on the bedside table. Keepsakes for Mom's girls.

The nurse came in again. "I'm sorry, but it's time to prepare *Señora* Beatriz's body for transport. I'm afraid your time is up."

"Her name is Poupée," I said, wiping away the deluge of tears from my face so I could look her straight in the eyes. The nurse looked back at me, confused. "To those that knew her."

Valentina gently hooked her arm in mine, pulling me off the bed and out of the room. Picking a fight with the nurse wasn't going to get us anywhere. She was just doing her job. As we left, I turned back. The golden light from the morning sunrise flooded the window and room, casting a soft spotlight on Mom's hospital bed. There Dad sat, desperately sobbing, "I'm sorry, *perdóname mi amor*," after "Forgive me, Poupi, I'm so sorry," deep into Mom's motionless chest. He'd saved hundreds of lives as a doctor. He was known for keeping alive even the sickest of patients battling end-stage cardiovascular disease. But the most important life of all—Mom's—he couldn't save.

Dad's words hung heavy in the air, amidst his and Mom's love story in pictures—their first dance; their second encounter at the horse races when Mom pretended she didn't know who he was (and dying inside as she did so); at the altar saying '*sí quiero*, I do'; holding their first child, Valentina; Mom rushing to the hospital after learning of Dad's car accident and praying to God not to take him; that hot summer day on June 30, 1974, when they arrived hand in hand to the Pittsburgh Airport with five young children in tow, ready to chase their dreams past the equator, through a menacing housefire that threatened to destroy everything they'd built, around the sun and over the moon until they disappeared into the horizon. They'd done it. They'd taken the chances so many only dream of. Some forty-five years after their first fateful encounter, one thing was clear: Mom was the love of Dad's life. She is the love of his life. Still to this day. As for me, the moment I'd always feared most had finally caught up with me.

That afternoon, as I sat with my family in the Van Orsdel Funeral Chapel in Miami's Design District picking out an urn for Mom's cremated remains, I replayed the hours leading up to her death over and over in my head. She'd just turned sixty-four one month to the day. She'd just passed her life insurance test, which was too ironic to bear. The insurance papers had arrived at the house, but she hadn't had a chance to sign them. How did things spiral so quickly? Why didn't we realize how dire the situation was? How'd she manage to slip past all of us?

I couldn't help but wonder if Mom had had a premonition that last day we'd spent together at her house in Pittsburgh. She seemed notably distant when I picked her up for Mass that morning, as if she was in a fog of sorts. And the whole thing about her jewelry. I'd found it annoying at the time. Did she know she'd soon be leaving us? Why else would she leave clear instructions as to which of her girls got what?

Mostly, I couldn't get over the fact that "you forgot my birthday" were the last words I spoke to Mom. The four most selfish words I'd uttered in my lifetime. By the time we got to her bedside, Mom had already slipped into a coma from which she never awoke. She never knew the lengths we took to get there. She never heard us tell her how much we loved her as we said our goodbyes. *Or did she?* While sepsis and cardiorespiratory arrest were listed as the cause of death, I felt she'd been long gone by the time we'd arrived at her hospital bedside. Her death was sudden, but it had been looming for months—ever since I visited *Abuelo* Alfredo's grave in Argentina the day before Dorita's birthday. I'd been so focused on leaving a legacy behind for Dorita, I'd all but neglected all the signs pointing towards Mom's imminent departure.

* * *

The following days, my sisters and I worked tirelessly to get Mom's memorial service in order. We'd decided to have it in Pittsburgh, since that's where the majority of her family and friends lived, on the eve of Christmas Eve. The morning of her service, Gastón, Dad, my brothers, sisters and I and our thirteen children headed next door to the golf course and released sixty-four red balloons in Mom's honor, one for each year of her life. We wrote notes all over them, saying goodbye and letting her know how much we loved her. It was a beautiful winter day in Pittsburgh with the clearest of blue skies up above. Still, Dad warned us that it was so cold the balloons may not fly. We took our chances and released them on the count of three, then sat watching as each one soared to the heavens.

Back at home, Gastón made *vitel toné* for lunch, a classic Christmas dish in Argentina originally from Italy. The Argentine version was composed of cold slices of *peceto* (eye of round) blanketed under an anchovy and tuna-based cream sauce studded with capers. Mom always said it was simply too odd not to adore it. To my relief, Gastón's sauce didn't include store-bought mayonnaise. Instead, he made his own aioli, combining it with tuna, capers, anchovies, oil and cream in a high-speed mixer. The result was a creamy tonnato sauce that, though a little grainy from the capers and anchovies, was also deliciously salty.

At *sobremesa*, Gastón looked at me from across the table. "*Gorda*, what else can I get you? You've barely touched your food."

"*Nada*. I'm okay. Just thinking about what I'm going to say this evening. Look at me. My eyes are so swollen from crying, I can barely keep them open. How am I going to deliver Mom's eulogy? Camila and Laura's kids are twelve and under and they have the courage to get up in front of the whole church to sing 'On Eagle's Wings.'"

"There won't be a dry eye in the house. That's going to be a hard act to follow. But you're going to get up and do as you do. Speak to your Mom from the heart, that's how." Gastón walked over to me, kissing me on my head. "I'm going to bathe the kids and put them down for a nap so they're ready for tonight's service."

As I sat there, alone at the table in the quiet of my dining room, the soapy floral scent of Escada Eau de Toilette with powdery-warm notes of coconut, peach, orange blossoms, warm and soft vanilla and sandal caught at my throat. It was the scent that hung in our dining room every time Mom came over. The perfume that clung on my babies after she'd spent an afternoon rocking and kissing them. It was the scent of loss.

I looked around. Hopelessly. "Mom? Are you there?"

I couldn't see her. But she was there in every way. Even in death, Mom filled a room with perfume. I pictured her as she walked in, pulling up a chair beside me. Mom never looked more elegant in her flame-red, St. John pantsuit she wore each Christmas. She was radiant with her blonde hair and golden skin. She glowed from within.

"Mom, where'd you go? Why didn't you fight? You just left. Dorita was the one we were worried about. She was the one who was sick. Not you. This is going to kill her. We never got to say goodbye." I gasped for air as a deluge of tears flooded the *vitel toné* I'd left untouched on my plate. "I don't know how to live without you."

I felt Mom take my hand in hers. I looked down at mine and saw hers. Our hands became one as a wave of clarity washed over my body. My heartrate slowed. My breath slowly came back. Mom brushed my hair behind my ear.

"You knew, Mom. Didn't you? You knew you were leaving. Why didn't you say anything? You tried and I didn't want to listen. I didn't want to hear it. I'm sorry. *Perdoname*. I'm so sorry." I gasped between hysterical tears. I looked into Mom's golden-hazel eyes that told me she understood every word I was saying. "What am I supposed to do now? In just a couple of hours I have to face a church full of people. What can I possibly tell them about you? About your life? How can I do you justice?"

Mom leaned over and whispered clearly in my ear. "*Es pan comido, hija.* It's simple—a piece of cake. Tell them I love them. Tell them *mi historia*. Our story. Tell them we lived between *las pampas* and the prairie and that they can always find me there. Waiting. Watching over them. And Josie, wear that red-wine velvet pantsuit of yours I love so much. *Nada de* black for my baby girl. You and me, we are one in the same."

And so I did.

Vitel toné (Sliced Eye of Round in Tuna Sauce)

SERVES A FAMILY OF SEVEN. *Or one bleeding heart.*

You can't get more surf and turf than *vitel toné*. I know, the thought of
meat and fish in one dish isn't at all appealing. But it somehow works,
and you just might get hooked. Its easy, prep-ahead nature makes this dish
a favorite appetizer or light second course among home cooks during
Argentina's summertime holiday season. *Vitello tonnato* started to appear
in cookbooks in the northern region of Piedmont, which was attached to
the coastal Liguria region at the time. This is the region where tuna was
canned, but also where oil, lemons and capers—other ingredients of tonnato sauce—were traded. At the time, tuna was actually considered a
condiment. Even though it is a rather traditional dish with a lot of history,
there is not one recipe of *vitel toné* but rather different variations based
on a basic premise. Some chefs say that you need to brown the roast in
olive oil, then simmer it with carrot, onion, celery and bay leaf. Other
chefs insist on braising the veal in unsalted water with vegetables. Some
make the sauce with olive oil and then add canned tuna in oil. Others
favor mayonnaise, either store-bought or homemade, and prefer to use
canned tuna in water, drained. In Argentina it's common to use *peceto*,
iron round, instead of veal. Whichever cut of beef you choose, you will
often see layers of meat entirely covered with sauce so much so that it
can barely be distinguished. You'll want to make this dish a day ahead.
The sauce is supposed to infiltrate the meat for several hours, sometimes
days. And make sure to reserve the leftover broth for soup or to make a
risotto. Another dish that keeps on giving.

MEAT

5½ pounds **eye of round roast**,
cleaned and trimmed of fat

1 tablespoon **salt**

1 tablespoon ground **black pepper**

2 tablespoons extra-virgin **olive oil**

2 medium **onions**, halved

3 medium **carrots**, peeled and
quartered

3 **celery sticks**, quartered

3 **garlic cloves**, peeled

1 cup of **white wine**

2 **bay leaves**

SAUCE

2 large **eggs**

1 **garlic clove**, peeled

1½ cups light **olive oil**

Juice of 1½ **lemons**

5 ounces best quality **canned tuna**, drained

8 **anchovy filets**, drained

2 teaspoons **capers**, drained

1 teaspoon **salt**

1¾ cups **heavy cream**

GARNISH

2 tablespoons **capers**, drained

Lemon slices

The day before, prepare the meat by removing its fat and skin. In a large stock pot over medium-high, season sides of roast with salt and pepper and then brown in olive oil, turning until golden brown on all sides. Remove roast from pan onto plate. Lower heat to medium and add onions, carrots, celery sticks, whole garlic cloves, salt and pepper to pan and sauté until onions are translucent, scraping the browned bits from the bottom of the pan. Adjust heat to high and add white wine to deglaze pan until reduced. Return seared meat to pan, add bay leaves and enough water to cover the roast. Bring to a boil, then reduce heat setting to medium-low. Cover and simmer until just tender, about two and a half hours. Remove pot from heat and, once fully cooled, place pot in the refrigerator to allow meat to cool down overnight in broth with vegetables so it continues to absorb the broth. The following morning, remove meat from broth, cover and allow to sit another twenty minutes or so. Strain and reserve the broth. Slice the meat very thinly (about ½ centimeter thick) with a sharp blade. (Too thick and the meat won't absorb the sauce.)

In a food processor, add the eggs, garlic and process until a pale yellow. Add in the light olive oil in a thin stream until the liquid seems to lighten and begins to emulsify and thicken. Add lemon juice, tuna (thoroughly drained), anchovy filets (thoroughly drained), capers (also thoroughly drained) and salt. Mix until well incorporated and creamy. Add heavy cream and mix until incorporated. If the sauce is too thick, add enough broth from the roast, a teaspoon at a time, to thin it to the consistency you like. The sauce has to be not too thick to pour, but also not so thin that it's runny.

Arrange the meat slices on a large serving plate. Cover with half the sauce. Put another layer of meat over and cover with remaining sauce. Garnish with grated capers and thin lemon slices. Leave the *vitel toné* in the fridge before serving for a few hours for the flavors to combine.

Chapter 12

El cambalache el que no llora, no mama
The Baby That Doesn't Cry, Doesn't Get Nursed

True to her Argentine heritage, Dorita enjoyed preparing *ñoqui* on the twenty-ninth of the month—*el día de ñoquis*—the day of gnocchi. On that day, Argentine tradition dictates that you eat the *ñoqui* with *pesos* under your plate to ensure good luck and prosperity. Carrying that money with you after the meal's *sobremesa* is said to bring you even more luck.

The story behind the old-fashioned, pasta-based superstition is twofold. In Argentina and Uruguay, a *ñoqui* is derogatory slang for a public worker who receives a monthly wage but performs little or no work. Some are the recipients of nepotism or political favors, while others work only to promote the government's agenda. Still others are disabled or continue to receive paychecks by mistake, such as those that have moved on to other positions or the retired. Some are even dead—long gone—yet their paychecks keep coming, and keep getting cashed. They're called *ñoquis* because many Argentines faithfully eat gnocchi just before payday. Most get paid on the first, so by the twenty-ninth, money is tight and often all that's left in the pantry is potatoes and flour. *Ñoqui* are the perfect solution as they're both filling and inexpensive.

The twenty-ninth was also the day when the Italian saint, Saint Pantaleon, was canonized. According to Italian legend, in the eighth century there was a young doctor by the name of Pantaleon, who traveled around performing miracles. Along his pilgrimage, he ran out of food and turned to a poor, rural family for help. Although they were poor, the family gave him what little bread they had, and in return for their kindness, Pantaleon predicted a great harvest the following year. His promise proved to be true, and Saint Pantaleon was then canonized as a Patron of Venice on the twenty-ninth day, forever marking it as a day to both commemorate the miracle and invite blessings of all sorts.

* * *

God knows we needed blessings. The pain of losing Mom left an emptiness I still haven't gotten over. I never will. Neither did *Abuela* Dorita. Shortly after Mom's passing, Dad, along with my *tío* Álvaro, decided it would be best to wait until after the new year to break the news to Dorita. Her health was fragile and slowly declining, day by day. Of course, she missed Mom's daily calls. After all, Mom called her like clockwork, and she never missed a day. But Dorita was also struggling with onset dementia. Like a loose plug in an electrical socket, she had moments of clarity mixed with total moments of dense fog. For that reason, my family decided to tell her Mom was sick in the hospital, but slowly improving. But the moment 2010 rolled in, Dad boarded a plane to Buenos Aires, and upon arriving, picked up his sister, my *tía* Ángela the nun, along with my sister Valentina and headed to Dorita's home to tell her the truth. I don't know what happened in her bedroom. Dad went in first, alone, to tell her. *Tía* Ángela followed shortly after, spending a while praying with her. Valentina spent many nights in Alfredo's back room making sure Dorita was okay.

She wasn't. But she did everything to appear to be, in a very stoic way that was unlike her. Just as she never spoke of things she didn't care to, such as her father's abandonment when she was a young girl, she stopped speaking of Mom altogether. Dorita tucked Mom's death away somewhere deep inside of her, somewhere she didn't have to think about it. Where it wouldn't kill her.

EL CAMBALACHE EL QUE NO LLORA, NO MAMA

It'd have been easier if it did, but Dorita proved herself a survivor. Her health kept hanging on by a thread whose spool was long and fortuitous. Still, grief tricked her into loneliness. But the reality is that the grief bound us. *We'd all lost. We all will.*

Three months after Mom's passing, Gastón woke me up in the middle of the night and asked the question we'd both been avoiding. "*Gorda,* are we going to see this through? La Dorita? The *dulce de leche?*"

Since getting into Whole Foods, we'd invested thousands of dollars in converting our old dining room into a commercial kitchen dedicated exclusively to making artisanal *dulce de leche.* Not to mention Mom's contribution. *Now what?*

Half asleep, I mumbled, "I lost Mom. I promised her I was going to leave a legacy for Dorita. I can't let her down." I wanted to move forward, but I didn't know how.

Gastón kissed me softly. "Go back to sleep." The following day he put in his two weeks' notice at PPG. He knew that one of us would have to devote themselves full time to our new culinary endeavor, especially if we attempted to turn it into a viable business. It was only fair to our children. And it gave Gastón, at the cusp of turning forty-one, a second chance. A reason to stay in the United States.

* * *

As time passed, I became consumed with missing Mom. Following her Irish exit, my grief became spare change I carried with me. No matter how many charity buckets I'd dump it all into, the change compounded, getting heavier and heavier with time—its jingle reminding me of its constant presence, no matter the size of my pockets. Gastón, on the other hand, found himself having to remind me that wine was not water as he'd watch me attempt to drown the possibilities of *what could have been* that haunted me: the *abuela* Mom would have been to our four young boys (*they'd never know what they were missing*); the business we could have built together; the birthdays we could have celebrated. *Sobremesa* would never be the same.

"I gave you my liver all those years ago. Along with my heart. It was always yours. Don't drink it away." Gastón poured the glass of Malbec I'd served myself for lunch down the sink. "I know it's tough without her. But don't forget that you're a mom, too. Your boys need you. *I* need you."

My first birthday without Mom was a rough one. Gastón did his best to recreate the mushroom sandwiches Mom would make me when I needed cheering up. He sautéed a variety of wild mushrooms and garlic in loads of butter. *Mom always used white button mushrooms.* He tucked them into an olive oil farmhouse loaf he'd found in the bread drawer. *Mom always used Town Talk white sandwich bread.* It was delicious. *It wasn't Mom's.* The bread was too crusty to sop up the buttery pan juices, along with my watershed of tears. It was just as Mom had told me all those years ago at *sobremesa* in her kitchen when I was nursing my breakup with Tripp: trying to recreate memorable moments at the table is almost always a recipe for heartache. That afternoon I went over to Dad's home in Fox Chapel to sit in Mom's kitchen for a while, alone with my thoughts.

"Mom, I'm home," I yelled as I walked through the back door. I was greeted with silence. No one was home. As usual, Dad was spending the holidays in Miami. But as I walked into the kitchen, a red helium balloon clinging to the ceiling floated over to greet me. *It couldn't be. Could it?* A month had passed since my family had gotten together to commemorate Mom's birthday, what would have been her sixty-fifth. We'd once again gathered to release a bunch of red balloons we'd written messages on to Mom from the golf course next door. It was slowly becoming a new family tradition. As we gathered that day in the kitchen writing our notes, I made sure to hide one of the helium balloons that had been flying at half-mast in that in-between place. *Not quite alive, not quite dead.* I'd been tempted to pop it, to put the deflated balloon out of its misery, but I understood it all too well. Knowing it wouldn't clear the trees that day, I hid it away in the hallway closet.

But now, thirty days later, here it was. Flying full steam; full of life. The balloon was anxiously waiting for me in the quiet of Mom's kitchen, begging for me to release her. I held the balloon between my hands, grabbed a black Sharpie and penned the first thing that came to mind.

Mom, from now on I promise to always celebrate my birthday twice: once for me and once for you. For the day you brought me into this world. For the day you began your passage into immortality. You're always with me. I'm always with you. Send me a sign you're okay. I just need to know you are. Te quiero *always—J.*

It was a brisk, twenty-seven degrees that afternoon, too cold for most balloons to fly high. But as I looked up, watching the balloon soar above the treetops on her way to Mom, I slowly came to understand that I, too, would have to decide whether I'd rise above my sadness or continue to live between two worlds. *Not quite alive, not quite dead.* Mom's words echoed in my head, "It's time to set your own table."

Mom got my message that day. And soon after, she began sending me messages of her own. The first one came in the form of blue herons. Mom and I had always shared a love for these majestic birds. They suddenly began appearing to me in the most unexpected of places, even in the dead of Pittsburgh winters. To this day, every time I see a blue heron, it goes straight to my heart, turning it on like a high-speed blender. "It's just me, JoJo, saying hello."

We rang in the new year that year at Nemacolin Woodlands, a resort in the Allegheny Mountains an hour outside of Pittsburgh. I hadn't been feeling well. For days I'd felt crampy after getting a period that didn't seem to want to end. The cramping intensified and the blood thickened. I made sure to get the first available appointment with my doctor when we got back home.

"You're pregnant," my OB told me.

"But that's impossible. I've been bleeding since before New Year's Eve."

"Bleeding can happen at your age. Especially after back to back pregnancies. We just need to watch it. According to the ultrasound, your due date is September 9. Congratulations. Is this a surprise?"

"Sure is. I just turned thirty-seven. It was the last thing I was expecting to hear. I finally just got my youngest out of diapers and pull-ups."

The year 2011 rolled in with a new year baby surprise—or so we thought. I'd barely broken the news to Gastón that we were once again expecting when I received a call from my doctor's office asking if I could come in for more testing. My blood tests had come back and they wanted to double check a couple of things. The subsequent test results were conclusive: I had an ectopic pregnancy that had implanted on my cervix. Gastón and I listened closely as the doctor explained the process that we'd have to follow to terminate the pregnancy. It would take at least a week or two, followed by a D&C.

Just as I'd begun feeling hopeful again, the rug was pulled out from underneath me. If I'd come to expect anything lately, it was that life could turn on a dime.

As I received my discharge papers the day of my D&C, my OB told me I needed to use extra birth control precautions for the following couple of months. "We scraped your uterus clean. It's like a teenager's, which means you'll be extra fertile until it begins to build up some lining again."

The next day, I braved the cold and went to Sunday Mass in search of some sort of inspiration. I didn't enter the main room, but instead listened to the sermon from the standing-only foyer. I rarely entered anymore. That church was one of the last places I'd been with Mom before she died. I often found myself staring at the pew we'd sat in, side by side, on that last day we spent together.

That particular Sunday, a baby was being baptized. Just as I was about to leave after receiving communion, I saw the priest raise up a little baby girl named Riley. She was a vision dressed in a beautiful white baptismal gown. The priest held her up over his head for all the church to take in. "Please join me in welcoming baby Riley to our family. She is the first baby to be baptized in 2011. Let this sweet baby girl's arrival stand as a beacon of hope for a prosperous 2011 for our entire congregation."

I hung on to every one of the priest's words. They took me back to a conversation I'd had with my sister Camila a month or two after Mom's death. Camila was in South Carolina at the time, helping my brother Oscar and his wife look for a new home in Charleston. Mom's sudden departure had been too much to bear

EL CAMBALACHE EL QUE NO LLORA, NO MAMA

for Oscar, who was in between jobs at the time. He took it as an opportunity to leave Pittsburgh altogether. As they were house hunting, Oscar's realtor stopped my sister, and, grabbing a hold of Camila's shoulder, asked if she knew a blonde woman who wore large, black Chanel sunglasses. Camila didn't quite know what to say.

"That sounds like my mother, but she passed several weeks ago."

"Well, she's here with us. She says she's your mom. She's talking a mile a minute. Does she speak another language? She's got a thick accent that makes it hard to understand her."

Oscar's realtor explained she'd been able to see spirits since she was a young girl. That day the three of them—Camila, Mom and the realtor—spoke. Camila called me later with a message from Mom. "It was the strangest thing. But this woman was spot on about things she could have had no way of knowing. She had a message for you too. She said, 'Tell the second to youngest—Riley.'"

"Riley? But I don't know a Riley. I've never known a Riley."

"That's what I thought, Josie. I don't know a Riley either. But that's what she told me to tell you. Maybe in time Mom's message will make sense."

It did. It was the sign I'd been looking for. I got home from church that day and kissed Gastón, telling him we were going to have a baby girl. I just knew it. I didn't bother to mention that Mom had sent me the message more than a year ago through a medium who spoke with a slow, southern drawl to Camila.

"*Gorda*, is that the meds talking? How many painkillers are you taking?"

Gastón thought I was crazy, but he certainly didn't stop me from trying. Two months later, we found ourselves back in my obstetrician's office.

The doctor placed my patient chart against his chest. "Didn't I tell you to be careful?"

"You did. But you should never tell a thirty-seven-year-old woman that she's like a teenager." I laughed. "You may want to rethink your choice of words next time."

"You have a point there. I think my wife would agree. So, it seems here your due date is somewhere around the week of November 17."

I turned to Gastón. "Mom's birthday."

* * *

The following June, I was four months pregnant as we were preparing to travel to Argentina with the kids to celebrate Gastón's *abuela* Helsa's ninetieth birthday. At that point, Lucas was nearing eight years old, Mateo six, Nico five and Nacho four. But once again, life made a sudden unexpected turn. Graciela called us crying early one morning to let us know Helsa passed suddenly from a blood clot in her leg, just six days before her birthday. We planned to travel regardless to celebrate Helsa and her life well lived. But as we sat in the Miami International Airport, awaiting to board the red-eye leg of our trip to Buenos Aires, our flight was cancelled indefinitely.

A volcano in the Puyehue-Cordon Caulle chain of southern Chile had burst into activity. It erupted after lying dormant for more than fifty years. The volcano spewed ash more than six miles into the sky, blanketing Villa La Angostura in a coat of cinders for more than nine months. The volcanic ash cloud cancelled hundreds of flights in and out of Chile and Argentina for more than a week. We were stranded mid-trip. It was the first time since Mom died that I'd have to go back to our home in Miami. I'd been avoiding the place at all costs. The city held too many raw memories of those last moments I'd been trying to forget for a year and a half now.

As we headed to Dad's apartment, I realized I'd only packed winter clothes since our original plans had us heading into the dead of Argentina's winter. I came up empty-handed after scouring the place for any remnants of children's clothes I'd hoped my nieces and nephews might have left behind. Instead, I found a pink helium balloon tucked away inside one of the back closets with the image of a baby holding a rattle and a *"Es una nena!"* message. *That's strange*, I thought, wondering who we knew that was having a girl. No one else in my family was pregnant at the

EL CAMBALACHE EL QUE NO LLORA, NO MAMA

time. I figured Camila must have had a baby shower for one of her friends at the apartment. The following morning Gastón and I decided to take the kids to TJ Maxx in South Beach to grab some summer clothes. To our surprise, it was the only TJ Maxx I'd ever been to that didn't have a children's department, and I'd been to most of them across the Eastern seaboard. Mom raised me and my siblings in TJ Maxx's along Interstate 95. Gastón decided to take the boys next door to Ross Dress for Less to let them pick out some shorts, short-sleeve tops and a bathing suit to tide us over until air travel to Argentina resumed. I was tired from the pregnancy and told Gastón to go ahead without me.

I sat on a bench in between the two stores while he shopped with the boys. Both store entrances were on the top floor of a covered parking garage. I sat down and must have dozed off, because I was startled when I felt a tap on my leg. An older man joined me on the other side of the bench, tipping his hat to say hello as he sat down. I straightened up—his white beard, khaki windbreaker, tweed pants and gentleman's cap gave him away immediately. My Gentleman Caller. I hadn't seen him since just before Mom died. He was back. But somehow, just when my natural instinct told me to get up and find Gastón, he smiled at me, putting me at ease. I smiled back.

He pointed, motioning for me to look up. I did. There was a balloon pinned against the cement parking garage ceiling that must have escaped an unlucky someone's grasp. It was just like the balloon I'd seen back at Dad's, except this one was in English. It was pink with a stork carrying a baby bundle in its beak with the words, "It's a girl!" I looked up for a good minute or two in awe, as if I was in a trance. But when I came to and looked back over at the man, my Gentleman Caller had, as usual, vanished into thin air.

A week later we arrived in Argentina. I hugged and kissed Graciela. Cradling my belly, I whispered in her ear, "*Es una nena.* We're having a girl."

She looked at me. "*¿Qué?* For sure?"

It was, I told her. Our baby girl was finally on her way.

Gastón, always supportive, tried suggesting that maybe we should wait until the five-month ultrasound to make such declarations. *Then maybe everyone won't think you're batshit crazy when we announce the birth of our fifth son.*

"Babes, I'm certain it's a girl. Mom's been sending me signs left and right. They're written clear as day." Not to mention my Gentleman Caller. I wondered if they were in on this together.

"I know, *Gordi*. But you're probably the first person ever to claim that a couple of helium balloons accurately predicted the sex of a baby. I know you, so I don't find it unusual. But I'm just saying. Others might."

Graciela was on my side. Always one to believe in superstitions, she decided to do some investigating of her own. "Let's find out if your *mamí's* right." Graciela grabbed two chairs with pillows and, covering my eyes, placed a spoon under one of the pillows and a fork under the other. "Okay, Josie. Now you must choose between the two chairs. If you sit on the one with the spoon, you're having a girl. If you choose the fork, a boy."

A southpaw, I chose the chair to the left. The one with the fork. The one that predicted a boy.

"See, *Gordita*? Let's just table the conversation about the baby's sex until we get the ultrasound."

"Okay. But I'm going with Mom on this one. She wouldn't steer me wrong."

That July, back in Pittsburgh, I had my twenty-week ultrasound. Our babysitter cancelled on us that morning, so Gastón and I took the boys with us to Weinstein Imaging Center. Once we were assured the baby was healthy, I couldn't wait another minute to find out the sex. We'd lined the four boys up against the wall. They knew not to make a peep as the technologist performed the scan. The anticipation was killing me. I could feel my heart throbbing in my head as I watched the images of our baby projected on the screen above.

"Do you want to know what you're having?"

"More than anything." I squeezed Gastón's hand.

"Are you sure?" The technician shot me a coy smile. She was enjoying herself.

"I'm sure. Look at them." I pointed to Lucas, Mateo, Nico and Nacho. All perfectly well-behaved, trying to make out the images on the screen. "My husband and I make boys." For the first time in months I was doubting my unwavering conviction that our girl was finally on her way.

"Brace yourself." She pointed to the screen. "Do you see these two lines here? They mean your boys are going to have a baby sister. Congratulations, Mom. You'll no longer be the odd one out."

Gastón and I were in shock. He laid his lips on my forehead, kissing it before uttering under his breath, "*Tenías razón, Poupée.* Your Mom was right." *Told you.* The boys were high fiving one another. Except for Nacho, who'd been hoping for a baby brother to boss around, they were over the moon that they'd soon have a little sister to corrupt.

I got up off the examination table and headed to the bathroom to clean the gel off my expanding waistline. Once inside, I collapsed to the floor and erupted into tears of joy. Mom had been right all along. She was still with us. My Gentleman Caller had also been right. *Was he helping Mom get her message across?* After all this time, I still didn't know who he was, but I'd come to understand that in one way or another he'd always been there, watching over me. Every time I'd begin to think I wouldn't see him ever again, he'd show up. Back at home that afternoon, our boys released four "It's a Girl" balloons up to the heavens to thank their *Bela* for our much-anticipated gift. Four months later, on the day before Thanksgiving, we welcomed María Poupée Oría, after Mom and our Blessed Mother, into our family.

* * *

I last visited *Abuela* Dorita on September 25, 2012, her ninety-third birthday, with a bottle of *dulce de leche* liqueur under one arm and my daughter wrapped in the other. Fresh off the plane, I'd decided to take a detour to Dad's apartment in Buenos Aires to freshen up and bathe and feed ten-month-old Poupée—who'd be meeting her great-*abuela* Dorita for the first time—before heading onto La Plata. As the taxi rounded the Ministry of Health Building—among the city's tallest structures on Avenida Nueve de Julio—we were greeted with twin, ten-story monumental images forged in steel of Evita's portrait towering over us.

"*Dios mío*, are those new?" I asked my driver.

"*Sí. Obra de la Cristina.*" He told me Argentina's second female president, Cristina Fernandez de Kirchner, a former First Lady herself who's been compared to Evita, commissioned the sky high monuments. The work on the south façade had been unveiled the year before, on the fifty-ninth anniversary of Evita's death. "Once the sun goes down, her face lights up against the night sky," the taxi driver quipped. "Even from the grave, she's still making political jabs."

"Really? How so?" I asked.

"There are two Evitas. The one that faces Buenos Aires' more affluent neighborhood on the building's northern façade shows her defiantly delivering a passionate speech into a microphone. I can hear her now, ranting about some oligarch or other who makes her want to bite them."

I laughed, finishing his thought, "Like one crunches into a carrot or a radish."

"*Tal cual.* Exactly." He laughed back. "Then you have Evita's official portrait on the other side that faces a much poorer area, where she's smiling in all her *gloria*, watching over her Argentine people."

While it was clearer than ever that Eva Perón's legacy lived on after all these years, I asked my driver, "But how much longer can her illusion last?"

"Tourists come and go, but Evita? She's not going anywhere." He met my eyes in his rearview mirror, as if to affirm his staunch position. "Sixty years after her death, she's still alive and kicking in Argentina. As for former *Presidente* Cristina, she's determined that no one in Argentina will forget her. But she's no Evita—her fairytale's coming to an end," he said, pulling into the toll booth as we exited the highway for La Plata.

* * *

After hugging *Abuela* tight and bathing her cheeks in kisses, I was faced with the hard truth that Dorita's Parkinson's and dementia had made her a shell of the grandma I'd grown up with. Still, she had moments of remarkable clarity that would some-

EL CAMBALACHE EL QUE NO LLORA, NO MAMA

times last hours at a time. Since Mom's passing, Dorita rarely left her bedroom, sleeping hours on end. I'd sit watching her, Poupée in my arms. When she was awake, I'd try to take advantage of every moment with her, brushing her hair, sometimes putting curlers in it or painting her nails. I'd read her the latest *chusmerío* from her favorite gossip magazines until Dorita would once again drift back into sleep. One particular afternoon, it seemed Dorita would sleep straight into the night. I sat on the chair next to her bedside, flipping through her tattered *Doña* Petrona cookbook, visiting each dog-eared page. I looked up when Dorita, still asleep, started calling for her dad under her breath. "*Papá, Papá, Papá . . .*" Dorita was visibly shaken, tossing and turning as if she was desperately searching for him.

Marta, Dorita's at-home nurse, heard her, too, and came in to check on her.

"She's asleep." I whispered. "She must be dreaming. I think she was calling for her father."

"Si, *señora* Josefina. She's been calling out to him in her sleep for the past several weeks. Sometimes frantically. I've tried asking her about him, but she won't speak a word of it."

"She never would. It's strange she would call after him. She never seemed to want anything to do with him, let alone say his name."

"That is interesting. She's been calling for him more and more," Marta said as she went to leave.

Moments later, Dorita awoke, still groggy. As I went to get her a *café con leche* for her *merienda*, Dorita grabbed my arm. "Josefinita, do you see him?"

"*¿Quién, Abuela?* Who?"

"There. Next to my bed." She pointed to the other side of her bed.

No one was there. "No. I must have just missed him. I'll be right back with our coffees. I got you an *alfajor* too. Are you up for a little?"

Dorita nodded yes. Barely.

Moments later, when I came back with two steaming mugs of coffee, Dorita was once again fast asleep. I turned to put her coffee down on her tall mirrored dresser before burning myself.

That's when I saw his reflection in the mirror. His silver beard. His herringbone cap laid carefully atop Dorita's comforter. Crouched next to Dorita's bedside, holding her, his hands tightly cupped around hers. The same way he'd held mine that night he pulled me from the wreckage when I lay between this world and the next. He'd been there to comfort me all of those years ago. My Gentleman Caller had been with me since that fateful day.

I blinked and shook my head. The two images—the one of him now, crouching beside Dorita who lay sleeping, holding her hands, and the one of him holding me on the side of Interstate 95 all those years ago—played over and over in my head on an endless loop. I'd always wondered if his visits might have had some greater purpose, as though he'd been watching over me for a reason, even if I wasn't sure what that might be.

But in that moment, he was there for Dorita. He didn't look up. Instead he kept his dark, compassionate eyes on my sleeping *abuela*, who too seemed caught between two worlds. Had he heard Dorita calling? "*Papá, Papá, Papá . . .*"

My head was flooded with questions: *Could it be? Her Dad? The man whose name she never again mentioned? Could my Gentleman Caller and Dorita's father be one in the same? Had he finally come home? Could it be he'd been trying to make his way back to her all these years?* I wanted to ask him, but I paused. Whoever he was, I didn't want to break the spell between him and Dorita. One thing was clear: he was there for her, and she'd seen him, too, moments before she fell back asleep.

Still, his hauntings throughout the years played like a movie in my head. Up until that moment, I'd never put two and two together. *He* was the mysterious stranger that pulled me out of the car during the night of my terrible car accident at just sixteen. That's why he seemed so familiar that night Tripp and I first saw him at my parents' home all those years ago in Pittsburgh. *He* tried warning me, on more than one occasion, of our imminent breakup. *He* invited Gastón into my dreams and made sure I noticed him at the airport in Córdoba. *He* followed me to Argentina and watched that fateful day at my *abuelo* Alfredo's grave as I discovered that my great-grandmother had died on Dorita's birthday.

He was trying to prepare me for what lay ahead—Mom's sudden passing on the heels of my own birthday. He appeared in some of my most trying times—sometimes warning me of their imminent arrival; sometimes assuring me that this too would pass, including the months that my son Mateo battled health issues of his own.

It was almost too much to take in at once. I don't remember how much time passed—it could have been ten seconds or ten minutes. But when I finally turned to take my seat on the other side of Dorita's bed, he was gone. I quickly turned to look back into the mirror but was met with my reflection alone. Other than Dorita, who was peacefully sleeping, it was just me in the room. *Or so I thought.*

The following day, the twenty-ninth of the month, was *el día de los ñoquis.* I made Dorita *ñoqui* for lunch. It was a good day for her. She'd showered that morning. We did her hair. Dorita sat on a stool in the kitchen watching as I rolled the *ñoqui* into small dumplings.

"Why *ricota* and not *papa* like we used to make together?"

"It's just easier. I love potato *ñoqui*, but you're much better at making it than I am. Plus, it's not consistent. I don't know what I do wrong, but sometimes it turns out great, while other times it turns out mushy."

"*You're* not consistent. It's not the recipe's fault. You're using the wrong potato. Not properly draining it. Or cooking it too long."

"Well, I prefer to blame it on the potato," I laughed. "Whatever it is I'm doing to it. But the boys love this ricotta gnocchi. It's lighter, and so much easier to make."

Dorita nodded in agreement. That day I prepared the *ñoqui* with a brown butter sage sauce. We usually ate in the kitchen, at Dorita's small breakfast table. But that morning I'd dressed her formal dining room table with a tablecloth and her best Delft china, creating a modern table to *Doña* Petrona's specifications and highest standards. I slid a *peso* under each of our plates along with a simple blessing—"¡*Buen provecho!* Bon Appetit, *Abuelita.*"

We ate a late lunch that day and topped it off with the post-meal *digestivo, dulce de leche* liqueur, in our coffees. At *sobremesa* I told Dorita about Mom, and how during my pregnancy she'd sent me messages through balloons letting me know we were expecting a baby girl. She didn't mention Mom by name. But she believed me. I could tell as she wiped away the tears pooling in her eyes.

"I was so honored when your *mami* named you after mine. I used to rock you as a baby and say your name over and over." Dorita draped her hand over mine. "It was the nicest gift anyone had ever given me. You must have loved her very much to name your daughter Poupée."

There. She'd finally said it. Mom's name. "I did. I do. I always promised Mom I'd name my first girl after her."

"Your first?"

I laughed. "In some ways, *Abuela,* I think—no, I know—Mom pulled some strings up there for me. She had everything to do with Poupée's arrival. Something tells me that if Mom were still with us, our daughter Poupée wouldn't be." I made sure to say my daughter's name over and over, hoping Dorita would start uttering it herself.

Dorita squeezed my hand tight. "A life for a life. Sometimes something has to give for something else to come in. But she wasn't supposed to go first."

"No, she wasn't. But somehow, I think she was at peace with it." I thought back to that last Sunday we'd spent together. How she'd stopped in the middle of the market, grabbing my shoulders to get my attention as she told me that she needed me to know I was a really good mom. To never forget it. And then later that afternoon when she'd asked me to write down what jewelry of hers went to each daughter once she was gone. She was slowly saying goodbye. Mom had known her days were numbered. She knew she was moving on.

Dorita raised her glass. We toasted to life that day. To her ninety-third birthday. To the forty-third anniversary of her mom's death. To Mom and her namesake, our new baby girl, Poupée.

Soon after, Dorita fell fast asleep tableside in her dining room chair after pouring a little too much liqueur in her coffee. Her head hung low as she mumbled, *"Papá, Papá, Papá . . ."*

Poupée woke up at the same moment crying out in hunger. She'd been peacefully sleeping in her carrier next to the table as we ate. *El cambalache, el que no llora, no mama . . .* The baby that doesn't cry, doesn't get nursed. I settled into the blue velvet couch next to the dining room table to feed her. In that moment, I found myself between these two glorious women, my *abuela* Dorita and the baby girl I'd dreamed of for so many years. I'd never felt more awake and alive.

In the quiet of Dorita's room, it dawned on me that my culinary quest to recreate Dorita's *dulce de leche* wasn't a gift for *Abuela*. It was a gift for me. And Gastón. It was the taste of Argentina we'd both been craving. As long as we continued to make the recipes passed down from generations of women in my family—Dorita, Mom, even my great-*abuela* and namesake, Josefina—lived on. And they were counting on us to remember.

As I sat quietly, feeding Poupée, the scent of Mom's perfume filled the room. Looking up, I was finally able to properly see in my mind's eye what was right in front of me. I looked over and saw Mom sitting at the table next to Dorita. She'd taken my seat. At her feet sat Sonny, licking the remnants of what was left of my plate of *ñoquis*. Mom was glowing. Like springtime in the Patagonia with its endless, carpeted meadows of striking purple and pink blooming lupines set against big blue skies and snow-capped, majestic peaks. A glorious sign of nature's revival. Across from Mom, to the left of Dorita, sat Josefina. I'd never had the chance to meet her, but she was just as I'd imagined from her pictures with her short, trimmed and tailored white hair, full face and understated grin. At the other end of the table was my *abuelo* Alfredo, who'd taken residence in his usual seat, smoking pipe in hand. As Dorita quietly went on with her *siesta*, they talked. Mom was smiling. *Her smile.* I'd never forgotten it. I never will. She rolled up the Argentine *peso* bill in front of her, set it aside and then winked at me and Poupée. I can still hear her now. "JoJo, baby girl, you did good. You chose the right name after all. I always knew you would. She's a doll. *She's our doll.*"

Thanks, Mom. Gracias. I miss you so much it hurts.

* * *

The room that afternoon was filled with a sort of peace I'd never known. I sat back and drank it all in, until something caught the corner of my eye coming from the hallway that led to the kitchen. I saw movement again and turned my head quickly, holding Poupée tightly, my breath catching in my chest as my Gentleman Caller, clad in his khaki windbreaker, hesitantly walked in with his hands in pockets.

I could hear the sound of his footsteps approaching. There he stood at arm's length. He stopped and looked at me and Poupée, acknowledging us with a small nod of his head as he removed his hat. Cap in hand, he turned and approached the table. He stopped at Dorita's chair and, gently placing his hands on her shoulder, kissed the top of her head and softly whispered, "*Mi Dorita*," before taking a seat next to Josefina.

Dear God, it is him. All those years I'd questioned his existence. Whether he was possibly a guardian angel or an ancestor I'd never met. All those years I'd looked over my shoulder, wondering if he'd be there. Why he was following me. He wasn't simply my ghost anymore. He was suddenly undeniably real—a vibrant, living version of Dorita's past that had never left her. One that was buried among the secrets of her youth. It had been decades since Dorita's father, my Gentleman Caller, walked out of her family's front door to never return. But that day, finally, he found his way back to her. Back home. And I, the casual observer, got to witness it all. *A rare glimpse of Heaven.*

The togetherness that came from that elbow-to-elbow *sobremesa* formed a bridge between us, giving voices to the ghosts that made us: my great-*abuela* Josefina, my *abuela* Dorita, my mom; to the ghosts that made me and my daughter, María Poupée. I'd finally come to understand why my Gentleman Caller had been watching over me all along: he couldn't do the same with his wife and daughter. I'd never know why he left; why he never returned. Was it of his own making? Or was it due to something out of his control? Dorita would carry that secret to the grave, or maybe she never even knew. Instead, he paid his penance by watching over me—Dorita's mom's namesake—all of those years. His apparitions, sporadic and polite as they were, were a stark reminder that, as Maya Angelou so eloquently put it in her poem "Our Grandmothers," "I go forth along, and stand as ten thousand."

In those moments of revelation, I'd never known a happier place than those two rooms: Dorita's dining room and kitchen in her home on Calle 39 in La Plata, Argentina. The place marking her slow exit from the world. The place Dorita spent a lifetime teaching me to live in.

I closed my eyes, giving myself over to the moment, and felt the steady rhythm in Poupée's chest as she nursed, drinking the milk that gave her life. With my baby girl in my arms, I found myself caught between those I loved the most—yet I was worlds removed from them. Even Dorita. I glanced over at her. Her chin resting on her chest. Her platinum white curls perfectly styled. Her perfectly manicured hands folded in front of her. Fast asleep in her chair at the head of the table, she seemed to be in and out of this world, on to the next. Resting peacefully. Dorita was the closest thing to Mom that I had left in this world. But it was clear the sun was slowly setting on her life. St. Peter would soon be calling her name. Dorita was moving on, and so was I, later that evening on the red-eye back to Gastón and the boys in Pittsburgh. I had to come to terms that it would be our last *sobremesa*. There'd be no more trips to Argentina to see her. My beloved *abuela* Dorita would soon be joining their side of the table. My Gentleman Caller was there at the ready to see his youngest daughter home.

Ñoqui de ricota (Ricotta Gnocchi)

SERVES 7. *Or one granddaughter coming to terms that she'll never again see her cherished abuela. In this world, at least.*

Making *ñoqui* is easier than you think. I promise. Especially this recipe. Gastón and I first tried *ricota ñoqui* in Philadelphia's Italian Market at a restaurant called Villa Di Roma. We were instantly hooked. These pillows of homemade pasta literally melt in your mouth. They're equally authentic as its potato relative, but lighter in texture and, again, so much easier to make, especially when you're feeding seven in one sitting. Even better, you get to skip the part of flicking potato *ñoqui* dumplings off the tines of a fork to give them their characteristic shape, although, growing up, that was my favorite part. You could always tell the ones Dorita had prepared from my own, as her dumplings were perfectly ridged on one side with a scooped indentation on the other, but she never minded. She'd mix my messy *ñoqui* among the rest, knowing I'd delight in eating them.

Thanks to Dorita, I'm a faithful follower of *el día de los ñoquis*. My family eats them most every twenty-ninth of the month, with a dollar bill under each plate. I'll never forget that last meal I shared with Dorita on September 29, 2012. Dorita didn't eat much by then, but from her face I could tell she relished each part. Especially the part where she sat in the kitchen by my side as I prepared them. It was rare that Dorita stepped into the kitchen anymore. That afternoon the weather was warming up, which is why we prepared a lighter brown butter sage sauce. But these pair beautifully with any type of preparation—marinara, a plum Marzano tomato sauce or a Bolognese. When we were kids, Dorita would simply toss them with loads of butter, Parmesan and pepper. Simplicity at its best.

2 15-ounce containers **ricotta cheese,** preferably whole milk	**Salt** and freshly ground **black pepper**
4 **eggs,** lightly beaten	1½ to 2 cups **flour**
2½ cups freshly grated **Parmesan,** plus more for serving	6 tablespoons **unsalted butter**
	20 or more **sage leaves,** whole

Drain the ricotta. Line a plate with cheese cloth or a clean kitchen towel, and then dump the ricotta onto it. Wrap cloth around ricotta and squeeze water out over a large bowl or sink. Once no more water comes out, place ricotta in a fine mesh strainer and allow it to rest over a bowl.

In a large bowl, combine ricotta, eggs and Parmesan. Add some salt and pepper. Add flour, starting with one cup and stir; add more flour until the mixture can form a ball. It should be very sticky in texture.

Bring a large pot of water to a boil and salt it.

Form the dough. Transfer your dough ball to a lightly floured work surface. Gently shape into a rectangle. Cut in half. Cut each half into even quadrants.

Working one quadrant at a time, roll the dough into a log. Use just enough flour to keep the dough from sticking completely to your work surface. A small amount of sticking is good—the added friction will help keep your log rolling nicely as you stretch it. Divide each of those logs in half with your bench scraper. Stretch out each half into a log about a foot long, and then repeat the process with all of the remaining dough. Cut the logs into individual gnocchi with your bench scraper.

Dust the cut *ñoqui* lightly with flour and transfer them to a rimmed baking sheet lined with parchment paper. At this stage, the gnocchi can be completely frozen and then transferred to a zip-top bag to store for up to 2 months (and they can be cooked directly from the freezer).

Make the sauce. Put the butter in a large skillet over medium heat. Swirl the pan occasionally to be sure the butter cooks evenly. As the butter melts, it will begin to foam. Continue to cook, swirling the pan occasionally, until the color goes from a lemony-yellow to golden-tan to, finally, a rich, nutty-brown color, about eight minutes. Add the sage, allowing it to crisp up for a minute or two, making sure not to burn them. Once crisp, remove pan from heat. Allow to cool slightly, then taste and season with salt and pepper as needed. Cover and set aside.

Cook the *ñoqui*. Once water is at a boil, drop the *ñoqui* in with a slotted spoon, giving them a very gentle stir at the beginning to ensure that they don't stick to the bottom of the pot or to one other. Allow the *ñoqui* to cook for approximately 2–3 minutes if fresh, or 5 minutes if frozen.

When the *ñoqui* rise to the surface, allow to cook for thirty seconds more. While you don't want to overcook the *ñoqui*, rendering it mushy, they need to heat all the way through for the raw flour and egg to set, giving the *ñoqui* a firmer—but light—bite. Remove with a slotted spoon and transfer to the skillet. When all the *ñoqui* are done, toss, taste and adjust the seasoning, and serve immediately.

Chapter 13

Pícaras and Spirited; *Dulce* and Sweet; *Picante* and Sharp

I have one last culinary confession: I've never liked Jell-O. *I know.* It's a national travesty to say such a thing. It's like an Argentine saying they don't like *dulce de leche.* ¿¡Qué?! Maybe it's because of my DNA, whose roots grow deep under the southern skies of Argentina, or possibly because my first memory of eating Jell-O was when I was in the hospital in the fifth grade after having my tonsils out. Jell-O wasn't a part of Dorita and Mom's everyday kitchen. Yet it's an emblem of home, a keeper of time in generation after generation of American kitchens. "Equal parts powder and water, nostalgia and modernity," according to *Jell-O Girls* author, Allie Rowbottom.

Still, I didn't like Jell-O. Until one afternoon when, in my mid-forties, Poupée asked me to make it for her. I didn't tell her it wasn't my favorite. I wanted her to decide for herself. Instead, I decided to make it our own. I got out a Bundt pan and set out to make a *dulce de leche* gelatin mold. Poupée, seven at the time, helped. We mixed two envelopes of unflavored gelatin with warm water. Then in a blender we added *dulce de leche*, whole milk, a teaspoon of vanilla extract and mixed it with the gelatin. We poured it into the mold and refrigerated it for six hours. We waited patiently. It felt like a lifetime. Then, after unmolding, I held back Poupée's long brown hair that flowed effortlessly down to her waist as she decorated the gelatin with fresh whipped cream.

The kids loved it. Gastón and I did, too. It was the perfectly delicious balance between our duel—and sometimes dueling—Argentine-American cultures.

* * *

Dorita peacefully passed away three months after that last *sobremesa* I shared with her in Argentina. My sister Valentina called me the morning of January 15, 2013 from Dorita's hospital room in La Plata to let me know she was no longer with us. As the first and oldest of her grandchildren, Valentina had always been Dorita's favorite, so it was only fitting she was the first to arrive to her bedside moments after she took her last breath. Dorita wanted it that way. Marta, Dorita's nurse, had been there in her last moments. She was in utter shock. Like us, she loved Dorita dearly.

Abuela's hands were still warm when Valentina arrived. Camila, Laura and I jumped on overnight flights to Buenos Aires that same evening to join Valentina in paying our respects to our dearly departed *Abuela*. Since Mom's death had preceded Dorita's, our extended family in Argentina felt it wasn't necessary that her grandchildren travel internationally to attend her funeral. But it was. Mom raised us girls to show up, with or without her. The love she instilled in us throughout her lifetime transcended the mold expected of her daughters and granddaughters. As women, Mom made sure we paved our own way.

Fresh off the plane, the four of us arrived at the funeral home just as they were sealing Dorita's casket. We were there to represent and pay tribute to our *abuela*, who, since Mom and Dad immigrated to the States decades before, had lived the latter half of her life straddling two cultures. Together, we lived in Spanglish. Dorita had always been our Argentina, and we, her United States of America.

Before leaving Dorita's house one last time, I grabbed the portrait my sister Valentina painted of her with oil pastels as an eightieth birthday gift. It was the same image of the portrait Valentina had given me years before to design the labels for our La Dorita *dulce de leche* jars. My oldest sister was always looking out for me, every step of the way. Before saying goodbye to Dorita's kitchen one last time, a black-covered book on the bookshelf grabbed my eye: her 1948, 26th edition of *Doña* Petrona's cookbook with yellowed scraps of paper sticking out of it—notes handwritten decades ago in Dorita's swirly cursive. I tucked it under my arm and took it home. Every once in a while I'll page through it and read the recipes Dorita cooked over and over for those she loved. It reminds me who she was. Who she is.

Four years to the day of Dorita's death, on January 15, 2017, I gave my six-month notice that I would be leaving my full-time job. At the ripe age of forty-three, I left a fifteen-year, C-level career to make *dulce de leche*.

I'd finally found the courage to follow my own dreams. Gastón was right there beside me, holding my hand each step of the way. Our culinary journey hasn't been without its own challenges. It's also taken us in directions we didn't see coming, such as opening Pittsburgh's first culinary incubator kitchen in 2013. But most importantly, it's my journey, of my own making. And Mom and Dorita are guiding me along the way.

*   *   *

I struggled for years with my parting words to Mom—"you forgot my birthday"—until almost ten years after her passing, when a dear family friend, Vivian Anne, whom I hadn't seen in close to fifteen years, private messaged me on Instagram. Growing up, our families spent Thanksgivings and New Year's Eves together in Pittsburgh, and later Miami Beach. Our dearly departed moms were five-foot, three-inch-tall spitfire best friends who lived life on their own terms, marching to the beat of Gloria Estefan's *Conga*. Vivian Anne's mom, Vivian, had bravely fought breast cancer for years before Mom passed. She was the first person I spoke with the night of Mom's death, and one of three people who I'd confided in, sharing the agony and guilt I felt about the last words I'd said to Mom. *How could I have been so selfish?* Vivian lost her battle with cancer just weeks after Mom's passing. She took the words I'd entrusted to her—*Mom, you forgot my birthday*—with her to the grave.

That is, until March 2019. Thanks to her daughter Vivian Anne's New Year's resolution to bring all of her family videos and memories into the twenty-first century by converting them to digital format, I finally received the closure I'd been seeking. Among her family treasures, Vivian Anne had found a clip of our moms at *sobremesa* on my seventeenth birthday surprise party celebration at the Fox Chapel Yacht Club. It was my *fiesta de quince* that Mom and Dad had thrown me Argentine style, fashionably late, two years later. My heart skipped a beat as I played the video.

"I'd like to wish Josephine a very beautiful and happy birthday. We love you," Mom said with a wink of her eye as the camera panned out. *She hadn't forgotten. She made sure I knew—even all those years later.* Mom's words made me realize that the heartbreak in life can be painfully beautiful. I'd been asking for a sign, and Mom and her band of *chicas* delivered. I'm so grateful to Vivian Anne for passing along Mom's message. At the time, she didn't understand its significance. But it was a true gift that I'll carry with me always.

* * *

Today, with twenty years of marriage to Gastón under my belt, I continue to be spoiled by his simple culinary genius. Like Mom and Dorita, Gastón commands our family of seven from the kitchen (or one of his five open-fire grill contraptions). To our five children, *Papi's* the family cook and *Mami's* the baker. Unlike some people who love to go out to dinner, Gastón loves to stay home. He wanders around the market for hours figuring out that night's menu. I still cook, quite often. But, mostly, I'm Gastón's "Juanita."

Cheesy eggs with *palta* continues to be a favorite staple we eat at least weekly. Except Gastón's swapped Argentina's Bimbo white sandwich bread with hearty Ezequiel toast and finishes the eggs off with a splash of Cholula hot sauce. And while I also enjoy cooking up a meal here and there, I'll often catch Gastón secretly doctoring my lentils, greens-n-beans, pumpkin chicken chili or *milanesas* with mashed potatoes with another pinch of salt and pepper, a sprinkling of lemon zest, a dash more of cumin or a couple extra pats of unsalted butter. It used to unnerve me, so much so that I used to call him the Kitchen Nazi, after the famed Soup Nazi character on *Seinfeld*. But it doesn't anymore. Like a finely aged cheese, I seem to have settled into my own skin. Now, I even find myself pretending not to notice. After all, I know we'll all be the better for it.

To this day, we continue to have our unassigned seats at the table. Gastón, like Dad, sits at the end farthest from the kitchen, but only after the rest of us are taken care of. That's the way he likes it; he insists upon it. Lucas, our oldest son, sits to his left, and is becoming quite the cook himself, often preparing family meals on his own. Nacho, our youngest boy and almost-blonde—like Mom—sits to his right. I sit on the end closest to the kitchen. Poupée sits to my right. Mateo, to my left. Nico, our middle child, sits in between Mateo and Nacho. We still call him *Nico pico y su amigo Federico*, or Nics for short. He still has enough personality for two. The seat across from Nico is empty. It's reserved for anyone who'd like to join us: friends, family, sisters, brothers, nieces and nephews. Our Argentine family. And our dearly departed loved ones: Mom, Dorita, Alfredo, Josefina. My paternal grandparents, Buby and Caminos. My father-in-law, Jorge Luis. My Gentleman Caller. It's a standing invitation for the ghosts we carry with us.

No matter our dinner guests, Gastón and I continue to try and instill our daily *sobremesa* ritual at home with our children, most weekdays and at least one weekend night. But I'm not going to lie, with packed schedules and extracurricular activities, it's challenging. But we make it a priority, because when we neglect *sobremesa*, things begin to unravel, and we lose touch with one another. Now that we run our own business, the post-meal tradition helps Gastón and I balance the business partner from the spouse. It centers us in our marriage and reminds us why we fought to be together in the first place. It reminds us that we're one another's homes.

Speaking of home, today, even after seventeen years of living in Pittsburgh, we still don't feel we've quite found our place yet. But as long as Gastón and I are together, no matter where we are, we're home. We still feel the water beckoning us. We hear Argentina calling. There are moments we're convinced the Patagonia will be our landing place. *Could we convince the kids to come with us?* It's one of our family's favorite *sobremesa* topics that we keep coming back to, meal after meal. But we also imagine long, carefree afternoons spent on a screened-in porch overlooking the endless marshlands on the banks of the Wando River in South Carolina. Sipping an unsweet tea with a splash of vodka and extra lemon for me, a Bloody Mary for Gastón. Listening to our favorite soundtrack: the symphony of crickets singing, frogs calling and cicadas humming as we watch lightning bugs dancing in the night, all grounded by a soft breeze rustling through the salt marsh. Together they form a low country boil that, bite after bite, leaves us hungry for more.

The Holy City treats us like we're home. Charleston's low country charm slowly steeped into our hearts and souls after Mom died. We've religiously visited Oscar's family home every spring and summer since, for weeks at a time. They even started referring to their guest bedroom as Josie's room. At *sobremesa* we discuss being torn between our two Deep South loves. It's not that we love Argentina more, just longer. Our Argentine roots run deep. We're counting on them to produce many offshoots for generations to come.

* * *

That ghosts exist is not something up for discussion. In my mind, at least. The question is, who recognizes them, who has the better story to tell or whose ghost helped to restore their faith in life at a time when they needed it most?

I've always felt my *abuelo* Alfredo was among my team of angels. He'd come to me more than once in the twilight between wakefulness and sleep, along with legions of ancestors, like my Gentleman Caller and great-*abuela* Josefina, and those that are still unknown to me. And, of course, Mom and *Abuela* Dorita have since joined the ranks. They knew I would someday need something to seize hold of when they were gone. So they gave me the gift of *dulce de leche*. And I've hung onto it. For dear life.

I haven't seen my Gentleman Caller since that last *sobremesa* with Dorita. I can't say if our paths will meet again, but I'm certain of one thing—he'd finally found his place at the table.

Since *Abuela* and Mom's passing and my daughter's birth, I've experienced other mystical, faceless angel encounters. I'm certain Poupée's guardian angel showed herself to me in all of her brilliant glory one day when she was just about two years old and ran out into the middle of the street into oncoming traffic, her angel saving her. *And me.* I marvel and give thanks to our guides who silently walk this earth with us.

As the years continue to pass, there's one thing I've come to know for sure: baking is my refuge. It brings me right back to being a young girl in the kitchen with *Abuela* Dorita. I loved rolling my sleeves up and baking anything and everything I could get my hands on—from boxed brownies to the homemade flan with *dulce de leche* that Dorita first taught me to bake when I was eight years old. That was my happy place, and in recent years I've consciously worked to reclaim it as an adult. I make a date with myself on Sunday afternoons when, after church (*if I make it*), I'll throw my favorite pajama bottoms back on, reach for my apron and dive into my Sunday baking therapy ritual that allows me to get back to being me. It's the time I set aside to celebrate the strong women in my life, my three *Marías*, who are always at the ready to be conjured back to mind through taste and smell in the everyday rituals of my family kitchen. It's in those precious moments, especially when I find myself watching over a pot of boiling milk or kneading pastry dough, that glimpses of my great-*abuela* Josefina, *Abuela* Dorita and Mom appear. In the food they made. In those who ate it. In the hearts of those they loved. They are there in every sense: *pícaras* and spirited; *dulce* and sweet; *picante* and sharp.

Dulce de leche Gelatin

SERVES 7. *Or 1 bicultural couple in search of common ground.*

Through her on-air career, Doña Petrona often prepared dishes with diverse culinary influences, the United States of America included. *Gelatina Royal* or Royal Gelatin Fantasy, which called for Royal's instant gelatin product, was among them. On one live TV episode, she decided to place the fruit-laden gelatin mold into the freezer "in order to keep it firm until the exact moment." The fact that there were no retakes meant that sometimes a recipe might flop on air. She often tried to cover up any errors. To her relief, she often succeeded. That episode, she tried to de-mold the gelatin with hot water four times without success. Finally, on the fifth try, she succeeded, mold intact. *Doña* Petrona later joked that foods made with gelatin should go only in the refrigerator and not the freezer. Like her audience, her delightful mistakes showed we're all just making it up as we go along.

This particular Argentine-inspired gelatin mold is a *dulce* delicious love story of me discovering the joys of Jell-O for the first time as a mother, with my daughter Poupée by my side. It takes almost no time to prepare, although it takes a while for the gelatin to set. It's best to prepare several hours ahead of time. And if your mold flops at the last second, put it back together as best you can and cover it with whipped cream *y, ya está.* There you have it. *¡Buen Provecho!*

1 ounce **unflavored gelatin**
(4 0.25-ounce pouches)

1½ cups **hot water**

3⅓ cups **dulce de leche**

3 cups **whole milk**

2 teaspoons **vanilla extract**

Fresh whipped cream for garnish

SPECIAL EQUIPMENT
High-speed blender

Mix gelatin and hot water in small bowl until dissolved; set aside. Grease a 10-inch fluted Bundt pan with baking spray.

Place dulce de leche, milk, gelatin mixture and vanilla extract in blender; cover. Blend until smooth. Pour mixture into prepared cake pan and cover with plastic wrap. Refrigerate overnight or until set (at least 6 hours).

When ready to serve, gently run a knife along edge of mold to separate from pan. Place an inverted serving plate on top of the cake pan and, using two hands to anchor the pan and plate together, carefully flip it over. Let the pan rest upside down on the plate for a minute to allow the mold to fully release from the pan. Gently shake the pan and plate together to help unmold the gelatin, being cautious to not break the mold, as it is very delicate. Remove pan and garnish the mold with fresh whipped cream.

P.D. Posdata.
P.S.

No matter where she was—Pittsburgh, Florida, even in the middle of Nowhere, Argentina—Mom had a standing Friday wash-and-style hair appointment with her faithful hair stylists, who she treated like family and longtime confidantes. Her ability and utter mastery of small talk with all in the hair salon, from the receptionist to the manicurist, never ceased to amaze me. Mom made everyone's presence known, and people noticed.

After her passing, I'd overlooked the slight detail that Mom simply stopped showing up to her weekly appointments without notice. It caused unintended grief and unresolved questions for Mom's fellow beauty salon family. In Buenos Aires, Gladys at Sergio Coiffeur on Cervino. In Miami Beach, Fernanda at Fernanda's Salon on Collins Avenue. In Pittsburgh, Karen at Hairdressers II on Highland. For the life of me, I honestly can't remember the name of the salon Mom frequented in Suardi, Argentina, or the lovely stylist. In any event, I should not have overlooked them, as they were an important part of Mom's life and fellowship.

For this reason, I offer a brief postscript that has been eating at me ever since her sudden and certainly unexpected passing: Should you ever lose a loved one suddenly, please make sure and call their hairdresser. Go sit in their chair and talk to them. It will save them much unnecessary heartache. Otherwise, they'll think they were left for another, and that's the last thing Mom would have wanted.

Acknowledgments
and gracias

I would not have written this book without my husband and true life partner, Gastón. Thanks to his unconditional love and unrelenting insistence, I found the courage to tell our story—and that of my beautiful Mom and *Abuela* Dorita, who I miss every single day. Without them, there would be no story to tell. Mom and Dorita filled me with enough love to last me several lifetimes. Today, I strive to do the same with my five children—Lucas, Mateo, Nico, Nacho and Poupée. The words within this book are for each and every one of them. So they know where they come from. So they'll always know how much their family loves them—especially those family members they were too young to remember, like Mom and Dorita. As long as we continue to honor those who've gone before us by cooking their faithful dishes and telling—and retelling—stories about them, their spirits live on.

I'd like to thank my Dad, the greatest storyteller I've ever known, for hiring Gastón on a whim all those years ago and then sending me to Argentina to audit him. And to my *abuelo* Alfredo —*gracias* for showing me your Argentina as a little girl. A special thank you also to my in-laws, Graciela and Jorge Luis, who made me feel like a part of the Oría family from day one. I'd also like to thank every person mentioned in my story, especially my brothers and sisters (by birth and marriage), first loves and dear friends. You've all left an unforgettable mark on my life.

Mil gracias to Sofía Pescarmona for her poetic forward. I couldn't think of a better woman to introduce my story. Also, to my agent, Leticia Gomez, who champions Latina voices that too often go unheard. Thank you to my publisher, Jennifer Baum, for giving me a chance and providing me a platform to tell my story, and her Scribe Publishing Company team—Mel Corrigan and Allison Janicki—for asking the tough questions and helping me string my words together to let my story sing. Finally, thank you to my faithful editor who always helps me find my story, Gina Mazza, and to my friends and fierce proof-readers—Amanda, Allie, Shannon, Olgita and Margie—for believing in me.

And to anyone reading this story, *gracias* from the bottom of my heart for letting my family into your home. There are three reasons I wanted to share my story. First, if I've learned anything about love, it's that you can't give up on it. It will find you—on its own terms. Second, because I believe there are signs everywhere. We just have to stay open to receiving them, and trust ourselves enough to know their meaning. I suffered tremendously after the sudden loss of my mom—as most who lose do (or will). However, it wasn't until I reconnected with my own spirituality and began recognizing her messages that I started to feel hopeful again. The final reason is that even though this is my story, I hope some part of it is yours too—maybe you have your own *abuela* Dorita whose spirit comes alive in these pages, or, like me, you are bicultural, Argentine, possibly even from the 'Burgh; perhaps you're in the midst of taking a chance on a second act (whether it be in love or professionally), or quite possibly you're simply looking to take your seat at *sobremesa's* endless table, where there's always room for one more. As they say in Argentina, *donde comen dos, comen tres.*

About the Author

Josephine Caminos Oría is an Argentine-American author, entrepreneur and mom. It was in her early 40s, with five young children in tow, that Josephine took a chance on herself, leaving a C-level career to make *dulce de leche*. Today Josephine, along with her Argentine husband, Gastón, is the founder of La Dorita Cooks, an all-natural line of *dulce de leche* products and Pittsburgh's first resource-based kitchen incubator for start-up and early stage food makers (see www.ladorita.net for more information). In addition, Josephine is the author of *Dulce de Leche: Recipes, Stories, & Sweet Traditions* (Burgess Lea Press, February 2017).

JosephineCaminosOria.com

Ladorita.net

Instagram/@JosephineCaminosOria

Facebook/Josephine.Oria

Twitter/@ddlladorita